PRACTICING HISTORY

Gabrielle Spiegel presents an essential new collection of key articles that examine the current status of the debate over the "linguistic turn" and attempt to rethink the practice of history in light of its implications. These are writings that operate within the framework of the linguistic turn, yet seek to move beyond its initial formulation and reception.

The introduction offers a synoptic overview of the last twenty-five years of theoretical analysis concerning historical writing, with a critical examination of the key concepts and positions that have been in debate. This collection traces the emergence of a new "practice theory" as a possible paradigm for future historical interpretation concerned with questions of agency, experience, and the subject.

Articles drawn from a mix of critical thinkers and practicing historians are presented together with clear and thorough editorial material. Complex ideas at the forefront of historical practice are revealed and made accessible to students, while for their teachers and other historians this new survey is an indispensable and timely read.

Contributors to this volume are: Mark Bevir, Richard Biernacki, Pierre Bourdieu, Michel de Certeau, Geoff Eley, Elizabeth Deeds Ermarth, Anthony Giddens, Andreas Reckwitz, Marshall Sahlins, Joan Scott, William H. Sewell Jr., Gareth Stedman Jones.

Gabrielle M. Spiegel is Dean of Humanities and Distinguished Professor of History at the University of California, Los Angeles. She is the author of *The Chronicle Tradition of Saint-Denis* (1978), *Romancing the Past* (1995), and *The Past as Text* (2000).

REWRITING HISTORIES
Series editor: Jack R. Censer

PRACTICING HISTORY

New Directions in Historical Writing after the Linguistic Turn

Edited by
Gabrielle M. Spiegel

 Routledge
Taylor & Francis Group

NEW YORK AND LONDON

First published 2005
by Routledge
270 Madison Ave, New York, NY 10016

Simultaneously published in the UK
by Routledge
2 Park Square, Milton Park, Abingdon, Oxon OX14 4RN

Routledge is an imprint of the Taylor & Francis Group

Typeset in Palatino by
Florence Production Ltd, Stoodleigh, Devon
Printed and bound in Great Britain by
MPG Books, Bodmin, Cornwall

Library of Congress Cataloging in Publication Data
New directions in historical writing after the linguistic turn/edited by
Gabrielle M. Spiegel
p. cm – (Rewriting histories)
1. Historiography.   2. Language and history.   3. Writing – History.
I. Spiegel, Gabrielle M.   II. Re-writing histories
D13.N427 2005
907'.2 – dc22   2004021793

British Library Cataloguing in Publication Data
A catalogue record for this book is available from
the British Library

ISBN 0–415–34107–8 (hbk)
ISBN 0–415–34108–6 (pbk)

CONTENTS

CONTENTS

CONTRIBUTORS

Mark Bevir is Professor of Political Science at the University of California, Berkeley who specializes in the philosophy of social science and the history of political thought, with a particular emphasis on British Studies. He is the author of *The Logic of the History of Ideas* (Cambridge, 1999) and co-author, with Rod Rhodes, of *Interpreting British Governance* (London, 2003). In addition, he edited *Critiques of Capital: Transatlantic Exchanges 1800 to the Present Day* (New York, 2003), with Frank Trentmenn. He has published over seventy articles on interpretation, postfoundationalism, British socialism, and other topics.

Richard Biernacki is Associate Professor of Sociology at the University of California, San Diego who specializes in theory, the history of labor, historical methods, and culture. His major work is *The Fabrication of Labor: Germany and Britain 1640–1941* (Berkeley and Los Angeles, 1995) as well as numerous articles on historiography and comparative methods in history.

Pierre Bourdieu is a renowned French sociologist, anthropologist, and philosopher whose work has spanned a broad range of subjects from ethnography to art, literature, education, language, cultural tastes, and television. Among his most famous books are *Distinction: A Social Critique of the Judgment of Taste* (London, 1990); *Outline of a Theory of Practice* (Cambridge Studies in Social and Cultural Anthropology, Cambridge, 1977); *The Logic of Practice* (Palo Alto, 1992); *Language and Symbolic Practice* (Cambridge, 1992); *The Field of Cultural Production: Essays on Art and Literature* (Cambridge, 1993); and *An Invitation to Reflexive Sociology* (Cambridge, 1992) among many others.

Michel de Certeau, French ethnologist, historian of ideas, and a member of the Freudian school of Paris, was one of the most wide-ranging and innovative thinkers of his generation, whose work combined principles from the disciplines of religion, history, ethnography, and psychology in order to redefine historiographical practice and theory. His major works include *The Writing of History* (New York, 1988); *Heterologies: Discourses on the Other*

(Minneapolis, 1986); *Cultural in the Plural* (Minneapolis, 1997); and *The Practice of Everyday Life* (Berkeley and Los Angeles, 1984).

Geoff Eley is Professor of History at the University of Michigan, specializing in German history of the nineteenth and twentieth centuries. He is the author of *Reshaping the German Right: Radical Nationalism and Political Change after Bismark* (New Haven, 1980); *The Peculiarities of German History: Bourgeois Society and Politics in Nineteenth-Century Germany* (Oxford, 1984), with David Blackbourn; *From Unification to Nazism: Reinterpreting the German Past* (London, 1986); *The Goldhagen Effect. History, Memory, Nazism: Facing the German Past* (Ann Arbor, 2000). He has edited several collections of essays that deal with current debates in social and cultural history, including *Culture/Power/History: A Reader in Contemporary Social Theory* (Princeton, 1993), with Nicholas B. Dirks and Sherry B. Ortner, and he is preparing a volume of his essays on historiography and theory called *History Made Conscious: The Politics of the Past at the Start of the Twentieth Century*.

Elizabeth Deeds Ermarth is Saintsbury Professor of English at Edinburgh University. Her books include *Sequel to History: Postmodernism and the Crisis of Representational Time* (Princeton, 1992); *The English Novel in History, 1840–1985* (London, 1997) and *Realism and Consensus in the English Novel: Time, Space and Narrative* (Edinburgh, 1998). She is currently working on a book to be called "Democratic Futures," which will deal with the cultural politics of postmodernity.

Anthony Giddens is Professor of Sociology at the University of Cambridge and Fellow of King's College. He also serves as the Chairman and Director of Polity Press, and as Chairman and Director of the Centre for Social Research. The author of more than 200 articles, review articles, and book reviews, his principal books include *Capitalism and Modern Social Theory* (Cambridge, 1971); *New Rules of Sociological Method* (New York, 1976); *Central Problems in Social Theory* (Berkeley, 1979); *The Constitution of Society: Outline of the Theory of Structuration* (Cambridge, 1984); *Social Theory and Modern Sociology* (Cambridge, 1987) among many others too numerous to list.

Andreas Reckwitz is Professor of Sociology at the European-University Viadrina in Frankfurt. He is the author of numerous articles on sociological and cultural theory as well as three books: *Structur. Zur sozialwissenschaftlichen Analyse von Regeln und Regelmässigkeiten* (Opladen, 1997); *Interpretation, Konstruktion, Kultur Ein Paradigmenwechsel in den Sozialwissenschaften* (Opladen, 2000); and *Die Transformation der Kulturtheorien. Zur Entwicklung eines Theorieprogramme* (Weilerswist, 2000).

Marshall Sahlins is Charles F. Grey Distinguished Service Professor of Anthropology at the University of Chicago and one of the most prominent

American anthropologists of our time. His numerous books include *Islands of History* (Chicago, 1985); *Waiting for Foucault* (Chicago, 2000); *Culture in Practice: Selected Essays* (New York, 2000); *Culture and Practical Reason* (Chicago, 1978); *How Natives Think: About Captain Cook, For Example* (Chicago, 1995); and has a forthcoming volume, *Apologies to Thucydides: Understanding History and Culture and Vice Versa* (to be published by the University of Chicago Press). A member of the National Academy of Sciences since 1991, his books have won numerous prizes.

Joan Scott is Professor of History in the School of Social Science at the Institute for Advanced Study in Princeton. Scott began her career as a social historian of nineteenth-century France, authoring works such as *The Glassmakers of Carmaux: French Craftsmen and Political Action in a Nineteenth-Century City* (Cambridge, MA, 1974) and *Women, Work and Family*, co-authored with Louise Tally (Cambridge, MA, 1974). It was her engagement with feminist history that led to her theoretical turn, leading her to challenge traditional historical practice, including the nature of historical evidence and experience and the role of narrative in the writing of history. This turn came to fruition in her groundbreaking book, *Gender and the Politics of History* (New York, 1988). Her latest book, *Only Paradoxes to Offer* (Cambridge, MA, 1996) joins the two strands of her work in examining the complexities and paradoxes of French law in mandating the equality of male and female candidates in local and national elections. In addition to these works, she has edited eight collections of articles on various aspects of history and feminism and published scores of articles.

William H. Sewell, Jr. is Frank P. Hixton Distinguished Service Professor of History and Political Science at the University of Chicago. His work centers on the history of early modern and modern Europe and on the theoretical relationship between history and social theory. He is the author of *Work and Revolution in France: The Language of Labor from the Old Regime to 1848* (Cambridge, 1980); *Structure and Mobility: The Men and Women of Marseille, 1829–1879* (Cambridge, 1985); and *A Rhetoric of Bourgeois Revolution: The Abbé Sieyes and "What is the Third Estate?"* (Durham, NC, 1994) as well as numerous articles dedicated to developing a theoretical vocabulary that speaks equally to history and the other social sciences. In 2004 he was elected a Fellow of the American Academy of Arts and Sciences.

Gabrielle M. Spiegel joined the University of California, Los Angeles as Dean of Humanities and Distinguished Professor of History in 2004, after serving as the Krieger-Eisenhower Professor of History at Johns Hopkins University. Her work focuses on French medieval history and historiography, literary and cultural theory, and postmodern historiography. She is the author of *The Chronicle Tradition of Saint-Denis: A Survey* (Medieval Classics: Texts and Studies, 10, Brookline and Leiden, 1978); *Romancing the Past: The Rise of Vernacular Prose Historiography in Thirteenth-Century France* (Berkeley and Los Angeles, 1993); *The Past as Text: The Theory and Practice of Medieval Historiography* (Baltimore, 1997); *Il Passato come Testo: Teoria e pratica della storiografia medievale* (Pisa and Rome, 1998); trans. with Stephen Nichols, *Kantorowicz: Stories of a Historian*, by Alain Boureau (Baltimore, 2001) as well as numerous articles on historiography and critical theory.

Gareth Stedman Jones is Director of the Centre for History and Economics, King's College, University of Cambridge and Professor of Political Science in the History Faculty at Cambridge University, where he is a Fellow of King's College. His most recent book is *An End to Poverty?* (London, 2004). His involvement with the linguistic turn is perhaps best seen in his 1983 book, *Languages of Class: Studies in English Working Class History, 1832–1982* (Cambridge, 1983), although he has also published numerous articles in the field in addition to books on English social history such as his well-known *Outcast London* (Oxford, 1971).

SERIES EDITOR'S PREFACE

Rewriting history, or revisionism, has always followed closely in the wake of history writing. In their efforts to re-evaluate the past, professional as well as amateur scholars have followed many approaches, most commonly as empiricists, uncovering new information to challenge earlier accounts. Historians have also revised previous versions by adopting new perspectives, usually fortified by new research, which overturn received views.

Even though rewriting is constantly taking place, historians' attitudes towards using new interpretations have been anything but settled. For most, the validity of revisionism lies in providing a stronger, more convincing account that better captures the objective truth of the matter. Although such historians might agree that we never finally arrive at the "truth," they believe it exists and over time may be better approximated. At the other extreme stand scholars who believe that each generation or even each cultural group or subgroup necessarily regards the past differently, each creating for itself a more usable history. Although these latter scholars do not reject the possibility of demonstrating empirically that some contentions are better than others, they focus upon generating new views based upon different life experiences. Different truths exist for different groups. Surely such an understanding, by emphasizing subjectivity, further encourages rewriting history. Between these two groups are those historians who wish to borrow from both sides. This third group, while accepting that every congeries of individuals sees matters differently, still wishes somewhat contradictorily to fashion a broader history that incorporates both of these particular visions. Revisionists who stress empiricism fall into the first of the three camps, while others spread out across the board.

Today the rewriting of history seems to have accelerated to a blinding speed as a consequence of the evolution of revisionism. A variety of approaches has emerged. A major factor in this process has been the enormous increase in the number of researchers. This explosion has reinforced and enabled the retesting of many assertions. Significant ideological shifts have also played a major part in the growth of revisionism. First, the crisis of Marxism, culminating in the events of Eastern Europe in 1989, has given rise to doubts about explicitly Marxist accounts. Such doubts have spilled over into the entire field of social history which has been a dominant subfield of the discipline for several decades. Focusing on society and its class divisions implied that these are the most important elements in historical analysis. Because Marxism was built on the same claim, the whole basis of social history has been questioned, despite the very many studies that directly had little to do with Marxism. Disillusionment with social history, simultaneously opened the door to cultural and linguistic approaches largely developed in anthropology and literature. Multi-culturalism and feminism further generated revisionism. By claiming that scholars had, wittingly or not, operated from a white European/American male point of view, newer researchers argued that other approaches had been neglected or misunderstood. Not surprisingly, these last historians are the most likely to envision each subgroup rewriting its own usable history, while other scholars incline towards revisionism as part of the search for some stable truth.

Rewriting Histories will make these new approaches available to the student population. Often new scholarly debates take place in the scattered issues of journals which are sometimes difficult to find. Furthermore, in these first inter-actions, historians tend to address one another, leaving out the evidence that would make their arguments more accessible to the uninitiated. This series of books will collect in one place a strong group of the major articles in selected fields, adding notes and introductions conducive to improved understanding. Editors will select articles containing substantial historical data, so that students – at least those who approach the subject as an object-ive phenomenon – can advance not only their comprehension of debated points but also their grasp of substantive aspects of the subject.

Theoretical underpinnings of historical work change just as much as do the fields defined by their subject matter. In fact, an important connection exists between these two kinds of inquiry. Scholarly embrace of specific explan-ations may encourage theoretical formulations. Likewise, shifts in the theor-ies applied can cause non-theorists to try new approaches. Regrettably, one problem faced by a large part of the historical community, from advanced undergraduates through to the most senior scholars, is that they do not understand theoretical issues well enough to see the connection to their work. In this circumstance, they cannot independently evaluate the interaction between the theoretical and the specifically historical.

This book addresses, among other matters, this lack of knowledge. The essays included provide an overview of the major theoretical issues of the last two decades up to the present. Significant and accessible, these essays explain the "linguistic turn" that has dominated theory for some time and inflected work in history. Those who adhere to this approach have argued, and still do, that the "realities" must be interpreted through cultural norms, discourses, and other faculties of the mind. Although the "linguistic turn" has hardly run its course, challenges to its dominance have emerged around the notion of "experience" and "practice." Several articles included here define this new theoretical approach which endeavors to open up a dialectic between action and cultural guideposts. This book also has an important role in this series which has charted revisionism in many fields but has devoted little space to the theoretical changes underpinning alterations in the interpretation of the past.

ACKNOWLEDGMENTS

Mark Bevir, "How to Be an Intentionalist," *History and Theory*, 41 (2002): 209–217.

Richard Biernacki, "Language and the Shift from Signs to Practices in Cultural Inquiry," *History and Theory*, 39 (2000): 289–310.

Pierre Bourdieu, *Outline of the Theory of Practice*, trans. Richard Nice (Cambridge, 1977): pp. 1–30; 72–97.

Michel de Certeau, *The Practice of Everyday Life*, trans. Steven Rendall (Berkeley, 1988). Chapter 3; slightly cut.

Geoff Eley, "Is All the World a Text? From Social History to the History of Society Two Decades Later," in Terrence J. McDonald, ed., *The Historic Turn in the Human Sciences* (Ann Arbor, 1996): 193–244; excerpted.

Elizabeth Deeds Ermarth, "Agency in the Discursive Condition," *History and Theory*, 40 (2001): 34–58; excerpted.

Anthony Giddens, *The Constitution of Society: Outline of the Theory of Structuration* (Berkeley, 1986). Excerpts from Chapter 1; also from pp. 281–284.

Andreas Reckwitz, "Toward a Theory of Social Practices: A Development in Culturalist Theorizing," *European Journal of Social Theory*, 5 (2002): 243–263.

Marshall Sahlins, "Individual Experience and Cultural Order," in *Culture in Practice: Selected Essays* (New York, 2000): 277–291.

Joan Scott, "The Evidence of Experience," *Critical Inquiry* (Summer, 1991): 773–797.

William H. Sewell, Jr., "A Theory of Structure: Duality, Agency and Transformation," *American Journal of Sociology*, 98 (1992): 1–29.

William H. Sewell, Jr., "The Concept(s) of Culture," in Victoria Bonnell and Lynn Hunt, eds, *Beyond the Cultural Turn* (Berkeley, 1999): 35–61.

Gareth Stedman Jones, "The Determinist Fix: Some Obstacles to the Further Development of the Linguistic Approach to History in the 1990s," *History Workshop Journal*, 42 (1996): 19–35.

Every effort has been made to contact the copyright holders and relevant parties. The publishers would be very grateful for notification of any omission.

Note

Some of the following texts have been abridged. Omissions are shown using [. . .] and any insertions are placed in square brackets.

INTRODUCTION

Gabrielle M. Spiegel

The aim of this book has been to gather a variety of writings, some published as early as the 1970s, some very recently, that represent current attempts to rethink the practice of history in light of the implications of what has come to be known as the "linguistic turn." These writings, while strongly influenced by the linguistic turn, are nonetheless driven by a degree of dissatisfaction with its basic postulates. "After the linguistic turn," thus, is intended to signal historical thought that operates within the framework of the linguistic turn, yet seeks to move beyond its initial formulation and reception. The collected articles represent a range of responses to "linguistic turn historiography" and the key issues embedded in it, drawing on earlier works by figures such as Bourdieu, de Certeau, and Sahlins, to mention only a few names, in order to rethink the historian's understanding of his or her practice in a way that acknowledges the powerful insights that a linguistic approach to society and culture has offered, yet to revise it from the perspective of a greater focus on questions of how society undergoes constant transformations in both its material and conceptual realms. Such a concern inevitably foregrounds issues of individual agents, historical actions, and the structural constraints that both enable and limit experience, around which much of the debate currently revolves. At base, the question turns on what we believe history is and how it happens.

It should be stressed that the writers included here represent only a sample of historians specifically engaged with these questions, drawn largely from among social historians (for reasons that will become clear) and the anthropologists and sociologists upon whose work they draw. Omitted from this discussion are many forms of historical inquiry—feminist, postcolonial, transnational, and gender studies—that were and remain equally if not more powerful, but which orient themselves in treating theoretical issues in ways rather different from the group appearing here. The book makes no claim for the primacy of the writings selected, except insofar as they directly, and from a determined theoretical perspective, address the question of the linguistic turn and its theoretical aftermaths. The introduction, therefore, lays out the basic framework of the semiotic model of culture that informed "linguistic turn" historical writing, and also traces the ways in which it is currently being

1

modified by historians, in part through the revival and adaption of earlier works, in part by the elaboration of new points of view, loosely grouped under a novel rubric of "Practice Theory." Although it can hardly be said that a consensus about the place of theory in history reigns today in the historical profession, there appears to be a movement of revision with respect to linguistic turn historiography sufficiently strong to warrant a book of this kind. But we need first to place the debate in relation to its own immediate historiographical and theoretical antecedents, in order to finally evaluate the goals and accomplishments of recent work.

Background

Historians' traditional understanding of the nature, epistemological grounding, truth-value, and goals of research and writing faced a significant challenge beginning in the late 1960s and 1970s with the emergence of what came to be known as the "linguistic turn," the notion that language is the constitutive agent of human consciousness and the social production of meaning, and that our apprehension of the world, both past and present, arrives only through the lens of language's precoded perceptions. Moreover, language, once understood as a relatively neutral medium of communication, sufficiently transparent to convey a reasonably accurate sense of reality, itself had been reconceptualized with the emergence of structural linguistics or semiotics, a movement that began with the publication in 1916 of Ferdinand de Saussure's *Course in General Linguistics*. For Saussure, language was not a transparent mode of referentiality but was, instead, a "system of differences with no positive terms." Thus, far from reflecting the social world of which it is a part, language, he believed, precedes the world and makes it intelligible by constructing it according to its own rules of signification. Since for Saussure such rules are inherently arbitrary, in the sense of being social conventions implicitly understood in different ways by differing linguistic communities, the idea of an objective universe existing independently of speech and universally comprehensible despite one's membership in any particular language system is an illusion.

Such was the "semiotic challenge" posed to the practice of historiography by the rise of structural linguistics and continuing with the successive emergence of structuralism, semiotics, and poststructuralism, including the elaboration of deconstruction.[1] The principal impact of these cognate developments was felt most intensely in the period after World War II; after 1965 they assumed the name "linguistic turn," disseminated through its use in an article on "Metaphysical Difficulties of Linguistic Philosophy" by the pragmatic philosopher Richard Rorty[2] and generalized to various disciplines throughout the course of the 1970s and after. The initial force of the "linguistic turn" in the work of a significant, though by no means universal, segment of historians sensitive to developments in theory was to throw into disarray the conventional postulates of positivist history by undermining its central notions of evidence, "truth," and objectivity. Despite considerable differences among the polemicists and practitioners of the "linguistic turn," I argued in 1990 (for details see note 1), "all began from the premise that language is somehow anterior to the world it shapes; that what we experience of 'reality' is but a socially (i.e. linguistically) constructed artifact or 'effect' of the particular language systems we inhabit," (p. 4). It was this belief in the fundamentally linguistic character of the world and our knowledge of it that formed the core of the "semiotic challenge." At stake in the debate occasioned by the "semiotic challenge" were a number of concepts traditionally deployed by historians in their attempts to understand the past: causality, change, authorial intent, stability of meaning, human agency, and social determination.

Twenty-five years after the adoption of the "linguistic turn," there is a growing sense of dissatisfaction with its overly systematic account of the operation of language in the domain of human endeavors of all kinds. To that extent, it is fair to say that the "semiotic challenge" has been addressed, absorbed, and—most important—is currently undergoing a process of alteration, at least with respect to the ways in which those who accept its basic premise of the social/linguistic construction of the world construe its relevance to, and operation in, the past understood both as an object of study and a subject of practice. We need, then to examine the current status of the debate over the "linguistic turn" by looking at a range of historians who seek to integrate some of its most important principles and yet to refashion them in a way more congenial to historians' traditional concerns with the role of historical actors in shaping the worlds they inherit, inhabit, and inform. Indeed, in a very real sense, the success of the "linguistic turn" among an important number of historians was so great that it has itself generated a new rethinking, not merely among those hostile to theory (which was true from the beginning), but significantly among those most receptive to its insights and advantages.

Among historians who have engaged in these debates, one response to the success of the semiotic/linguistic view of culture and society has taken place via a refocusing on precisely the categories of causality, change, human agency and subjectivity, experience, and a revised understanding of the master category of discourse that stresses less the structural aspects of its linguistic constructs than the pragmatics of their use. Thus practice and meaning have been at least partially uncoupled from the impersonal workings of discursive regimes and rejoined to the active intentions of human agents embedded in social worlds. Rather than being governed by impersonal semiotic codes, historical actors are now seen as engaged in inflecting the semiotic constituents (signs) that shape their understanding of reality so as to craft an experience of that world in terms of a situational sociology of meaning, or what might be called a social semantics.[3] This shift in focus from semiotics to semantics, from given semiotic structures to the individual and social construal of signs; in short, from culture as discourse to culture as practice and performance entails, I would argue, a recuperation of the historical actor as an intentional (if not wholly self-conscious) agent, the precise meaning of which will require an extended discussion below. For the moment, suffice it to say that from a historiographical point of view, what results is the restoration, albeit in a now de-essentialized form, of a version of phenomenology akin, although not identical, to that phenomenology against which the generation of French theorists who articulated the basic premises of poststructuralism struggled. Although it is premature to say that historical writing has managed, through this refocusing, to "save the phenomena," that is, to return to a notion of history as an objective science capable of describing past reality *"wie es eigentlich gewesen,"* it has nonetheless, I believe, reached a point where it is on the verge of "saving the phenomenological," of restoring the historical actor and his or her consciousness of the world, however thoroughly mediated by discourses of one sort or another, to the center of historical concerns.

A notable shift in recent years is the highly visible role that social historians have assumed in current debates, in contrast to the 1970s, when those most strenuously engaged in importing "French theory" tended to draw on literary theorists and to ponder the immediate impact of semiotics in transforming the fields of intellectual and, ultimately, cultural history. Thus, the original phase of the "linguistic turn" in the social sciences revolved around issues of "textuality" and the application of Clifford Geertz's semiotically inspired "text analogy" to a wide range of historical questions and domains.[4] This literary phase in the reception of French theory seems now to be over and historians are turning more to social and sociological theory for inspiration. Indeed, the prominence of social historians in the ongoing reconfiguration of the place of theory in historical writing suggests the degree to which the deepest challenge posed by the "linguistic turn" was to the practice of social history and discloses the extent to which the rise of cultural history (and its socio-cultural cognates in anthropology and sociology) was governed by discontents arising from the then dominant practice of social history, Marxist and non-Marxist alike.

In light of these developments, it is perhaps to be expected that the current movement away from structuralist and poststructuralist readings of history and historiography is similarly governed by the needs and goals of social history, albeit of a kind quite different from that which preceded the advent of the "linguistic turn." In the pages that follow, then, we shall be centrally, although not exclusively, concerned with revisions to social and cultural history taking place in response both to the appropriation *and* the retreat from positions staked out during the high tide of "linguistic turn" historiography. To understand the dynamics of this accomodationist strategy it is important to understand the image of poststructuralism that was polemically deployed in the first place, since it was a particular version of it that set the terms of the original debate, although at issue were not necessarily the most accurate readings of Saussure, Foucault, Barthes, Lyotard, Derrida, and other avatars of the movement that came more generally to be known as postmodernism.

History and semiotics

In the debates that raged among historians throughout the 1970s and 1980s and on into the 1990s, the "linguistic turn" tended to be presented in a highly structuralist version, despite the fact that it entered the academy in the guise of poststructuralism, itself both a continuation and critique of fundamental features of Saussurean linguistics. Thus historians advocating a semiotic view of culture and society tended to emphasize the impersonal operation of semiotic codes as prefiguring, and hence constitutive of, "reality"; to quote without cease Derrida's assertion that poststructuralism marked the moment "when language invaded the universal problematic and everything became discourse"; and to repeat with even greater fervor his lapidary maxim "il n'y a pas de hors texte" ("there is no outside the text"), a phrase that Derrida insists was universally misinterpreted.[5]

Entailed in the adoption of a semiotic model was a far-ranging belief, as Lloyd Kramer explained, in "the active role of language, texts and narrative structures in the creation ... of historical reality."[6] All parties to structural (and poststructural) linguistics agreed that no direct, unmediated apprehension of "reality," however conceived, was possible. In postmodern thought "things" as such, have no social reality apart from their linguistic construction; they are not objective givens in themselves, but rather the product of a linguistic process of "objectification." Hence society is not an "objective structure" to which meanings and actions can be referred as expressions. To understand its operation requires one to understand the constitutive and determining force of the structure of language in all forms and phases of life.

Moreover, by focusing on a specifically Saussurean conception of language (*langue*) as an autonomous structure, distinct from its actualization in speech (*parole*), historians who adopted a semiotic model argued that language was not solely a medium of communication but a structure of objective relations that constituted the condition of possibility for both the production and deciphering of discourse. The analytic priority of language over speech, *langue* over *parole*, meant that "discursive," "literary," "symbolic," "cultural," and, indeed, "social" phenomena were to be deciphered by reference to the underlying linguistic code of a given society, a code composed of a structure of signs whose relation to one another is "arbitrary," in the sense of being based on differential rather than referential values.[7] All cultural practices, all discourse, all forms of activity, whether literary or social, merely "execute" the code-governed properties of the linguistic model, and are to be understood in its terms, rather than with respect to the functions that speech acts, deeds, and practices fulfill. Moreover, since *langue* in its totality is a structure of rules or codes, rather than a realized practice, it governs, but cannot be known by, those who inhabit it, so that all practice is shaped by largely unconscious structures that have effects on behavior but do not contribute to the individual agent's understanding of it.[8]

One inference common among historians dubious about the linguistic turn, was, as John Toews maintained in a highly influential article, that "the creation of meaning is impersonal, operating 'behind the backs' of language users whose linguistic actions can merely exemplify the rules and procedures of the languages they inhabit but do not control."[9] In that sense, the objectivity of the linguistic model in a Saussurean scheme remains essentially virtual, yet paradoxically is hypostatized in the analytic priority and realism granted to the structure. "Structures," in a structuralist vocabulary, tend, as William Sewell has complained, "to assume a far too rigid causal determinism in social life ... while the events or social processes they structure tend to be seen as secondary, and superficial." Structures appear "as impervious to human agency, to exist apart from, but nevertheless to determine the essential shape of the strivings and motivated transactions that constitute the experienced surface of social life." A social science which relies on a notion of structure, he argues, "tends to reduce actors to cleverly programmed automatons."[10] Marshall Sahlins, himself heavily influenced by structuralism and remaining faithful to some of its fundamental ideas, concurs, believing that "poststructuralism, postmodernism and other afterological studies developed a sense of cultural determinism so oppressive, an idea of social order so totalizing, as to conjure up the 'superorganic' notions of culture produced in the 1950s."[11] In Sahlins's view, discourse, when viewed as the embodiment of linguistic structure, is "the new cultural superorganic—made even more draconian as the expression of a 'power' that is everywhere, in all quotidian institutions and relations."[12] Structuralism in general, whether linguistic as in the case of Saussure, or anthropological as in the case of Claude Lévi-Strauss, or sociological, as in the early writings of Pierre Bourdieu, privileges the hidden, unconscious operation of synchronic structures over conscious, purposive individual activity. By stressing the structural and systematic nature of the underlying linguistic model, historians espousing the linguistic turn proclaimed the discursive condition to be a set of available languages, preordained scripts, and semiotic codes that created not only the condition of possibility for all thought and behavior, but also served as their determining mechanisms of production.

To be sure, another reading of Saussure was always possible, one that stressed language not only as a differential—that is, non-referential—system of meaning, but which also insisted on the disjunction between potential and practice (*langue* and *parole*), and which, as Elizabeth Deeds Ermarth points out, saw linguistic systems as forever incompletable, incapable, as long as they remained living languages, of becoming "totalized" because always capable of new specifications.[13] For Ermarth, there exists an all-important "gap" between the potential capacities of a given semiotic code, on the one hand, and any particular specification of it on the other.[14] Indeed, deconstruction and most forms of poststructuralism focused precisely on this "supplementarity" in language, its non-totalizable, indeterminate, ambiguous, discontinuous, and heterodox nature. Yet this did not prevent historians from emphasizing language's structural, and *structuring*, aspects. It is a mark of this reading of semiotic theory that the French theorist who most influenced *historians* was the early (that is, archeological, or pre-genealogical) Foucault.[15]

The cultural turn

The structuralist thrust of this early phase in the advent of the linguistic turn was favored for the ways in which it enabled cultural historians to free themselves from the governing paradigm of social history, dominant everywhere in the historical profession from the 1930s on.[16] The fundamental orientation of social history as it had emerged in the various schools of Marxist history (England), *Annaliste* historiography (France) or the New History in the United States (originating in the 1930s and revived powerfully in the 1960s) derived from social science models that posited society as an objective structure of relations of which individual thought and activity was the unmediated, subjective expression. Culture was to society as subjective to objective, and social science models put their faith in the determining status of the latter. The primary causal forces in history thus resided in deep social structures of *longue durée* (in the French case seen as virtually immobile, as in the writings of Ferdinand Braudel). Culture, while not necessarily an epiphenomenon or "superstructure" in the Marxist sense, nonetheless was viewed as a secondary element, the subjective enactment of underlying interests and identities generated, in the first instance, by the terms and demands of social being.

Yet discontent with the classic model of social history mounted as anomalies accumulated, difficulties born of the inability to coordinate individual and even class social behaviors and cultural expressions with the objective structures that in theory produced them.[17] Increasingly, as Roger Chartier, a pioneer of cultural history in France, explained:

> work in history has shown that it is impossible to characterize cultural themes, objects, and practices in immediately sociological terms, and, furthermore, that the distribution and uses of those themes, objects and practices in a given society are not necessarily compatible with preexisting social divisions established on the basis of differences of status and wealth.[18]

At the same time, British Marxists, and E.P. Thompson above all, were expressing similar dissatisfactions with the overly deterministic explanatory thrust of social theory. They responded by elaborating a concept of "experience" as the domain in which, as Thompson proclaimed, "structure is transformed into process and the subject re-enters history,"[19] not merely as an expression of larger forces but as a conscious agent who interprets his or her life in terms of cultural norms, traditions, moral and familial values and feelings, and religious beliefs. Thus "experience" emerged in Thompson's work as an intermediate category, the place where social forces and interests were interpreted and handled in both voluntary and normative fashion to produce a broad form of social (class, in his case) consciousness created by social actors themselves. Yet to the extent that Thompson and others remained faithful to the original premise of social history—that social life is governed, at base, by circumstances not of mens' choosing—they preserved the material, "objective" side of social determination and left intact social history's distinction between objective and subjective in which the fundamental vector of causal explanation ran from society to consciousness. Or as Thompson himself put it: "Experience . . . has, in the last instance, been generated in 'material life,' has been structured in class ways, and hence 'social being' has determined 'social consciousness.'"[20] An analogue of this development in France can be seen in the emergence of the study of *mentalités*, which had a brief period of prominence in the 1960s in the work of LeGoff and others and which, like its English counterpart, preserved the basic contours of the social history paradigm and, therefore, its inherent—and problematic—mechanism of social causality.[21]

The "linguistic turn," with its reliance on Saussurean semiotics, addressed the problems that had accumulated in the practice of social history by carving out, as we have seen, an arena of genuine autonomy for culture as a self-enclosed, non-referential mechanism of social construction that precedes the world and renders it intelligible by constructing it according to its own rules of signification. As a result, cultural history emerged as a field that attempted to overcome the division between society and culture; to avoid the social determinism that was a by-product of the mechanistic causal model and functionalist methodology employed in the social sciences; and to propose culture as an autonomous realm in which the principal stakes were not the pursuit of individual or class interests but the creation of domains of meaning. In this, cultural historians were powerfully influenced—in ways far too well known to rehearse here—by the rise of symbolic anthropology and, in particular, by the adoption of Geertz's conception of culture as "an interworked system of construable signs"[22] whose goal was expressive rather than instrumental and by the application of his "text analogy" to the analysis and interpretation of social behavior.

Although cultural history never abandoned a belief in the objective reality of the social world (and, therefore, is perhaps more properly termed sociocultural history), the enthusiasm for interpretive approaches and above all the shift in the focus of investigation from social phenomena to discourses—a mark of the overwhelming influence of Foucault—tended to occlude the differences between the cultural turn and the linguistic turn.[23] Throughout the 1980s, the growing attention to language and discursive structures challenged the causal model of the old social history and tended to substitute discursive models of culture that claimed to demonstrate, with the aid of Saussurean linguistics, the culturally (i.e. linguistically) constructed nature of society and the individual's experience of the world. So thorough-going was this reversal that social historians like Geoff Eley were led to query: "Is All the World a Text?"

The revisionist critique

Current dissatisfaction with the "linguistic turn" has fastened on its overly systematic account of the operation of language. Richard Biernacki, for example, has criticized what he calls its "formalizing" and "essentializing" premises, inherited from the past and never adequately overcome. To explain the "formalizing premise," Biernacki points to the structuralist concept that "meaning is generated by the synchronic relations among signs in a sign system," requiring researchers interested in cultural meaning "to isolate the contrasts and systematic relations among the signs employed in a semiotic community,"[24] hence to undertake a formal analysis of the totality of the semiotic system as that which comprises the architecture or structure of a culture. Implicit in this approach is a belief in a given culture's ultimate coherence on the level of *langue*, if not on the level of practice.

Moreover, Biernacki contends, the theory of culture as sign system led inexorably to the second of the two major assumptions infiltrating historical work in the 1980s, namely an "essentializing premise," attributable to the manner in which "cultural investigators mistook the concepts of 'sign' and 'sign reading' for parts of the natural furniture of the world, rather than as historically generated 'ways of seeing.'"[25] Paradoxically, the paradigm of the sign system became the only exception to the rule that all concepts are conjured by convention, are arbitrary and historical, not natural in origin, including those of historians. In Biernacki's opinion, the "linguistic turn" in historical study was solidified only when historians found they could persuasively combine both formalizing and essentializing premises: "the proposal that culture consists of a (partially) cohesive, intelligible system of signs fused with the proposal that our general notion of a sign system reflects a basic and irreducible sphere of being." Hence the irreducibility of culture substituted for the social historian's belief in the irreducibility of experience, and was thereby naturalized, despite repeated protestations to the contrary.

In this combination, the "formalizing premise" provided a methodological tool for the analysis of discourses as formal semantic systems while the "essentializing premise" asserted the primacy and autonomy of culture in historical processes, an assertion shored up by formalism's ability to make a sign system constitutive and definitive of the conduct of historical actors;[26] together they made it possible to bridge the gap between the abstract semiotic system and agents' use of signs as tools for "reading" the world. Small wonder that Gareth Stedman Jones has less elegantly, but perhaps more forthrightly, named the combined workings of these premises the "determinist fix," which he attributes to cultural history's canny use of a linguistic approach while remaining loyal to the "undead residue of historical materialism" that has been, in his opinion, the legacy of Michel Foucault to postmodernism.[27]

Current efforts to modify the basic postulates of poststructuralism have concentrated on the issues most hotly contested during the high tide of the "linguistic phase" of the postmodern turn. At present, a widespread movement of revision is underway, directed toward new understandings of the key concepts, or master terms, around and through which the debate has been channeled: discourse, subject, agency, practice, experience, in short, meaning and culture as historical phenomena. Thus, as some historians in France, Britain, and America have begun to remark, the "linguistic turn" in the social sciences has now been succeeded by a "historical turn,"[28] although the meaning of this statement remains to be specified. In order to understand its possible significance, it will be helpful to focus on the series of key terms that serve as vehicles for the present movement of revision.

Discourse

To begin with, there is a more nuanced and much broader understanding of discourse as a field of practices that far exceeds the linguistic, taking into account complex phenomena such as "institutions," "political events," "economic activities," and the like, that is, arenas of human endeavor traditionally thought to lie beyond or outside the discursive realm. (Socio-cultural history, for example, had always left to the side of discourse an understanding of material reality as context, against which it elaborated its discursive readings.) This broader understanding of discourse, of course, was already present in Foucault, especially if attention was paid to the ways that his interpretation of "discourse" and "discursive structures" changed over the course of his career. In his early work, Foucault tended to focus on vast discursive structures, or *epistemes*, as composed of fundamental "codes of culture ... that establish for every man the empirical order with which he will be dealing." Such codes formed the "mental grids" according to which people processed information and thus lived their lives, constituting individual perception as an effect of "the already encoded eye."[29] After the mid-1970s, Foucault's "genealogical" orientation,[30] as well as his elaboration of the notion of knowledge/power, gave greater emphasis to the material and institutional practices and technologies of knowledge that underlie, support, and/or contest discursive formations, themselves multiple and undergoing constant processes of change, a shift in focus that was especially pronounced in his last essays on governmentality. The state, the prison, the clinic, society, sex, and the "soul" are produced by particular technologies of knowledge—they are the "objectifications" to which discursive regimes give rise—and in this way are themselves discourses.[31] In that sense, Foucault's later use of the term discourse, as Nicholas Dirks has emphasized, should not be confused with "language" or textuality—indeed is defined in ways that sharply distinguish it from language. Discourse is, rather, "about the conditions under which the world presents itself as real, about the way institutions and historical practices become regimes of truth and of possibility itself."[32] And since discourse in this meaning is synonymous with knowledge, which is in turn inseparable from power, it does not stand outside of or analytically prior to its social embodiments—as does Saussurean *langue*—but is dispersed throughout the entire range of the social, institutional, and material practices of a society. Discourse thus assumes the place of a specific social realm involving structures of domination and systems of power, ones that operate according to their various internal "logics," within which practices of every kind are embedded.

From this perspective, current work on "discourse" has in a sense *rediscovered* and come newly to emphasize the ways in which discourse is tied to institutions and social practices, and similarly has insisted that any given society is constituted through a multiplicity of dynamic, fluid, and ever-changing systems of meaning (discourses), which create regimes of practical rationality and action as well as regimes of "truth."[33] When discourse is understood in this larger sense, questions of practice, hence of self and agency, are newly foregrounded.

Self, subjectivity, and agency

As William Reddy noted recently, "a chorus of dissatisfaction has sounded against the 'linguistic turn,' and 'agency' has arisen as a catchword for what is missing from recent linguistic theories."[34] The dissatisfaction arises from the highly structuralist interpretation of subjectivity that had prevailed earlier. Indeed, a revised understanding of subjectivity was intrinsic to the abandonment of phenomenology from the earliest days of structuralism. No one stated it more clearly than Foucault when, recalling his first encounter with Saussure in the late 1940s while attending lectures of Maurice Merleau-Ponty, he said:

> I remember clearly [that] . . . the problem of language appeared and it was clear that phenomenology was no match for structural analysis in accounting for the effects of meaning that could be produced by a structure of the linguistic type, in which the subject (in the phenomenological sense) did not intervene to convey meaning.[35]

The subject, instead, like the meaning conveyed, was an "effect" of discourse, not an individual, centered, unitary person as humanism had envisaged him/her, so much as a position assigned by and within discursive practices. Thus what was paramount and primary was discourse, which logically preceded the construction of the subject, as Foucault made abundantly clear in the early chapters of *The Archeology of Knowledge*, announcing his decision to "abandon any attempt to see discourse as a phenomenon of expression." "Discourse," he declared, "is not the majestically unfolding manifestation of a thinking, knowing, speaking subject, but, on the contrary,

11

a totality, in which the dispersion of the subject and his discontinuity with himself may be determined."[36] Discourse *produces* the subject, who is not a self-conscious or self-determining agent, but rather a "subject position" created by discourse and occupying a determinate space within it. Hence Foucault famously announced the "death of man," who, in the closing lines to *The Order of Things*, Foucault predicted "would soon disappear like a face drawn in sand at the edge of the sea" (New York, 1970, 386–387).

The consequences for historical analysis of the "death of the subject" were to throw the concepts of agency, experience, and practice into disarray, since absent a purposive historical actor and any concept of intentionality, it is impossible to establish a ground from which the individual can fashion his or her destiny on the basis of his or her experience of the world. The self has been reduced to an entirely constructed and "plastic nodal point in a discursive or cultural system."[37] Agency in the discursive condition, Elizabeth Deeds Ermarth notes, "is not a singularity but a process, a happening, a particular expression of systematic value."[38] The person (or subject) is construed as a "moving specifier," which cannot be encompassed by sociological generalizations. What disappeared in this treatment of the subject was the historian's traditional attempt to connect presence and sense, act and intention, practice and meaning, leaving in its place a *moleculating*,[39] dispersed subjectivity, deriving from the multiple discursive conditions within which, at each moment, a complex subjective specification involving multiple codes takes place. Poststructuralism defined the subject not only as discursively constituted but also as controlled, ultimately, by the social as hegemonically, that is, discursively thought (knowledge/power). Such a view of the postmodern self was spelled out most clearly by Joan Scott, for whom "being a subject means being '*subject to*' definite conditions of existence, conditions of endowment of agents and conditions of exercise."[40] As a consequence, in the view of David Gary Shaw, "the self as articulated in much [poststructuralist] historical theory is so divested of autonomy and control that it can't really operate as a cause, as an agent; and the postmodern self doesn't even aspire to be a center."[41]

Recent literature on the topic of self and agency has been sharply critical of the fracturing, decentering effects of structuralist and poststructuralist formulations. Most historians are disposed to agree with Judith Newton that the fact that subjects are culturally (historically) determined does not mean that the subject is dead or that "human agency in a changing world is for the most part illusory."[42] It is precisely by focusing on the question of how subjects effect change that the rehabilitation of agency—of "human intentionality and forms of empowerment to act"[43]—has centered. At present, there exists a wide range of responses to the question of agency, from those who remain—like de Certeau, Scott, and Ermarth—fully within a semiotic framework, while focusing on practices, to scholars like Bevir, who attempt to recuperate something akin to a humanist conception of the individual considered as the source and generator of social and intellectual meaning.

12

Others, like Bourdieu, Giddens, Sahlins, Sewell, and Biernacki (and in a slightly different fashion de Certeau as well) tend to focus on the adaptive, strategic, and tactical uses made of existing cultural schemes by agents who, in the very act of deploying the elements of culture, both reproduce and transform them. In that sense, all the authors represented in this collection, to one degree or another, take an actor-centered, or neo-phenomenological approach, one defined primarily in ethnomethodological terms.[44] Put more simply, these scholars begin from a belief in individual perception as the agent's own source of knowledge about, and action in, the world, a perception mediated and perhaps constrained, but *not* wholly controlled, by the cultural scaffolding or conceptual schemes within which it takes place. Even here, there are wide differences of emphasis on the relative contexts of freedom and constraint within which agents operate, depending on the degree to which a given author emphasizes structure over process, or vice versa.

A key aspect of this neo-phenomenological approach is that it seeks, as Bourdieu explains (although dissenting from its analytic utility),

> to make explicit the primary experience of the social world, i.e. all that is inscribed in the relationship of familiarity with the familiar environment, the unquestioning apprehension of the social world which, by definition, does not reflect on itself and excludes the question of the conditions of its own possibility.[45]

Insofar as they share this view, many historians are deploying a (largely implicit) concept of "social phenomenology," in which, as Andreas Reckwitz explains,

> the aim of social analysis is to take over the "subjective perspective," i.e. to reconstruct the sequence of mental acts of consciousness which are located "inside" and are directed in the form of phenomenological "intentionality" at outward objects to which the consciousness ascribes meanings. The social then is ... the subjective *idea* of a common world of meanings ... The aim of social-as-cultural analysis from the point of view of social phenomenology, then, is to describe the subjective acts of (mental) interpretations of agents and their schemes of interpretation.[46]

Such a return to the "subjective perspective" of historical beings and their "mental acts of consciousness" might appear as a revival of earlier notions of the "individual" as a freely acting agent and thus as a return to the status ante quo of the "linguistic turn." The most pronounced version of this reassertion of the unconstrained character of individual meaning-making appears in the work of Mark Bevir, whose reclamation of an intentional theory of meaning—albeit a "weak intentionalism"—entails the hermeneutic actions of what he calls the "procedural individual."[47] Despite the somewhat awkward and arcane terminology, Bevir's argument, set forth in his recent book *The Logic of the History of Ideas* (Cambridge, 1999), clearly aims at the recuperation of the liberal subject, understood as an individual operating within received traditions but in ways that, while conditioned by intellectual traditions and social inheritances that exercise their influences on him/her, are nonetheless wholly unconstrained by such cultural legacies. Bevir insists that although he defends the capacity of the individual for agency (in the sense just stipulated), he explicitly rejects the idea of the individual as autonomous—what he labels "atomistic individualism"—since "individuals only ever can come to hold beliefs or perform actions against the background of a social tradition that influences them."[48] Yet Bevir's desire that his argument be understood against the linguistic turn's rejection of the liberal, humanist subject emerges clearly in his declaration that

> [r]ecent theories disclose a virulent anti-humanism in which the individual is apparently portrayed as a mere dupe of language, discourse, or power/knowledge, lacking any capacity to reflect on, let alone innovate within, the iron constraints of . . . social contexts.[49]

In contrast to structuralist and poststructuralist anti-humanism, Bevir contends, he seeks to "grapple with concepts tied to the creativity of the individual subject—concepts such as agency, intentionality and intuition."[50] In the light of such statements, it is difficult to distinguish his insistence on the free exercise of individual reason from the beliefs of earlier humanist historians. At the very least, there is a clear departure here from the wholly public notion of culture critical to a semiotic understanding of language as it had been deployed by writers as diverse as Foucault and Geertz. Although Bevir may represent a somewhat extreme pole in terms of the positions being staked out on questions of self and agency, his forthright reclaiming of a voluntarist individualism is symptomatic of more general tendencies.

Among historians less willing to abandon the structural insights of the linguistic turn, the reinsertion of the agent as effective actor has been achieved largely by highlighting the disjunction between culturally given meanings and individual uses of them in contingent, historically conditioned ways. Historical agency, from this perspective, represents the individual's relationship to the cultural order, "the embodiment of collective powers in individual persons," as Sahlins puts it.[51] It may, but for some thinkers need not, include the sort of conscious intentionality in relation to things and behavior suggested above by Reckwitz. Thus Bourdieu's famous notion of *habitus*, comprising the conceptual schemes and dispositions that guide and govern an individual's life strategies and tactics, remains a largely unconscious source of behavior. In *Outline of a Theory of Practice*, Bourdieu defines *habitus* as "an acquired system of generative schemes objectively adjusted to the particular conditions in which it is constituted; the *habitus* engenders all the thoughts, all the perceptions, and all the actions consistent with those conditions and no others."

It constitutes, in Bourdieu's view, an "immanent law . . . [a] *lex insita* laid down in each agent by his earliest upbringing," one that "makes coherence and necessity out of accident and contingency," that, in effect, turns history into nature.[52] The *habitus* thus functions as "the strategy-generating principle enabling agents to cope with unforeseen and ever-changing situations"[53] without in any way being the product of obedience to rules, despite the fact that, as in the earlier quote, it defines the parameters and schemas within and according to which all thoughts and behaviors take place, allowing for those "and no others."

At its root, minimalist definition, agency refers to the individual's capacity to act, to *do* something (intentionally or otherwise), implying at the very least an agent's practical knowledge and mastery of the common elements or conventions of culture, a form of cultural competency founded "less upon discursive than practical consciousness."[54] Thus for Michel de Certeau the examination of cultural and interpretive practices emphatically "does not imply a return to individuality" or individual consciousness because, as Jonathan Carter similarly suggests from a semiotic perspective, the problem of individualism does not arise, since "signs are intrinsically social . . . and even in the case of perception, we mediate experience in shared, public terms."[55] In both versions, the emphasis on understanding culture from the actor's point of view as a process of doing and practical meaning-making retains, yet modifies, the earlier stress on the systematic character of culture as a structure or web of signification.

Formulations like this continue to regard the structure of practice as an unintended and unconscious locus of meaning construction for historical actors, a sort of intermediate structure in and of itself. Biernacki, for example, argues that the pragmatics of sign usage comprises a "structure" and generator of meaning in its own right. As a structure, a set of organizing principles, "practice" need not be fully conscious in order to shape conduct and interpretation.[56] In a similar vein, Jacques Revel has warned historians not to give terms like "strategy" too reductive a meaning, or to make it too simply instrumental, for the choices exercised by historical agents are themselves a product of socialization

> in that they are inseparable from the representations of relationships, space, the resources which it places at their disposal, the obstacles and constraints which it imposes on them and which define the perpetually changing configurations in the interior of which they must situate themselves, evaluate and then exploit their possibilities.[57]

Yet such an approach would seem, at the very least, to reintroduce a thinking, cognizing subject able to negotiate within his or her cultural repertoire, whether the subject is understood to be fully conscious or not.

Essential to this approach is an understanding of practices of *resignification* and their recursive nature by means of which, as Anthony Giddens has argued, the structure teaches agents who help to form the structure, in a circular process that Giddens terms "structuration." A fundamental aspect of the concept of structuration is Giddens' claim on behalf of the "duality of structure," according to which "the structural properties of social systems are both medium and outcome of the practice they recursively organize."[58] The theory of structuration relies neither on the experience of the individual actor nor the existence of any form of social totality. Rather, human practices and activities are seen as "recursive," that is to say "they are not brought into being by social actors, but continually *recreated* by them via the very means whereby they express themselves as actors."[59]

By insisting on the "duality" of structure and the recursive character inherent in its social reproduction, Giddens is able to preserve some principal insights of a semiotic concept of culture while loosening its totalizing and determining influence on individual practices. Structure persists as a set of "rules and resources," "procedures of action," and aspects of praxis, but exists as such only in a virtual state, made palpable and thus socially real through their deployment by human actors. Structure, in that sense, effectively comes into being and is sustained through the continuity generated by the social practices of human actors; their practical activities embody and enact, but never perfectly replicate its constituent components. This is because Giddens accepts a hermeneutic starting point for the theory of structuration, one that considers the discursive formulation of a rule to be "already an interpretation of it that may in and of itself alter the form of its application,"[60] making structure itself a process (hence "structuration") rather than a stable scheme or system.

A more openly semiotic, though similarly revisionist, understanding of culture as a process of continual reappropriation and differential use of structural components (i.e. signs) can be seen in Michel de Certeau, whose *The Practice of Everyday Life* proposes that historians adopt the point of view of enunciation (*parole*) rather than structure (*langue*) as the focus of investigation, so that enunciation becomes the heuristic model by which to understand the practical activity of human agents/actors. The situated nature of language use makes of enunciation, says de Certeau:

> a nexus of circumstances, a nexus adherent to the "context" from which it can be distinguished only by abstraction. Indissociable from the present instant, from the particular circumstances and from a *faire* (a peculiar way of doing things, of producing language and of modifying the dynamics of a relation), the speech act is at the same time a use of language and an operation performed within it.[61]

Arts of speaking, like arts of "doing" disclose the ways that agents adopt and adapt—in effect practice—culture in loosely regulated ways, achieving through use the tactical, strategic, and personal aims and behaviors that take place in the interstices of normative spaces. Practices function like improvisations, individual ruses and devices, presuming (as improvisation while playing the piano does, for example) the knowledge and application of codes, but according to a logic of action relative to situations, without a specific field of action. Everyday practices generate an *uncodable* difference within systems, operating as a silent, illegible *poesis* of "doing," "making," and signification. Meaning here operates not at the level of code or structure, but on that of the semantics of ordinary language use, constructing the world through its continual and practical creation and recreation over time.

By proposing "semantic" in place of "semiotic" constructivism, these historians argue that no past use of a term determines its application to the next case, hence there always exists a domain of indeterminacy about which concept or convention is relevant and how it is to be construed. Taken together, the varying modalities of use account for how culture is "sustained, mediated, replicated and changed."[62] Agency, thus, consists in the adaptive and individual deployment of available, circulating meaning. It therefore signals, and relies upon, the linguistic and practical competence of historical actors, which Bernard Lepetit defines as

> the capacity to recognize the plurality of normative fields and to identify their respective specific contents; the aptitude to discern the characteristics of a situation and the qualities of its protagonists; the faculty, finally, of inserting themselves into the interstitial spaces that the universe of rules manages between them, to mobilize for their own profit the most adequate system of norms and taxonomies, to construct on the basis of disparate rules and values the interpretations that differentially organize the world.[63]

A notable feature of this focus on agency in the present context is the new attention given to enactment rather than discourse, together with a fresh awareness of the productive openness and individualizing potential created by the gap between *langue* and *parole* as a space of indetermination, hence of individual intention and action. Indeed, David Gary Shaw would go so far as to suggest that the attempt to rehabilitate notions of agency and self allows a refurbished role for the rational,[64] a rationality that emerges in the context of choice and interests, rather than functioning as a specified, discursive logic. By reappropriating meanings (by *resignifying*) as a way of responding to or making sense of events as they happen, historical actors construe their culture from the point of view of their self-preservation and self-presentation, and creatively bend it to the conditions of daily life. Agency, therefore, becomes, as Kathleen Canning indicates,

> a site of mediation between discourses and experiences [that] serves not only to dislodge the deterministic view in which discourse always

seems to construct experience, but also to dispel the notion that discourses are shaped by everything but the experiences of the people texts claim to represent.[65]

Experience and practice

As should be clear by now, the new master concepts in post-linguistic turn historiography are experience and practice. Indeed, no term in the post-modern lexicon has been as vexed as that of experience, for it rapidly became the center around which dissent against the linguistic turn revolved. Few historians were as resolute as John Toews in pronouncing the irreducibility of "experience," while urging that, in the face of what he held to be the semi-otic reduction of experience to meaning, historians needed to

> reaffirm in new ways that, in spite of the relative autonomy of cultural meanings, human subjects still make and remake the worlds of meaning in which they are suspended and that ... these worlds are not creations ex nihilo but responses to, and shapings of, changing worlds of experience ultimately *irreducible* to the linguistic forms in which they appear.[66]

In an impassioned jeremiad, Toews quotes Keith Baker's warning that to accept a structuralist approach to language is to extend "an offer of the entire world as a domain of meaning, but at the cost of our historical souls."[67] The language is symptomatic of many historians' instinctive recoil before the notion that experience, the bedrock of social history, might be a mere "effect" of discourse, since it seems to deny a host of putatively pre-discursive, bodily sensations that could be thought both to exceed and to escape discursive construction. Feminist historian Joan Scott remains almost alone in pursuing a (post)structuralist logic to the end when she proclaims that: "Experience is a subject's history. Language is the site of history's enactment. Historical explanation cannot, therefore, separate the two."[68] With impeccable consistency, Scott argues that an acceptance of the mediated and constructed nature of the world in language commits one to a view of "experience" as insepar-able from discursive formations, since in effect "experience is a linguistic event."[69] For Scott, the insistence on "experience" represents an attempt to re-essentialize the subject, whereas, she believes, "a refusal of essentialism seems particularly important once again these days within the field of history, as disciplinary pressure builds to defend the unitary subject in the name of his or her experience."[70]

Scott's appraisal of the underlying motive for preserving "experience" as a primary category of historical analysis is surely correct. Yet it is notable that even feminist historians, who were among the earliest to espouse the "linguistic turn" because of its evident utility in denaturalizing sexual differ-ence, have cast a dubious eye on the notion that discourses position subjects and *produce* their experiences. Language is, more often, seen as the locus for the articulation of experience, which therefore does not, as Ricoeur once commented, "arrive *in* language but only comes *to* language."[71] Experience, understood in this manner, represents all the ways that persons have of responding to or making meanings of events as they occur, that process by which action in the world is construed via a "creative appropriation of the conditions of daily life."[72] Similarly, historians doing microhistory and *Alltagsgeschichte*, both centrally concerned with the everyday life-experiences of individual historical actors, have tended to present experience as the "ground of a new knowledge that is located in bodily and material conditions" of existence, "situated outside textually mediated discourses in the actualities of everyday lives."[73]

Thus a renewed emphasis on bodily dispositions—*habitus* and *hexis*—has appeared in recent discussions among cultural historians, stressing the ways in which "agents call on bodily competencies that have their own structure and coordinating influence, incorporating corporeal principles of practical knowledge."[74] The hallmark of this approach is a new conceptualization of the body, no longer seen as an "instrument" used by an agent in order to act, but the place where mental, emotional, and behavioral routines are inscribed. Such routines are not necessarily the result of reflection but are better understood as the product of social practices imbibed primarily, though not exclusively, at an early age simply by virtue of living in the world—what Bourdieu felicitously calls "the hidden persuasion of an implicit pedagogy."[75] As such, they never attain the level of conscious principles of action. Rather, the principles embodied in this way, Bourdieu asserts, "are placed beyond the grasp of consciousness, and hence cannot be touched by voluntary, deliberate transformation, cannot even be made explicit." For Bourdieu, bodily dispositions (including motor functions or *hexis*) represent a transference of the logic of the structure, now em-*bodied* in practical techniques of the body as a sort of *pars totalis*.[76] Everyday practices combine to construct the "socially informed body" which, in its incorporated state, possesses "the instruments of an ordering of the world, a system of classifying schemes which organizes all practice and of which the linguistic scheme . . . is only one aspect."[77]

As in the case of linguistic competence, bodily competence permits the agent to "perform" the world, to speak the social, as it were. Understood in this way, social practices *are* routinized bodily performances, incorporating both a way of "knowing how"—to act, to be an agent, to do something—and a (practical, unreflexive) knowledge of the world. Knowledge is itself a social practice—a mental routine—one largely implicit and always culturally specific, transforming the agent into a body/mind that "carries" and "carries out" the social world.[78] In that sense, Reckwitz points out, the routinized practices conducted by bodied agents collapse the traditional distinction "between inside and outside, between mind and body."[79] The body is not the instrument but the constituent of action, and bodily dispositions construct the world, Biernacki and Jordan argue, from within the order of the body *in situ*.[80]

Given this renewed emphasis on the body, it is not surprising that Patrick Joyce has recently pointed to the emergence of something like a new "material turn" in the social sciences.[81]

It is in the domain of practice where bodily dispositions are enacted, and it is to concepts of practice that post-linguistic turn historiography has resorted to recuperate the historical through a reinterpretation of culture itself as an "organizing style" of practice. As William Sewell points out, "the past decade and a half has witnessed a pervasive reaction against the concept of culture as a system of symbols and meanings," inclining rather to the belief "that culture is a sphere of practical activity shot through by willful action, power relations, struggle, contradiction and change."[82] In this view, culture emerges less as a systematic structure than as a repertoire of competencies, a "tool kit," a regime of practical rationality or a set of strategies guiding action, whereby symbols/signs are mobilized to identify those aspects of the agent's experience which, in this process, are made meaningful, that is experientially "real."

Culture, thereby, is recast as a "performative term," one realized only processually (diachronically) as "signs put to work" to "reference" and interpret the world. Historical investigation, from this perspective, would take practices (not structure) as the starting point of social analysis, since practice emerges here as the space in which a meaningful intersection between discursive constitution and individual initiative occurs. This initiative is, in the first instance, cognitive, a subject's ongoing reformulation of values, priorities, interests, and behaviors in terms provided, but not governed, by available discourses or languages (i.e. sign systems).[83] Skills, competencies, language as tool kit, strategies, and the like are seen as pervasive constituents of agents' surroundings, but also embody their practical/discursive grasp of the world and articulate their individual possibilities for understanding. Hence praxis takes its place as a situational sociology of meaning—or "sémantique des situations" as Lepetit calls it[84]—which assumes that individuals who are members of a semiotic community are capable not only of recognizing statements made in a semiotic code, but of using the code as well, of putting it into practice in the sense of "attaching abstractly available symbols to concrete things and circumstances and thereby to posit something about them."[85]

Meanings, in this approach, are never simply "inscribed on the minds or bodies of those to whom they are directed, but are always reinscribed in the act of reception."[86] Culture, therefore, William Sewell argues, should be understood as a dialectic of system and practice, the former understood structurally, but modified in its effects by the contradictory, contested, and constantly changing ways in which it is implemented in the latter.[87] To engage in any form of cultural practice means drawing upon a set of socially conventional, thus commonly shared, meanings in order to be understood and to be consequential. In that sense, practice implies system, while the system itself— as almost all the advocates of a revised semiotics/structuralism seem to insist—exists only in the continuity bestowed upon it by the succession of practices that instantiate it. Hence, for Sewell, system and practice consti-tute an indissoluble duality (or dialectic) and the important theoretical question is not, as he says, "whether culture should be conceptualized as practice or as a system of symbols and meanings, but how to conceptualize the articulation of system and practice."[88]

Sewell's argument on behalf of a dialectical understanding of culture as the interplay between system and practice in social life seems to me indicative of the theoretical negotiations inherent in the "accomodationist" strategy governing much of the critique of the "linguistic turn." To maintain the systematicity of culture while carving out large areas for human autonomy in its pragmatic application, Sewell is compelled to propose a notion of culture's "thin" coherence, one that is always at stake due to its inherently loose, ill-integrated, contradictory nature, and centrifugal tendencies.[89]

In ways not dissimilar, Marshall Sahlins has argued that every practical act is at the same time a form of cultural reproduction, and every repro-duction of received cultural categories is also "an alteration, insofar as in action, the categories by which a present world is orchestrated pick up some novel empirical content." Like Sewell, Sahlins sees history as a dialogue between "received categories and perceived contexts, between cultural sense and practical reference," a dialogue that puts into question any rigidly structuralist concept of culture as discursive regime by examining how cultural concepts are used to engage the world.[90] When put to work, lan-guage is "exposed to the profound dynamism of sign usage and acquires novel meaning."[91] Thus all perception, all meaning-making occurs within historically contingent, sociologically situated contexts, produced by agents who function as purposive users and semantic resignifiers of historically constructed sign systems or discourses. And it goes without saying that agents' understandings of themselves—of their individual and collective iden-tities—are encom-passed by the very historicity within which their lives, hence perceptions, take place.

Although Sahlins's work remains, as he indicates, "informed by a compre-hensive sense of culture as the order of the symbolic," his principal goal is to describe how history can be culturally ordered without being culturally prescribed.[92] To Sahlins, structure is always "at risk" both from events and from the semantic improvisations incident to the everyday enactment of culture.[93] Inherited language (or discourse), can never fully encompass or adequately describe the vast variety of empirical realities or experiences presented for categorization and interpretation, and in that sense life outruns the capacity of culture to account for it.[94] If every use of cultural categories represents a reproduction of them, every reference is also a difference. The *conventional* (systematic, conceptual) values of signs are constantly modified through the *intentional* values that they accrue when implemented by subjects. Praxis is, then, as Sahlins puts it, "a risk to the sense of signs in the culture-as-constituted." Hence "man's symbolic hubris becomes a great gamble

21

played with the empirical realties." This is the gamble Sahlins calls the "double contingency" of the "risk of categories in action," a risk at once objective, due to a certain intractability of the world in its resistance to facile categorization, and subjective, resulting from the individual's intentional and practical construal of meaning.[95] Cultural categories, as historically generated phenomena, are subject to the constant effects of functional re-evaluation and resignification on the part of agents and thus can never be fully stabilized; culture in its entirety, as system, is always under pressure to change. In that sense, culture, Sahlins stresses, "functions as a synthesis of stability and change, past and present, diachrony and synchrony."[96] In this dialectical play between system and practice, not only is culture a realm of relative autonomy with respect to the social world, but social practice also achieves a relative autonomy from the discursive categories by which it is ultimately defined and understood. "Weak structures," "thin coherence," "weakly continuous processes of change," "relatively autonomous" forms of thought, action and agency, even "weak" notions of truth[97]—all mark the revisionist accommodation that is in progress, one that retains a belief in the mediating force of discourse and culture in creating *meaningful* forms of life but at the same time eschews any return to transcendence, identity, essence, teleology, totality, or the deterministic implications of the constructivist phase in the understanding of the linguistic turn.

Practicing history/theorizing practice

Taken as an ensemble, recent theoretical initiatives by historians are shaping a body of historical writing—primarily social in inspiration but with strong cultural components—that Andreas Reckwitz has recently grouped together under the rubric of "Practice Theory," all the while recognizing its unsystematic character.[98] Drawing on diverse—and sometimes incompatible— congeries of theories that include Bourdieu's project of a "praxeology" and its semiotic variant found in de Certeau; Giddens' "theory of structuration"; the "ordinary language investigations" of late Wittgenstein[99]; a deeper understanding and appreciation of Foucault's late work, which intersects with theories of the body, both feminist and sociological; combined with neo-hermeneutical models of embodied agency that takes much of its force from the ethnomethodological or neo-phenomenological models supplied by writers like Garfinkel, "Practice Theory" asserts the continuing relevance of semiotic insights proferred by the linguistic turn, yet reinterprets them in favor of a rehabilitation of social history by placing structure and practice, language and body into dialectical relation in systems construed as "recursive," "thinly coherent," "weakly continuous," and always "at risk." In that sense, as Bonnell and Hunt have recently argued, it would appear that scholars are engaged in a redefinition and revitalization of the concept of the "social" that had been weakened, if not altogether obliterated, by poststructuralism.[100]

Granted the as yet unsystematic character of this emerging school,[101] it still seems legitimate to inquire: how "thin" (or "thick") is structural coherence, how finely or loosely integrated are both symbols (on the level of system) and practices (on the level of behaviors and interpretive refashioning of semiotic codes), and what is the dominant vector in the dialectical interplay of system and practice? Even if we assume, as Giddens and, following him, Sewell, would, that the influence always runs in both directions—that is, is reciprocal—on the basis of what calculus can the stipulated "articulation" of system and practice be determined, assuming that system and practice are not perfectly isometrical in the force of their determinations in history? What is the place of the subject and/or individual in this loosely articulated structure and to what degree is s/he a freely acting or constrained agent? To the extent that all revisionists focus on intentionality, does this entail a renewed faith in consciousness, or does it not? Psychoanalytic models suggest that one can have intentions without consciousness, but can the same be said of neo-phenomenological models? And if "Practice Theory" relies upon neo-phenomenological and hermeneutic theories of intentionality, what is to vouchsafe the socially viable nature of agents' perceptions, or to distinguish them from delusional miscontruals, given the absence of any strong notion of rationality and the partially privatized nature of cultural appropriation, at least by comparison with the wholly public nature of semiotic models of culture, in which individual intentions do not intervene?[102] Furthermore, if everyday practices, as de Certeau maintains, make only uncodable differences in systems, how do they achieve historical visibility, that is to say, how do they leave sufficient traces in the archival or literary record to allow us to know about them?

Finally, how does the historian write up the multi-dimensional, semi-coherent, semi-inarticulate dynamics of practice in the face of traditionally felt needs to represent the past in some kind of narrative logic and/or form of emplotment, a not insignificant problem when one remembers the origins of linguistic turn historiography in the narrativist schools of White, LaCapra, Kellner, Ankersmit, and the like, who argued that *no* historical account is possible without some form of troping or emplotment? What, one asks, is the *narrative* logic of bodily dispositions, unsystematic resignification, and interstitial behavior? Compared to semiotics, structuralist and/or poststructuralist theory, whose overly systematic and putatively "idealist" principles it seeks to redress, "Practice Theory" sets forth a series of theoretical compromises inherent in its complex and often contradictory goals. Is it likely to offer a persuasive modification of the "linguistic turn" on these grounds? As I argued already in 1990,

> the ability of semiotics to sweep the theoretical field was testimony
> to the power of its challenge to traditional epistemologies, to the tech-
> nical virtuosity of its practitioners, and to the underlying coherence
> of its theory, against which those advocating a return to history rather

23

weakly invoke collective "common sense" or individual, subjective experience. But while there are good historical reasons for historians to insist on the autonomy of material reality, they are not necessarily reasons which make for good history, and the semiotic challenge cannot be met simply by an appeal to common or individual sense and experience.[103]

In addition, there seem to be some missed opportunities in this emerging body of "theory" in the neglect of writers whose work seems better adapted to its underlying agenda than some of the theorists deployed. What, for example, explains the absence of Maurice Merleau-Ponty, whose phenomenology of perception, with its grounding in the body, would appear to be perfectly matched to the needs of theorizing practice in a materialist vein?[104] More striking still is the absence of Mikhail Bakhtin, whose belief in the thoroughly social nature of language and whose emphasis on heteroglossia as embodying the dialects of personal experience and social stratification in the social diversity of speech types offers an exemplary demonstration of the ways that social location and individual intention inflect and refract discourses, giving voice to the multiplicity of meanings that lies at the heart of all linguistic phenomena.[105] To be sure, Merleau-Ponty and Bakhtin were much in vogue in the 1970s and 1980s, but the same could be said of most of the work under consideration here. Indeed, to the extent that the group associated with "Practice Theory" draws on a body of work for the most part available since the 1970s and 1980s, if not earlier, one may legitimately ask whether this recent turn in historiography represents a final phase in the reception of linguistic turn historiography—a sort of intellectual exhaustion (in all senses of the word) of its potential—or a genuinely novel initiative that strikes out in new directions? In the end, this question seems less important, and less readily answered, than the question of what might be thought to be the perceived stakes in the current project of revision, whatever its sources or ambitions.

It could be postulated that what is at stake in this process of accommodation and revision is that historians are looking, in the wonderful phrase of Václec Havel, "for an objective way out of the crisis of objectivism."[106] But to assume that this is the case is to underestimate the profoundly, even radically, historicist nature of the current critique of "linguistic turn" historiography. Instead, it seems more likely that at issue is not the abandonment of culture as structure so much as a reconsideration of the "being of structure *in* history and *as* history."[107] In shifting the focus of historical investigation from the level of totalized images of "culture" and "society" to local sites of practice and everyday life, post-linguistic turn historiography does, however, tend to dissolve notions of structure and the theories that depend on them, since it is usually the case that such generalizing theories fail to account for internal variations and incommensurabilities in the systems they purport to describe.[108] It is in this sense that the "linguistic turn" is giving way to a "historical turn," since historicism—understood as an acknowledgment of the contingent, temporally, and socially situated character of our beliefs, values, institutions, and practices[109]—subtends both the retention of an attenuated concept of discourse as that which creates the conditions of possibility for, and the constituents of, a given culture, and the revisionist emphasis on practice, agency, experience, and adaptive uses of historically specific cultural resources. In valorizing once again a fundamentally and deeply ingrained historicist posture, historians implicitly give up essentialist constructions of human nature.

In many ways, this was a central appeal of the "linguistic turn" from the beginning, at least as far as its anti-essentializing, political agenda was concerned. It was the de-essentializing potential of "discourse" as a category of historical analysis that made it attractive to a wide variety of new members of the profession beginning in the late 1960s and early 1970s—women, blacks, the postcolonial subject, etc.—since the ability to show that concepts like "male" and "female," "black" and "white," "master" and "slave," "colonist" and "subaltern," were historically and discursively constructed was at the same time to maintain that they could always be so constructed otherwise. The compelling character of the de-essentializing agenda, both intellectually and politically, has remained a strong factor among historians, even as they retreat from the structuralist strands of argumentation and analysis that made it so persuasive initially. And to the extent that the same political goal can be achieved via a radical historicism, we are now witnessing what Dorothy Ross has described as "the diffusion of historicism across disciplinary boundaries into the humanities and social sciences, producing works that are recognizably historicist" yet recognizably different in approach from the historicism that had been intrinsic to poststructuralist theories.[110]

Although "Practice Theory" as such has scarcely attained the status of a viable "theory" in any real sense of the word, the accent it places on the historically generated and always contingent nature of structures of culture returns historiography to its age-old concern with processes, agents, change, and transformation, while demanding the kind of empirically grounded research into the particularities of social and cultural conditions with which historians are by training and tradition most comfortable. At the same time, it retains some of the more powerful insights of poststructuralism, even as it advocates weak versions of it. "Practice Theory" is not likely soon to fulfill a demand for rigorous theorizing in history, nor to placate those who remain faithful to an unmodified semiotic concept of culture and language. Its very looseness and theoretical incoherence, on the other hand, may prove to be a historiographical benefit, carving out a space where the differential concerns of a broad group of historians, anthropologists, sociologists, and philosophers can find a common space within which to address each other. It is simply too early to tell. But as a form of historical reasoning that focuses on the

selective cultural organization of experience "Practice Theory" seems sufficiently capacious to accommodate a host of revisionist impulses, whose
ultimate configuration remains to be realized.

NOTES

1 On these developments see my article, "History, Historicism and the Social Logic
of the Text in the Middle Ages," *Speculum*, 65 (1990): 59–86, reprinted in *The Past
as Text: The Theory and Practice of Medieval Historiography*, (Baltimore and London,
1997): 3–28. I would like to thank David Nirenberg, Lynn Hunt, Miguel Cabrera,
Peter Jelavich, Brigitte Bedos Rezak, Nancy Partner, Carol Gluck, Carroll Smith-
Rosenberg, Judith Walkowitz, and Linda Orr, as well as the members of the Johns
Hopkins History Seminar, for reading an earlier version of this introduction and
for their comments on and insights into some of its initial confusions.
2 See Richard Rorty, *The Linguistic Turn: Essays in Philosophical Method with Two
Retrospective Essays*, Richard Rorty, ed. (Chicago and London, 1992).
3 "Semantics" here would pertain not only to "meaning" or "signification" as such
but would include the relationship of propositions to reality.
4 As articulated in Geertz' classic essay, "Deep Play: Notes on the Balinese Cockfight,"
The Interpretation of Cultures (New York, 1973): 412–453.
5 Jacques Derrida, "Structure, Sign and Play in the Discourse of the Human Sciences,"
in *Writing and Difference*, trans. Alan Bass (Chicago, 1978): 280.
6 Lloyd Kramer, "Literature, Criticism and Historical Imagination: The Literary
Challenge of Hayden White and Dominick LaCapra," in Lynn Hunt, ed., *The New
Cultural History* (Berkeley and Los Angeles, 1980): 97–98.
7 For a full discussion of this character of Saussurean linguistics see Pierre Bourdieu,
Outline of a Theory of Practice, trans. Richard Nice (Cambridge, 1977): 22 ff.
8 The latter point stressed by Andreas Reckwitz, "Toward a Theory of Social Practices:
A Development in Culturalist Theorizing," *European Journal of Social Theory*, 5 (2)
(2002): 254. Partially reprinted here in Chapter 13.
9 John Toews, "Intellectual History After the Linguistic Turn: The Autonomy of
Meaning and the Irreducibility of Experience," *American Historical Review*, 92 (1987):
882.
10 William H. Sewell, Jr., "A Theory of Structure: Duality, Agency and Transformation,"
American Journal of Sociology, 98 (1992): 2. See Chapter 7, this volume.
11 Marshall Sahlins, "Introduction" in *Culture in Practice Selected Essays* (New York,
2000): 11.
12 Ibid., p. 12.
13 Elizabeth Deeds Ermarth, "Agency in the Discursive Condition," *History and Theory*,
40 (2001): 43. See Chapter 4.
14 Ibid., p. 44.
15 Geoff Eley has similarly noted the pervasive influence of Foucault, in "Is All the
World a Text?: From Social History to the History of Society Two Decades Later,"
in Terrence J. McDonald, ed., *The Historic Turn in the Human Sciences* (Ann Arbor,
1996): 203. See Chapter 1.
16 For a general discussion of this evolution see Dorothy Ross, "The New and Newer
Histories: Social Theory and Historiography in an American Key," in *Imagined
Histories: Americans Interpret the Past*, Anthony Mohlo and Gordon S. Wood, eds.
(Princeton, 1998): 85–106. Also Miguel A. Cabrera, *Postsocial History An Introduction*,
trans. Marie McMahon (New York, Toronto, 2004). I would like to thank the author
for letting me read a copy of his book while still in manuscript.

17 For an insightful account of these developments see Miguel A. Cabrera, "Linguistic Approach or Return to Subjectivism? In Search of an Alternative to Social History," *Social History*, 24 (1991): 75 ff.

18 Roger Chartier, "The World as Representation," in Jacques Revel and Lynn Hunt, eds., *Histories, French Constructions of the Past*, Vol. I, *Postwar French Thought*, trans. Arthur Goldhammer *et al.* (New York, 1995): 548–549.

19 E.P. Thompson, "The Poverty of Theory," in *The Poverty of Theory and Other Essays* (New York, 1978): 362.

20 Ibid., p. 363.

21 It is interesting that French dissatisfaction with this paradigm began to appear as early as the late 1980s with two signal editorials that appeared in the *Annales*: "Histoire et sciences sociales: Un Tournant Critique," *Annales ESC*, (1988): 291–293; and the following year with an article presciently advocating a turn to "experience": "Tentons l'Expérience," Ibid., (1989): 1317–1323. Within a decade, a full-scale treatment of new approaches based on "practice" and "experience" was published in a collection edited by Bernard Lepetit, *Les Formes de l'Expérience Une autre histoire sociale* (Paris, 1995). For a critical review of these developments by British historian Gareth Stedman Jones, see "Une autre histoire sociale? (note critique)," *Annales HSS*, 53 (1998): 383–394.

22 Clifford Geertz, "Thick Description: Toward an Interpretive Theory of Culture," in *The Interpretation of Cultures* (New York, 1973): 14.

23 For a recent discussion of this phenomenon see Ronald Grigor Suny, "Back and Beyond: Reversing the Cultural Turn?," *American Historical Review*, 107 (2002): 1482 ff.

24 Richard Biernacki, "Language and the Shift from Signs to Practices in Cultural Inquiry," *History and Theory*, 30 (2000): 292. See Chapter 12.

25 Ibid., p. 293.

26 Ibid., p. 295.

27 Gareth Stedman Jones, "The Determinist Fix: Some Obstacles to the Further Development of the Linguistic Approach to History in the 1990s," *History Workshop Journal*, 42 (1996): 21. See Chapter 2.

28 For France, see Bernard Lepetit, ed., *Les Formes de l'Expérience* (Paris, 1995); for the United States see Dorothy Ross, "The New and Newer Histories: Social Theory and Historiography in an American Key," in *Imagined Histories: American Historians Interpret the Past*, Anthony Mohlo and Gordon S. Wood, eds. (Princeton, 1998): 85–106, as well as Terrence J. McDonald, ed., *The Historic Turn in the Human Sciences* (Ann Arbor, 1996); and for Britain, among many others, see Gareth Stedman Jones, "The Determinist Fix: Some Obstacles to the Further Development of the Linguistic Approach to History in the 1990s," *History Workshop Journal*, 42 (1996).

29 Michel Foucault, *The Order of Things: An Archeology of the Human Sciences*, (New York, 1973): xxi.

30 On Foucault's genealogical phase see my article: Gabrielle M. Spiegel, "Foucault and the Problem of Genealogy," *The Medieval History Journal*, 4 (1), January–June 2001: 1–14.

31 On this aspect of Foucault see Patricia O'Brien, "Michel Foucault's History of Culture," in Lynn Hunt, ed., *The New Cultural History* (Berkeley and Los Angeles, 1989): 35 ff.

32 Nicholas B. Dirks, "Is Vice Versa? Historical Anthropologies and Anthropological Histories," in Terrence J. McDonald, ed., *The Historic Turn in the Human Sciences* (Ann Arbor, 1996): 34.

33 See Miguel A. Cabrera, "On Language, Culture and Social Action," *History and Theory*, 40 (2001): 82–100; John E. Toews, "Intellectual History After the Linguistic Turn," *American Historical Review*, 92 (1987): 890; Nicholas B. Dirks, "Is Vice Versa? Historical Anthropologies and Anthropological Histories," in Terrence

J. McDonald, ed., *The Historic Turn in the Human Sciences* (Ann Arbor, 1996): 34. Also, see the recent collection of articles edited by Patrick Joyce, most of which tend in this direction: Patrick Joyce, ed., *The Social in Question: New Bearings in History and the Social Sciences* (London and New York, 2002).

34 William M. Reddy, "The Logic of Action: Indeterminacy, Emotion and Historical Narrative," *History and Theory*, 40 (2001): 11.

35 Michel Foucault, *Politics, Philosophy and Culture: Interviews and Other Writings 1977–1984*, Lawrence Kritzman, ed. (New York, 1988): 21. For a discussion see Michael J. Fitzhugh and William H. Leckie, Jr., "Agency, Postmodernism and the Causes of Change," *History and Theory*, 40 (2001): 62.

36 Michel Foucault, *The Archeology of Knowledge and the Discourse on Language*, trans. A.M. Sheridan Smith (New York, 1972): 55.

37 Victoria E. Bonnell and Lynn Hunt, eds., *Beyond the Cultural Turn* (Berkeley, 1999): 22.

38 Elizabeth Deeds Ermarth, "Agency in the Discursive Condition," *History and Theory*, 40 (2001): 46.

39 I derive the term "moleculating" from Sylvère Lotringer and Sande Cohen, *French Theory in America* (New York and London, 2002): 6.

40 Joan Scott, "The Evidence of Experience," *Critical Inquiry*, 17 (1991): 793. See Chapter 10. Scott insists that

> treating the emergence of a new identity as a discursive event is not to introduce a new form of linguistic determinism nor to deprive subjects of agency. It is to refuse a separation between "experience" and language and to insist, instead, on the productive quality of discourse.

41 David Gary Shaw, "Happy in Our Chains?," *History and Theory*, 40 (2001): 4.

42 Judith Newton, "History as Usual?," *Cultural Critique* (1988): 99.

43 The definition is that of Sherry B. Ortner, ed., *The Fate of Culture Geertz and Beyond* (Berkeley and Los Angeles, 1999): 5.

44 A basic introduction to ethnomethodology can be found in Harold Garfinkel, *Studies in Ethnomethodology* (Cambridge, 1984).

45 Pierre Bourdieu, *Outline of a Theory of Practice* (Cambridge, 1977): 3. It should be noted that Bourdieu explicitly rejects phenomenological reconstitution of lived experience as the basis for a theory of practice.

46 Andreas Reckwitz "Toward a Theory of Social Practices: A Development in Culturalist Theorizing," *European Journal of Social Theory*, 5 (2) (2002): 247. See Chapter 13.

47 Bevir gives a definition of the meaning of these terms in his statement that, in rejecting "scheme-oriented" concepts of culture, we are

> led to an intentional theory of meaning, albeit a weak intentionalism that allows for the unconscious, for changes of intent and for the relevant intentions being of a reader rather than the author. Weak intentionalism consists of a principal of procedural individualism according to which hermeneutic meanings exist only for specific individuals.

Mark Bevir, "Author's Introduction" and "A Reply to Critics" in "Constructing the Past: Review Symposium of Bevir's *The Logic of the History of Ideas*," *History of the Human Sciences*, 15 (2002): 100.

48 Ibid., p. 130–131.

49 Ibid., p. 129.

50 Ibid., p. 126. For an insightful discussion of Bevir, see Andreas Reckwitz,"The Constraining Power of Cultural Schemes and the Liberal Model of Beliefs," in "Constructing the Past: Review Symposium on Bevir's *The Logic of the History of Ideas*": 119.

51 Marshall Sahlins, "Introduction," in *Culture in Practice: Selected Essays* (New York, 2000): 25.

52 Pierre Bourdieu, *Outline of a Theory of Practice* (Cambridge, 1977): 81, 87.

53 Ibid., p. 72.

54 The phrase comes from Anthony Giddens, *The Constitution of Society: Outline of the Theory of Structuration* (Berkeley and Los Angeles, 1986): 9.

55 Michel de Certeau, *The Practice of Everyday Life*, trans. Steven Rendall (Berkeley, Los Angeles, London, 1984): xi; Jonathan A. Carter, "Telling Times: History, Emplotment and Truth," *History and Theory*, 42 (2003): 3.

56 Richard Biernacki, "Language and the Shift from Signs to Practice in Cultural Inquiry," *History and Theory*, 39 (2000): 302 and 289.

57 Jacques Revel, "L'Institution et le social," in *Les Formes de l'Expérience*, Bernard Lepetit, ed.: 80.

58 Anthony Giddens, *The Constitution of Society: Outline of the Theory of Structuration* (Berkeley and Los Angeles, 1986): 24 and *passim*.

59 Ibid., p. 2.

60 Ibid., p. 23.

61 Michel de Certeau, *The Practice of Everyday Life*, trans. Steven Rendall (Berkeley, Los Angeles, London, 1984): 33.

62 David Gary Shaw, "Happy in Our Chains?," *History and Theory*, 40 (2001): 6.

63 Bernard Lepetit, "Histoire des pratiques, pratique de l'histoire," in Bernard Lepetit, ed., *Les Formes de l'Expérience* (Paris, 1995): 30.

64 David Gary Smith, "Happy in Our Chains?," *History and Theory*, 40 (2001): 8.

65 Kathleen Canning, "Feminist History after the Linguistic Turn: Historicizing Discourse and Experience," *Signs*, 19 (1994): 378.

66 John E. Toews, "Intellectual History After the Linguistic Turn," *American Historical Review*, 92 (1987): 882.

67 Ibid., p. 882.

68 Joan Scott, "The Evidence of Experience," *Critical Inquiry*, 17 (1991): 793.

69 Ibid., p. 793.

70 Ibid., p. 791.

71 Cited in Martin Jay, "Should Intellectual History Take a Linguistic Turn? Reflections on the Habermas-Gadamer Debate," in Dominick LaCapra and Steven L. Kaplan, eds., *Modern European Intellectual History: Reappraisals and New Perspectives*, (Ithaca, NY and London, 1982): 108.

72 Kathleen Canning, "Feminist History after the Linguistic Turn: Historicizing Discourse and Experience," *Signs*, 19 (1994): 377.

73 The citation comes from Dorothy Smith, *The Everyday World as Problematic* (1987), cited in Canning, ibid., p. 374.

74 See Richard Biernacki, "Method and Metaphor after the New Cultural History," in Victoria E. Bonnell and Lynn Hunt, eds., *Beyond the Cultural Turn* (Berkeley, 1999): 75.

75 Pierre Bourdieu, *Outline of a Theory of Practice* (Cambridge, 1977): 94.

76 Ibid., p. 94.

77 Ibid., pp. 123–124.

78 See Andreas Reckwitz, "Toward a Theory of Social Practices," *European Journal of Social Theory*, 5 (2002): 256.

79 Ibid., p. 251.

80 Richard Biernacki and Jennifer Jordan, "The Place of Space in the Study of the Social," in Patrick Joyce, ed., *The Social in Question: New Bearings in History and the Social Sciences* (London and New York, 2002): 134.

81 Patrick Joyce, *The Social in Question* (London and New York, 2002): 14.

82 William Sewell, "The Concept(s) of Culture," in Victoria E. Bonnell and Lynn Hunt, eds., *Beyond the Cultural Turn* (Berkeley, 1999): 44.

83 See Chris Lorenz, "Some Afterthoughts on Culture and Explanation in Historical Inquiry," *History and Theory*, 39 (2000): 350.

84 Bernard Lepetit, "Histoire des pratiques, pratique de l'histoire," in Bernard Lepetit, ed., *Les Formes de l'Expérience* (Paris, 1995): 14.

85 William Sewell, "The Concept(s) of Culture," in Victoria E. Bonnell and Lynn Hunt, eds., *Beyond the Cultural Turn* (Berkeley, 1999): 51.

86 John E. Toews, "Intellectual History After the Linguistic Turn," *American Historical Review*, 92 (1987): 884.

87 William Sewell, "The Concept(s) of Culture," in Victoria E. Bonnell and Lynn Hunt, eds., *Beyond the Cultural Turn* (Berkeley, 1999): 52.

88 Ibid., p. 47. For a critique of Sewell's position see Richard Handler, "Cultural Theory in History Today," *American Historical Review*, 107 (2002): 1515 ff.

89 William Sewell, "The Concept(s) of Culture," in Victoria E. Bonnell and Lynn Hunt, eds., *Beyond the Cultural Turn* (Berkeley, 1999): 53 ff.

90 Marshall Sahlins, *Islands of History* (Chicago and London, 1985): 145.

91 A position Sahlins shares with Paul Ricoeur, from whom this phrase is taken. See Aletta Biersack, "Local Knowledge, Local History: Geertz and Beyond," in Lynn Hunt, ed., *The New Cultural History* (Berkeley and Los Angeles, 1980): 91.

92 See *Culture in Practice* (New York, 2000): 16, 26.

93 Marshall Sahlins, *Islands of History* (Chicago and London, 1985): x.

94 Or as Michel Bréal felicitously put it (quoted in ibid., pp. 147–148):

> It cannot be doubted that language designates things in an incomplete and inexact way ... Substantives are signs attached to things: they include just part of the *vérité* that can be included by a name, a part necessarily all the more fractional as the object has more reality. ... [Hence] our languages are condemned to a perpetual lack of proportion between the word and the thing ... The expression is sometimes too wide, sometimes too narrow.

95 Ibid., pp. 145; 149–150.

96 Ibid., p. 144.

97 Thus David D. Roberts argues that "we must do away with strong, certain truth in history ... the poststructuralists have deepened our understanding of why and how." "Postmodern Continuities: Difference, Dominance and the Question of Historiographic Renewal," *History and Theory*, 37 (1998): 394.

98 See Andreas Reckwitz, "Toward a Theory of Social Practices: A Development in Culturalist Theorizing," *European Journal of Social Theory*, 5 (2002): *passim*.

99 On this see especially Theodore R. Schatzki, *Social Practices: A Wittgensteinian Approach to Human Activity and the Social* (Cambridge, 1996).

100 Victoria E. Bonnell and Lynn Hunt, *Beyond the Cultural Turn* (Berkeley, 1999): 11.

101 As Reckwitz himself acknowledges, "Toward a Theory of Social Practices," *European Journal of Social Theory*, 5 (2002): 257.

102 On the uncertain boundary between perception and phantasm see chapter I of Maurice Merleau-Ponty, *The Visible and the Invisible*, Claude Lefort, ed., trans. Alphonso Lingis (Evanston, IL, 1968).

103 Gabrielle M. Spiegel, "History, Historicism and the Social Logic of the Text," in *The Past as Text*, (Baltimore and London, 1997): 19.

104 See, for example, his *The Visible and the Invisible* (Evanston, IL, 1968).

105 See M.M. Bakhtin, *The Dialogic Imagination*, Michael Holquist, ed., trans. Caryl Emerson and Michael Holquist (Austin, TX, 1981).

106 Cited in Elizabeth Deeds Ermarth, "Agency in the Discursive Condition," *History and Theory*, 40 (2001): 52.

107 The phrase is Sahlins's, *Islands of History* (Chicago and London, 1985): 145.

108 I am grateful to Simon During of the English Department of Johns Hopkins University for this insight.
109 The definition is that of David Hollinger, "How Wide the Circle of 'We'? American Intellectuals and the Problem of the Ethnos since World War II," *American Historical Review*, 98 (1993): 310.
110 Dorothy Ross, "The New and Newer Histories: Social Theory and Historiography in an American Key," in *Imagined Histories* (Princeton, 1998): 100. This difference lies primarily in the renewed emphasis on materialism and the body.

Part I

DISCOURSE AND THE PROBLEM OF SOCIAL HISTORY

1

IS ALL THE WORLD A TEXT? FROM SOCIAL HISTORY TO THE HISTORY OF SOCIETY TWO DECADES LATER

Geoff Eley

Geoff Eley, a social historian of modern Germany, here offers a masterful survey of the fundamental transformation that overtook the practice of social history between the 1970s and 1990s, a transformation that witnessed the rise of cultural history as a response to the challenges to traditional forms of social history posed by the linguistic turn. In his view, the decisive shift occurred around 1980, as a new generation of historians trained in the 1960s and early 1970s came to professional maturity. Under the impact of changing political contexts and the rise of feminism and women's history, there occurred a turn to linguistically conceived forms of cultural history, which split the generation between those who remained committed to what Eley characterizes as "a restlessly aggrandizing social history" and those who came to define themselves as cultural historians, that is, who focused on discourse and its operation in the cultural construction of social life.

Eley stresses the importance of the writings of Michel Foucault to this development. Not only did Foucault's early work demonstrate the operation of discourse, or what Foucault called "epistemic regimes" in defining the conditions of possibility for what can and cannot be thought in particular historical epochs (defined by the episteme of that era). Foucault's elaboration of the idea of the indissoluble connection between knowledge and power (or what is sometimes called the knowledge/power nexus) also formulated a new understanding of power as decentered and dispersed as a "microphysics" throughout the entire range of society and its social practices, hence challenging the utility of social history's conventional focus on the state and classes as the centers of domination and power. As Eley explains, the thrust of Foucault's work was to undermine the materialist view of society and culture in favor of linguistic analysis, a movement aided by the rise of narrativist schools of history indebted in various ways to Hayden White's Metahistory, *to the symbolic anthropology popularized among historians by the writings of Clifford Geertz, and, though in a less thorough way, to Derrida and deconstruction. As a result of their combined influence, as Eley indicates, "textuality has become a metaphor for reality in general."*

It is precisely this textualized view of reality that the authors represented in this volume are beginning to question, without wishing to abandon it entirely, thus the question posed by Eley's essay: "Is All the World [really?] a Text?" Eley shares the sense of unease with a wholly textualized, discursive approach to social history, without at the same time wishing to abandon its critical insights. His article figures as an early moment in the new movement of revision advocating a return to "history," and seeks to occupy a "middle ground" between the older school of social theorists and the new cultural historian's deployment of discourse as the determinative force in social construction.

* * *

In the beginning

In 1971 Eric Hobsbawm called it "a good moment to be a social historian" (1971, 43).[1] Ten years later this was still the case, despite a certain fractiousness and the readiness of some to find a crisis in the field. The main thing was the continuing growth of activity (the proliferation of journals, conferences, subdisciplinary societies, international networks, curricular initiatives, and dissertations, despite the contraction of history graduate programs), and in light of such expansion conflicts of direction were perhaps the normal signs of diversification and growth. That social historians could argue over theory and method was evidence of vitality more than ill health, and only those with narrow or sectarian views of social history's proper orientation could be upset by conflict as such.[2]

Ten years further on, though, such confidence is harder to sustain. I am not the only person to have detected a general discursive shift in the rhetoric and practice of the profession from "social" to "cultural" history, effected via what we have become accustomed to calling the "linguistic turn." Clearly this observation needs to be elaborated and specified, but a good barometer of the change in historiographical sensibility has been Gareth Stedman Jones. From his invigorating polemic against the liberal complacencies and positivistic assumptions of the British historiographical tradition in 1967 to a variety of critical and substantive essays in the mid-1970s, Stedman Jones developed a project of "non-empiricist" and "theoretically informed history" that was Marxist, open to other forms of social theory, and naturally materialist, as the unifying problematic of contemporary social history then took that to mean.

For many social historians, therefore, it was very disconcerting when in 1983 Stedman Jones seemed to embrace a form of linguistic analysis that was decidedly nonmaterialist in the classical sense and seemed to call the given assumptions of social history into doubt. Moreover, since that time things have moved fast. Stedman Jones's own rather cautious formulations have been left behind, disappearing in a more radical polarity of so-called deconstructionists and unrepentant materialists.[3] Of course, the social history that emerged from the 1960s was never a unitary project. But some notion of social determination, conceptualized on the ground of material life, whether in demographic, political-economic, labor-process, class-sociological, or class-cultural terms, generally provided a tissue of common assumptions. From a vantage point at the end of the 1980s, by contrast, a rough division seems to have opened within this "broad church" between those who have been rethinking their assumptions to the point of radically subverting the determinative coherence of the category of the social and those who continue defending the particular social-historical materialism that formed them.

In this respect, social history has become one site of a general epistemological uncertainty that characterizes large areas of academic-intellectual life in the humanities and social sciences in the late twentieth century. This flux is perhaps more extensive in some places than in others (in the sense that it pervades more disciplines more completely) and more central to disciplinary discussion in, say, literature and anthropology than in, say, sociology and the "harder" social sciences. Not by accident, the most radical and influential discussions have been occurring in areas that lack the constraining power of disciplinary traditions—especially women's studies and the emerging field of cultural studies. [. . .] By 1990, I would argue, interest in Foucault and Derrida extends far beyond a few "professionally marginal historians whose primary allegiance was to interdisciplinary communities with membership made up largely of literary theorists, cultural critics, and philosophers" (Novick 1988, 605).

It is difficult to periodize this movement with any precision [. . .].

My own sense is that things began to change around 1980 [. . .].

To a great extent, I want to argue, this reflects a process of complex generationally internal revision. [. . .] The turn to linguistically conceived forms of cultural history by the end of the 1970s, moved by a combination of changing political contexts and autonomous theoretical engagement, most sharply registered in feminism and women's history, marked the fracturing of the same broad generational consensus. To some extent, these tensions expressed themselves in early conflicts over theory per se, as in the acrimonious attacks on "structuralist Marxism," which dominated left intellectual life in Britain for much of the later 1970s.[4] Moreover, the salience of this particular generation and its disagreements was magnified by the drastic reduction in the number of graduate historians in the later 1970s and early 1980s. Mainly for that reason, the succeeding generation has had little opportunity to declare its own distinctive voice—by contrast (one might guess) with the one qualifying in the later 1980s and early 1990s, which will have a great deal to say in the areas of gender history and cultural studies.

[. . .]

So we have entered "new times." What is striking to me, in this conjuncture, is the degree to which historians have been willing to become their own theoreticians. This seems to me not to have been as true of the 1960s, when social history declared its presence via a more eclectic and dependent turn to

sociology (and sometimes anthropology), and the most self-conscious appropriations of social science focused on methodology (as in demography, family
history, mobility studies, urban history, and so on) rather than theory per se.
To that extent, Stedman Jones's essays of 1967–76, which called on historians
to emancipate themselves from a junior relationship to social science and
begin producing theory of their own, bespoke an accurate reading of the
relationship.[5] [. . .]

But the most salient sites of such independent theorizing, I would argue,
are ones where uncritical borrowing is harder because of the absence of an
existing practice to rationalize, as well as the paucity of relevant theory to
use—where innovation, initiative, and interdisciplinarity have been inscribed
more centrally in the very conditions and processes of knowledge production
from the start, one might say—namely, the new and "un-disciplined" fields of
feminist theory/women's history and cultural studies. Of course, no theory is
ever conjured out of nothing, and it might be objected that historians in these
latter areas are no less dependent on external theory than their predecessors
(or previous incarnations) as new social historians. It is simply that a different
kind of theory, literary rather than social-scientific, is in play. But it is no accident that several of the key influences in this domain, such as Michel Foucault
or Stuart Hall, are distinguished precisely by their disobedience to conventional disciplinary classification (was Foucault a historian, or what?). And it
does seem to me that historians (Joan Scott and Richard Johnson would be
perfect respective examples) have become far more active participants in this
new theoretical conversation than in the old.[6]

[. . .]

The current landscape

In his 1971 essay, Hobsbawm suggested that most interesting social history
was clustered around six complexes of questions:

1   Demography and kinship
2   Urban studies in so far as these fall within our field
3   Classes and social groups
4   The history of "mentalities," or collective consciousness, or of
    "culture" in the anthropologists' sense
5   The transformation of societies (for example, modernization or
    industrialization)
6   Social movements and phenomena of social protest.

(Hobsbawm 1971, 12)

In reviewing this list two decades later, it is hard simply to add to the topical
inventory because (as I am arguing) the main change is an underlying shift
of perspective rather than the opening up of new areas.[7] The first three of
Hobsbawm's categories are clearly alive and well. Thus, the machinery

of historical demography continues to grind out its findings, often with the barest relationship to broader questions but at its best with a meticulous grounding in the classical materialist problematic of social change—usually from an eclectically sociological perspective.[8] Likewise, while, theoretically, urban history remains too loose and ill defined a category, the urban community study has become the main practical medium for investigating class formation.[9] The historiography of class has also unfolded to a great extent within parameters outlined by Hobsbawm, and to the research on the working class may now be added a burgeoning literature on peasants and a more recently developing one on the bourgeoisie and the petite bourgeoisie/ lower middle class.[10]

But as a descriptive framework for "the actual practice of social history," Hobsbawm's list no longer serves. This is partly because new topical clusters need to be added—recent growth areas of social history include crime and punishment, medicine and public health, sexuality, popular religion, work, and popular memory, while social policy and education are older ones perhaps oddly missing from Hobsbawm's original list. More to the point, though, the entire construction of social history as a (sub)disciplinary field has been shifting during the last decade, so that a body of discussion has developed parallel to the existing research in a way that calls into question the conventionally constituted social-historical knowledge—with profound implications for all six of Hobsbawm's categories. Rather than just elaborating a longer inventory of topics, therefore, it is important to mention certain aspects of the surrounding flux.

First, it needs to be said straight away that gender theory is transforming the basis on which we think about history. Whether as a dimension of analysis or an area of empirical work, women's history is absent from Hobsbawm's account, and to read older accounts such as his is to be reminded of how radical a change has occurred since the 1960s.[11] [. . .]

While this move remains controversial, it is only more recently, with the conceptual shift from the history of women to the historical construction of sexual difference, that the protected central spaces of the discipline have started to give way. Of course, a large amount of work is being done on sexual representations as such. But major areas, like the history of work,[12] class formation,[13] citizenship and the public sphere (Landes 1988; Pateman 1988; Outram 1989; Catherine Hall 1985), and the study of popular culture[14] are all being reshaped by the application of a gender perspective. The latter also promises to recast understandings of nationalism and fascism, although some of the emerging work on masculinity tends to settle too easily into the study of men alone rather than in their relations with women.[15] We should not paint too optimistic a picture, of course. For instance, the core of historical demographers and historians of the family have remained remarkably resilient in their defense of an older-defined project.[16] But the insistent pressure for a recognition of gender as a "useful category of historical analysis" is only likely to become more intense (Scott 1988, 28–50).

It is important to note the now pervasive influence of Foucault. It would be a mistake to exaggerate retrospectively the instigating centrality of Foucault's ideas to the departures we are discussing, and in practice they have achieved their resonance only within the broader universe of thinking I will be dealing with subsequently. Nor can the speed of his reception be overstated. The works themselves were actually available in translation quite early. But Foucault was completely absent from the pioneering works in the social history of crime, the law, and imprisonment in the 1970s [. . .]. It was only by the early 1980s that historians were explicitly beginning to take note (Weeks 1982; Harrison and Mort 1980). Since that time, work on sexuality (particularly the late nineteenth- and twentieth-century constructions of sexual categories), on prisons, hospitals, asylums, and other institutions of confinement, on social policy and public health, and on the history of science and the academic disciplines has been shot through with Foucault's formative influence.

Moreover, aside from directing attention in this way to new areas of research, Foucault's reception has had some vital theoretical effects. It has fundamentally redirected the understanding of power away from conventional, institutionally centered conceptions of government and the state and from the allied sociological conceptions of class domination, toward a dispersed and decentered conception of power and its "microphysics." It has sensitized us to the subtle and complex forms of the interrelationship between power and knowledge, particularly in the latter's forms of disciplinary and administrative organization. It has delivered the extraordinarily fruitful concept of discourse as a way of theorizing both the internal rules and regularities of particular fields of knowledge (their "regimes of truth") and the more general structures of ideas and assumptions that delimit what can and cannot be thought and said in particular contexts of time and place. It has radically challenged the historian's conventional assumptions about individual and collective agency and their bases of interest and rationality, forcing us to see instead how subjectivities are constructed and produced within and through languages of identification that lie beyond the volition and control of individuals in the classical Enlightenment sense.

[. . .]

Another body of cultural analysis, contemporary cultural studies, has produced relatively little historical work so far. A still emergent cross-disciplinary formation, cultural studies comprises a varying miscellany of influences—sociologists, literary scholars, and historians in Britain (but not anthropologists) and mass communications, literary theory, and, potentially, reflexive anthropology in the United States. Strong existing traditions (e.g., in critical ethnography, cultural anthropology, and ethnomethodology) have worked preemptively against cultural studies in the social sciences in the United States, outside departments of communications, while their relative weakness in Britain allowed greater corresponding space for cultural studies to emerge. Thus, so far the main U.S. initiatives have come more from the humanities (e.g., the Unit for Criticism and Interpretive Theory at Illinois–Urbana or the Program in Comparative Studies in Discourse and Society at Minnesota), whereas the proliferating interdisciplinary programs and institutes in the social sciences have shown very little interest. On the other hand, feminist theory has played a key part in both Britain and the United States, as has the post-Saidian critique of colonial and racist forms of thought. Again, individual influences will vary (e.g., Gramsci or psychoanalytical approaches in Britain), but the linguistic turn, together with the fascination with postmodernism, has been common to both.

[. . .]

I would like to end this series of observations with a paradox. On the one hand, the earlier ambition of a "total history," of writing the history of society in some integrated and holistic way, has come radically into question. In one of my own less memorable essays published over a decade ago, I argued that the most interesting feature of social history at the end of the 1970s was "its new totalizing potential." Now, it is possible to maintain some version of this claim still (e.g., the possibility of considering all phenomena and practices in their social dimensions), but the stronger form of the argument— "attempting to understand *all* facets of human existence in terms of their social determinations," as I put it—has become very problematic (Eley 1979, 55f). As I will argue in the following, the confident materialist conception of social totality—"society" in its Marxist and non-Marxist sociological forms—has for many social scientists and cultural theorists ceased to be the natural organizing belief.

But, on the other hand, a considerable body of historical sociology continues to be written much as before, that is, organized within the established problematics of state-making, the rise of capitalism, comparative political development, revolutions, and so on (e.g., Tilly 1990; Wallerstein 1988). More than that, in fact, there has developed a new genre of world histories, extending literally from Mesopotamia to the global confrontation of the twentieth century, produced by leading British sociologists, seeking presumably to recapture the memories of their grammar school (or perhaps public school) history syllabus, essentially an attempt to rebuild social theory by writing the history of the world (Giddens 1981, 1985; Mann 1986; John Hall 1985). This creates an interesting juxtaposition. On the one hand, the radical diagnoses of the "postmodern condition" are proclaiming the demise of all master narratives; on the other hand, the most ambitious historical sociologists are defining their project by producing . . . a new range of grand narratives.

[. . .]

All the world's a text

Surveying the intellectual landscape of the social sciences at the end of the twentieth century then, it is hard not to be impressed by the power and popularity of literary theory, linguistic analysis, and related forms of theoretical

41

address. Whether we look to the revival of intellectual history and the influence of Dominick LaCapra, to the potential convergence of intellectual historians with literary critics in a "new historicist" mold, to the enormous impact of Edward Said and now Gayatri Spivak on intellectuals writing in and about the Third World, to the interest of Joan Scott and other feminists in theories of gender and language, to the pull of reflexive anthropology toward the narrative ordering of the experienced world, to formal analysis of the "rhetoric" of economics and other apparently nonliterary disciplines, or simply to the common currency of terms like *discourse* and *deconstruction*— in all of these areas there seems to be no escape.

In many ways, Hayden White is the patron saint of this development for at an early stage (1973) his *Metahistory* problematized the boundaries between the humanities and the social sciences and showed how works in the latter are also constructed around particular narrative and rhetorical strategies, even when bound at their most rigorous and single-minded to the rules of evidence and scientific methodology. Moreover, White mounted this challenge from the older resources of literary criticism and his own original and idiosyncratic imagination, confronting "objectivist" history with the moral and aesthetic principles that order and inform its production (White 1973, 1978). In the meantime, the transformation of literary studies by the impact of (among others) Derrida and De Man has radicalized the challenge. The complexities of reading (and writing) have brought the category of the text and the work of interpretation into question. From focusing on authorial intention and the text's single attainable meaning (a chimera that obscures the indeterminacy and necessary openness of the text, its "undecidability," its multiplicity of meanings), literary theory has sharpened the practice of reading to a point of technical sophistication where meanings can seemingly be endlessly disclosed. For outsiders it has often been hard to break into this magic circle without devoting oneself full-time to learning a new language of cleverness and gesture, and sometimes it has seemed that a reprofessionalizing of literature and an authorizing of the theorist—a technocracy of the word—has been precisely the point.

Yet such suspicions cannot occlude the actual influence of such theory beyond its immediate domain. For some modified appropriation of deconstruction's basic program—at its simplest, "a reading which involves seizing upon [texts'] inconsistencies and contradictions to break up the idea of a unified whole" (*HWJ* editors 1980, 1)—has become very commonplace. For the social historian in particular, some notion of externality, what Derrida has called "the diachronic overdetermination of the context" or Raymond Williams's notion of determination as the setting of limits, is bound to loom as important (Derrida 1988, 606). Probably this means focusing on two kinds of moves—back, to the contexts of the text's production, and out, to the ways in which its meanings get constructed. Rather than what the text "means," in fact, it may be more fruitful to understand how it "works." As Tony Bennett puts it, with the characteristic Gramscian inflection on British cultural studies: "the text is a site on which varying meanings and effects may be produced according to the determinations within which the work is inscribed—determinations that are never single and given but plural and contested, locked in relations of struggle" (Bennett 1982, 235). Moreover, this mode of analysis has been increasingly extended from written texts in the more conventional sense to all manner of documents, and indeed to experience, behavior, and events as well. From assailing the transparency of the text in the discourse of literary criticism, textuality has become a metaphor for reality in general.

[...]

The excitement of those days, the sense of participating in a continuous and unsettling process of revision, is worth remembering. And while the voice at this point is clearly personal (with a British accent), it is also worth recognizing this as a remarkable generational achievement, which both internationalized (or at least Europeanized) a previously parochial intellectual culture, wrenched it into an openly theorized mode of exchange, and simultaneously problematized the latter's terms of address. At the same time, there is also a danger of presenting this process as more unified, coherent, and logically continuous than it was (or could have been), so that one move followed rationally on another, causally inscribed in the contradictions and insufficiencies that preceded it. Yet intellectual histories are seldom as rationally constructed as this; and the process of revision was divisive rather than harmonious, instigated by conflicts and disruptions as much as by its own logical momentum.

Feminism is by far the most important influence of this kind, and the reader may have noticed its regular reappearance in my text—not quite as a disruption, as my understanding of its importance is too controlled for that, but not quite as a fully integral primary theme either. I have puzzled over what to do about this, and perhaps this accurately captures the relationship of feminist to general theory or social historical discussion (always assuming that "general" in this context is more than a synonym for androcentrism). Better, that is, to keep the sense of relative apartness and ability to disturb the narrative and logical coherence of the account than to be smoothly assimilated to its structure (which would also be a dishonesty of its own). On the one hand, as Terry Lovell observes, contemporary feminist writing shows a trajectory that is recognizable in the terms I am using:

> The journey begins with Marxist- or socialist-feminist writings (in history, social science *and* cultural studies), seeking to uncover the material conditions of women's oppression under capitalism; it advances with the recognition that certain aspects of that oppression do not yield very readily to Marxist categories and that a more adequate account of feminine subjectivity is required for an understanding of the ways in which that oppression is *lived*, which might be sought in psychoanalysis rather than Marxism. Then, via Lacan

and modern theories of language, the journey continues into the "poststructuralism" and "deconstructionism" whose luminaries include Foucault, Derrida and Kristeva. Some travellers continue beyond feminism itself, into a "postfeminism" and "postmodernism" which understand both Lacanian psychoanalysis and Marxism to have been mere staging-posts along the way.

(Lovell 1990, 21f.)

On the other hand, it is still necessarily apart. As Sally Alexander puts it in an essay that is still rather notable among social historians for its willingness to engage theoretically with this issue:

If feminism has been only one of the detonators of "crisis" in marxist thought and practice it has been the most insistently subversive because it will not give up its wish to speak in the name of women; of women's experience, subjectivity and sexuality. ... We were asking the impossible perhaps. As a feminist I was (and still am) under the spell of those wishes, while as a historian writing and thinking in the shadow of a labour history which silences them. How can women speak and think creatively within marxism when they can neither enter the narrative flow as fully as they wish, nor imagine that there might be other subjectivities present in history than those of class (for to imagine that is to transgress the laws of historical materialism)?[17]

[...]

As the hold of the economy has been progressively loosened, and with it the determinative power of the social structure and its causal priorities, therefore, the imaginative and epistemological space for other kinds of analysis has grown. In fact, for many who have gone down this route, the classical materialist connection has been broken once and for all. "Society" as a unitary object can no longer be maintained. There is no structural coherence deriving easily from the economy, from the functional needs of the social system and its central values, or from some other overarching principle of order. Particular phenomena—an event, a policy, an institution, an ideology, a text—have particular social contexts, in the sense of conditions, practices, sites, which conjoin for an essential part of their meaning. But there is no underlying given structure to which they can necessarily be referred, as its essential expression or necessary effects. In other words, the major casualty of this intellectual flux has been the confidence in a notion of social totality in its various Marxist and non-Marxist forms.

[...]

Thus, the last two decades have seen a dizzying intellectual history. We have moved from a time when social history and social analysis seemed to be capturing the central ground of the profession and the force of social determinations seemed axiomatic to a new conjuncture in which "the social" has come to seem ever less definite and social determinations have surrendered their previous sovereignty. The road from "relative autonomy" and "structural causality" (the hard-won gains of the 1970s) to the "discursive character of all practices" (the poststructuralist axiom of the 1980s) has been rapid and disconcerting, and the persuasiveness of the antireductionist logic has been extraordinarily hard to withstand (rather like an up escalator with no way down).

But if "society" as a totalizing category is dissolving, does that mean that social explanation as such has lost all independent efficacy? There is a sense in which the reception of Foucault and subsequent poststructuralisms has collapsed the distinction between the social and the cultural altogether (where the latter becomes a summary description for the entire discursive domain), so that the social formation (and hence the bases of interconnectedness) becomes redefined agnostically as the aggregate of "discursive practices"— as "equivalent to the non-unified totality of these practices" or as "a complex, overdetermined and contradictory nexus of discursive practices" (Hall 1978, 12). In that case, if social reality is only accessible via language (in the constitutive theoretical sense as well as in the commonsense descriptive one that most would accept) and "the social" is only constituted *through* discourse, then what place is left for specifically social determinations at all?

This is the point that I take the discussion to have reached. A relatively small number of historians have taken the train to the end of the line, through the terrain of textuality to the land of discourse and deconstruction, to a radical epistemology that "relativizes the status of all knowledge, links knowledge and power, and theorizes these in terms of the operations of difference" (Scott 1988, 4). This can be alternately *empowering*, in that its revelation of the "nonfixity" of meaning shows how social and political definitions may be questioned and how the terms of the given are always in play and therefore susceptible to challenge, in the present no less than the past, and *disabling*, to the extent that the critique of epistemology in its most radical forms undermines the idea of historical knowledge as such and reduces the historian's task to more or less elaborate forms of historiographical critique (history not as the archival reconstruction of what happened but as the continuous contest over how the past is approached or invoked). A much larger group of social historians continues much as before, generally aware of what is happening but uninterested in the theory behind the linguistic turn and essentially wishing that it would go away. And then there are the rest of us, partly there for the ride, partly curious to see where it goes, and not at all sure we'll stay very long at the destination.

Now, this intermediate place (I hesitate to call it the "middle ground" because it certainly involves accepting the basic usefulness and interest of poststructuralist theory to begin with—that is, being willing to get on the train in the first place) is in my view a very good one to be in. It has some important virtues, pluralism chief among them. But it also has some real costs.

It means giving up the claim to a distinct form of historical knowledge, let alone the aggrandizing and oft repeated claim to being somehow the "queen of the disciplines." History in the sense of the (mostly unreflected) practice of many or most historians does tend to a definite epistemology, which usually amounts to some brand of empiricism—that is, the belief in a know-able past, whose structures and processes are able to be distinguished from the forms of documentary representation, conceptual and political appropriations, and historiographical discourses that construct them. By now, I take the epistemological critique of this naive practice (or, more radically, the critique of epistemology per se as "a theoretical domain that tries to state a mechanism of correspondence between a discourse and objects existing outside discourse which can be specified and made the measure of it") to be basic (Hirst 1985b, 138).

But this does not mean that history becomes pointless or undoable. On the one hand, rejecting a correspondence theory of truth does not mean that doing history becomes completely arbitrary, that the historian can somehow invent documents at will, or that rules of evidence become irrelevant (fears typically voiced by the opponents of the linguistic turn). It does mean that criteria of truth have to be thought [of] very differently. Knowledge is as "good" or "bad" as the quality of questions that constitute it: "Historical knowledge works by posing, re-posing and displacing questions, *not* by accumulating 'evidence' independently of them. Facts are not given, it is only relative to a question that we can begin to assess the value of those materials which are to constitute evidence for the answer to it" (Hirst 1985a, 54). As Stedman Jones said in his 1976 article, "history like any other 'social science' is an entirely intellectual operation which takes place in the present and in the head" and "[t]he fact that the 'past' in some sense 'happened' is not of primary significance since the past is in no sense synonymous with history." In fact, the "real" past is beyond retrieval. Instead, the historian both evaluates documentary residues by the technical procedures of the profession and assigns them relevance via the construction of a significant problem. Accordingly, the common distinction between "history" and "theory" makes no sense: "The distinction is not that between theory and non-theory, but between the adequacy or inadequacy of the theory brought to bear" (Stedman Jones 1976, 296, 297). Moreover, the test of history's knowledge (its "truth") is not some general notion of epistemological validity ("truth-in-general") but the particular criteria of adequacy and appropriateness that history, no less than other particular fields (from biblical scholarship to automobile mechanics), has tended to devise (and which will always themselves be subject to varying degrees of consensus and disagreement).

On the other hand, history is simply unavoidable. It is constantly in play at the level of both everyday understanding and the formal discourses affecting social, economic, cultural, and political exchange. It is invoked and appropriated as a matter of course either implicitly or explicitly in order to make arguments. And for such arguments to be made (or countered) effectively, appropriate attention to the evidentiary conventions of the history profession will often need to be paid. But such conventions should not be mistaken for a viable epistemological claim. History's value is not as an archive or a court of "real experience." It is as a site of difference, a context of deconstruction—partly because it is *de facto always* being fought over (i.e., invoked and appropriated in contestatory ways) and partly because it affords the contexts in which the ever seductive unities of contemporary social and political discourse, the naturalizing of hegemonies, can be upset. History is different not in the sense that it reveals earlier stages in our own story or as an unapproachable realm of the exotic but in the sense that the very notion of a single coherent and unified story can be unpicked: "If [history] does not consist merely in the vindication of our own views of ourselves or in triumphalist accounts of modernity, it is because some historians can recognize that the past is different, not merely an earlier stage of our 'story,' but a means of unsettling ourselves and investigating, however partially, what we *are*."[18]

Turning to history

Of course (the hard-bitten realists of the profession will say, patrolling their practice against these suggestions), such theory is all very well, but what difference does it really make? Worse, all this endless theorizing, the self-sustaining industry of critique, deflects one from more concrete and extended engagements with the past (whose pursuit, after all, remains the mundane justification for separate and specialized departments of history). Such attacks have become a familiar rhetorical move, intended to preempt, rather than to consider seriously, the theory concerned. But in an innocent form the complaint does contain a reasonable request. If the earlier assumptions of social history no longer hold and the older notions of social totality and social determination cannot suffice, then how can the practical project of a critical social history—in dissertation and monographic form, as opposed to essay-critique—be reaffirmed? Some exemplary answer to this question, in however indicative a form, is clearly owed.

There are no ready-made solutions to the conundrum, but one extremely fruitful response to current uncertainties has been to historicize the category of "society" itself by specifying the terms of its own social, political, and intellectual history—that is, by looking at the terms under which "the social" first became abstracted into an object of theory-knowledge, a target of policy, and a site of practice, so that the material context in which society could be convincingly represented as an ultimately originating subject became gradually composed.[19] Here "the social" refers not to the global analytical category of "society" in some unproblematic social science sense but to the historically located methods, techniques, and practices that allowed such a category to be constructed in the first place. The impetus for such a perspective is unmistakably Foucault.

GEOFF ELEY

Foucault's concept of the disciplinary society is concerned directly with this process. At one level, it profoundly shifts our understanding of politics, carrying the analysis of power away from the core institutions of the state in the national-centralized sense toward the emergence of new individualizing strategies "that function outside, below and alongside the State apparatuses, on a much more minute and everyday level" (Foucault 1980a, 60). But at another level, it is precisely through such individualizing strategies that *society* ("the social" or the "social body") became recognized, constituted, and elaborated as the main object of science, surveillance, policy, and power. Population (fertility, age, mobility, health), economics, poverty, crime, education, and welfare became not only the main objects of government activity but also the measure of cohesion and solidarity in the emerging nineteenth-century social order. If we are to understand the latter, it is to the new social science and medico-administrative discourses, their technologies, and effects that we must look—to the new knowledges "concerning society, its health and sickness, its conditions of life, housing and habits, which served as the basic core for the 'social economy' and sociology of the nineteenth century" (Foucault 1980b, 176). In the late nineteenth- and early twentieth-centuries, the repertoire of power-producing knowledges then further expands—through psychiatry and psychology, social work and the welfare state, youth policy, industrial relations, public health, social hygiene, eugenics, and so on. As Donzelot and others have argued, the family becomes a particular object of such interventions and expertise. Moreover, as feminist scholars and Foucault's own final works have shown, sexuality provides an especially rich field for showing such power relations under construction (Donzelot 1979; Mort 1987; Copley 1989).

This "discursive" move—from the assumption of an objective "society" to the study of how the category of "the social" was formed—may be taken as paradigmatic for a variety of areas, and here I want to consider briefly two in particular, the process of working-class formation and the growth of citizenship ideals in the early nineteenth century, both of which have attracted some attention in this respect.[20] Since Thompson it has been harder and harder to present the process of working-class formation as the logical unfolding of an economic process and its necessary effects at the levels of social organization, consciousness, and culture. But nor can we conduct the alternative analysis simply as a process of empirical disaggregation, so that a fuller grasp of the working class's compositional complexities (its sectional variety across industries; its internal differentiation by hierarchies of seniority, status, and skill; and its cultural segmentation along lines of gender, religion, ethnicity, and race) and the time scale of its coalescence can emerge. To understand class as a political factor, in fact, we have to go further and accept the intractable methodological and theoretical difficulties of analyzing working-class politics (the rise of labor movements and socialist parties) as the causal expression of an economically located class interest and social structural position, indeed the futility of ever achieving historiographical consensus to this

48

effect (quite apart from the epistemological problems with such a notion of social causality as I have been describing them).

In this sense, class as a political and cultural *postulate* (the assertion of a particular model of social identity) was just as crucial to the process of class formation as the existence of class as a demonstrable social fact (the creation of new social positions defined by the relationship to the means of production or some other material criteria). The *ideology of class*, the insistence that class was the organizing reality of the emerging capitalist societies and the growth of specific practices and organizations around that insistence (like trade unions and socialist parties), is arguably a better starting point for the study of class formation than the classical one of economics and social structure because it was at this discursive level that the operational collectivity of class—who got to be included, who set the tone, and who received the recognized voice—was defined. In these terms, the history of a class is inseparable from the history of the category. Class emerged as a set of discursive claims about the social world seeking to reorder that world in terms of itself.

A move of this kind helps us free analysis from the teleology of a class consciousness thought to be inscribed in the structures of class interest and class-collective experience—and from the need to find special explanations when that class consciousness is imperfectly, if at all, achieved. Indeed, it converts the notion of "interest" itself into a problem, a discursive effect of complex histories rather than a given, coherent, and agreed basis for action that is causally prior. Rather than asking which working-class interests were reflected in which organizations and forms of action (so that working-class consciousness becomes expressively derived), we should start asking how the prevailing understandings of working-class interest were produced, how particular practices and institutions encouraged or hindered particular constructions of working-class interest, and how one specific set of images of what the working class was came to be entrenched. From this perspective, "interest" is far more an effect than a cause.

Focusing on the construction of class as a structuring and motivating category in this way gives us better access to the partialities and indeterminacies of class formation and to the processes of exclusion on which its solidarities grew. And in exploring the always incomplete process of construction that thus defines class as an operative phenomenon, we should concentrate less on uncovering an underlying coherence in the languages of class than on understanding their lines of fracture and difference. As Robbie Gray observes, reflecting on Stedman Jones's intervention, such language is "multi-layered, complex, fractured, composed of incoherences and silences, as well as the smooth flow of would-be authoritative public discourses," and as such it must be read for its exclusions as well as for its unifying appeals (Gray 1986, 367). The most important and continuous of such exclusions has concerned women and is ordered along lines of gender.

The positive identity of the working class as it became elaborated during the nineteenth century—the ideal of the skilled male worker in industry—

rested on powerfully dichotomous assumptions about what it meant to be a man or woman. Those assumptions were ordered into a pervasive dualism that aligned men with the worlds of work and the public domain of politics and women with the home and the private realm of domesticity—the one a site of control and rationality, the other a site of affect and subordination. Inscribed in the language of class were definite notions of masculinity and femininity that limited "women's access to knowledge, skill and independent political subjectivity" (Alexander 1984, 137). Consequently, the importance of gender, sexuality, and family cannot be bracketed from an account of the politics of working-class formation. On the contrary, the social construction of sexual difference in such a way that it did work to separate the private sphere of family from the worlds of work and class—the gendering of class formation—actually had a powerful impact on how working-class identity came to be understood. Moreover, the fixing of class identity in this way presupposed the suppression of alternative possibilities. Such a fixing presumed, indeed required, the silencing of alternative meanings that threatened to outgrow its terms. In the case of "class," the discourse marginalized the role of women through the fixity of its assumptions in this way. It seems to me enormously important to uncover such structures and their operation and convert the assumed meanings of class into a problem. It is vital, in other words, to upset the unity of meaning.

In fact, we need an opposing conception of identity that stresses its nonfixity and sees it as an unstable ordering of multiple possibilities whose provisional unity is managed discursively through language and is only ever constituted through incompletely ordered factors of difference. If the purpose is to understand the ways in which processes and structures of exclusion have ordered historical constructions of class, then overcoming such exclusions means recognizing the indeterminate multiplicity of identity. How we see ourselves as a basis for action and how we are addressed in the public arena are not fixed. We recognize ourselves variously—as citizens, as workers, as parents, as consumers, as enthusiasts for sports or hobbies, as religious believers, and so on. Those recognitions are inflected with power relations of different kinds, and they are heavily gendered by assumptions defining us as women or men. At one level, this complexity and nonfixity of subject positions is a banal observation. But the important thing is that politics is usually conducted as if identity is fixed. The issue then becomes: on what bases, in different places and at different times, does identity's nonfixity become temporarily fixed in such a way as to enable individuals and groups to behave as a particular kind of agency, political or otherwise? How do people become shaped into acting subjects, understanding themselves in particular ways? In effect, politics consists of the effort to "domesticate the infinitude" of identity (Mouffe 1989). It is the attempt to *hegemonize* identity, to order it into strong programmatic commitments. If identity is decentered, politics is about the *attempt to create a center*.

[. . .]

Thus, the "unity" of the working class, though postulated through the analysis of production and its social relations, is a never attainable object of construction, a fictive agency, a contingency of political action. Moreover, notions of citizenship can be similarly deconstructed, particularly if we push these back to the ideal of the rationally acting individual subject usually located in the traditions of thought descending from the Enlightenment. It has become a commonplace of feminist critique that modern political thought is highly gendered in its basic structures, particularly in the Enlightenment context of the later eighteenth century when the key elements of liberal and democratic discourse were first composed. In other words, the constitutive moment of modern political understanding was itself constituted by newly conceived or rearranged assumptions about woman and man: this was not only visible in constitutions, legal codes, and political mobilizations, but it also ordered the higher philosophical discourse around the universals of reason, law, and nature, grounding this in an ideologically constructed system of differences in gender.

The new category of the "public man" and his "virtue" was elaborated via a series of oppositions to "femininity," which both drew upon older notions of domesticity and women's place and rationalized them into a set of formal claims concerning woman's "nature." At the most fundamental level, specific constructions of "womanness" defined the quality of being a "man," so that the *natural* identification of sexuality and desire with the feminine allowed the *social* and *political* construction of masculinity to take place. In this sense, modern politics, among other things, was constituted "*as* a relation of gender" (Landes 1988, 204). In the rhetoric of the 1780s and 1790s reason was counter-posed conventionally to "femininity, if by the latter we mean (as contemporaries did) pleasure, play, eroticism, artifice, style, politesse, refined facades, and particularity" (Landes 1988, 46). Then, in the concentrated circumstances of the French Revolution, women were to be silenced to allow masculine speech—in the language of reason—full rein. Together with others (class, race, ethnicity, religion, age, etc.), gender and sexual identity were the powerful exclusions from which the modern political subject became formed— indeed, which allowed that idea of rational subjectivity first to emerge.

There is no need to explicate this further. The point is to suggest how particular discursive formations—whose emergence and elaboration can be carefully located historically—are themselves centrally implicated in social history, in constituting the basic categories of understanding and therefore the social, cultural, and political environment in which people acted and thought rather than being predicated on "experience" or following unproblematically from a social cause. The nineteenth-century discourse of citizenship, no less than the related conceptions of class-collective identity, were immensely complex and powerful formations of this type, which finely ordered the social and political world and structured the possibilities of what could and could not be thought. Gender was crucial not only to the patterning and containment of one's class identity but also to the endowment and delimitation of one's political capacities. Recent feminist theory has acutely sensitized us to the procedures and assumptions that regulate access to a political voice. On the one hand, there is the synthesizing critique of patriarchy as a continuous figure of European political thought from Hobbes through Locke to the Enlightenment and beyond. In the latter, women are essentially confined within the household: "Within this sphere, women's functions of child-bearing, child-rearing and maintaining the household are deemed to correspond to their unreason, disorderliness and 'closeness' to nature. Women and the domestic sphere are viewed as inferior to the male-dominated 'public' world of civil society and its culture, property, social power, reason and freedom" (Keane 1988, 21). But on the other hand, the beauty of recent work is that it has shown how this pattern of subordination was reformulated and recharged in the midst of that major political cataclysm —the French Revolution—through which the ideal of human emancipation was otherwise radically enlarged. In other words, the emerging liberal model of rational political exchange was not just vitiated by persisting patriarchal structures of an older sort. The very inception of the liberal public sphere was itself shaped by a new exclusionary discourse directed at women.

In highlighting the exclusionary treatment of women, such work is also subverting the existing terms of the story—enabling not just the retrieval of a previously neglected aspect but a set of insights that fundamentally reconstructs our sense of the whole. There are now rich demonstrations in a variety of fields to this effect. Thus, Davidoff and Hall (1987) have shown how classical bourgeois society and politics no less than the nineteenth-century working-class presence were also produced by gendered processes of class formation. They stress *both* the constitutive importance of gender (i.e., the historically specific structuring of sexual difference) in the ordering of the middle-class social world via particular patterns of family and domesticity and particular styles of consumption *and* the reciprocal interactions between this private sphere and the public sphere of associational life and politics, in which the latter both reflected and actively reproduced the gendered distinctions of class identity generated between home and work. The remarkable associational activity of the early nineteenth century strictly demarcated the roles of women and men via a mobile repertoire of ideologies and practices, which consistently assigned women to a nonpolitical private sphere, "having at most a supportive role to play in the rapidly expanding political world of their fathers, husbands and brothers" (Catherine Hall 1985, 11). Moreover, this separation of spheres—between the masculine realm of public activity and the feminine realm of the home, which certainly did not preclude (and was finely articulated with) relations of interconnectedness between business/occupation and household and engendered a particular conception of the public and the private for the emergent nineteenth-century bourgeoisie— was replicated in the situation of the working class, as work on Chartism and nineteenth-century socialist movements as well as the social history of the working class has amply shown (Alexander 1984; Rose 1991).

Conclusion

In this essay I have tried to take stock of the last twenty years not to provide an accurate inventory of recent work but to provide a sense of current direction. However, while the 1970s were still characterized by a sense of forward movement, borne by the unlimited power of social explanation, the 1980s have seen far more a mood of uncertainty and flux. As I have suggested, this is partly a generational story, as one part of the social history cohort of the 1960s has detached itself from the previous materialist consensus (as we can minimally call it) to pursue the antireductionist logic of structuralist and poststructuralist theory, leaving another part (probably the majority) in considerable disarray—some dogmatically reaffirming older positions (which I have tended to call "classically materialist"), some opting for a more eclectic and anthropologically oriented cultural history, and many more continuing in their hard-won social-historical practice of the 1970s. At the risk of over-simplifying, I tend to see two main tributaries among English-speaking social historians to the linguistic turn: one is the large corpus of British post-Althusserian Marxism/post-Marxism (including a separate but convergent feminism) and the other is the remarkable North American impact of decon-structive literary theory, increasingly mediated through specifically feminist discussion. (Where this leaves the specifically anthropological contribution is less clear.) At this point, the radical pressure of feminist theory seems to me to be primary.

Critics of the so-called linguistic turn from the left (and the more mischiev-ous ones from the right) happily reduce it to a particular kind of social project—as the self-indulgent acrobatics of left intellectuals who have lost their way, constructing seductive but self-serving rationalizations for their own ivory tower isolation, seeking a substitute for the working class that refuses their ministrations, and losing their nerve for the well-tried yet difficult radical projects (Wood 1986; Palmer 1990). In response, the construc-tive relationship between the theoretical perspectives I have been exploring and the chances of articulating a politics more adequate to the diverse and complex bases of collective identity at the end of the twentieth century is one I would—on the contrary—readily affirm. Moreover, the social and political histories of the last quarter century—in the so-called real world—that have induced such widespread skepticism about more traditional ideas of class-political agency among their putative bearers—as a primary and suffi-cient basis for understanding and acting on the world—certainly inform the appeal of those perspectives for those socialists such as myself who would like to reelaborate some viable basis of left-wing politics from the contem-porary wreckage of the state-socialist traditions. There is also an available social analysis—of post-Fordism, post-modernity, and the transnational restructuring of the global capitalist economy—that can begin to ground the conditions of possibility for a politics of "new times." But such a social analysis of the intellectual history I have been recounting is not necessary to the theoretical and epistemological challenge it contains. It certainly can't be invoked as some kind of normalizing materialist move.

Indeed, the exact relationship between intellectual life—in this case a specific shift of theory and its effects in the doing of history—and general social and political conditions is anything but clear, and one of the purposes of my essay has been to point to the difficulties of bringing them causally together. It would be perverse—an act of materialist faith—to call the argument back to an older conception of the social and thereby to make harmless the very questions it is trying to raise. At all events, social history in its amorphous but aggrandizing form of the 1970s has ceased to exist: it has lost its coherence as an intellectual project (which derived, I suggested, from the sovereignty of social determinations within a self-confident materialist conception of social totality, both of which have been subjected to compelling critique) and it has lost its prestige as the natural location for the more radical, innovative, and experimental intellectual spirits in the profession, particularly in the generations currently being recruited. The "new cultural history" or cultural studies is currently taking its place.

I do not see this as a crisis or a cause for regret. But there is certainly no shortage of voices that do. In the most recent—and book-length—example, Bryan Palmer denounces the linguistic turn as "unmistakably an adversary maneuver" directed against historical materialism and social history. It represents a "hedonistic descent into a plurality of discourses that decenter the world in a chaotic denial of any acknowledgment of tangible structures of power and comprehensions of meaning"; a "reduction of analysis and theory to the puns and word games of scholastic pretension"; and "a messianic faddism" that has disastrously captured the imagination of social historians (Palmer 1990, 188). Palmer's is truly a bizarre book, oscillating abruptly between sympathetic exegeses of poststructuralist contributions and constructive appropriations on the one hand and wild condemnations on the other. In the end, the linguistic turn for Palmer has resulted straightforwardly in ". . . crap, a kind of academic wordplaying with no possible link to anything but the pseudo-intellectualized ghettoes of the most self-promotionally avant-garde enclaves of that bastion of protectionism, the University" (Palmer 1990, 199). Against this kind of intellectual police action ("These are refusals that must be made, and made clearly"—but according to what authority?), which is depressingly reminiscent of the worst excesses of Edward Thompson's *The Poverty of Theory* and the surrounding debate, *we* should insist on the need for pluralism. And that is the note on which I prefer to end. Whether individually we decide to take the linguistic turn or not, there will remain a diversity of histories in the profession, and as in practice there is no way of finally resolving these debates short of driving the opponents from the field and burning their books; the best we can ask is openness and intellectual seriousness in the exchange. Understanding advances through conflict and the polemical clarification of difference. But in the end it is the differences that have to remain.

NOTES

This essay was written during the summer of 1990 and reflects both the state of disciplinary discussion and my own thinking at that time. During the intervening years an enormous amount of publication, debate, and clarification has occurred, though arguably not a huge change in the basic epistemological landscape my essay describes. More historians have begun to explore the excitement of the new perspectives, but probably an equal number continue to rail against the pernicious effects of a demonized,"postmodernism," and the field of difficulty continues much as before. Rather than trying to bring my citations up to date (an entire project in itself), I've left the text and footnotes in their original form, as a kind of snapshot of a history still in motion. On the other hand, the subsequent publications of Kathleen Canning and Peggy Somers deserve to be acknowledged, as they reflect earlier discussions that helped shape my own arguments about class formation. See Kathleen Canning, "Gender and the Politics of Class Formation: Rethinking German Labor History," *American Historical Review* 97 (1992): 736–68; "Feminist History after the Linguistic Turn: Historicizing Discourse and Experience," *Signs* 19 (1994): 368–404; *Languages of Labor and Gender: Female Factory Work in Germany, 1850–1914* (Ithaca, 1996); and Margaret R. Somers, "Workers of the World, Compare!" *Contemporary Sociology* 18 (1989): 325–30; "Narrativity, Narrative Identity, and Social Action: Rethinking English Working-Class Formation," *Social Science History* 16 (1992): 591–630. More generally, I would like to thank my friends and colleagues in the Program for the Comparative Study of Social Transformations (CSST), who provided the context of intellectual generosity and exploration that allowed this essay to be written. I owe a particular debt to Nick Dirks, Mike Kennedy, Sherry Ortner, Bill Sewell, and Peggy Somers, but especially Terry McDonald, who organized the conference from which this [essay] derived, and whose intellectual friendship and intelligence has been a vital part of my Michigan years. For an indication of developments since 1990, readers may wish to consult the Introduction to Nicholas B. Dirks, Geoff Eley, and Sherry B. Ortner, eds., *Culture/Power/History: A Reader in Contemporary Social Theory* (Princeton, 1994): 3–45; and Geoff Eley, "Playing It Safe. Or: How Is Social History Represented? The New Cambridge Social History of Britain," *History Workshop Journal* 35 (1993): 207–20.

1 The bibliographical context for this essay is potentially huge. Rather than cluttering the text itself with absurd numbers of citations or multiplying the footnotes, I have tried to indicate this context by citing only one or two representative titles on each occasion while collecting the full references in the bibliography at the end. Thus, the bibliography is intended to provide a reasonably full guide to the wider reading on which the argument of the essay is based.

2 Several essays from the later 1970s have been repeatedly cited for these polemical disagreements: Fox-Genovese and Genovese (1976); Stedman Jones (1976); Stone (1977); Judt (1979). They were followed by Stone (1979); and Eley and Nield (1980).

3 See the following of Stedman Jones's essays: 1972, 1975, 1976, 1977a, 1977b. The essay on language was Stedman Jones (1983), in a volume that also republished several of the earlier essays. The best guide to the trajectory of his thinking is the introduction to that volume, together with an interview conducted by Stuart Macintyre (1977).

4 See Thompson (1978) and the coinciding debate around Johnson (1978). Other contributions include Anderson (1980), and the debate between Stuart Hall, Richard Johnson, and Edward Thompson at the Thirteenth History Workshop in Oxford in December 1979 and published in Samuel (1981). (A fourth, feminist, speaker withdrew from the History Workshop debate on the grounds that the tone and terms of the proceedings made her presence inappropriate. My favorite among the many subsequent commentaries is Magarey (1987)).

5 See especially Stedman Jones (1972, 1976). For a particular case, see McDonald (1985). The best general illustration of the point is *Past and Present* between the late 1950s

and late 1960s, when the generation of British Marxists who mainly left the communist party in 1956–57 turned to non-Marxist social theory to help their general
rethinking. Philip Abrams and Eric Hobsbawm were key in the exchange with sociology; Jack Goody, Peter Worsley, Keith Thomas, and Hobsbawm again in that with
anthropology.

6 See Scott (1988) and Johnson (1978, 1979a, 1979b, and more recently 1986–87). Both
began their careers in the 1960s in the more dependent relationship criticized by
Stedman Jones, cultivating their analyses in the sun of sociology—Scott in a classic
of the new social history, Johnson as a historian of education within a perspective of
social control. See Scott (1974) and Johnson (1970).

7 This is reflected in the introduction to Thane and Sutcliffe (1986), which is consciously
framed to update Hobsbawm's survey, but which presents a rather disorganized
mélange of topics and trends. Ultimately, a general shift from "class" to "culture" in
the organizing categories of British social history seems to be their overriding theme.

8 The apogee of achievement is Wrigley and Schofield (1981). The launching in 1986
of a new journal, *Continuity and Change. A Journal of Social Structure, Law and
Demography in Past Societies*, may presage a broadening of vision. In the meantime,
see Levine (1987); Seccombe (1983); and Hochstadt (1982).

9 Specific urban phenomena naturally retain their importance, in contrast to urban
history's claims of constituting a coherent field in itself. Urban planning, the fiscal
dimensions of the local state, Third World urbanization since the 1960s, the city as
the cultural ideal of modernism—these and other themes come readily to mind. It
is the exaggerated expectations invested in urban history as a subdisciplinary
specialism that seem to have come aground.

10 The literature on peasants may be best approached through the *Journal of Peasant
Studies*, founded in 1973–74. For the petite bourgeoisie, see Blackbourn (1985); and
Crossick and Haupt (1984). The most elaborate recent project on the bourgeoisie has
been German-centered with extensive comparative ambitions and was coordinated
by Jürgen Kocka at the University of Bielefeld. See especially Kocka (1988); and for
an English-language collection in counterposition, Blackbourn and Evans (1990).
There is also much activity in Italy, for which see the reports in the *Bollettino di infor-
mazion a cura del gruppo di studio sulle borghesie del xix secolo* (1985–). The role of gender
in bourgeois class formation has also received important attention. See especially
Davidoff and Hall (1987); Ryan (1981); Frevert (1988).

11 On the other hand, Hobsbawm was well aware of the importance of matters like the
sexual division of labor or women's political emancipation, and his labor history
writings showed both the relative strengths and the blindnesses of the communist
political tradition in this respect. The difference can be gauged by considering
someone of a similar generation whose lack of awareness was genuinely crass: Perkin
(1981).

12 For work on Britain, see Alexander (1976, 1984); Rose (1986, 1991); Freifield (1986);
John (1986); and the special issue of *Social History* on "Gender and Employment"
(1988). Similar lists could be given for Germany, France, and the United States. But
progress should not be overestimated: astonishingly, one recent imposing handbook
of international research, Tenfelde (1986), contains among its *twenty* mainly thematic
essays not a single entry on women.

13 Here the influence of Scott (1988) is obviously important, together with works such
as Ryan (1981), and Davidoff and Hall (1987). I should also acknowledge the work
on gender and class formation in Germany by my colleague Kathleen Canning.
Again, the impact on more orthodox discussions of class formation, even where these
profess innovation, should not be overstated. See Katznelson and Zolberg (1986),
where gender relations are glaring in their absence (apart from a lamely exculpatory
footnote on the second page of the introduction, 4).

14 This has become an area of great activity, most of which is strongly present-based and can be found in a range of new journals, including *New Formations* (1987–); *Block* (1979–89); *Cultural Studies* (1987–); *Social Text* (1982–); *Cultural Critique* (1985–); *Representations* (1983–); *Media, Culture, and Society* (1978–); and the women's studies journals. Key works would include: Mulvey (1989); Williamson (1986); Coward (1984); Gamman and Marshment (1988); Radway (1984); Modleski (1982); and Kaplan (1987). Conceptually, such work can be used by historians to excellent effect. For two examples relating to film, see Petro (1989); and Kuhn (1990). For an older genre, excellent in its kind, that treats film as a source of social commentary but from which both women as such and the new cultural theory are absent, see Stead (1989). Stead's book falls within the 1960s/1970s problematic of left-inclined British social history, doubly influenced by Thompson (1963) and Williams (1958), with all the virtues and limitations, which include the by-now-familiar innocence on questions of gender. See Swindells and Jardine (1990). Historical discussion within the newer cultural perspectives can be found in the film journals, *Screen* (1959–) and *Jump Cut* (1974–).

15 See Bridenthal, Grossmann, and Kaplan (1984); Macciocchi (1979); Caplan (1979); and Theweleit (1987, 1988). A good way into current work on masculinity is Chapman and Rutherford (1988), and review essays by Tosh, Roper, and Bristow in Roper (1990).

16 For an example of the continuous reduction of family history to the technical and procedural parameters of a demographic problematic, however compelling those imperatives in their own terms, see the response of Houston and Smith (1982) to Chaytor's dissenting article (1980). For indications of how recent theory might allow the history of the family to be (de/re)constructed, see Barrett and Mcintosh (1982), and Riley (1983), Barrett and McIntosh (1982: 95–105) also provide a useful critique of an influential post-Foucauldian text, Donzelot (1979).

17 Alexander (1984), 127. The same passage is quoted by Swindells and Jardine (1990), 93, and by the introduction to Lovell (1990), 25, where the Alexander essay is also reprinted. I have always thought that there is a kind of presumption in male historians trying to speak for women's history. Yet the alternative of more incidental forms of reference cannot escape the effect of tokenism. There is no easy solution. For some useful thoughts, see Todd (1988), 118–34.

18 Hirst (1985b), 28. Hirst's essays, mostly produced between the late 1970s and early 1980s, are a useful guide through these questions. See also the following comment from Hirst (1979), 21:

> We would argue that discourses and practices *do* employ the criteria of appropriateness or adequacy (not of epistemological validity) but these are specific to the objectives of definite bodies of discourse and practice. None will pass muster as a general criterion of validity, but there is no knowledge process *in general* and, therefore, no necessity for such a criterion. Techniques of criticism of biblical texts are of no use in garage mechanics. Questions of priority and relation in the Gospels, of the state of wear of a gearbox elicit different types of tests and disputes about them. The referents and constructs, Gospels, motor cars, depend on conditions which differ, so do criteria and tests. Tests, etc., develop within the discourses and practices to which they relate and are subject to dispute. As tests they are radically different, they seek to establish or challenge different things according to the objectives and circumstances of the practice in question.

19 Whereas this approach derives strongly from Foucault, it has affinities with the "keywords" method of Raymond Williams and with the work of Reinhart Koselleck and the West German tradition of *Begriffsgeschichte*. See Williams (1983); Brunner, Conze, and Koselleck (1972–89); Tribe (1989).

20 For important work in a similar direction, see Somers (1989, 1992) and Canning (1992, 1994).

REFERENCES

Alexander, Sally. 1976. "Women's Work in Nineteenth-Century London." In Juliet Mitchell and Ann Oakley, eds., *The Rights and Wrongs of Women*, 55–111. Harmondsworth.

Alexander, Sally. 1984. "Women, Class and Sexual Difference." *History Workshop Journal* 17: 125–49.

Anderson, Perry. 1980. *Arguments within English Marxism*. London.

Barrett, Michele, and Mary McIntosh. 1982. *The Anti-Social Family*. London.

Bennett, Tony. 1982. "Text and History." In Peter Widdowson, ed., *Re-Reading English*, 223–36. London.

Blackbourn, David. 1985. "Economic Crisis and the Petite Bourgeoisie in Europe during the Nineteenth and Twentieth Centuries." *Social History* 10: 95–104.

Blackbourn, David, and Richard J. Evans, eds. 1990. *The German Bourgeoisie*. London.

Bridenthal, Renate, Atina Grossman, and Marion Kaplan, eds. 1984. *When Biology Became Destiny: Women in Weimar and Nazi Germany*. New York.

Brunner, Otto, Werner Conze, and Reinhart Koselleck, eds. 1972–89. *Geschichtliche Grundbegriffe*. 5 vols. Stuttgart.

Canning, Kathleen. 1992. "Gender and the Politics of Class Formation: Rethinking German Labor History." *American Historical Review* 97: 736–68.

Canning, Kathleen. 1994. "Feminist History after the Linguistic Turn: Historicizing Discourse and Experience." *Signs* 19: 368–404.

Caplan, Jane. 1979. "Introduction to Macciocchi: 'Female Sexuality in Fascist Ideology.'" *Feminist Review* 1: 59–66.

Chapman, Rowena, and Jonathan Rutherford, eds. 1988. *Male Order: Unwrapping Masculinity*. London.

Chaytor, Miranda. 1980. "Household and Kinship: Ryton in the Late Sixteenth and Early Seventeenth Centuries." *History Workshop Journal* 10: 25–60.

Copley, Antony. 1989. *Sexual Moralities in France, 1780–1980: New Ideas on the Family, Divorce, and Homosexuality: An Essay on Moral Change*. London.

Coward, Rosalind. 1984. *Female Desires: How They Are Sought, Bought, and Packaged*. London.

Crossick, Geoffrey, and Gerhard Haupt, eds. 1984. *Shopkeepers and Master Artisans in Nineteenth-Century Europe*. London.

Davidoff, Leonore, and Catherine Hall. 1987. *Family Fortunes: Men and Women of the English Middle Class, 1780–1850*. London.

Derrida, Jacques. 1988. "Like the Sound of the Sea Deep within a Shell: Paul De Man's War." *Critical Inquiry* 14: 590–652.

Donzelot, Jacques. 1979. *The Policing of Families*. New York.

Eley, Geoff. 1979. "Some Recent Tendencies in Social History." In Georg G. Iggers and Harold T. Parker, eds., *International Handbook of Historical Studies: Contemporary Research and Theory*, 55–70. Westport, CT.

Eley, Geoff, and Keith Nield. 1980. "Why Does Social History Ignore Politics?" *Social History* 5: 249–71.

Foucault, Michel. 1980a. "Body/Power." In Colin Gordon, ed., *Power/Knowledge*, 55–62. Brighton.

Foucault, Michel. 1980b. "The Politics of Health in the Eighteenth Century." In Colin Gordon, ed., *Power/Knowledge*, 166–82. Brighton.

Fox-Genovese, Elizabeth, and Eugene Genovese. 1976. "The Political Crisis of Social History: A Marxian Perspective." *Journal of Social History* 10: 205–20.

Freifield, Mary. 1986. "Technical Change and the Self-Acting Mule." *Social History* 11: 319–43.

Frevert, Ute, ed. 1988. *Bürgerinnen und Bürger: Geschlechterverhältnisse im 19. Jahrhundert*. Göttingen, Germany.

Gamman, Lorraine, and Margaret Marshment, eds. 1988. *The Female Gaze. Women as Viewers of Popular Culture*. London.

Giddens, Anthony. 1981. *A Contemporary Critique of Historical Materialism*. Vol. 1, *Power, Property and the State*. London.

Giddens, Anthony. 1985. *A Contemporary Critique of Historical Materialism*. Vol. 2, *The Nation-State and Violence*. Cambridge.

Gray, Robert. 1986. "The Deconstruction of the English Working Class." *Social History* 11: 363–73.

Hall, Catherine. 1985. "Private Persons versus Public Someones: Class, Gender, and Politics in England, 1780–1850." In Carolyn Steedman, Cathy Urwin, and Valerie Walkerdine, eds., *Language, Gender and Childhood*, 10–33. London.

Hall, John A. 1985. *Powers and Liberties: The Causes and Consequences of the Rise of the West*. Oxford.

Hall, Stuart. 1978. "Some Problems with the Ideology/Subject Couplet." *Ideology and Consciousness* 3: 120.

Harrison, Rachel, and Frank Mort. 1980. "Patriarchal Aspects of Nineteenth-Century State Formation: Property Relations, Marriage and Divorce, and Sexuality." In Philip Corrigan, ed., *Capitalism, State Formation, and Marxist Theory*, 79–109. London.

Hirst, Paul Q. 1979. *On Law and Ideology*. London.

Hirst, Paul Q. 1985a. "Collingwood, Relativism, and the Purposes of History." In *Marxism and Historical Writing*, 43–56. London.

Hirst, Paul Q. 1985b. "Interview with Local Consumption." In *Marxism and Historical Writing*, 121–48. London.

History Workshop Journal. 1980. Editorial: "Language and History," *History Workshop Journal* 10: 1–5.

Hobsbawm, E. J. 1971. "From Social History to the History of Society." *Daedalus* 100: 20–45.

Hochstadt, Steve. 1982. "Social History and Politics: A Materialist View," *Social History* 7: 75–83.

Houston, Rab, and Richard Smith. 1982. "A New Approach to Family History?" *History Workshop Journal* 14: 120–31.

John, Angela, ed. 1986. *Unequal Opportunities: Women's Employment in England, 1800–1918*. Oxford.

Johnson, Richard. 1970. "Educational Policy and Social Control in Early-Victorian England." *Past and Present* 49: 96–119.

Johnson, Richard. 1978. "Thompson, Genovese, and Socialist-Humanist History." *History Workshop Journal* 6: 79–100.

Johnson, Richard. 1979a. "Culture and the Historians." In John Clarke, Chas Critcher, and Richard Johnson, eds., *Working-Class Culture: Studies in History and Theory*, 41–71. London.

Johnson, Richard. 1979b. "Three Problematics: Elements of a Theory of Working-Class Culture." In John Clarke, Chas Critcher, and Richard Johnson, eds., *Working-Class Culture: Studies in History and Theory*, 201–37. London.

Johnson, Richard. 1986–87. "What Is Cultural Studies Anyway?" *Social Text* 16: 38–80.

Judt, Tony. 1979. "A Clown in Regal Purple: Social History and the Historians." *History Workshop Journal* 7: 66–94.

Kaplan, E. Ann. 1987. "Gender Address and the Gaze in MTV." In *Rocking around the Clock: Music Television, Postmodernism, and Consumer Culture*, 89–142. New York and London.

Katznelson, Ira, and Aristide R. Zolberg, eds. 1986. *Working-Class Formation: Nineteenth-Century Patterns in Western Europe and the United States*. Princeton, NJ.

Keane, John, ed. 1988. Introduction to John Keane, ed., *Civil Society and the State: New European Perspectives*, 1–31. London and New York.

Kocka, Jürgen, ed. 1988. *Bürgertum im 19. Jahrhundert: Deutschland im europäischen Vergleich*. Munich.

Kuhn, Annette. 1990. *Cinema, Censorship, and Sexuality, 1909–1925*. London.

Landes, Joan B. 1988. *Women and the Public Sphere in the Age of the French Revolution*. Ithaca, NY.

Levine, David. 1987. *Reproducing Families. The Political Economy of English History*. Cambridge.

Lovell, Terry, ed. 1990. *British Feminist Thought: A Reader*. Oxford.

Macciocchi, Maria-Antonietta. 1979. "Female Sexuality in Fascist Ideology." *Feminist Review* 1: 67–82.

McDonald, Terrence J. 1985. "The Problem of the Political in Recent American Urban History: Liberal Pluralism, and the Rise of Functionalism." *Social History* 10: 323–45.

Macintyre, Stuart. 1977. "Interview with Gareth Stedman Jones." *Red Shift* 4: 19–23,

Magarey, Susan. 1987. "That Hoary Old Chestnut, Free Will and Determinism: Culture vs. Structure, or History vs. Theory in Britain." *Comparative Studies in Society and History* 29: 626–39.

Mann, Michael. 1986. *The Sources of Social Power, I: A History of Power from the Beginning to A.D. 1760*. Cambridge.

Modleski, Tania. 1982. *Loving with a Vengeance: Mass-Produced Fantasies for Women*. New York.

Mort, Frank. 1987. *Dangerous Sexualities: Medico-Moral Politics in England since 1830*. London.

Mouffe, Chantal. 1989. "Rethinking Pluralism." Comparative Studies of Social Transformations (CSST) lecture, 21 Sept. 1989, University of Michigan, Ann Arbor, MI.

Mulvey, Laura. 1989. *Visual and Other Pleasures*. Bloomington and Indianapolis, IN.

Novick, Peter. 1988. *That Noble Dream: The "Objectivity Question" and the American Historical Profession*. Cambridge.

Outram, Dorinda. 1989. *The Body and the French Revolution: Sex, Class, and Political Culture*. London and New Haven, CT.

Palmer, Bryan D. 1990. *Descent into Discourse: The Reification of Language and the Writing of Social History*. Philadelphia, PA.

Pateman, Carole. 1988. *The Sexual Contract*. Cambridge, MA.

Perkin, Harold. 1981. "What Is Social History?" In *The Structured Crowd: Essays in English Social History*, 1–27. Brighton.

Petro, Patrice. 1989. *Joyless Streets: Women and Melodramatic Representation in Weimar Germany*. Princeton, NJ.

Radway, Janice. 1984. *Reading the Romance: Women, Patriarchy, and Popular Culture*. Chapel Hill, NC.

Riley, Denise. 1983. *War in the Nursery: Theories of the Child and Mother*. London.

Roper, Michael, ed. 1990. "Recent Books on Masculinity" (reviews by John Tesh, Michael Roper, and Joseph Bristow). *History Workshop Journal* 29: 184–93.

Rose, Sonya O. 1986. "Gender at Work: Sex, Class, and Industrial Capitalism." *History Workshop Journal* 21: 113–31.

Rose, Sonya O. 1991. *Limited Livelihoods*. Berkeley, CA.

Ryan, Mary P. 1981. *Cradle of the Middle Class: Family and Community in Oneida County, New York, 1780–1865*. Cambridge.

Samuel, Raphael, ed. 1981. *People's History and Socialist Theory*. London.

Scott, Joan. 1974. *The Glassworkers of Carmaux: French Craftsmen and Political Action in a Nineteenth-Century City*. Cambridge, MA.

Scott, Joan. 1988. *Gender and the Politics of History*. New York.

Seccombe, Wally. 1983. "Marxism and Demography." *New Left Review* 137: 22–47.

Somers, Margaret R. 1989. "Workers of the World, Compare!" *Contemporary Sociology* 18: 325–30.

Somers, Margaret R. 1992. "Narrativity, Narrative Identity, and Social Action: Rethinking English Working-Class Formation." *Social Science History* 16: 591–630.

Stead, Peter. 1989. *Film and the Working Class: The Feature Film in British and American Society*. London.

Stedman Jones, Gareth. 1972. "History: The Poverty of Empiricism." In Robin Blackburn, ed., *Ideology in Social Science: Readings in Critical Social Theory*, 96–115. London.

Stedman Jones, Gareth. 1975. "Class Struggle and the Industrial Revolution." *New Left Review* 90: 35–69.

Stedman Jones, Gareth. 1976. "From Historical Sociology to Theoretical History." *British Journal of Sociology* 27: 295–305.

Stedman Jones, Gareth. 1977a. "Class Expression versus Social Control? A Critique of Recent Trends in the Social History of 'Leisure'." *History Workshop Journal* 4: 162–70.

Stedman Jones, Gareth. 1977b. "Society and Politics at the Beginning of the World Economy." *Cambridge Journal of Economics* 1: 77–92.

Stedman Jones, Gareth. 1983. "Rethinking Chartism." In *Languages of Class: Studies in English Working-Class History, 1832–1982*, 90–178. London.

Stone, Lawrence. 1977. "History and the Social Sciences in the Twentieth Century." In Charles F. Delzell, ed., *The Future of History*, 3–42. Nashville, TN.

Stone, Lawrence. 1979. "The Revival of Narrative." *Past and Present* 85: 3–24.

Swindells, Julia, and Lisa Jardine. 1990. *What's Left? Women in Culture and the Labour Movement*. London.

Tenfelde, Klaus, ed. 1986. *Arbeiter und Arbeiterbewegung im Vergleich: Berichte zur internationalen historischen Forschung*. Historische Zeitschrift-Sonderheft 15. Munich.

Thane, Pat, and Anthony Sutcliffe, eds. 1986. *Essays in Social History*. Oxford.

Theweleit, Klaus. [1987] 1988. *Male Fantasies*. Minneapolis, MN.

Thompson, Edward P. 1963. *The Making of the English Working Class*. London.

Thompson, Edward P. 1978. *The Poverty of Theory and Other Essays*. London.

Tilly, Charles. 1980. "Two Callings of Social History." *Theory and Society* 9(5): 679–81.

Tilly, Charles. 1990. *Coercion, Capital, and European States, A.D. 990–1990*. Oxford.

Todd, Janet. 1988. "Men in Feminist Criticism." In Mary Eagleton, ed., *Feminist Literary Theory: A Reader*, 118–34. London.

Tribe, Keith. 1989. "The *Geschichtliche Grundbegriffe* Project: From History of Ideas to Conceptual History." *Comparative Studies in Society and History* 31: 180–4.

Wallerstein, Immanuel. 1988. *The Modern World-System*. Vol. 3, *The Second Era of Great Expansion of the Capitalist World-Economy*. New York.

Weeks, Jeffrey. 1982. "Foucault for Historians." *History Workshop Journal* 14: 106–19.

White, Hayden. 1973. *Metahistory: The Historical Imagination in Nineteenth-Century Europe*. Baltimore, MD.

White, Hayden. 1978. *Tropics of Discourse: Essays in Cultural Criticism*. Baltimore, MD.

Williams, Raymond. 1958. *Culture and Society, 1780–1950*. London.

Williams, Raymond. 1983. *Keywords: A Vocabulary of Culture and Society*. 2nd edn. London.

Williamson, Judith. 1986. *Consuming Passions: The Dynamics of Popular Culture*. London.

Wood, Ellen Meiksins. 1986. *The Retreat from Class: A New "True" Socialism*. London.

Wrigley, E. A., and Roger S. Schofield. 1981. *The Population History of England, 1541–1871*. Cambridge.

2

THE DETERMINIST FIX

Some obstacles to the further development of the linguistic approach to history in the 1990s

Gareth Stedman Jones

In this article, British labor historian Gareth Stedman Jones traces the adoption of "linguistic turn" historiography among formerly Marxist social historians, who saw in it a way to free themselves from the determinism intrinsic to the Marxist tendency to represent culture as belonging to a "superstructure," whose meaning was to be deciphered by reference to a material, essentially economic, "base." At the same time, he argues, the discursive approach, with its insistence on language as a self-contained system that precedes and constructs social reality, was only incompletely employed by social historians, who remained committed to a notion of social causation as the ultimate explanation for social and intellectual formations, hence the "determinist fix" indicated in the title. In Stedman Jones's view, this awkward mix of linguistic and social approaches was due to what he calls "the undead residue of historical materialism, [that] has been the legacy of Michel Foucault," a materialism now lodged in the mechanisms of disciplinary coercion constituted by discursive regimes of "knowledge-power," rather than Marxist modes and relations of production. On this reading, the effect of Foucault's legacy to social and intellectual history was to substitute relations of power in place of relations of production as the principle of social causation, a form of explanation which remains fundamentally materialist, despite its espousal of the linguistic turn. As such, it poses a severe obstacle to the further development of a linguistic approach to history.

* * *

From the end of the 1970s, the Marxist approach to history, which had flourished in Britain and elsewhere for over two decades, entered a period of abrupt and terminal decline. Signs of this crisis were visible in many different areas. Politically, the growth of feminism posed questions about experience which could not be explained in class terms. The doubts of feminist critics about the status and content of inherited historical narratives were now reinforced by work in literary theory and history. Similarly, with the growth of dissident protests from Eastern Europe and the advent of the Green movement, Radicals and liberals were increasingly repelled by the Marxist dismissal of justice and rights, ecologists were increasingly repelled by the Marxist emphasis upon the conquest of nature. [...]

Finally, among historians the demise of Marxism was hastened by the emergence of an alternative theoretical approach to history, derived originally from linguistics. What was significant about this approach was not so much attention to language itself. This had long been practised by more sophisticated historians. In the field of modern social history, Asa Briggs's essay on 'the language of class' in industrialising England and William Sewell's work on the language of labour in eighteenth- and nineteenth-century France were good examples of what had been achieved in pre-existing genres.[1] What was distinctive about the new approach was its insistence upon language as a self-contained system of signs the meanings of which were determined by their relationship with each other rather than to some primordial or transcendental extra-linguistic terrain. What attracted interest in this new approach was firstly that by its refusal to derive language – or more properly discourse – from an external pre-linguistic reference point, it by-passed the idea of language as a reflection of reality. Potentially this represented a serious challenge to the core assumption of historical materialism and all the different versions of Marxist history – the determination of thought by social being. Secondly, as a distinct method of enquiry, it offered new ways of connecting social and intellectual history free from the problems embodied in the Marxian notion of ideology, whose effect was always to turn thought into a derivative second order entity, the product of a set of practices belonging to a 'superstructure' whose meaning was ultimately to be deciphered by reference to the ('material' or 'economic') 'base'.

This was the promise held out by the linguistic approach. Since the middle of the 1980s, however, the hope that the linguistic approach might offer a new way of unifying the historical field has faded.[2] Whatever the possibilities in theory, there has been little practical interest in surmounting the gulf between social and intellectual history. In Britain and the United States, those most interested in a linguistic approach to history have simply turned away from questions raised by the history of society and shifted their attention to questions traditionally demarcated as 'political history'. In France, from where so many of the original theoretical innovations had begun, enthusiasm has also declined. In a recent work detailing the new *Annaliste* agenda for social history, for instance, it is stated that interest in Saussurean linguistics has now been replaced by an interest in situational semantics and that the 'linguistic turn' has now been followed by a 'historical turn'.[3]

I shall argue that the main reason why the adoption of a discursive approach has not become more widespread among historians in the 1990s is that it is still too identified – not inaccurately in some cases – with a set of assumptions deriving from the 1970s, which in crucial respects remain little more than a variant of the Marxist position which it so noisily and repetitively claims to have displaced. This has been a consequence of the incomplete way in which accounts with Marxism were settled among historians in the 1980s.[4] What *was* dislodged and dismantled was a particular narrative: a narrative which had connected the origins, trajectory and destiny of the modern industrial working class (and other classes) with particular phases in the development of the capitalist mode of production or which related the 'making' of the working class with its particular experience of capitalist exploitation and political oppression. What was *not* dislodged was a set of basic reflexes in relation to social causation, the functioning of state and the role of ideology. Indeed in many versions the new discursive approach retained a conception of social and political thought, of law, of religion and of the state, no less reductionist than that which had preceded it. In other words, what so often continued to tie the new discursive or even 'post-modernist' conception of history to its officially buried Marxist predecessor was an inveterate habit of mind – a determinist fix.

Particularly responsible for this bizarre fusion between a linguistic approach and the undead residue of historical materialism has been the legacy of Michel Foucault. It has been the preparedness of historians in English-speaking countries to adopt this or that Foucauldian proposition in an eclectic manner, apparently unaware of its proximity to the structuralist Marxism which preceded it, which has been in large part responsible for the continuing confusion about what a discursive approach might entail. Too often a discursive approach is still simply taken as just another name for Foucault's writings. Or at the very least, any resort to the employment of discursive categories is presumed to be weighed down with Foucauldian baggage.

If a linguistic approach to history is to be further developed, it is important to refuse this identification. The 'linguistic turn' did not begin with Foucault, nor did it – nor does it – in any sense depend upon Foucault's version of what it meant. Foucault's theory was only one of many possible variants of a linguistic approach. It will be argued here that if there is a concept of discourse capable of unifying social and intellectual history, it is not likely to develop from the 'new' social theory proclaimed by Foucault and his followers, but rather from an extension of the insights pioneered in other branches of intellectual and cultural history.

Such a position does not mean the denial of the original importance of Foucault's work as a challenge and a source of renewal in history. At the most general level, Foucault's work represented a challenge to all historians. Through his substitution of terms like *archaeology* and *genealogy* for the historian's vocabulary of 'change' and 'development', his assault upon the hidden teleological assumptions contained in the notion of 'origins' and his provocative reassertion of the randomness of historical conjunctures, Foucault left a deep and lasting impression upon the writing of history. His emphasis upon the radical contingency of the sequence of historical events echoed that of Lévi-Strauss.[5] But unlike Lévi-Strauss, Foucault also attempted to spell out what such an approach to the writing of history might mean in practice.

In his own work, Foucault brilliantly historicised the appearance of 'the clinical gaze', the drastic shifts in the Western treatment of madness, the invention of 'society' and the 'social', the emergence of new forms of punishment and disciplinary mechanisms involving control of the mind in place of the mutilation of the body and finally the unfinished survey of ancient and modern discourses of sexuality.[6] Whatever the defects in his writings, it is clear that his powerful if partial insights retain a capacity to disturb and that the prevailing picture of modern social administration and the character of the modern state have been powerfully affected by his intervention.

But an acknowledgement of Foucault's specific insights should be sharply distinguished from an endorsement of his overall vision of society and politics; and even more so, from the claim apparently accepted by many sociologists and even by some historians, that his work set the agenda for a new kind of history. It is well known that Foucault repeatedly made such claims, but it is surprising that so many have accepted them so uncritically. For not only is it possible to doubt how large a break in continuity was really created by his writings, but it may also be suggested that one of their principal defects is precisely the extent of their continuity with a now largely discredited 1960s structuralism. In particular, in two crucial respects at least, Foucault's work represented not a break in continuity or a change in direction, but a renewal and a philosophically souped-up restatement of the assumptions and procedures of the two principal sources of social history in post-war France: the *Annales* and Marxism.

The main theme derived from the *Annales*, was that which has come to be called 'the death of the author'. In Foucault's work, discourses are dissociated from agents or individual speech-acts. They are conceived as impersonal, anonymous, non-interactive and objective systems of rules which construct the subjects and objects of their world. The possibility of space or indetermination in the relationship between agent, function and discourse is removed, a construction which was grandiloquently declaimed by Foucault to be 'the death of Man'.[7] Closer scrutiny of the signs and portents heralding this dramatic event reveal that the point of reference was not to Armageddon, to the Holocaust or to Hiroshima, or even to the disappearance of the metaphysical underpinnings of faith evoked in Nietzsche's 'death of God'. Instead, nothing more momentous than a change in the posture of literary criticism. Furthermore, it is interesting to note that this relegation of the author or historical agent to the mere occupation of 'a subject position' in the new conception of discourse was not much more than the accentuation of a long tradition of emphasis upon historically situated unconscious and habitual mental processes, associated particularly with the work of Lucien Febvre and encapsulated in the *Annales* conception of 'mentalité'.[8] It is also true, as Peter Schöttler has pointed out, that the whole theme of the demotion of authorship – interestingly paired with a novel interest in post-Saussurean linguistics – was in fact inaugurated by *Annales* in two articles by Greimas and Barthes published in 1958 and 1960.[9]

In the case of Marxism, Foucault's objections are well-known. They were strongly stated in *The Order of Things*: Marxism belonged to a preceding episteme, that of the beginnings of the nineteenth century, it was teleological and anchored to a simplistic account of economic determination.[10] Nevertheless, some of the assumptions which shaped the alternative construction elaborated by Foucault in *Discipline and Punish* and elsewhere, strongly resembled those which had underpinned Marxism. In particular, there were strong similarities between Foucault's position and the anti-humanist, anti-historicist structuralist version of Marxism being elaborated in France at the time by Althusser and his followers.[11] This was especially true of Foucault's treatment of law, politics and ideology. What he shared with the Marxists was a conception of law as no more than a veiled form of violence and the refusal of any reality to normative conceptions of right.

These views not only shaped Foucault's contemporary political philosophy, but also his vision of history. According to Foucault, the association of power with law and sovereignty – that law had to be the 'form of power', and 'power' had to be 'exercised in the form of law' belonged to a specific historical stage in the history of power. It was that of 'the juridical state' of the Middle Ages when the monarchy raised itself over competing feudal magnates by proclaiming its sole right to pronounce the law. But this juridical state was replaced by a second form, 'the administrative state, born in the territoriality of national boundaries in the fifteenth and sixteenth centuries and corresponding to a society of regulation and discipline'. Finally, sometime in the eighteenth and early nineteenth centuries, this administrative state was in turn replaced by 'the governmental state', no longer defined primarily by territoriality, but in terms of 'the mass of its population with its volume and density'. This last form of state was now juxtaposed to civil society, henceforth constituted as an independent domain with its own regularities; its role was to foster this independence and forward these regularities through the minimum degree of regulation or application of power.[12] Traversing these three temporal strata designated by the three forms of the state was a fundamental shift in the nature of power analysed in *Discipline and Punish*. In that book Foucault argued that in the period after 1700, in place of a type of power based on a juridical notion of sovereignty (unitary power exercised through external and repressive political will), there emerged a new form of power (the pervasive, polymorphous and panoptic varieties of power-knowledge associated with the human sciences, operating internally and constructively upon subjects). This was and remains the characteristic form of the operation of power in modern society.[13]

[. . .]

According to Foucault's account, there emerged in the seventeenth and eighteenth century 'a new mechanism of power', 'absolutely incompatible with the relations of sovereignty' so that, 'by rights' the old juridical theory of sovereignty should have disappeared. But, as Foucault admitted, 'the theory of sovereignty has continued not only to exist as an ideology of right, but also to provide the organising principle of the legal codes which Europe acquired in the nineteenth century, beginning with the Napoleonic Code'.[14] Having reached this point, a mere historian might have wondered whether he or she had missed something important in the way in which the supposed problem of the juxtaposition between old and new forms of power had been constructed in the first place. Not Foucault, however, who attempts to repair the holes in his original story by adding on further dubious and unproven assertions. He states that there were two reasons why relations of sovereignty did not disappear. First, a democratised form of the theory of sovereignty served as 'an instrument of criticism of all the obstacles that can thwart the development of disciplinary society'. Second, 'it allowed a system of right to be superimposed upon the mechanisms of discipline in such a way as to conceal its actual procedures'.[15] In other words, the late eighteenth century democratic revolutions were primarily means by which the spread of a new carceral archipelago could be both legitimated and concealed.

This purported explanatory gloss gives some idea of the ingredients of Foucault's conception of non-history. [. . .] It is a clear demonstration of just how large a part of Foucault's theory is built upon a crude functionalist notion of social control. Foucault treats individuals as the assignees of subject positions within discursive practices, but he ignores the extent to which these practices changed as effects of the changing utterances and activities of these same individuals. He reduces law and concepts of right to simple ideologies of legitimation. Indeed, in a project worthy of King Cnut he expels all normative conceptions from history and instead links discursive positions unilaterally to relations of power. Far from fulfilling the promise of a new history, Foucault's approach was a striking example of the reductionist practices of the gauchiste sociology and social history of the 1970s. His was a form of social theory superimposed upon history; unremittingly grim and yet at the same time whimsical in its magnification of certain forms of evidence and its wilful disregard of others. [. . .]

[. . .]

In fact there is no reason why the acceptance of a discursive approach to history should lead to an acceptance of Foucault's particular conception of discourse. Nor is there any reason to endorse his persistent practice of merging the ambition to improve with the ambition to control, the aspiration to emancipate with the desire to punish. It is upon the basis of such shoddy historiographical procedures that Foucault constructs his tendentious picture of the Enlightenment, in which by covertly continuing to rely upon a Marxist conception of the bourgeoisie and its history, Foucault is able to imply that those who sought to establish civil equality and the representative state also in some way colluded in 'the dark side of these processes'.[16]

Recently, Foucault's ambiguous proximity to aspects of the Marxist picture of modern history has been further highlighted by an emphasis among some of his followers upon what *divided* Foucault from a linguistic approach to that history. For from the time of *The Archaeology of Knowledge*, it is claimed,

Foucault began to establish a distance between himself and 'the sovereign, sole independence of discourse' and in that book he distinguished between 'discursive formations' and 'non-discursive domains' (institutions, political events, economic practices and processes).[17] How far Foucault moved in this direction is not known, for in his later work on sexuality this problem was not clearly posed. But in the work of followers like Michel de Certeau and Roger Chartier this distinction has been considerably sharpened.[18] Chartier, for instance, distinguishes between discursive and non-discursive practices, even though he concedes that they are equally 'real' and that historical access to these non-discursive practices is only possible through the texts which describe them. Nevertheless, he insists that social realities are not to be assimilated to discursive practices, nor should the practices which make up the social world be 'reduced' to 'the rationality' that governs discourse.[19]

It is not clear what is meant by a non-discursive practice or an activity which is not informed by rationality in the minimal sense of being imbued with meaning. For if activities can be considered in text-like ways, it is not because they are deemed to be the straightforward acting out of discourses in the way in which, for instance, Chartier attacks notions of the French Revolution as the acting out of the discourse of the Enlightenment. It is rather because activities generate meaning – or to be more accurate a myriad of meanings – which reside in, and can be deciphered through their juxtaposition to other meanings within a vast and practically infinite semiological field. Complex phenomena like 'institutions', 'political events' or 'economic practices' are not non-discursive in the sense that they lack, or have not acquired, meaning or particular sets of meanings. On the contrary, they represent concentrates of meaning, arenas within which large numbers of often heterogeneous discursive practices of different weight, different temporality and different provenance, overlap and intersect. Such phenomena are never prior to meaning; rather from the beginning they are prone to be overloaded with different and often incompatible meanings – hence the difficulty, perhaps impossibility of unambiguous signification. Substantively, therefore, it is difficult to know how to interpret Chartier's (and Foucault's) claim that, 'the late eighteenth and early nineteenth centuries were fundamental ... because they constructed a new figure of power, anonymous, autonomous, and operating through practices that are not accompanied or legitimated by any discourse'.[20]

The danger of following the path proposed by Chartier and others is that it appears to re-open the old split between social and intellectual history and to relegate intellectual history to its former superstructural role (first come the new practices and subsequently the ideologies which give them legitimation). By the same token, the discursive clash occurring in the political arena is once more relegated to a second order reality. Thus a revamped version of the social interpretation of history is re-established. Formerly, this interpretation was justified by the appeal to an unmediated pre-discursive notion of experience, now the appeal is to an unmediated pre-discursive notion of practice. It is not surprising that according to this conception, intention is relegated to a marginal role in the intelligibility of such practice. This at least seems to be what is implied by Chartier's warning that 'the reflective and voluntary portion of human action does not necessarily provide the meaning of historical processes'.[21]

It would be foolish to deny that there are processes in the past which are not encompassed – or at least not sufficiently or adequately encompassed – by the languages and discourses of the past. Urbanisation and population change would be good examples of processes too diffuse to be considered the product of any particular set of discursively framed intentions on the part of contemporaries. It is also often the case that in so far as contemporaries attempted to take account of such processes, the discourses by which their speculations were shaped often led them to mistaken conclusions. It is noteworthy that in Britain in the late eighteenth century until the publication of the results of the 1801 Census, it was widely believed that the population had been declining. It is also true that the advent of the modern world was accompanied by the increasing scale and frequency of processes whose outcomes far exceeded what could be grasped by an examination of individual intentions. The behaviour of markets provided the most obvious evidence of this growing gap between intention and result and of the need to understand forms of activity which could not be aligned with the intentions of any particular set of actors. These were indeed the major challenges posed to any attempt to theorise the behaviour of commercial societies. In all these instances, it is possible to refer to social processes which were not governed by the rationality of individual agents, or whose macro-social effects bore only a paradoxical relationship with individual intentions: the much-cited relation between public virtue and private vice dramatised in Mandeville's *Fable of the Bees*. But it is highly questionable whether a problem of an analogous kind was posed in the sphere of discipline and punishment. In particular, it is implausible to imagine forms of *power* without agency.

There is an alternative to these attempts to construe the discursive approach as an extension of the radical social history of the 1970s. For there is no reason why such an approach should continue to be saddled with its residues of a structuralist reading of *mentalité*, its reductionism, its functionalism, its dismantling of the subject, its subordination of politics and – in Foucault's case – its substitution of relations of power in place of the relations of production. A conviction that intellectual and social history are not different in kind can start from the opposite end of the spectrum and attempt to extend the procedures and discriminations developed in the study of intellectual and cultural history to encompass the broader domains of social and political history. If all action is meaningful, meaning arises through the multiple and diverse relationships between subjectivities, while the sum total of such relationships constitutes society. Therefore, in place of the conventionally sharp disciplinary demarcations between social and intellectual history, historical investigation would range across the whole spectrum of social activity without encountering more than differences of degree. It would start from

those forms of activity traditionally assigned a pre-cultural or purely behavioural significance, especially, for example, in the cruder positivist versions
of economics, geography or demography. In these areas historians have only
recently paid serious attention to the deciphering of the languages – verbal,
gestural, ritual – organising and articulating the always specific investments
of meaning attending such primal 'actions' or 'passions' as for example, birth,
death, pain, illness, the consumption of food or the most elementary forms
of the labour process. However formidable and tenaciously embedded in the
assumptions of Western culture, the only differences separating the rules
attending the excavation of meaning and decoding of intention in these cases
from forms of activity clustered at the opposite pole – the traditional realms
of literary or philosophical high culture – are those inherited from the conventions of disciplinary demarcation. In other words, there is no reason why the
meticulous techniques devoted to the analysis of texts embodying more
explicit, self-consciously reflective forms of thought or specialised forms of
knowledge and mediated through highly formalised forms of communication, should not be extended to other kinds of text dispersed across the
social-cultural spectrum.[22] The poles of this spectrum would not coincide in
any predictable manner with traditional distinctions between 'elite' and
'popular' or the conventional division of interest between social history
and the history of ideas. For, on the one hand, the habitual or routinised
components of activity, or the predictable or unremarked dimensions of
experience pertain no less to the domain of the 'elite' than to the domain of
the popular and deserve as much historical investigation. Conversely, techniques designed to specify the novel components of a particular political
text by inferring its point of intervention from a reconstruction of the larger
field of utterance in which it was situated, are equally applicable to the
analysis of forms of creative innovation in the modification or transformation
of conventions governing performance in popular culture.[23] Similarly, and in
contrast to the traditional approach to 'social movements', there is no reason
why the 'intellective' elements of popular politics should not be analysed
as rigorously and scrupulously as is customary in studies of the history of
ideas. Such changes have in fact been occurring for some time. Once upon a
time, Chartism, popular millenarianism and witchcraft tended to be relegated
to the domain of behaviourist or functionalist interpretation. Each have
benefited greatly by being made the object of the more precise enquiries and
linguistic sensitivities of intellectual and cultural historians. More recently,
other seemingly familiar phenomena have been imbued with quite different
and unexpected types of meaning and importance through the application of various forms of discursive approach to research upon the history
of medicine, of family and household, of friendship, entrepreneurship,
commerce and migration.[24]

Broadening insights pioneered by intellectual historians to encompass the
larger domains of political and social history undoubtedly requires shifts of
emphasis. Existing methods have been largely devised to solve problems

accompanying the interpretation of formal and systematic texts produced by individuals. Furthermore, much of the most innovative work in this field has clustered in the early modern period and concerned the circulation of ideas among small and highly literate groups.[25] Few have ventured into, and even fewer beyond, the revolutions at the end of the eighteenth century. Thus the change of tempo and scale arising from the democratisation of political discourse [. . .] has only just begun to be addressed. Nor has sufficient attention so far been paid to the connections between this large expansion of the political public and the emergence of a new subject matter of political discourse – urbanisation, population increase and the condition of the inhabitants of the new factory districts. Similarly, few attempts have so far been made to identify and trace the presence and interactions of different political, religious and other languages in the utterances and activities of large movements, mass parties, churches, religious groups or newspapers and their readerships in the modern era.

In the investigation of these issues, analysis of authorial intention, though essential, is clearly not sufficient. It must be matched by the equal or greater attention paid by the best cultural historians to questions of intended constituency, to the different forms of appropriation of particular texts – what meanings were actually conveyed, how they were understood and interpreted. Here Chartier's question about the gap between intention and effect becomes central. For clearly the ability of authors or even political and legal authorities to police meanings is limited. Utterances may possess meaning within more than one language game. Meanings may change when they are shifted from one discourse to another. In nineteenth- and twentieth-century Britain, one need only think of the often disputed and contextually shifting meanings of supposedly familiar Victorian terms like 'independent' or 'respectable'. New dimensions of experience – and often grievance – may be opened up through the play or combination of discourses. In the case of the 'sans-culottes', Michael Sonnenscher demonstrates that it owed its existence to a confluence of the language of the popular theatre, of the sermon and of the law under the pressure of events in the early months of the French Revolution.[26] Not all meanings may be intended. Authorless meanings, sometimes of political and historical importance, may be produced innocently through misunderstanding or conflictually through mistrust. Rumoured or misheard remarks were frequently the originating occasion of medieval European crowd attacks on Jews,[27] or sixteenth- and seventeenth-century witchcraft denunciations. In extreme situations, political authorities may wholly lose control over the interpretation of utterances and actions; intended meanings, may be disregarded, may be appropriated by others, qualified or extended in unwanted ways. The loss of linguistic and political authority generally amount to the same thing.

[. . .]

Only by acknowledging that politics occurs wholly within discourse and by refusing to counterpose discourse to an extra-discursive reality, is it possible to arrive at a historically grounded sense of the significance of the place of law, authority and legitimacy in historical development. Systems of thought, like those of Marxism and perhaps of the later Foucault, which juxtapose discursive practices to extra-discursive domains and accord a primary reality to the extra-discursive, tend also to reduce law to ritualised violence, and authority, legitimacy and justice to post-hoc forms of ideological justification. What is lacking in such accounts is an explanation of the way in which such norms are historically formed and the means by which they are sustained, or indeed how as discursive artefacts such norms come to appropriate and articulate basic forms of human emotion.[28]

Theories like those of Foucault erase the distinction between nature and culture. They possess no account of how in modern constitutional states legal and ethical norms are produced through participation in the institutions of civil society. They dismiss as unimportant the mechanisms of a political culture which may be defined as a set of discourses and symbolic practices through which the competing claims of individuals and groups upon one another and upon the whole are articulated, negotiated and enforced.[29] In the case of Chartism and its extensive employment of the language of constitutionalism, it is possible to explore the process by which new claims emerged through a process of disputation over the meaning of terms within shared political languages. Such an account of Chartism – but it could equally well be applied to the language of Republicanism in nineteenth-century France, or of high church Toryism in eighteenth-century England – suggests why notions of right are indispensable to the task of historical explanation. For they provide the features which distinguish the formation of competing and conflicting claims within civil society from the putatively pure struggles of power which characterise Foucault's picture of power and government. In other words, the reductionist character of Foucault's vision of 'governmentality' renders it incapable of distinguishing between states which abide by norms of legality and those that do not. For similar reasons, a central feature of Foucault's non-historical appropriation of the past is that it is disabled from accepting that changing norms of right may – in favourable circumstances and conjunctures – provide the most powerful means through which the weak are occasionally enabled to combine together and defeat the strong.

What has been highlighted by this discussion of the obstacles to the further development of a linguistic approach to history has been the stultifying effect of the survival, sometimes in disguised form and often barely self-aware, of a residue of reductionist and determinist assumptions dating from the 1970s. There are no doubt several sources of this determinist fix. But certainly, the legacy of Foucault has been of prime importance and behind him the lopsided and incomplete character of the break between Marxism and new forms of theoretical radicalism in the 1960s and 1970s. Rather than jumping from a half-discarded Marxism to a sketchily defined idea of 'post-modernity',[30] such a conclusion suggests, at present the best contribution that might be made by *historians* is to ponder how 'modernity' came to be constituted as it was in the first place: a journey back to the eighteenth century, to the seed-bed of the critique of reason and the theory of commercial society in order to retrace the conditions of existence of the appearance of various forms of 'social science' and 'socialism' and to re-examine what might be considered the necessary and the contingent components in the growth of critiques of commercial society.

[. . .]

Only when all this is done and historical scholarship like politics can clear away, assess and move on from the unsorted debris left by the death of Marxism, will it be possible to ask again what insights Marx's work might give us. We continue to learn from Aristotle or Machiavelli without having to become Aristotelians or Machiavellians. One day, I hope we shall be able to learn again from Marx in the same fashion.

NOTES

1 A. Briggs, 'The Language of Class', in A. Briggs and J. Saville (eds), *Essays in Labour History*, London and New York, 1960; W. H. Sewell, *Work and Revolution in France: The Language of Labour From the Old Regime to 1848*, Cambridge, 1980.

2 See D. LaCapra and S. Kaplan (eds), *Modern European Intellectual History: Reappraisals and New Perspectives*, Ithaca (NY), 1982; D. LaCapra, *Rethinking Intellectual History: Texts, Contexts, Language*, Ithaca (NY), 1983; J. E. Toews, 'Intellectual History after the Linguistic Turns: The Autonomy of Meaning and the Irreducibility of Experience', *American Historical Review* 92, 1987, pp. 879–907.

3 B. Lepetit (ed.), *Les Formes de l'expérience: une autre histoire sociale*, Paris, 1995, p. 14.

4 I discuss the shortcomings of both my criticisms of Marxist history and my presentation of a linguistic approach as they appeared in *Languages of Class*, Cambridge, 1982, in the preceding section of the full version of this essay.

5 C. Lévi-Strauss, 'History and Dialectic', in *The Savage Mind*, London, 1966, Chapter 9.

6 M. Foucault, *The Birth of the Clinic: An Archaeology of Medical Perception*, New York, 1973; idem, *Madness and Civilisation: A History of Insanity in the Age of Reason*, London, 1972; idem, *The Order of Things: An Archaeology of the Human Sciences*, New York, 1973; idem, *Discipline and Punish: The Birth of the Prison*, London, 1977; idem, *The History of Sexuality*, volume I (*The Use of Pleasure*), Harmondsworth, 1984 and volume II (*The History of Sexuality*), Harmondsworth, 1986.

7 See Foucault, *The Order of Things*.

8 See J. Revel, 'Mentalités', in A. Burgière (ed.), *Dictionnaire des sciences historiques*, Paris, 1985.

9 A. J. Greimas, 'Histoire et liguistique', *Annales* 13, 1958, pp. 110–14; R. Barthes, 'Histoire et littérature: à propos de Racine', *Annales* 15, 1960, pp. 524–37.

10 See Foucault, *The Order of Things*.

11 It is difficult to know from the texts who influenced whom; Althusser referred to Foucault as a former pupil, but also acknowledges Foucault's work, as a support for his own position. See Althusser, *Reading Capital*, London, 1970, pp. 323–4.

12 These themes are explored in M. Foucault, *Power/Knowledge: Selected Interviews and Other Writings, 1972–1977*, C. Gordon (ed.), New York, 1980 and in G. Burchell, G. Gordon and P. Miller, *The Foucault Effect: Studies in Governmentality*, Chicago, 1991.

13 Foucault, *Discipline and Punish*.

14 Foucault, 'Two Lectures', in *Power/Knowledge*, pp. 104–5.

15 Ibid.

16 Foucault somewhat flippantly rejected any charge of anti-Enlightenment animus in his approach: 'What reader will I surprise by stating that analysis of the disciplinary practices of the eighteenth century is not a way of making Beccaria responsible for the Gulag?', M. Foucault, 'La Poussière et la nuage', in M. Perrot (ed.), *L'impossible prison: recherches sur le système pénitentiaire au XIXe siècle*, Paris, 1980, p. 36. But Foucault's reasons for rejecting the charge were scarcely reassuring. They were 1) that ideology is not the determining instance in social operations, and 2) by ascribing the mobile and problematic figures of the division between the true and the false to a referential, original rationality, given once and for all as 'the rationality'. In other words, once again, the neo-Marxist notion of superstructure and the structuralist 'death of the author'.

17 Foucault, *Archaeology of Knowledge*, p. 164, cited in R. Chartier, 'The Chimera of the Origin: Archaeology, Cultural History and the French Revolution', in *Foucault and the Writing of History*, Oxford, 1994, p. 174.

18 See M. de Certeau, *Histoire et psychoaanalyse entre science et fiction*, Paris, 1987; Chartier, 'Chimera'.

19 Chartier, 'Chimera', p. 184.

20 Ibid., p. 183.

21 Ibid., p. 178.

22 K. Baker, *Inventing the French Revolution*, Cambridge, 1990, p. 14.

23 Ibid.

24 See for example on the cultural-religious context of demographic behaviour A. Bourgière 'Les changements sociales. Brève histoire d'un concept', in B. Lepetit (ed.), *Les Formes de l'expérience*, Paris, 1995. On the meaning of family in the eighteenth century see N. Tadmor, 'The Concept of the Household-Family in Eighteenth-Century England', *Past and Present* 151, 1996, pp. 111–41; on the political ramifications of economic phenomena see E. Rothschild, 'An Alarming Commercial Crisis in Eighteenth-Century Angoulême: Sentiments in Economic History', Centre for History and Economics Papers, March, 1996.

25 For a representative sample of works see J. G. A. Pocock, *Politics, Language and Time: Essays on Political Thought and History*, Chicago, 1960; *idem, The Machiavellian Moment: Florentine Political Thought and the Atlantic Republican Tradition*, Princeton (NJ), 1975; *idem, Virtue, Commerce and History: Essays in Political Thought and History, Chiefly in the Eighteenth Century*, Cambridge, 1985; J. Dunn, *The Political Thought of John Locke*, Cambridge, 1969; Q. R. D. Skinner, *The Foundations of Modern Political Thought*, 2 vols, Cambridge, 1978; *idem, Machiavelli*, Oxford, 1981; R. Tuck, *Hobbes*, Oxford, 1989; *idem, Philosophy and Government, 1580–1715*, Cambridge, 1993; J. Tully, *A Discourse on Property: John Locke and his Adversaries*, Cambridge, 1980; D. Wooton, *Paolo Sarpi: Between Renaissance and Enlightenment*, Cambridge, 1983.

26 M. Sonnenscher, 'The Sans-Culottes of the Year II: Rethinking the Language of Labour in Evolutionary France', *Social History* 9, 1984, pp. 301–28; *idem, Work and Wages: Natural Law, Politics and Eighteenth-Century French Trades*, Cambridge, 1989, Chapter 10.

27 M. Rubin, *Gentile Tales*, New Haven (CT), 1999.

28 This is another area in which it is essential to take issue with Foucault. Throughout his career Foucault remained hostile to the findings of psychoanalysis; initially for Sartrean reasons, and subsequently because it disrupted his antinomian approach to madness. The historian should, however, make careful and discriminating use of the insights of psychoanalysis in an attempt to situate a range of powerful and repeatedly encountered human emotions articulated in various forms of political and religious discourse. For instance, phobias about contamination, fears about corruption, conspiracy and the subversion of virtue, anxieties about loss or lack of sexual identity, fantasies of identification or election, anger about exclusion, obsessive fixations upon honour, insult and betrayal, and so on.

29 See Baker, *Inventing the French Revolution*, p. 4.
30 The alignment of a new social history with post-modernity is made in P. Joyce, 'The End of Social History', *Social History* 20, 1995, pp. 73–93; see also J. Vernon, 'Who's Afraid of the "Linguistic Turn"? The Politics of Social History and its Discontents', *Social History* 19, 1994, pp. 81–97; N. Kirk, 'History, Languages, Ideas and Post-Modernism: A Materialist View', *Social History* 19, 1994, pp. 21–41; G. Eley and K. Nield, 'Starting Over: The Present, the Post-Modern and the Moment of Social History', *Social History* 20, 1995, pp. 355–65.

3

THE CONCEPT(S)
OF CULTURE

William H. Sewell, Jr.

In this article, William H. Sewell, Jr., political scientist and historian, examines the new master category of "culture." He shows how the concept of culture currently encompasses both a theoretical meaning, as a category abstracted from social experience and its complex realities, as well as a term that stands for a bounded world of beliefs and practices, usually employed to refer to a concrete, historically specific entity that is more or less equivalent to or synonymous with a "society." For Sewell, the distinction between culture as a theoretical category and culture as a determinate body of beliefs and practices is crucial for rethinking the place that "culture" as a category of social life and determinant of history has held since the 1980s, particularly since the rise of cultural history and its displacement of social history as the focus of historical analysis.

In its theoretical sense, culture has been treated as "an institutional sphere devoted to the making of meaning," and social life itself is seen as concerned with the pursuit of meaning, rather than interests or material gain. Indeed, under the impact of cultural anthropology, culture came to be understood as a system of symbols and meanings, operating as a determinative structure of human behavior. In the last decade and a half, however, there has been a reaction against this view and scholars now tend instead to approach culture as a sphere of practical activity, "shot through," as Sewell says, "by willful action, power relations, struggle, contradiction and change." From this perspective, culture is understood less as an autonomous structure of meaning and is, instead, recast as a performative term, as a realm of meaning constantly produced and reproduced by historical actors, whose performance of meaning is unsystematic, changeable and often fragmented in nature. In this treatment, culture loses its coherence and systematicity and becomes a "tool kit," or repertoire of strategies for action on the part of historical agents, whose enactment (performance) of culture is grounded in everyday experiences and practices. It is, thus, viewed analytically as "processual," as a body of signs put to work to interpret the world.

Rather than espousing either the culture-as-system or culture-as-practice model of culture, Sewell argues for a dialectical approach that defines culture as "the semiotic dimension of human social practice in general" and assumes that culture as a

76

structural element is always interacting with culture as practice and that both aspects of culture—as structure and as practice—are relatively autonomous dimensions of social organization that are in constant, dialectical engagement with one another. In this sense, culture remains a structure, but is modified in its effects by the contradictory, contested, and constantly changing ways in which it is implemented in practice. If practice implies system, system exists only in the continuity bestowed upon it by the series of practices that instantiate it. The problem for the historian, then, becomes how to conceptualize the articulation, or interaction, of system and practice.

In order to maintain the systematicity of culture while carving out large areas of human autonomy in its pragmatic application, Sewell is compelled to propose a notion of culture's "thin" coherence, a coherence always at stake due to the unstable and varying applications made of it in practice. Despite the appeal of this dialectical approach to cultural practices, the reader of Sewell's article is entitled to ask just how "thin" is culture's coherence and how finely or loosely integrated are symbols or signs (on the level of culture-as-system) and practices (on the level of behavior)? Sewell's answer to these questions is, quite sensibly, that it depends on the historical culture under examination, to which no independent theory can offer a precise guide or specification. In many ways, Sewell's formulation represents the current state of the problem of "culture" in its effort to modify a purely semiotic approach by means of a historically determinate understanding of social practice.

* * *

The aim of this chapter is to reflect upon the concept—or more properly the concepts—of culture in contemporary academic discourse. Trying to clarify what we mean by culture seems both imperative and impossible at a moment like the present, when the study of culture is burgeoning in virtually all fields of the human sciences. Although I glance at the varying uses of "culture" in a number of disciplines, my reflection is based above all on the extensive debates that have occurred in anthropology over the past two decades—debates in which some have questioned the very utility of the concept.[1] I feel strongly that it remains as useful, indeed essential, as ever. But given the cacophony of contemporary discourse about culture, I also believe that the concept needs some reworking and clarification.

The current volatility of the concept of culture sharply contrasts with the situation in the early 1970s, when I first got interested in a cultural approach to social history. At that time it was clear that if you wanted to learn about culture, you turned to the anthropologists. And while they by no means spoke in a single voice, they shared a widespread consensus both about the meaning of culture and about its centrality to the anthropological enterprise. I began borrowing the methods and insights of cultural anthropology as a means of learning more about nineteenth-century French workers. Cultural analysis, I hoped, would enable me to understand the meaning of workers' practices that I had been unable to get at by using quantitative and positivist methods—my standard tool kit as a practitioner of what was then called "the new social history."[2] I experienced the encounter with cultural anthropology as a turn from a hardheaded, utilitarian, and empiricist materialism—which had both liberal and *Marxisant* faces—to a wider appreciation of the range of human possibilities, both in the past and in the present. Convinced that there was more to life than the relentless pursuit of wealth, status, and power, I felt that cultural anthropology could show us how to get at that "more."[3]

Anthropology at the time had a virtual monopoly on the concept of culture. In political science and sociology, culture was associated with the by then utterly sclerotic Parsonian theoretical synthesis. The embryonic "cultural studies" movement was still confined to a single research center in Birmingham. And literary studies were still fixated on canonical literary texts—although the methods of studying them were being revolutionized by the importation of "French" structuralist and poststructuralist theory. Moreover, the mid-1960s to the mid-1970s marked the glory years of American cultural anthropology, which may be said to have reached its apotheosis with the publication of Clifford Geertz's phenomenally influential *Interpretation of Cultures* in 1973.[4] Not only did anthropology have no serious rivals in the study of culture, but the creativity and prestige of cultural anthropology were at a very high point.

During the 1980s and 1990s, the intellectual ecology of the study of culture has been transformed by a vast expansion of work on culture—indeed, a kind of academic culture mania has set in. The new interest in culture has swept over a wide range of academic disciplines and specialties. The history of this advance differs in timing and content in each field, but the cumulative effects are undeniable. In literary studies, which were already being transformed by French theory in the 1970s, the 1980s marked a turn to a vastly wider range of texts, quasi-texts, paratexts, and text analogs. If, as Derrida declared, nothing is extratextual ("il n'y a pas de hors-texte"), literary critics could direct their theory-driven gaze upon semiotic products of all kinds—legal documents, political tracts, soap operas, histories, talk shows, popular romances—and seek out their intertextualities.[5] Consequently, as such "new historicist" critics as Stephen Greenblatt and Louis Montrose recognize, literary study is increasingly becoming the study of cultures.[6] In history the early and rather self-conscious borrowing from anthropology has been followed by a theoretically heterogeneous rush to the study of culture, one modeled as much on literary studies or the work of Michel Foucault as on anthropology. As a consequence, the self-confident "new social history" of the 1960s and 1970s was succeeded by an equally self-confident "new cultural history" in the 1980s.[7]

In the late 1970s, an emerging "sociology of culture" began by applying standard sociological methods to studies of the production and marketing of cultural artifacts—music, art, drama, and literature. By the late 1980s, the work of cultural sociologists had broken out of the study of culture-producing institutions and moved toward studying the place of meaning in social life more generally. Feminism, which in the 1970s was concerned above all to document women's experiences, has increasingly turned to analyzing the discursive production of gender difference. Since the mid-1980s the new quasi-discipline of cultural studies has grown explosively in a variety of different academic niches—for example, in programs or departments of film studies, literature, performance studies, or communications. In political science, which is well known for its propensity to chase headlines, interest in cultural questions has been revived by the recent prominence of religious fundamentalism, nationalism, and ethnicity, which look like the most potent sources of political conflict in the contemporary world. This frenetic rush to the study of culture has everywhere been bathed, to a greater or lesser extent, in the pervasive transdisciplinary influence of the French poststructuralist trinity of Lacan, Derrida, and Foucault.

[. . .]

If, as I believe, Clifford is right that we cannot do without a concept of culture, I think we should try to shape it into one we can work with. We need to modify, rearticulate, and revivify the concept, retaining and reshaping what is useful and discarding what is not.

What do we mean by culture?

Writing in 1983, Raymond Williams declared that "culture is one of the two or three most complicated words in the English language."[8] Its complexity has surely not decreased since then. I have neither the competence nor the inclination to trace out the full range of meanings of "culture" in contemporary academic discourse. But some attempt to sort out the different usages of the word seems essential, and it must begin by distinguishing two fundamentally different meanings of the term.

In one meaning, culture is a theoretically defined category or aspect of social life that must be abstracted out from the complex reality of human existence. Culture in this sense is always contrasted to some other equally abstract aspect or category of social life that is not culture, such as economy, politics, or biology. To designate something as culture or as cultural is to claim it for a particular academic discipline or subdiscipline—for example, anthropology or cultural sociology—or for a particular style or styles of analysis—for example, structuralism, ethno-science, componential analysis, deconstruction, or hermeneutics. Culture in this sense—as an abstract analytical category—only takes the singular. Whenever we speak of "cultures," we have moved to the second fundamental meaning.

In that second meaning, culture stands for a concrete and bounded world of beliefs and practices. Culture in this sense is commonly assumed to belong to or to be isomorphic with a "society" or with some clearly identifiable sub-societal group. We may speak of "American culture" or "Samoan culture," or of "middle-class culture" or "ghetto culture."[9] The contrast in this usage is not between culture and not-culture but between one culture and another

—between American, Samoan, French, and Bororo cultures, or between middle-class and upper-class cultures, or between ghetto and mainstream cultures.

[. . .]

Here, I will be concerned primarily with culture in the first sense—culture as a category of social life. One must have a clear conception of culture at this abstract level in order to deal with the more concrete theoretical question of how cultural differences are patterned and bounded in space and time. Once I have sketched out my own ideas about what an adequate abstract theory of culture might look like, I will return to the question of culture as a bounded universe of beliefs and practices. [. . .]

Culture as a category of social life

Culture as a category of social life has itself been conceptualized in a number of different ways. Let me begin by specifying some of these different conceptualizations, moving from those I do not find especially useful to those I find more adequate.

Culture as learned behavior. Culture in this sense is the whole body of practices, beliefs, institutions, customs, habits, myths, and so on built up by humans and passed on from generation to generation. In this usage, culture is contrasted to nature: its possession is what distinguishes us from other animals. When anthropologists were struggling to establish that differences between societies were not based on biological differences between their populations—that is, on race—a definition of culture as learned behavior made sense. But now that racial arguments have virtually disappeared from anthropological discourse, a concept of culture so broad as this seems impossibly vague; it provides no particular angle or analytical purchase on the study of social life.

A narrower and consequently more useful conceptualization of culture emerged in anthropology during the second quarter of the twentieth century and has been dominant in the social sciences generally since World War II. It defines culture not as all learned behavior but as that category or aspect of learned behavior that is concerned with meaning. But the concept of culture-as-meaning is in fact a family of related concepts; *meaning* may be used to specify a cultural realm or sphere in at least four distinct ways, each of which is defined in contrast to somewhat differently conceptualized noncultural realms or spheres.

Culture as an institutional sphere devoted to the making of meaning. This conception of culture is based on the assumption that social formations are composed of clusters of institutions devoted to specialized activities. These clusters can be assigned to variously defined institutional spheres—most conventionally, spheres of politics, economy, society, and culture. Culture is the sphere devoted specifically to the production, circulation, and use of meanings. The cultural sphere may in turn be broken down into the subspheres of which it is composed: say, of art, music, theater, fashion, literature, religion, media, and education. The study of culture, if culture is defined in this way, is the study of the activities that take place within these institutionally defined spheres and of the meanings produced in them.

This conception of culture is particularly prominent in the discourses of sociology and cultural studies, but it is rarely used in anthropology. Its roots probably reach back to the strongly evaluative conception of culture as a sphere of "high" or "uplifting" artistic and intellectual activity, a meaning that Raymond Williams tells us came into prominence in the nineteenth century.[10] But in contemporary academic discourse, this usage normally lacks such evaluative and hierarchizing implications. The dominant style of work in American sociology of culture has been demystifying: its typical approach has been to uncover the largely self-aggrandizing, class-interested, manipulative, or professionalizing institutional dynamics that under-gird prestigious museums, artistic styles, symphony orchestras, or philosophical schools. And cultural studies, which has taken as its particular mission the appreciation of cultural forms disdained by the spokesmen of high culture—rock music, street fashion, cross-dressing, shopping malls, Disneyland, soap operas—employs this same basic definition of culture. It merely trains its analytical attention on spheres of meaning production ignored by previous analysts and regarded as debased by elite tastemakers.

The problem with such a concept of culture is that it focuses only on a certain range of meanings, produced in a certain range of institutional locations—on self-consciously "cultural" institutions and on expressive, artistic, and literary systems of meanings. This use of the concept is to some extent complicit with the widespread notion that meanings are of minimal importance in the other "noncultural" institutional spheres: that in political or economic spheres, meanings are merely superstructural excrescences. And since institutions in political and economic spheres control the great bulk of society's resources, viewing culture as a distinct sphere of activity may in the end simply confirm the widespread presupposition in the "harder" social sciences that culture is merely froth on the tides of society. The rise of a cultural sociology that limited itself to studying "cultural" institutions effected a partition of subject matter that was very unfavorable to the cultural sociologists. Indeed, only the supercession of this restrictive concept of culture has made possible the explosive growth of the subfield of cultural sociology in the past decade.

Culture as creativity or agency. This usage of culture has grown up particularly in traditions that posit a powerful "material" determinism—most notably Marxism and American sociology. Over the past three decades or so, scholars working within these traditions have carved out a conception of culture as a realm of creativity that escapes from the otherwise pervasive determination of social action by economic or social structures. In the Marxist tradition, it was probably E. P. Thompson's *Making of the English Working Class* that first conceptualized culture as a realm of agency, and it is particularly English Marxists—for example, Paul Willis in *Learning to Labor*—who have elaborated this conception.[11] But the defining opposition on which this concept of culture rests—culture versus structure—has also become pervasive in the vernacular of American sociology. One clear sign that American anthropologists and sociologists have different conceptions of culture is that the opposition between culture and structure—an unquestioned commonplace in contemporary sociological discourse—is nonsensical in anthropology.

In my opinion, identifying culture with agency and contrasting it with structure merely perpetuates the same determinist materialism that "culturalist" Marxists were reacting against in the first place. It exaggerates both the implacability of socioeconomic determinations and the free play of symbolic action. Both socioeconomic and cultural processes are blends of structure and agency. Cultural action—say, performing practical jokes or writing poems—is necessarily constrained by cultural structures, such as existing linguistic, visual, or ludic conventions. And economic action—such as the manufacture or repair of automobiles—is impossible without the exercise of creativity and agency. The particulars of the relationship between structure and agency may differ in cultural and economic processes, but assigning either the economic or the cultural exclusively to structure or to agency is a serious category error.

This brings us to the two concepts of culture that I regard as most fruitful and that I see as currently struggling for dominance: the concept of culture as a system of symbols and meanings, which was hegemonic in the 1960s and 1970s, and the concept of culture as practice, which has become increasingly prominent in the 1980s and 1990s.

Culture as a system of symbols and meanings. This has been the dominant concept of culture in American anthropology since the 1960s. It was made famous above all by Clifford Geertz, who used the term "cultural system" in the titles of some of his most notable essays.[12] The notion was also elaborated by David Schneider, whose writings had a considerable influence within anthropology but lacked Geertz's interdisciplinary appeal.[13] Geertz and Schneider derived the term from Talcott Parsons's usage, according to which the cultural system, a system of symbols and meanings, was a particular "level of abstraction" of social relations. It was contrasted to the "social system," which was a system of norms and institutions, and to the "personality system," which was a system of motivations.[14] Geertz and Schneider especially wished to distinguish the cultural system from the social system. To engage in cultural analysis, for them, was to abstract the meaningful aspect of human action out from the flow of concrete interactions. The point of conceptualizing culture as a system of symbols and meanings is to disentangle, for the purpose of analysis, the semiotic influences on action from the other sorts of influences—demographic, geographical, biological, technological, economic, and so on—that they are necessarily mixed with in any concrete sequence of behavior.

Geertz's and Schneider's post-Parsonian theorizations of cultural systems were by no means the only available models for symbolic anthropology in the 1960s and 1970s. The works of Victor Turner, whose theoretical origins were in the largely Durkheimian British school of social anthropology, were also immensely influential.[15] Claude Lévi-Strauss and his many followers provided an entire alternative model of culture as a system of symbols and meanings—conceptualized, following Saussure, as signifiers and signifieds. Moreover, all these anthropological schools were in a sense manifestations of a much broader "linguistic turn" in the human sciences—a diverse but sweeping attempt to specify the structures of human symbol systems and to indicate their profound influence on human behavior. One thinks above all of such French "structuralist" thinkers as Roland Barthes, Jacques Lacan, or the early Michel Foucault. What all of these approaches had in common was an insistence on the systematic nature of cultural meaning and the autonomy of symbol systems—their distinctness from and irreducibility to other features of social life. They all abstracted a realm of pure signification out from the complex messiness of social life and specified its internal coherence and deep logic. Their practice of cultural analysis consequently tended to be more or less synchronic and formalist.

Culture as practice. The past decade and a half has witnessed a pervasive reaction against the concept of culture as a system of symbols and meanings, which has taken place in various disciplinary locations and intellectual traditions and under many different slogans—for example, "practice," "resistance," "history," "politics," or "culture as tool kit." Analysts working under all these banners object to a portrayal of culture as logical, coherent, shared, uniform, and static. Instead they insist that culture is a sphere of practical activity shot through by willful action, power relations, struggle, contradiction, and change.

In anthropology, Sherry Ortner in 1984 remarked on the turn to politics, history, and agency, suggesting Pierre Bourdieu's key term "practice" as an appropriate label for this emerging sensibility. Two years later the publication of James Clifford and George Marcus's collection *Writing Culture* announced to the public the crisis of anthropology's culture concept.[16] Since then, criticisms of the concept of culture as a system of symbols and meanings have flowed thick and fast. The most notable work in anthropology has argued for the contradictory, politically charged, changeable, and fragmented character of meanings—both meanings produced in the societies being studied and meanings rendered in anthropological texts. Recent work in anthropology has in effect recast culture as a performative term.

Not surprisingly, this emphasis on the performative aspect of culture is compatible with the work of most cultural historians. Historians are generally uncomfortable with synchronic concepts. As they took up the study of culture, they subtly—but usually without comment—altered the concept by stressing the contradictoriness and malleability of cultural meanings and by seeking out the mechanisms by which meanings were transformed.

The battles in history have been over a different issue, pitting those who claim that historical change should be understood as a purely cultural or discursive process against those who argue for the significance of economic and social determinations or for the centrality of concrete "experience" in understanding it.[17]

[. . .]

Culture as system and practice

Much of the theoretical writing on culture during the past ten years has assumed that a concept of culture as a system of symbols and meanings is at odds with a concept of culture as practice. System and practice approaches have seemed incompatible, I think, because the most prominent practitioners of the culture-as-system-of-meanings approach effectively marginalized consideration of culture-as-practice—if they didn't preclude it altogether.

This can be seen in the work of both Clifford Geertz and David Schneider. Geertz's analyses usually begin auspiciously enough, in that he frequently explicates cultural systems in order to resolve a puzzle arising from concrete practices—a state funeral, trances, a royal procession, cockfights. But it usually turns out that the issues of practice are principally a means of moving the essay to the goal of specifying in a synchronic form the coherence that underlies the exotic cultural practices in question. And while Geertz marginalized questions of practice, Schneider, in a kind of *reductio ad absurdum*, explicitly excluded them, arguing that the particular task of anthropology in the academic division of labor was to study "culture as a system of symbols and meanings in its own right and with reference to its own structure" and leaving to others—sociologists, historians, political scientists, or economists—the question of how social action was structured.[18] A "cultural account," for Schneider, should be limited to specifying the relations among symbols in a given domain of meaning—which he tended to render unproblematically as known and accepted by all members of the society and as possessing a highly determinate formal logic.[19]

Nor is the work of Geertz and Schneider unusual in its marginalization of practice. As critics such as James Clifford have argued, conventional modes of writing in cultural anthropology typically smuggle highly debatable assumptions into ethnographic accounts—for example, that cultural meanings are normally shared, fixed, bounded, and deeply felt. To Clifford's critique of ethnographic rhetoric, I would add a critique of ethnographic method. Anthropologists working with a conception of culture-as-system have tended to focus on clusters of symbols and meanings that can be shown to have a high degree of coherence or systematicity—those of American kinship or Balinese cockfighting, for instance—and to present their accounts of these clusters as examples of what the interpretation of culture in general entails. This practice results in what sociologists would call sampling on the dependent variable. That is, anthropologists who belong to this school tend to select symbols and meanings that cluster neatly into coherent systems and pass over those that are relatively fragmented or incoherent, thus confirming the hypothesis that symbols and meanings indeed form tightly coherent systems.

Given some of these problems in the work of the culture-as-system school, the recent turn to a concept of culture-as-practice has been both understandable and fruitful—it has effectively highlighted many of the earlier school's shortcomings and made up some of its most glaring analytic deficits. Yet the presumption that a concept of culture as a system of symbols and meanings is at odds with a concept of culture as practice seems to me perverse. System and practice are complementary concepts: each presupposes the other. To engage in cultural practice means to utilize existing cultural symbols to accomplish some end. The employment of a symbol can be expected to accomplish a particular goal only because the symbols have more or less determinate meanings—meanings specified by their systematically structured relations to other symbols. Hence practice implies system. But it is equally true that the system has no existence apart from the succession of practices that instantiate, reproduce, or—most interestingly—transform it. Hence system implies practice.[20] System and practice constitute an indissoluble duality or dialectic: the important theoretical question is thus not whether culture should be conceptualized as practice or as a system of symbols and meanings, but how to conceptualize the articulation of system and practice.

The autonomy of culture

Let me begin this task by stating some assumptions about practice. I assume that human practice, in all social contexts or institutional spheres, is structured simultaneously both by meanings and by other aspects of the environment in which they occur—by, for example, power relations or spatiality or resource distributions. Culture is neither a particular kind of practice nor practice that takes place in a particular social location. It is, rather, the semiotic dimension of human social practice in general. I further assume that these dimensions of practice mutually shape and constrain each other but also that they are relatively autonomous from each other.[21]

The autonomy of the cultural dimension of practice can also be understood by thinking about culture as a system. The cultural dimension of practice is autonomous from other dimensions of practice in two senses. First, culture has a semiotic structuring principle that is different from the political, economic, or geographical structuring principles that also inform practice. Hence, even if an action were almost entirely determined by, say, overwhelming disparities in economic resources, those disparities would still have to be rendered meaningful in action according to a semiotic logic—that is, in language or in some other form of symbols. For example, an impoverished worker facing the only manufacturer seeking laborers in that district will have no choice but to accept the offer. Yet in accepting the offer she or he is not

simply submitting to the employer but entering into a culturally defined relation as a wageworker. Second, the cultural dimension is also autonomous in
the sense that the meanings that make it up—although influenced by the
context in which they are employed—are shaped and reshaped by a multitude of other contexts. The meaning of a symbol always transcends any
particular context, because the symbol is freighted with its usages in a multitude of other instances of social practice. Thus, our worker enters into a
relationship of "wageworker" that carries certain recognized meanings—of
deference, but also of independence from the employer and perhaps of solidarity with other wageworkers. These meanings are carried over from the
other contexts in which the meaning of wage work is determined—not only
from other instances of hirings but from statutes, legal arguments, strikes,
socialist tracts, and economic treatises. They enter importantly into defining
the local possibilities of action, in this case perhaps granting the worker
greater power to resist the employer than the local circumstances alone would
have dictated.

To understand fully the significance of this second sort of autonomy, it is
important to note that the network of semiotic relations that make up culture
is not isomorphic with the network of economic, political, geographical,
social, or demographic relations that make up what we usually call a
"society." A given symbol—mother, red, polyester, liberty, wage labor, or dirt
—is likely to show up not only in many different locations in a particular
institutional domain (motherhood in millions of families) but in a variety of
different institutional domains as well (welfare mothers as a potent political
symbol, the mother tongue in linguistic quarrels, the Mother of God in the
Catholic Church). Culture may be thought of as a network of semiotic relations cast across society, a network with a different shape and different
spatiality than institutional, or economic, or political networks.[22] The meaning
of a symbol in a given context may therefore be subject to redefinition
by dynamics entirely foreign to that institutional domain or spatial location
[. . .]. This fact is what makes it possible—indeed virtually guarantees—that
the cultural dimension of practice will have a certain autonomy from its
other dimensions.

If culture has a distinct semiotic logic, then by implication it must in some
sense be coherent. But it is important not to exaggerate or misspecify the
coherence of symbol systems. I assume the coherence of a cultural system to
be semiotic in a roughly Saussurian sense: that is, that the meaning of a sign
or symbol is a function of its network of oppositions to or distinctions
from other signs in the system. This implies that users of culture will form a
semiotic community—in the sense that they will recognize the same set of
oppositions and therefore be capable of engaging in mutually meaningful
symbolic action. To use the ubiquitous linguistic analogy, they will be capable
of using the "grammar" of the semiotic system to make understandable
"utterances."

It should be noted, however, that this conception actually implies only a quite minimal cultural coherence—one might call it a thin coherence. The fact that members of a semiotic community recognize a given set of symbolic oppositions does not determine what sort of statements or actions they will construct on the basis of their semiotic competence. Nor does it mean that they form a community in any fuller sense. They need not agree in their moral or emotional evaluations of given symbols. The semiotic field they share may be recognized and used by groups and individuals locked in fierce enmity rather than bound by solidarity, or by people who feel relative indifference toward each other. The posited existence of cultural coherence says nothing about whether semiotic fields are big or small, shallow or deep, encompassing or specialized. It simply requires that if meaning is to exist at all, there must be systematic relations among signs and a group of people who recognize those relations.

That this Saussurian conception implies only a thin cultural coherence seems consonant with certain deconstructionist arguments. The entire thrust of deconstruction has been to reveal the instability of linguistic meaning. It has located this instability in the signifying mechanism of language itself—claiming that because the meaning of a linguistic sign always depends on a contrast with what the sign is opposed to or different from, language is inevitably haunted by the traces of the very terms it excludes. Consequently, the meaning of a text or an utterance can never be fixed; attempts to secure meaning can only defer, never exclude, a plethora of alternative or opposed interpretations.

Cultural analysts who—like me—wish to argue that cultural systems are powerfully constraining have often drawn back from deconstructionist arguments in horror. I think this is a major mistake; indeed, I would maintain that a broadly deconstructionist understanding of meaning is essential for anyone attempting to theorize cultural change. Deconstruction does not deny the possibility of coherence. Rather, it assumes that the coherence inherent in a system of symbols is thin in the sense I have described: it demonstrates over and over that what are taken as the certainties or truths of texts or discourses are in fact disputable and unstable. This seems entirely compatible with a practice perspective on culture. It assumes that symbol systems have a (Saussurian) logic but that this logic is open-ended, not closed. And it strongly implies that when a given symbol system is taken by its users to be unambiguous and highly constraining, these qualities cannot be accounted for by their semiotic qualities alone but must result from the way their semiotic structures are interlocked in practice with other structures—economic, political, social, spatial, and so on.[23]

Thus far in this section I have mainly been considering culture as system. But what I have said has implications for how we might conceptualize culture as practice. First, the conception of culture as semiotic implies a particular notion of cultural practice. To engage in cultural practice is to make use of a semiotic code to do something in the world. People who are members of a semiotic community are capable not only of recognizing statements made in a semiotic code (as I have pointed out above) but of using the code as well, of putting it into practice. To use a code means to attach abstractly available symbols to concrete things or circumstances and thereby to posit something about them. I would also argue that to be able to use a code means more than being able to apply it mechanically in stereotyped situations—it also means having the ability to elaborate it, to modify or adapt its rules to novel circumstances.

What things in the world *are* is never fully determined by the symbolic net we throw over them—this also depends on their preexisting physical characteristics, the spatial relations in which they occur, the relations of power with which they are invested, their economic value, and, of course, the different symbolic meanings that may have been attributed to them by other actors. The world is recalcitrant to our predications of meaning. Hence, as Marshall Sahlins has pointed out, every act of symbolic attribution puts the symbols at risk, makes it possible that the meanings of the symbols will be inflected or transformed by the uncertain consequences of practice. Usually, such attributions result in only tiny inflections of the meaning of symbols. But on some occasions—for example, when Hawaiian chiefs used the category of tabu to enforce their monopoly on trade with Western merchants—novel attributions can have the result of transforming the meaning of a symbol in historically crucial ways.[24]

Part of what gives cultural practice its potency is the ability of actors to play on the multiple meanings of symbols—thereby redefining situations in ways that they believe will favor their purposes. Creative cultural action commonly entails the purposeful or spontaneous importation of meanings from one social location or context to another. I have recently worked on a telling example of the importation of meaning. The men and women who captured the Bastille in July of 1789 were unquestionably characterizable as "the people" in the common sense of "the mob" or the "urban poor." But Parisian radicals and members of the French National Assembly played on the ambiguity of the term to cast those who took the Bastille also as a concrete instance of the abstract category of "the people" who were said to be sovereign in radical political theory. Importing the association between the people and sovereignty from the context of political theory into that of urban crowd violence had the not inconsequential effect of ushering the modern concept of revolution into the world.[25]

Cultures as distinct worlds of meaning

Up to now, I have been considering culture only in its singular and abstract sense—as a realm of social life defined in contrast to some other noncultural realm or realms. My main points may be summarized as follows: culture, I have argued, should be understood as a dialectic of system and practice, as a dimension of social life autonomous from other such dimensions both in its logic and in its spatial configuration, and as a system of symbols possessing a real but thin coherence that is continually put at risk in practice and therefore subject to transformation. Such a theorization, I maintain, makes it possible to accept the cogency of recent critiques yet retain a workable and powerful concept of culture that incorporates the achievements of the cultural anthropology of the 1960s and 1970s.

But it is probably fair to say that most recent theoretical work on culture, particularly in anthropology, is actually concerned primarily with culture in its pluralizable and more concrete sense—that is, with cultures as distinct worlds of meaning. Contemporary anthropological critics' objections to the concept of culture as system and their insistence on the primacy of practice are not, in my opinion, really aimed at the concept of system as outlined above—the notion that the meaning of symbols is determined by their network of relations with other symbols. Rather, the critics' true target is the idea that cultures (in the second, pluralizable sense) form neatly coherent wholes: that they are logically consistent, highly integrated, consensual, extremely resistant to change, and clearly bounded. This is how cultures tended to be represented in the classic ethnographies—Mead on Samoa, Benedict on the Zuni, Malinowski on the Trobriands, Evans-Prichard on the Nuer, or, for that matter, Geertz on the Balinese. But recent research and thinking about cultural practices, even in relatively "simple" societies, has turned this classic model on its head. It now appears that we should think of worlds of meaning as normally being contradictory, loosely integrated, contested, mutable, and highly permeable. Consequently the very concept of cultures as coherent and distinct entities is widely disputed.

Cultures are contradictory. Some authors of classic ethnographies were quite aware of the presence of contradictions in the cultures they studied. Victor Turner, for example, demonstrated that red symbolism in certain Ndembu rituals simultaneously signified the contradictory principles of matrilineal fertility and male bloodletting. But he emphasized how these potentially contradictory meanings were brought together and harmonized in ritual performances.[26] A current anthropological sensibility would probably emphasize the fundamental character of the contradictions rather than their situational resolution in the ritual. It is common for potent cultural symbols to express contradictions as much as they express coherence. One need look no farther than the central Christian symbol of the Trinity, which attempts to unify in one symbolic figure three sharply distinct and largely incompatible possibilities of Christian religious experience: authoritative and hierarchical orthodoxy (the Father), loving egalitarianism and grace (the Son), and ecstatic spontaneity (the Holy Ghost). Cultural worlds are commonly beset with internal contradictions.

Cultures are loosely integrated. Classic ethnographies recognized that societies were composed of different spheres of activity—for example, kinship, agriculture, hunting, warfare, and religion—and that each of these component parts had its own specific cultural forms. But the classic ethnographers

typically saw it as their task to show how these culturally varied components fit into a well-integrated cultural whole. Most contemporary students
of culture would question this emphasis. They are more inclined to stress
the centrifugal cultural tendencies that arise from these disparate spheres
of activity, to stress the inequalities between those relegated to different
activities, and to see whatever "integration" occurs as based on power or
domination rather than on a common ethos. That most anthropologists now
work on complex, stratified, and highly differentiated societies, rather than
on the "simple" societies that were the focus of most classic ethnographies,
probably enhances this tendency.

Cultures are contested. Classic ethnographies commonly assumed, at least
implicitly, that a culture's most important beliefs were consensual, agreed on
by virtually all of a society's members. Contemporary scholars, with their
enhanced awareness of race, class, and gender, would insist that people who
occupy different positions in a given social order will typically have quite
different cultural beliefs or will have quite different understandings of
what might seem on the surface to be identical beliefs. Consequently, current
scholarship is replete with depictions of "resistance" by subordinated groups
and individuals. Thus James Scott detects "hidden transcripts" that form the
underside of peasants' deference in contemporary Malaysia and Marshall
Sahlins points out that it was Hawaiian women who most readily violated
tabus when Captain Cook's ships arrived—because the tabu system, which
classified them as profane (*noa*) as against the sacred (*tabu*) men, "did not sit
upon Hawaiian women with the force it had for men."[27] Cultural consensus,
far from being the normal state of things, is a difficult achievement; and when
it does occur it is bound to hide suppressed conflicts and disagreements.

Cultures are subject to constant change. Cultural historians, who work on
complex and dynamic societies, have generally assumed that cultures are
quite changeable. But recent anthropological work on relatively "simple"
societies also finds them to be remarkably mutable. For example, Renato
Rosaldo's study of remote Ilongot headhunters in the highlands of Northern
Luzon demonstrates that each generation of Ilongots constructed its own logic
of settlement patterns, kinship alliance, and feuding—logics that gave successive generations of Ilongots experiences that were probably as varied as
those of successive generations of Americans or Europeans between the late
nineteenth and late twentieth centuries.[28]

Cultures are weakly bounded. It is extremely unusual for societies or their
cultural systems to be anything like isolated or sharply bounded. Even the
supposedly simplest societies have had relations of trade, warfare, conquest,
and borrowing of all sorts of cultural items—technology, religious ideas,
political and artistic forms, and so on. But in addition to mutual influences
of these sorts, there have long been important social and cultural processes
that transcend societal boundaries—colonialism, missionary religions, inter-
regional trading associations and economic interdependencies, migratory
diasporas, and, in the current era, multinational corporations and trans-

national nongovernmental organizations. Although these transsocietal processes are certainly more prominent in more recent history than previously, they are hardly entirely new. Think of the spread of such "world religions" as Islam, Christianity, Hinduism, or Buddhism across entire regions of the globe or the development of extensive territorial empires in the ancient world. I would argue that social science's once virtually unquestioned model of societies as clearly bounded entities undergoing endogenous development is as perverse for the study of culture as for the study of economic history or political sociology. Systems of meaning do not correspond in any neat way with national or societal boundaries—which themselves are not nearly as neat as we sometimes imagine. Anything we might designate as a "society" or a "nation" will contain, or fail to contain, a multitude of overlapping and interpenetrating cultural systems, most of them subsocietal, transsocietal, or both.[29]

Thus all of the assumptions of the classic ethnographic model of cultures— that cultures are logically consistent, highly integrated, consensual, resistant to change, and clearly bounded—seem to be untenable. This could lead to the conclusion that the notion of coherent cultures is purely illusory; that cultural practice in a given society is diffuse and decentered; that the local systems of meaning found in a given population do not themselves form a higher-level, society-wide system of meanings. But such a conclusion would, in my opinion, be hasty. Although I think it is an error simply to assume that cultures possess an overall coherence or integration, neither can such coherences be ruled out a priori.

How coherence is possible

Recent work on cultural practice has tended to focus on acts of cultural resistance, particularly on resistance of a decentered sort—those dispersed everyday acts that thwart conventions, reverse valuations, or express the dominated's resentment of their domination.[30] But it is important to remember that much cultural practice is concentrated in and around powerful institutional nodes—including religions, communications media, business corporations, and, most spectacularly, states. These institutions, which tend to be relatively large in scale, centralized, and wealthy, are all cultural actors; their agents make continuous use of their considerable resources in efforts to order meanings. Studies of culture need to pay at least as much attention to such sites of concentrated cultural practice as to the dispersed sites of resistance that currently predominate in the literature.[31]

Even in powerful and would-be totalitarian states, centrally placed actors are never able to establish anything approaching cultural uniformity. In fact, they rarely attempt to do so. The typical cultural strategy of dominant actors and institutions is not so much to establish uniformity as it is to organize difference. They are constantly engaged in efforts not only to normalize or homogenize but also to hierarchize, encapsulate, exclude, criminalize, hegemonize, or marginalize practices and populations that diverge from the

91

sanctioned ideal. By such means, authoritative actors attempt, with varying degrees of success, to impose a certain coherence onto the field of cultural practice.[32] Indeed, one of the major reasons for dissident anthropologists' discomfort with the concept of culture is that it is so often employed in all of these ways by various powerful institutional actors—sometimes, alas, with the help of anthropologists.

The kind of coherence produced by this process of organizing difference may be far from the tight cultural integration depicted in classic ethnographies. But when authoritative actors distinguish between high and low cultural practices or between those of the majority ethnicity and minorities or between the legal and the criminal or between the normal and the abnormal, they bring widely varying practices into semiotic relationship—that is, into definition in terms of contrasts with one another. Authoritative cultural action, launched from the centers of power, has the effect of turning what otherwise might be a babble of cultural voices into a semiotically and politically ordered field of differences. Such action creates a map of the "culture" and its variants, one that tells people where they and their practices fit in the official scheme of things.

The official cultural map may, of course, be criticized and resisted by those relegated to its margins. But subordinated groups must to some degree orient their local systems of meaning to those recognized as dominant; the act of contesting dominant meanings itself implies a recognition of their centrality. Dominant and oppositional groups interact constantly, each undertaking its initiatives with the other in mind. Even when they attempt to overcome or undermine each other, they are mutually shaped by their dialectical dance. Struggle and resistance, far from demonstrating that cultures lack coherence, may paradoxically have the effect of simplifying and clarifying the cultural field.

Moreover, dissenting or oppositional groups work to create and sustain cultural coherence among their own adherents, and they do so by many of the same strategies—hierarchization, encapsulation, exclusion, and the like—that the authorities use. Once again, it is notable that the concept of culture is as likely to be deployed politically by dissident groups as by dominant institutions, and with many of the same exclusionary, normalizing, and marginalizing effects as when it is deployed by the state. To take an obvious example, dissident nationalist and ethnic movements nearly always attempt to impose standards of cultural purity on those deemed members of the group and to use such standards to distinguish between those who are and are not group members.

None of this, of course, implies that cultures are always, everywhere, or unproblematically coherent. It suggests instead that coherence is variable, contested, ever-changing, and incomplete. Cultural coherence, to the extent that it exists, is as much the product of power and struggles for power as it is of semiotic logic. But it is common for the operation of power, both the efforts of central institutions and the acts of organized resistance to such institutions, to subject potential semiotic sprawl to a certain order: to prescribe (contested) core values, to impose discipline on dissenters, to describe boundaries and norms—in short, to give a certain focus to the production and consumption of meaning. As cultural analysts we must acknowledge such coherences where they exist and set ourselves the task of explaining how they are achieved, sustained, and dissolved.

It is no longer possible to assume that the world is divided up into discrete "societies," each with its corresponding and well-integrated "culture." I would argue forcefully for the value of the concept of culture in its non-pluralizable sense, while the utility of the term as pluralizable appears to me more open to legitimate question. Yet I think that the latter concept of culture also gets at something we need to retain: a sense of the particular shapes and consistencies of worlds of meaning in different places and times and a sense that in spite of conflicts and resistance, these worlds of meaning somehow hang together. Whether we call these partially coherent landscapes of meaning "cultures" or something else—worlds of meaning, or ethnoscapes, or hegemonies—seems to me relatively unimportant so long as we know that their boundedness is only relative and constantly shifting. Our job as cultural analysts is to discern what the shapes and consistencies of local meanings actually are and to determine how, why, and to what extent they hang together.

NOTES

I have received valuable comments on this chapter from a number of friends and colleagues. Even though I heeded their good advice only intermittently, I would like to thank Anne Kane, David Laitin, Claudio Lomnitz, Sherry Ortner, William Reddy, Marshall Sahlins, Paul Seeley, Ann Swidler, Lisa Wedeen, members of the Social Theory Workshop at the University of Chicago, the audience at a Sociology Department Brown Bag at the University of Arizona, and my fellow authors in this volume, who gave me critical comments at our conference at the University of California at Berkeley in April 1996.

1 For a discerning analysis of this debate, see Robert Brightman, "Forget Culture: Replacement, Transcendence, Relexification," *Cultural Anthropology* 10 (1995): 509–46.
2 One outcome of these efforts was William H. Sewell, Jr., *Work and Revolution in France: The Language of Labor from the Old Regime to 1848* (Cambridge, 1980).
3 This turn of historians to anthropology was quite widespread in the 1970s, not only in America, where it informed the work of such scholars as Natalie Davis and Robert Darnton, but also in France, England, and Australia, where anthropology influenced such scholars as Emmanuel Le Roy Ladurie, Jacques Le Goff, Keith Thomas, Peter Laslett, and Rhys Isaac.
4 Clifford Geertz, *The Interpretation of Cultures: Selected Essays* (New York, 1973).
5 Jacques Derrida, *Of Grammatology*, trans. Gayatri Chakravorty Spivak (Baltimore, 1976).
6 A good introduction to this current of scholarship is H. Aram Veeser, ed., *The New Historicism* (New York, 1989).
7 Lynn Hunt, ed., *The New Cultural History* (Berkeley, 1989).

8 Raymond Williams, *Keywords: A Vocabulary of Culture and Society*, rev. ed. (London, 1983), p. 87. See also Raymond Williams, *Culture and Society: 1780–1950* (New York, 1958).

9 The two types of meanings I have distinguished here can be overlaid, so that the cultural aspects of the life of a people or a social group are distinguished from the noncultural aspects of its life. Hence, "Balinese culture" may be contrasted to "Balinese society" or "the Balinese economy." In anthropological usage, however, "culture" also is commonly used to designate the whole of the social life of a given people, so that "Balinese culture" becomes a synonym for "Balinese society" rather than a contrastive term.

10 Williams, *Keywords*, pp. 90–1.

11 E. P. Thompson, *The Making of the English Working Class* (London, 1963); Paul Willis, *Learning to Labor: How Working Class Kids Get Working Class Jobs* (New York, 1981).

12 Clifford Geertz, "Religion as a Cultural System" and "Ideology as a Cultural System," in *Interpretation of Cultures*, pp. 87–125, 193–233; "Common Sense as a Cultural System" and "Art as a Cultural System," in *Local Knowledge: Further Essays in Interpretive Anthropology* (New York, 1983), pp. 73–93, 94–120.

13 David M. Schneider's most influential book is *American Kinship: A Cultural Account* (Englewood Cliffs, N.J., 1968). The most systematic statement of his conception of a cultural system is David M. Schneider, "Notes toward a Theory of Culture," in *Meaning in Anthropology*, ed. Keith H. Basso and Henry A. Selby (Albuquerque, 1976), pp. 197–220.

14 Talcott Parsons, *The Social System* (Glencoe, Ill., 1959). Geertz and Schneider were both students of Talcott Parsons and Clyde Kluckhohn in the Harvard Department of Social Relations and they taught together during the 1960s at the University of Chicago, then the epicenter of cultural anthropology.

15 Victor W. Turner, *The Forest of Symbols: Aspects of Ndembu Ritual* (Ithaca, N.Y., 1967), *The Ritual Process: Structure and Anti-Structure* (Chicago, 1969), and *Revelation and Divination in Ndembu Ritual* (Ithaca, N.Y. 1975).

16 Sherry Ortner, "Theory in Anthropology Since the Sixties," *Comparative Studies in History and Society* 26 (1984): 126–66; Pierre Bourdieu, *Outline of a Theory of Practice*, trans. Richard Nice (Cambridge, 1977); Clifford and Marcus, *Writing Culture: The Poetics and Politics of Ethnography* (Berkeley, 1986).

17 Joan W. Scott has been at the center of much of this polemic. "On Language, Gender, and Working-Class History," *International Labor and Working Class History*, 31 (spring 1987): 1–13, was a response to Gareth Stedman Jones, *Languages of Class: Studies in English Working Class History, 1832–1982* (Cambridge, 1984). This essay was published with responses in the same issue by Bryan D. Palmer (14–23), Christine Stansell (24–29), and Anson Rabinbach (30–36); Scott then responded to their critiques in no. 32 ([fall 1987]: 39–45). Scott criticizes John Toews, "Intellectual History after the Linguistic Turn: The Autonomy of Meaning and the Irreducibility of Experience," *American Historical Review* 92 (1987): 879–907, in "Experience," in *Feminists Theorize the Political*, ed. Joan W. Scott and Judith Butler (New York, 1992), pp. 22–40. Laura Lee Downs criticizes Scott in "If 'Woman' is Just an Empty Category, Then Why Am I Afraid to Walk Alone at Night? Identity Politics Meets the Postmodern Subject," *Comparative Studies in Society and History* 35 (1993): 414–37; Scott's response, "The Tip of the Volcano" (438–43), and Downs's reply (444–51) are published in the same volume. Perhaps the most blistering denunciation of discursive history is Brian D. Palmer, *Descent into Discourse: The Reification of Language and the Writing of Social History* (Philadelphia, 1990). For a discussion of many of these issues, see Joyce Appleby, Lynn Hunt, and Margaret Jacob, *Telling the Truth about History* (New York, 1994), pp. 198–237.

18 Schneider, "Notes toward a Theory of Culture," 214.

19 See, e.g., Schneider, *American Kinship*.
20 Readers of Marshall Sahlins should find this formulation familiar. See especially *Islands of History* (Chicago, 1985), pp. 136–56.
21 For a fuller exposition of this perspective, see William H. Sewell, Jr., "Toward a Post-Materialist Rhetoric for Labor History," in *Rethinking Labor History: Essays on Discourse and Class Analysis*, ed. Lenard R. Berlanstein (Urbana, Ill., 1993), pp. 15–38.
22 On the spatial aspect of culture, see Claudio Lomnitz-Adler, "Concepts for the Study of Regional Culture," *American Ethnologist* 18 (1991): 195–214.
23 This is not, of course, the usual conclusion arrived at by deconstructionists, who would insist that these "other structures" are no less textual than semiotic structures and that making sense of them is purely a matter of intertextuality. This epistemological and perhaps ontological difference between my position and that of deconstruction should make it clear that I am appropriating from deconstruction specific ideas that I find useful rather than adopting a full-scale deconstructionist position.
24 Marshall Sahlins, *Historical Metaphors and Mythical Realities* (Ann Arbor, 1981), esp. pp. 67–72, and *Islands of History*, pp. 136–56.
25 William H. Sewell, Jr., "Political Events as Transformations of Structures: Inventing Revolution at the Bastille," *Theory and Society* 26 (1996): 841–81.
26 Turner, *Forest of Symbols*, pp. 41–3.
27 Sahlins, *Historical Metaphors*, p. 46. See also James Scott, *Weapons of the Weak: Everyday Forms of Peasant Resistance* (New Haven, 1985).
28 Renato I. Rosaldo, *Ilongot Headhunting, 1883–1974: A Study in Society and History* (Stanford, 1980).
29 Arjun Appadurai's work on recent forms of transnational cultural forms has been particularly influential. See, e.g., "Global Ethnoscapes: Notes and Queries for a Transnational Anthropology," in Richard G. Fox, ed., *Recapturing Anthropology* (Santa Fe, N.M., 1991), pp. 191–210, and *Modernity at Large: Cultural Dimensions of Globalization* (Minneapolis, 1996).
30 For a critical discussion of such work, see Sherry B. Ortner, "Resistance and the Problem of Ethnographic Refusal," *Comparative Studies in Society and History* 37 (1995): 173–93.
31 For a fascinating study of state cultural practices, see Lisa Wedeen, *Ambiguities of Domination: Politics, Rhetoric, and Symbols in Contemporary Syria* (Chicago, 1999).
32 This characterization seems to me to be roughly consonant with a Gramscian idea of hegemony; see Antonio Gramsci, *Selections from the Prison Notebooks*, ed. and trans. Quintin Hoare and Geoffrey Nowell Smith (New York, 1971). For two quite different Gramscian cultural analyses of politics, see Stuart Hall, *The Hard Road to Renewal: Thatcherism and the Crisis of the Left* (London, 1988), and David D. Laitin, *Hegemony and Culture: Politics and Religious Change among the Yoruba* (Chicago, 1986).

Part II

SELF AND AGENCY

4

AGENCY IN THE DISCURSIVE CONDITION

Elizabeth Deeds Ermarth

Literary critic and historian Elizabeth Deeds Ermarth in this article sets forth the hypothesis that the claims of postmodernity undermine the historically generated bases upon which political democracy in Europe and the West have traditionally rested through its attacks on "objectivity" and the humanist individual that, together with their related values, continue to sustain much of what comprises democratic political practice. For Ermarth, modernity's belief in the stability of individual identity was inextricably linked to an accompanying belief in the objectivity of the world, since it is the individual "agent" of modernity and his or her subjectivity that makes possible the existence of the "objective" by means of the Cartesian split between subject and object. Postmodernity has undermined humanist conceptions of the individual as a unitary, self-conscious agent, and in so doing has equally undermined the independent existence of the individual's correlative, the objective world. Ermarth proposes a new conception of individual agency that accepts and operates within the framework of the postmodern "discursive condition." She invents the term "anthematic subjectivity" to express the multiple, fragmented, and ever-fluid specifications of the subject within postmodern discourse, taking a lead from the Greek word anthemion, meaning "a floral pattern of particular complexity, whose interlaced design is made up of themes or patterns that arrive and depart from various posting places, recurring and recrossing without exact repetition, yet providing an open system of patterning." Unlike most of the articles in this collection, Ermarth's remains committed to a fully semiotic understanding of language and its constitutive force in fashioning the individual and the world, yet seeks to make it available as a support for the kind of collective practices that continue to shape democratic politics.

* * *

[. . .]

The Discursive Condition

The Discursive Condition is a phrase I favor over Lyotard's Postmodern Condition because it features language. I suppose that by now most interested readers remember the "moment" when in Derrida's words "language invaded the universal problematic" and "everything became discourse—provided we can agree on this word."[1] The idea that all systems operate like language—one of the most powerful ideas of the twentieth century—informs postmodernity and thus its provision for agency. The implications of this idea still have not been fully explored and they even have been resisted by the very professors of language and literature whom one would expect to welcome these developments that bring literature and language back from marginality.

The postmodern "move" to language involves a complete redefinition of what language is and how it operates. So important is this redefinition of language to understanding the Discursive Condition and its possibilities that I will state some key points even at the risk of reiterating what is by now obvious to many.

The fundamental ideas appear in the work of the Swiss linguist, Ferdinand de Saussure. His premature death prevented him from publishing (had he been so inclined) the famous lectures he gave at Geneva during the first decade of the twentieth century, and we have only the collated notes of his students which were published in 1915 as *Cours de Linguistique Générale* and translated into English as *Course in General Linguistics* in 1959. Ever since, this little book has provided inspiration to philosophers and cultural historians intent upon re-inventing social, intellectual, and political practice. While the *Cours* is more useful as a quarry than as a finished argument, nevertheless its venturesome formulations continue to inspire creative solutions. Unfortunately, less creative readers have treated its diagrams as scientific descriptions rather than as student notes.

Saussure took two steps of particular interest for the present argument. The first new idea appears in a passage from the section on "Linguistic Value." "Value"—as artists have always known—is a formal matter, not a matter of (so-called) "content." Saussure claimed that linguistic value is "purely differential," that is, only intelligible systemically, not positively or in isolation from systemic relationships. [. . .]

In other words, every linguistic value is determined by its relations with other values in its particular system. This is obvious as soon as one reflects on the difference between linguistic referents in two languages. *Chien* and *dog* do not refer to the "same" thing because their meaning is determined by reference within their respective linguistic systems. So, says Saussure, we understand the word "dog" not because it refers to a hairy four-legged creature which the French call "chien" but because in English "dog" is "not-log"

100

and "not-bog" and "not-doll" and "not-dot." In short, knowledge of linguistic value is reflexive in the sense that it arises from a complex, subliminal, nearly miraculous knowledge of an entire system of differentiations which tells us how to understand the word "dog" and its function (whether it is a noun or a verb). Dog is most precise when we know most about what it is not.

The cultural relevance of this description of the "linguistic fact" was obvious, even commonsensical, to Saussure and to his many readers since. In asserting the arbitrariness, that is, the non-natural condition of the linguistic sign, and in asserting the differential (self-referential) functioning of languages, Saussure anticipated and often grounded the critique of modernity that has spread from philosophy and linguistics to cultural description. He said, apparently almost as an aside, that his approach to linguistics would develop into a new science called "semiology" thus anticipating speech-act theory and the general use of reflexive linguistic systems as models for analysis of cultural value. The new science's

> main concern will still be the whole group of systems grounded on the arbitrariness of the sign. In fact, every means of expression used in society is based, in principle, on collective behavior or—what amounts to the same thing—on convention. Polite formulas, for instance, though often imbued with a certain natural expressiveness (as in the case of a Chinese who greets his emperor by bowing down to the ground nine times), are nonetheless fixed by rule; it is this rule and not the intrinsic value of the gestures that obliges one to use them. Signs that are wholly arbitrary realize better than the others the ideal of the semiological process; that is why language, the most complex and universal of all systems of expression, is also the most characteristic; in this sense linguistics can become the master-pattern for all branches of semiology although language is only one particular semiological system.[2]

This description of language as systemic and differential flew in the face of five centuries of positivist development in which language was treated as a neutrality: one of the powerful, neutral, and transparent media of modernity. It is a coincidence to savor that, at almost precisely the same cultural moment as Saussure was dismissing the neutrality of language, Einstein was arriving at a new description of nature that also rejected the transparency or neutrality of scientific measurement and that required scientific measurement to take itself into account when describing any putatively "objective" phenomenon or event.

Saussure's second big step was to treat *all* systems of meaning and value as languages: that is, as semiotic systems that produce meaning through differential function. This means that, for example, the human sciences can understand human practices—domestic, political, scientific—only if they approach them as functions of differential systems, never as freestanding positivities or objects. When Derrida traces the shift beyond modernity to the "moment when language invaded the universal problematic," and when Foucault says that we do not choose to make a difference, because "we are difference,"[3] they both invoke the simple but revolutionary terms represented by Saussure's claim that all identities, meanings, and values, are differential, not positive in nature. It was practically another Reformation. Where one semantic universe formerly was, multiple semantic universes now are. Where once there was a distinction between language and so-called Reality, now languages constitute realities so that the term "reality" must wear quotes to indicate its systemic function. Inhabiting a language means inhabiting a reality, and that so-called "reality" (one begins to search for ways to qualify such once-unproblematic terms) changes with the language. Complexity increases with the fact that one inhabits several or many languages simultaneously.

[. . .]

The clue to a new construction of subjectivity, and thus of agency, lies in Saussure's emphasis on language as a differential, not referential (structural) model. He distinguishes between the language system as potential (*langue*) and the particular specification of that system, or usage (*parole*). This difference between the potential and the practice renders a linguistic system forever incomplete-able. So long as it remains a living language the system does not become "totalized" (Lévi-Strauss's term), in other words, dead because fully realized and incapable of new specification. The implications of this creative gap between system and specification have not been adequately explored.

[. . .] The speech act is finite; the language is not. Whatever "English" is, it is entirely disseminated. Its rules are the implicit knowledge of all (and only) native speakers. That sum of speakers both contains and yet exceeds the language. In short, English demonstrably exists but is unrecoverable. We can only "recognize" it in this or that specification, never in the abstract, as in grammar books and diagrams.

For "English," read, "Discourse": a term that leads beyond verbal languages to all the differential systems of meaning and value that Saussure identified as constituting the field of semiotic play. The possibilities are infinite, including body languages, garment languages, the languages of international diplomacy, of various nationalisms, of organizations, of political influence, of aesthetic value, of domestic violence, of fashion, of economics, and so on. Whatever the *langue*, or discursive system of potential, the arena of subjectivity and freedom lies in that all-important gap between the potential capacities of a given semiotic code on the one hand and, on the other hand, any particular specification of it. This "Tender Interval" (Nabokov's phrase for something only slightly different) lying between language (*langue*) and enunciation (*parole*) brings to subjectivity a set of conditions entirely different from those belonging to the unified subject of modernity. To reconceive subjectivity for this discursive condition entails a radical change of tools. [. . .]

Anthematic subjectivity in the Discursive Condition[4]

Emphasis upon a *discursive condition* has taught us to search for "code" rather than for "structure": a shift with substantial implications for subjectivity. Once everything has become discourse, and subjectivity becomes a function of systems of differential relationships, what becomes of that wonderful windowless monad known as the "free" and "in-dividual" agent: the one who carries the ethical responsibilities of freedom?

[. . .]

The positive meaning of the term "self" taken for granted today only flourished after the mid-nineteenth century and for many different reasons, including religious history, evolutionary science and narrative, and changing patterns of social and economic life. That profound mutation depended, in its turn, on a revolution in the meaning of the term "society." In their positive meanings, "individual" and "self" are by definition social terms. "Self" had no dignity compared to God and has no place in the pilgrimages of early modernity; but "self" does develop dignity in comparison with other, equal people. This version of individuality, Foucault's founding subject of history, is the singularity essential to (and created for) the consensus that maintains universal common denominators like "time" and "space," the neutral media of modernity "in" which the events of modern causality can happen.

To reformulate this singular "self" or "subject" for postmodernity—as an element of differential systems, a function of discourse—means to reject once again the singularity of what was, rather briefly, "the individual" or non-divisible identity. The discursive condition insures that subjectivity never operates in one language or discourse at a time, in some kind of prim, impossible sequence, but instead operates simultaneously in several discursive systems at once, be they verbal languages or other semiotic systems (gender relations, fashion, politics). In these conditions, it makes less and less sense to consider subjectivity in terms of simple location at all. And so, the familiar questions arise about autonomy, freedom, and responsibility. "The subject" appears to be no longer the originator of language, but its creature. What independent or moral life can be expected of a subjectivity controlled by systems into which it is born and over which it has little control? What uniqueness is possible for a subjectivity thus positioned? If discourses pre-ordain subject positions, do they also pre-ordain what we once called individual history? What becomes of concepts like social justice and even "human rights" when their epistemological grounds are discredited and their founding subject distributed throughout the functions of systems?

[. . .]

The differential linguistic model inspired by Saussure tells us two things about semiotic systems that bear on the problem of agency: first, that structure is always potential, never explicit; and second, that explicit statements or speech acts (*paroles*) can push the limit of an available systemic potential without ever exhausting it, at least not so long as that system or *langue* "lives,"

103

that is, remains capable of new usages. The subjectivity embedded in semiotic systems by no means loses political relevance and responsibility, on the contrary, those are built in and are inevitably part of the process of specifying language. The more experimental the usage, the more potential it has for political and social creativity. In fact, revitalizing usage is precisely what great writers do and why their work contributes so directly to social health. Agency in these contemporary conditions is not a singularity but a process, a happening, a particular expression of systemic value. [. . .] Saussure [implies] that "identity" and "agency" appear not as discrete essentials but as the practices of a lifelong activity of specifying the available rule regimens (*langues*).

Furthermore, we operate in several regimens simultaneously. Code-multiplicity means that we no longer have only a subject-in-process, or even a subjectivity-in-process, but something more like subjectivity-in-processes. In more Saussurian terms, identity can appear only as the sequence of specifications of the available rule regimens. I am not first a parent, then an author, later a consumer. I am all simultaneously, each interlaced with the other so that what I do as a parent influences what I do as a consumer. This is not news to most people, but it is not accounted for in the matter-and-motion explanatory models of modernity. The interpretive and intellectual tools inherited from modernity exclude and even depreciate this messy and unpredictable interlacement and continue to encourage assertion of impossible unanimities.

Adequate discussion of identity in the discursive condition, then, must accommodate its *"palimpsestuousness"*—to use the delicious term coined by the Scottish poet and scholar, Michael Alexander. Identity is not something essential and atomic, like the vestigial "soul" of early modernity; identity is sequence and palimpsest. Its singularity exists in the unique and unrepeatable sequence of a life, but not in some essential "subject." Its palimpsestuousness derives from the multiplied discursive condition in which each moment involves a complex subjective specification of multiple codes. This moving specifier, including its role in any collectivity, cannot be encompassed by sociological generalizations, which confuse its crucial singularity and flatten its palimpsestuousness with "the weeds of statistics and waist-high generalizations."[5] Instead, this discursive identity consists in the unique and unrepeatable sequence of complex enunciation. It is a form of materialization resembling poetry.

This idea of a distributed subjectivity, far from being a loss or a lack, allows for the actual complexity of conscious life more fully and precisely than the modern "subject" ever did. A complex, multilaminated subjectivity actually seems a fairly commonsense description of lived experience in our time: more than does the abstract *cogito* or "miserable treasure" inherited from Christian and Romantic absolutes. It seems particularly pointless, even wrong, to impose that monadic idea of "the subject" upon a personal knowledge that is more random and radical than that traditional model allows.

The idea of agency is correspondingly altered. During a bygone era of modernity, political activists used to talk about trying to make a difference, as if exceptional intervention were requisite to "action." But in the discursive condition it is impossible *not* to make a difference. "We are difference" as Foucault says[6]; the real question then is, do we make the difference we intend? We are difference: not "selves" or "subjects" or "enunciators" conceived independently from discourse, but instead, a kinetic subjectivity-in-multicoded-process. Instead of a static singularity, postmodern subjectivity is more like a moving nexus or intersection: a point of empowerment or suppression, and the agent first of a unique and unrepeatable sequence that is constantly being specified from the potentials available in the discursive condition. Such a subjectivity is individual in its sequence, not in some irreducible core. Its uniqueness lies in its trajectory, impossible to anticipate, within which an unpredictable series of specifications are made from among the available languages. The volatility of discourse—language's resonance, its power of poetic, associative linkage—provides precisely the varied opportunities for selective specification that constitute the unique and unrepeatable poetry that makes life more than a cartoon.

Personal agency takes on new and different kinds of importance in this environment of semiotic multiplicity. Postmodernity provides for an assertion of personal uniqueness that is far more complex and creative than what Cartesian philosophy once asserted: a personal uniqueness not given, but constructed; a uniqueness I create as I go from day to day, specifying in particular ways my multiple shared potentials. From that aura of possibility, and with all my limitations upon me, I construct—you construct, he and she and they construct—the unique and unrepeatable poetry of an individual life. [...]

While coining a term for this new subjectivity may be premature, something is needed to counter the gravitational pull of "the" subject/individual/enunciator/self. So for the sake of argument, I propose the term *anthematic subjectivity*. The term "anthemion" comes to me from the work of Vladimir Nabokov, poet, novelist, and keeper of the keys to English for our time. *Anthemion* is a Greek word meaning a floral pattern of particular complexity. [...]. Nabokov's "anthemion" indicates an interlaced, flower-like design where themes or patterns arrive and depart from various posting places, recurring and recrossing without exact repetition, and yet providing a kind of open system of rhythmic iteration and patterning.

[...]

Anthematic subjectivity is born within that volatility. Discursive sequences completely scramble what might have become a "history" of persons—their obscure objects of desire, their lasting identities and conventional lives, their explanations that are only well-dressed mistakes, and especially their fatal attempts to recapture the past.

[...]

105

Political practice in the discursive condition

Along with the modern individual subject, what vanishes into the discursive condition is the entire humanist apparatus of infinities, objectifiers, and common denominators upon which so much has depended, including representational politics. The consensus apparatuses of representational art, of democratic systems, and even of history are in doubt. If the "founding subject" is in question, then it would be necessary to think again about what it founds, including the nature of the sequence, the nature of the series.[7] Where once the individual sustained the grammars of perspective on which "time" rested, now even history, even "time" as modernity has taught us to assume it, belongs to the palimpsest of codes, to the game of language or, as Julio Cortázar called it "this dirty game of substitutions."[8]

[. . .]

In the discursive condition, there is no infinite, neutral envelope for "events" and "individuals," not even time, or, at least not even the neutrality of historical time but instead only new forms such as "rhythmic times" or "ph(r)ase times" appropriate to the discursive condition.[9]

If the anthematic subjectivity cannot be deployed in the same way as the modern "individual" as the basis for a universally rationalized consensus apparatus, then (one might be tempted to ask) on what basis do anthematic subjectivities make sense to each other and produce results, including political results? Without the modern grammars of perspective that produce the common arenas of neutral time and space, what becomes of the entire culture of representation, especially democratic institutions? How does anthematic subjectivity avoid merely babbling incoherently or lapsing into "madness?" Do "anthematic" recognitions allow for any kind of collective practice recognizable as democratic politics? Is meaningful connection possible, in other words, can we group many "anthematic" subjectivities so they "add up" in some way that makes their practices intelligible as meaning, or are they just random relative to one another? Can we describe events and take actions in anything like collective terms?

[. . .]

The first step in solving a problem of this magnitude is fairly to state it; the problem of agency has to be re-thought from the ground up, beginning with functional recognition that practice takes place in the discursive condition, not "in" the neutral media of modernity. From this recognition new questions arise, new values come into play. What languages do I employ and how? How does History function? If making a difference is not a choice but a condition—if we are not essential agents picking up tools in neutral space and time but simply "are difference"—then how do we learn to recognize the differences we make? How do we describe practice without using the objectifying models of modernity? What kind of formulae would be suitable to anthematic subjectivity and to the discursive condition? We especially need to resist the temptation to find History and its founding subject in places where it was not constituted and thus, with the inexorable gesture of modernity, to subsume all potential languages into one. Perhaps, considering the radioactivity of the languages inherited from modernity, and considering the terminological revolution that postmodernity requires, it would be a good idea to reiterate periodically—say, the first day of every month—that terms like "truth," "real," "object," and "subject" are the tools of the devil.

To rewrite the possibilities of collective agreement it is first of all necessary to think outside History and to find alternatives to its founding subject and its narrative (explanatory) habits. For most academics in the human sciences this is easier said than done, because quantitative and temporal distance markers seem almost to constitute the building blocks of intellectual life conducted outside relatively "hard" science. Course material is often organized historically; scholarly attention respectfully stops at chronological "period" boundaries and accepts the correlative subdivision of "knowledge" into ever-narrowing tracks. The division of knowledge in universities—the emphasis on "disciplines" and on categories of disciplines—is a modern system par excellence, a grammar of perspective institutionalized. [. . .] [T]he instruments of modernity entirely fail to register the crossings, inscriptions, interlacements, mysterious mental maneuvers of imagination performed in the discursive condition and constitutive of life whether or not our intellectual models acknowledge them.

The shift toward postmodern solutions would involve a shift away from the quantitative values that modernity emphasizes: the quantities and distances of Renaissance perspective systems, of empirical science, and of so much history. The practices appropriate to the discursive condition emphasize qualitative values. [. . .] Instead of questions such as "how long?" and "how much?" the emphasis shifts to questions such as "how complex?" "how proportioned?" "how flexible?" "how innovative?" [. . .]

Recognizing discursive complexity would have implications for method, especially in arenas where the objectifying methods of science are employed or imitated. Where modernity favors a productive positivism, discursive practice involves a continuing, even open-ended project of interlacement in which negative value has substantial importance. Where modernity favors structural formalities, with their progressive and objectifying results, postmodernity substitutes a digressive formality of sustained interruption. Where modern science is hostile to whatever threatens to digress, postmodernity emphasizes precisely the digressive play that confirms discursive vitality. Where modern causalities produce stable results in a unanimous world, the anthematic sequences of postmodernity involve continuing disequilibrium, exploratory repetition, irreducible discursive variety.[10]

Possible achievements in the discursive condition seem considerably humbler than those always implicit in the infinite horizons and emergent forms of modern history. Discursive opportunities lie ready-to-hand in the small, daily iterations or revisions of discursive potentials; the detail and the moment, far from being mere disposable clues, become the only springboards

107

of practice, the indispensable sites of the only real opportunity. Such activity does not lead to a politics involving appearances on the World Stage, but instead to a more localized politics composed of those specifications that enhance or erode available discursive languages. [. . .] As Jean-François Lyotard put it, politics is "the threat of the differend": a difference that is not a thing, not a positivity, but instead a perpetual and systemic relationship through division.[11] That differend must be negotiated constantly. Where the political agendas of modernity reduced, even sublimated or denied differences in order to produce a putatively common world, the political agendas of postmodernity treat difference as constitutive and irreducible. That shift of emphasis forecloses on all the endless wars for possession of Truth. It constrains all activity to the play of systems wherein all definition is differential and internal to a system, and thus no basis for truth claims. This relativizing extends beyond the familiar "conflict of valid claims" of nineteenth-century political philosophy because it denies the possibility of *any* mediating common denominator, including especially the possibility of "historical time" within which events are mutually informative because they belong to one and "the same" world.[12]

The given codes that constitute the discursive condition are precise taskmasters. Certain things work and others do not. Certain things can be said, other things are simply not speakable. The only way to influence or alter these commanding codes is through practical iterative alterations.

[. . .]

Postmodernity thus presents difficulty for the modern political problem of collective action, a difficulty often mentioned by those keen to denounce postmodernity from a modern point of view. [. . .]

In the discursive condition, however, it is impossible *not* to act under collective obligation because the bases of all practice are the discursive systems or "languages," including the language we call History; these systems have been collectively created, revised, and sustained. The "individual" specification of those available languages (the poetry of a life) can be original, or conventional, or a bit of both; it can reconfirm familiar usage or attempt new ones; open new solutions or keep repeating old ones. The one thing the individual contribution cannot be is detached from collective enterprise. Any "writing" in a shared language is only possible in the first place because that potential has been provided by others, most of them long dead; and such individual specifications confirm or extend the possibilities of that shared language which will survive them and an infinite number of future specifications. Each specific usage potentially affects all others either by adding the weight of repetition or by opening the possibility of new practice. Such local influences intersect and radiate unpredictably.

[. . .]

My intention in this essay has been to focus a problem rather than offer solutions. The problem is this: how can the political optimism about exercising agency in democratic societies endure in the anthematic regimens of the discursive condition? If, as has been suggested, representational institutions and their grammar of perspective have depended on the "subject" of modernity, what happens to the institutions when that "subject" becomes a specifying function of multiple codes where the codes themselves are half-inaccessible to scrutiny? Modernity would encourage answering those questions from a spectator's position located outside and above the arena of practice: perhaps in order to control it, or perhaps only to replicate speculative positions invalidated by practice. Postmodernity, on the other hand, always emphasizes practice, and practice defined to include what is local and continuous, aleatory and imaginative compared to the rationalizations of modernity.

The critique of modernity is an international phenomenon deeply rooted in Europe and its politics. If Eurocentric societies, perhaps especially the US, fail to refocus modern democratic politics for postmodernity, they may consign democracy to inconsequence. The novelist Milan Kundera has said that the loss of Central Europe after World War II was the beginning of the end of Europe, and that the recent liberation of Central Europe from superpower domination is Europe's second chance. Whatever we make of Kundera's interested remark, it focuses on the fact that Eurocentric cultures including the United States now stand at a liminal phase, a threshold that marks an epoch not in terms of years or decades only, but in terms of centuries. In confronting this considerable problem, it would be encouraging to see more modest, more self-aware use of habitual terms in discussing our supposedly "free" choices and actions. It would be encouraging to see more therapeutic recognition of the insistent power of discursive systems.

NOTES

1 Jacques Derrida, "Structure, Sign and Play in the Discourse of the Human Sciences," *Writing and Difference*, trans. Alan Bass (Chicago: University of Chicago Press, 1978), 280.
2 Ferdinand de Saussure, *Course in General Linguistics* [1915], trans. Wade Baskin (New York: McGraw Hill, 1959), 68.
3 Michel Foucault, *The Archaeology of Knowledge and the Discourse on Language* (originally *L'Archaeologie de savoir* [Paris: Gallimard, 1979] and *L'Ordre du discours* [Paris: Gallimard, 1971]), 131.
4 Much of this section and some passages in the preceding and following sections are reprinted (sometimes modified) from "Beyond the Subject: Individuality in the Discursive Condition," *New Literary History* 31 (Summer 2000), 405–419.
5 Vladimir Nabokov, *Ada, or Ardor: A Family Chronicle* (New York: McGraw-Hill, 1969), 76.
6 Foucault, *The Archaeology of Knowledge*, 131.
7 Foucault, *The Discourse on Language*, published with *The Archaeology of Knowledge*.
8 Julio Cortázar, *Hopscotch* [1963], trans. Gregory Rabassa (New York: Random House, 1966), 345.
9 See Ermarth, "Ph(r)ase Time: Chaos Theory and Postmodern Reports on Knowledge," *Time and Society* 4 (1995), 91–110; "Time and Neutrality: The Media of Modernity in the Postmodern World" in *Time and Value*, ed. S. Lash, A. Quick, and R. Roberts

(Oxford: Blackwell, 1998, 197–209); and throughout *Sequel to History* (Princeton: Princeton University Press, 1992).

10 See Ermarth, "Language and Time" and "Time as Rhythm," in *Sequel to History*, 45–71; 139–210.

11 Jean-François Lyotard, *The Differend: Phrases in Dispute*, trans. Georges van den Abbeele (Minneapolis: University of Minnesota Press, 1988), 136, paragraph 184.

12 See Ermarth, "Ph(r)ase Time."

5

INDIVIDUAL EXPERIENCE AND CULTURAL ORDER

Marshall Sahlins

Just as historians were beginning to turn to anthropology for theoretical and method-ological inspiration during the 1970s and 1980s, some anthropologists, most notably among them Marshall Sahlins, were making the reverse journey into history. The effect of anthropology's involvement with history was to direct the attention of anthropologists to questions of historical change, a relatively rare orientation for anthropology, which at the time was strongly influenced by structuralism, whether that of Lévi-Strauss, as in the early writing of Pierre Bourdieu, or the linguistic model derived from the application of semiotics to culture, as in the case of anthro-pologist Clifford Geertz. Like these scholars, Sahlins began his life in anthropology during the 1960s and 1970s strongly committed to structuralism. However, in work produced during the 1980s and 1990s he began moving toward a more historical, and more ethnographically grounded, approach than in his earlier writings, although he never abandoned a belief in the importance of structure as a force in history or a focus of anthropological investigation. The latter reveals itself in his conviction that, as he says in the "Introduction" to the essays collected in Culture in Practice, *"to speak of the ways in which people meaningfully construct their existence goes back to the symbolic side . . . of anthropology" (p. 13).*

*   The essay reprinted here on "Individual Experience and Cultural Order" origin-ally appeared in 1982, and so falls within the "historical" phase of Sahlins's corpus. It takes up the problem of "cultural determinism," or the relation between individual action and cultural order. In ways similar to historian William Sewell, Sahlins distances himself from the idea that culture is a "super-organic object" that exists independently of the human subjects who enact it. And like Sewell as well (who, it should be noted, partially derives his ideas from the work of Sahlins), Sahlins opts for a dialectical understanding of the relationship between cultural order and indi-vidual experience and action. In contrast to Sewell, however, Sahlins does not postulate culture's "thin" coherence, in order to make room for social practices. Rather, he adapts Saussure's distinction between language (*language*) and speech (*parole*) as a way of conceptualizing the differential status that culture has in its dual modes of existence: as a general structure or system (comparable to language*

in Saussure) and as it appears and is used in human projects (comparable to the enunciative speech acts (or parole) in Saussurean linguistics). As Sahlins describes it, structure is a state, while human action unfolds sequentially and consequentially in a temporal process, through which the sign is "substantialized" in action by reference to the world. In this process, the conventional meanings of words are endowed with human intentionality, and thus become subject to new interpretations. Although Sahlins insists that action, both interpretative and practical, begins and ends in structure, he stipulates that if, in the interim, signs are displaced by being set into novel relationships with one another then by definition the structure is transformed. This lived, pragmatic re-evaluation of signs in use sets culture-as-system into motion, and thus opens a space for historical development, which results from the cumulative and collective effects of practice. Sahlins's position is close to that espoused by William Sewell, and, in its fidelity to Saussurean linguistics, to that articulated in Michel de Certeau's The Practice of Everyday Life *as well.*

*   *   *

I am going to resurrect an issue that anthropologists these days hate to think about, even though as students of culture they have a main responsibility for discussing it. I mean the problem of "cultural determinism," or the relation between individual action and cultural order. True, an older generation with some strong ideas on the subject has now died off and a younger one having other preoccupations taken its place; and, while such is the normal definition of progress in the social sciences, we are not really free to forget the problems that plagued the ancestors. The issue was important; and, besides, we have been speaking it all this time while pretending not to know it. What I propose to do is to reflect (in a much too schematic way) on the implications of current interests in symbolism and structuralism for the received idea that culture is sui generis, a so-called superorganic object independent of the human subjects who enact it.

Utilitarian individualism and cultural determinism

It must be recalled that the concept of the superorganic developed in anthropology – and also, with the Durkheimian "social fact," in sociology – by opposition to the complete theory of culture already present in Western society and consciousness – present, indeed, as the way this society takes consciousness of itself. I refer to the mainstream idea of an "economic man" whose rational choices precipitate, as if by an Invisible Hand, not only the well-being of the Nation but its very social forms. Marxism perhaps excepted, this utilitarian individualism is the only coherent analysis of culture the West has produced. Our colleagues in the University of Chicago Economics Department are brilliantly engaged in quantitative demonstrations of it, but even on the basis of naive experience we can be sure in advance of their success. For since the development of the self-regulating market, we have had this certain, if peculiar, knowledge of ourselves as businesslike social beings, bent on maximizing life's benefits and minimizing its costs. "Utility dominates the study of culture," as A.M. Hocart said, "because it dominates the culture that studies."

Rendering all kinds of goods and services commensurable in their capacity as monetary values, the market society did not merely disguise to itself the meaningful differences between things. To an anthropologist, the historical peculiarity is that the kinds of acts he recognizes in a tribal context as instances of "social organization," "politics," "kinship," "art," even "religion," appear, when he returns from the field, as so many quests for "utilities." For in the context of a total market, no matter what the nature of such acts taken in themselves, our relationship to them is decisively economic. Whether one chooses to go to a baseball game or to a concert, vacation in Hawaii, or buy the *Oxford English Dictionary*, all such actions and options must first be translated into their apparent common denominator of "pleasures" or "satisfactions," among which we prudently allocate our limited pecuniary means. In the translation, then, their distinctive social content is lost, with the result that from the natives' point of view all of culture seems constituted by (and as) the businesslike economizing of autonomous individuals. I have to admit that many Western anthropologists have been tempted to reproduce this indigenous folklore in their own studies, as a consciousness also of the others. For when a society makes a fetish of the commodity, its anthropology is disposed to make a commodity out of the fetish.

Bourgeois life turns culture into the hidden a priori of a calculus of pragmatic action. The symbolic order is subsumed in hierarchies of means and ends, as motives and interests located within the subject and realized by a process of rational choice also natural to him/her. Culture thus becomes a presupposition, we are left unaware of other logics inscribed in our intentions. I refer not merely to the difficulties of making other judgments of a Weberian sort on rational action; for example, that the collective disutilities of a system of private transport are not envisioned in the way that buying and driving a car, as a project of economizing, appears in personal experience. More significant yet is the qualitatively different logic of symbolic value that enters into action as an unreflected premise.

[...]

Yet as Nietzsche remarked, "Man does not seek happiness; only Englishmen do that." Anthropology has been forced to reconcile its own cultural presuppositions with the experience of other natives. In the event, the indigenous Western concepts were turned inside out. The response to individualism was to alienate man from his own activity and creativity, transferring these instead to a kind of supersubject, Culture, which for its part was accorded all powers of movement and determination. Admittedly this "culture" had no phenomenal existence apart from human beings, but it had autonomous characteristics and functions, and men could do no more than express its internal constitution and dynamics. The naive consciousness of capitalist society was thus exchanged for its historic Unhappy Consciousness.

[. . .]

To sum up: Utilitarianism concealed culture within a faulty human episte-mology, while the "superorganic" dissolved humanity in a fantastic cultural ontology. One is inclined to wish a plague on both their houses. But not before exhausting certain anthropological observations, such as the absence of any necessary relation between what people do and the reasons they may have for doing it.

Intention and convention

Eskimo are famous for customs of gift-giving. "Gifts make slaves," they some-times explain, "as whips make dogs." By contrast, a people famous for belligerence may have equally paradoxical motives for fighting. "They fought, they beat each other," writes a longtime resident among the Yanomamö of Brazil. "I don't know why; they said it was in order to be more peaceful and to be friends." There seems to be no adequate relation between the character of conventional practices, such as giving gifts or making war, and the inten-tions that predicate them, whether these intentions be described in social terms (for example, gaining status) or as subjective dispositions (for example, belligerence). The cross-cultural argument, moreover, can be supported from our own social experience. Psychoanalysis as well as common experience documents that an aggressive intent can be realized in an act of sex or on a field of football, by being excessively polite to someone, ignoring him or insulting him, by presenting a lecture or writing a book review ("that'll teach 'em"). Any given intention may correspond to an indefinite set of cultural practices and vice versa, since the intention is connected to the convention by a relative and contextual scheme of significance.

But if the connection is arbitrary, it is not for all that aleatory, inasmuch as it is motivated within the cultural order. This would be true even if the act had unprecedented social effects. Say that gift-giving established a novel form of social advancement: it would still find some logical motivation – it would "make sense" – in the culture as constituted. The disparity between conven-tions and intentions thus becomes a strong argument for culture as sui generis. It seems incorrect to deny that individual action is culturally determined, since this is all it can be.

The same dismal prospect appears implied by intrinsic features of symbolic consciousness and discourse. Nothing is socially known or communicated except as it is encompassed in the existing cultural order. From the first moment, experience undergoes a kind of structural co-optation: the incorpor-ation of the percept within a concept of which the perceiver is not the author. This is Durkheim's famous "sociological epistemology." Likewise, Walker Percy remarks, "It is not enough to say that one is conscious of some-thing; one is also conscious of something as *being something*." Perception is instantaneously a *re*-cognition, a matching of the percept with some received social category – "There goes a bird." Human or symbolic consciousness thus consists of acts of classification involving the subsumption of an individual perception within a social conception. Hence, as percept belongs to concept in the way that an instance belongs to its class, so does experience belong to culture.

Moreover, we know – at least since Saussure and Cassirer – that the cultural category by which experience is appropriated is for its part referentially arbitrary. It does not follow directly from the world but from a set of principled relationships between categories. The contrast in French between the terms "fleuve" and "rivière" entails a different segmentation of fluvial objects than the usual English glosses "river" and "stream," inasmuch as the French distinction does not turn on relative size but on whether or not the water flows into an ocean. There is no necessary starting point for any such cultural scheme in "reality," as Stuart Hampshire writes – while noting that many philosophers have believed there is. Rather, the particular conceptual scheme or "language game" constitutes the possibilities of worldly reference for the people of a given society, even as that scheme is constructed on principled distinctions among signs which, in relation to objects, are never the only possible distinctions. It follows that there is no such thing as an immaculate perception.

The argument from symbolic discourse has the same apparent implication. Insofar as a sentence asserts, it does so by seating a specific identification within a cultural class. A sentence is minimally a grammatical subject and a predicate – "There goes a bird." The grammatical subject identifies something in particular – "[it] there." But the predicate describes it in the terms of (relative) generals – "bird," "going": once more a class whose criteria are values of the prevailing cultural scheme.

On the other hand, it is well known that in speaking the individual puts the entire cultural scheme at his own personal disposition. The famous "shifters" of discourse – the pronouns "I" and "you," adverbs of time and place ("now" and "then," "here" and "there"), tenses of the verb, and so on – contextualize all abstract categories by the speaker's reference to himself and his particular situation. Speech invents a Cartesian world, developed outward from the true and certain knowledge of the "I." In practice, the individual is the Archimedean point of the cultural universe: for on the coordinates of his standpoint, hence of his interests, all of culture is transcendentally laid out, and all meanings, which without him are merely virtual or possible, become actual, referential, and intentional.

Yet here linguistics joins up with certain clear and distinct ideas of social psychology, sociology, and anthropology: the common finding that "I is another" (*Je est un autre*). Such was the point of George Herbert Mead's sustained demonstration that the self becomes known as an object by assuming the attitude of another toward one's own act or gesture – an identification with the other that alone permits reflection upon the self and to

115

which language is indispensable. For Mead, as for Schütz, this "interchange-ability of standpoints" is essential both to the origin of the self and the origin of human society. For Rousseau, it was the origin of human society itself: uniquely endowed with the sentiment of *pitié* which places him in the position of the one who suffers, man begins by experiencing himself as identical to his fellows. But that too, as Benveniste teaches, is the true character of the apparently egocentric symbolic discourse.

For the "I" of speech necessarily predicates a "you," and vice versa, even as the two are always reversible. No matter how egocentrically the world is laid out in speech, "I" am never alone in it. In dialogue, "I" and "you" exchange places: referential standpoints are necessarily reversed – shall we not say? – between *us*. This interchangeability is indispensable to interpretation and communication, since without it I could not know that your "here" is my "there." It must follow that the "you" to whom I speak, and who becomes "I" in speaking to me, is in some fundamental sense like me, namely, in the capacity of social person.

The consequences, as Benveniste says, spread out in all directions. We can understand why Lévi-Strauss founds the passage from nature to culture on reciprocity as the decisive (that is, objectified) form of overcoming the opposition of self and other. Since reciprocity in this parallels the essential characteristics of symbolic discourse, we might even credit his explanation by inherent principles of the human mind. But more consequential for present purposes are inherent qualities of human society. If there are other "I"s whose standpoints I make my own, it becomes uniquely possible for humans to constitute social universals, categories, and groups that extend indefinitely in space and time.

[. . .]

Never present as such to individual experience, the institutions of society thus become capable of ordering subjective interests and actions – that is, by virtue of a common membership with "the generalized other." Nor will my purposes be completely idiosyncratic: even when opposed to some other they are formulated on a common cultural logic. Yet this further allusion to Mead reminds us that different values of the social logic, some more particularistic, some more universal, intersect in the person. The individual is a social being, but we must never forget that he is an individual social being, with a biography not the same as that of anyone else. Here is someone to whom "attention must be paid." For, to adopt Mead's vocabulary, if there is a "me" that incorporates the attitude of some group at some level of generality, there is also an "I" that retains a potential freedom of reaction to the "generalized other." This means that life in society is not an automatic genuflection before the superorganic being but, rather, a continuous rearrangement of its categories in the projects of personal being. In the final section of this paper, I will describe this dialectic, which is nothing less than structural transformation, as a symbolic process.

Dialectics of structure and action

The word "interest" derives from a Latin impersonal verbal construction meaning "it makes a difference." An interest in something is the difference it makes for someone. Happy etymology, since it runs parallel to the Saussurean definition of conceptual value. The sign is determined as a concept by its differential relation to other signs. The meaning of "blue" is fixed by the co-presence of other terms, such as "green"; if, as is true in many natural languages, there were no "green," the term "blue" would have greater conceptual and referential extension [. . .]. The same goes for God the Father, a dollar bill, motherhood, or filet mignon: each has a conceptual sense according to its differential place in the total scheme of such symbolic objects. On the other hand, the symbolic object represents a differential interest to various subjects according to its place in their life schemes. "Interest" and "sense" are two sides of the same thing, the sign, as related respectively to persons and to other signs. Yet my interest in something is not the same as its sense.

Saussure's discussion of linguistic value helps make the point, as it is framed on an analogy to economic value. The value of a five-franc piece is determined by the dissimilar objects with which it can be exchanged, such as so much bread or milk, and by other units of currency with which it can be contrastively compared – one franc, ten francs. By these relationships the significance of five francs in the society is constituted. Yet this general and abstract sense is not the value of five francs *to me*. To me, it appears as a specific interest or instrumental value, and whether I buy milk or bread with it, give it away, or put it in the bank, all depends on my particular circumstances and objectives. As implemented by the subject, the conventional value acquires an intentional value, and the conceptual sense an actionable reference.

I am suggesting that the classic distinction between language and speech be expanded into an argument about culture in general – that culture likewise has a dual mode of existence. It appears both in human projects and intersubjectively as a structure or system. Intentionally arranged by the subject, it is also conventionally constituted in the society. But, as a symbolic process, it is differently organized in these two dimensions.

[. . .] [I]mmediately we see that culture-as-lived has a different kind of phenomenal existence than culture-as-constituted. The sign enjoys an actual being, *in praesentia*, only as it is inscribed in human action. As a scheme of relationships between symbolic categories, the "system" is merely virtual. It exists *in absentia*, in the way that the English language, as distinct from people's actual utterances, exists perfectly or as a whole only in the community as a whole. We can say that, as lived, the symbolic fact is a phenomenal "token," whose "type" is its mode of existence in culture-as-constituted. Besides, in culture-as-constituted the sign has an abstract sense, merely signifying, by virtue of all possible relations with other signs, all its possible uses; it is thus "stimulus-free," not bound to any particular worldly referent. But people live in the world as well as by signs, or better, they live in the world by signs, and in action they index the conceptual sense by reference to the objects of their existence. In naive and evidently universal human experience, signs are the names of things "out there."

[. . .]

[C]ulture-as-constituted is a mutual determination of significant forms, and as the significance of any given form depends on the co-presence of the others – as God the Father is defined by God the Son, and vice versa – the "system" is indeed systemic on the condition that it is synchronic. Structure is a state; but action unfolds as a temporal process. And in intentional action the logic of relationship between signs lies precisely in their orientation: sequentially and consequentially, as means and ends of people's purposes. Moreover, I (the others) are constantly putting these signs in various and contingent relationships. Today I decide to humiliate someone by giving him a gift he cannot repay; no, better perhaps to call him the name he deserves; or then again, I could review his book. In structure, the sign is fixed by differential relationships to other signs; in action, it is variously combined with other signs in implicational relationships.

I have said that the sign is substantialized in action by reference to the world. But, as every such context by which the sign is substantially defined is unique, so then is every individual's expression of the culture-as-constituted. Moreover, in their several projects people effect contingent relationships between signs which are not necessarily those ordained in the culture-as-constituted. Recall Mead's observations on the possible slippage between intentional values and conventional values, figured as a distinction between the "I" and the "me." Now, it seems incorrect to deny that people can change their culture, because, as Mead concluded, that's all they ever do.

The two dimensions of culture are indeed mutually irreducible, but we are now in a position to show that they are dialectically interpenetrable. First, however, some ground rules. The possibility that a personal arrangement of symbolic forms will have structural effect clearly depends on many conditions of the culture-as-constituted: the improvisations that can be logically motivated, as by analogy, metaphor, or the like; the institutional freedom to do so; the position of the actor in a social hierarchy that gives his action structural weight, makes it more or less consequential for others. All such conditions vary from society to society and may be empirically ascertained; but they are not here matters of theoretical principle. Here I am concerned solely with the ways – if you want, the mechanisms – by which structure and project interact as a symbolic process. I identify two such ways: the functional displacement of sign relationships in personal action, and the practical revaluation of signs in the famous "context of the situation."

Action begins and ends in structure, begins from the biography of the individual as a social being to end by the absorption of his action in a cultural practico-inert, the system-as-constituted. But if, in the interim, signs are functionally displaced, set into novel relationships with one another, then

118

by definition the structure is transformed; and in this interim the condition of the culture-as-constituted may actually amplify the consequences of an individual's action.

[. . .]

The pragmatic revaluation of signs has to do with their determination in a particular worldly context, a process specific to culture in the dimension of action. Signs are notoriously "polysemic" as conceptual values; they have multiple meanings. But as human interests they acquire determinate representations, amounting to some inflection of the conceptual sense. And because the "objective" world to which they are applied has its own refractory characteristics and dynamics, the signs, and by derivation the people who live by them, may then be categorically redefined. I give an exotic example of such meaningful relations between praxis and structure, though I believe the process is commonplace.

When great numbers of ordinary Hawaiian women flocked aboard Captain Cook's ships in 1779 demanding sexual relations with the too-willing British seamen, they were acting on traditional considerations. To sire a child by a god or chief – for such the British were – was all the women wanted. Then, as Hawaiians say, "the bones of the grandparents will live": the kinship connection traced through the half-chiefly child will be the source of many benefits. As it turned out, the common women thus put themselves in opposition to their own chiefs, who, likewise acting on the traditional code, sought to engross all trade with the foreigners, since it represented a *mana* uniquely consistent with their own.

Although the women had made no material stipulations on their paramours, the British seamen knew how to repay the services done them – indeed, defined the women's acts as "services" or "prostitution" by giving them gifts. These gifts, moreover, included iron tools for the kinsmen – fathers, brothers, or husbands – who had gladly brought the women aboard: precisely the goods in which chiefs had interest and to which they demanded a privileged access. Thus was initiated a collective interest between commoner men and women that set them against the Hawaiian powers that be.

In particular, the commoners were set against the tabu system orchestrated by chiefs and priests. And this in a double way. For one, commoner women were consistently tempted, as well as encouraged by the British, to violate the tabus by which the chiefs controlled relations with Cook's ships. Second, the women were less inclined to observe the domestic tabus that separated them from their own men, such as eating with them, and of certain foods reserved as sacrifices to ancestral and greater gods. The men alone could eat these things, because relative to women they had tabu status, which made them kinds of domestic chiefs. But onboard the ships, women tasted the forbidden fruits as well as tabu pork, and in the company of men – the British seamen.

To appropriate Bateson's bon mot: *plus c'est la même chose, plus ça change.* Chiefs, men, and women were all following their traditional self-conceptions

119

and interests. Yet, in this particular pragmatic situation, the entailed definitions of social and ritual categories were revalued and relationships between
them transformed. The effects of practice, returning then to structure, would
have subsequent meaningful impact on the historic course. Eating with the
British men, the Hawaiian women polluted them. The English in general
lost their divine status, and a cultural separation set in that was not supposed
in the initial interpretation of the foreigners as Hawaiian gods. Moreover,
when certain chiefs finally decided in 1819 to abolish the tabu system
by eating with women – an apparently spectacular "cultural revolution," as
anthropologists have called it, undertaken before the first Christian
missionary set foot on the Islands – they were merely ratifying an accomplished fact. The chiefs found many commoners ready to join them, since
people had been doing the same for decades.

As I say, the paradigm here suggested does not really require such unusual
circumstances. The deployment of received cultural understandings to
specific worldly contexts always harbors the possibility that things will never
again be the same – precisely because the "objective" things, as well as the
social persons, thus represented in the terms of a conventional reason also
have their own reasons. The world is under no obligation to correspond to
the categories by which it is thought – even if, as Durkheim said, it can only
exist for people in the way that it is thought. Thus, in the dialectic of culture-
as-constituted and culture-as-lived, we also discover some possibility of
reconciling the most profound antinomy of social science theory, that between
structure and practice: reconciling them, that is, in the only way presently
justifiable – as a symbolic process.

NOTE

Originally published in William Kruskal, ed., *The Social Sciences: Their Nature and Uses*
(Chicago: University of Chicago Press, 1982). © 1982 The University of Chicago Press.

6

THE CONSTITUTION OF SOCIETY: OUTLINE OF THE THEORY OF STRUCTURATION

Elements of the theory of structuration

Anthony Giddens

Like Bourdieu, British sociologist Anthony Giddens seeks to make social practices ordered across space and time, rather than the experiences of individual actors or any kind of societal totality, the focus of social scientific investigation. Unlike Bourdieu, who stresses the unconscious and, in that sense determinative, source of behavior in the generative schemes produced by the form of social conditioning he calls habitus, Giddens emphasizes the productive role that actors themselves play in the maintenance and recreation of social codes and norms. For Giddens, structure teaches agents who help to form the structure, in a circular process that Giddens terms "structuration."

A fundamental aspect of the concept of "structuration" is Giddens's claim on behalf of the "duality of structure," according to which "the structural properties of social systems are both medium and outcome of the practice they recursively organize." Human practices and activities are seen as "recursive," that is to say "they are not brought into being by social actors, but continually recreated by them via the very means whereby they express themselves as actors." It is through such practices of resignification (of the recreation of underlying codes) that structure itself exists and is transformed. Thus, rather than seeing social structure as an unconscious generative scheme of behavior, as in effect Bourdieu does, Giddens emphasizes the active, practical consciousness that social actors deploy in the course of their lives; their practical use of society's structural components (norms, rules, institutions) thus effectively "constitutes" society.

By insisting on the "duality" of structure and the recursive character inherent in its social reproduction, Giddens is able to preserve some principal insights of a semiotic concept of culture while loosening its totalizing and determining hold on individual practices. Structure persists as a set of "rules and resources," "procedures of action," and aspects of praxis, but exists as such only in a virtual state, made palpable and thus socially real through their enactment by human actors. Structure, in that sense, effectively comes into being and is sustained through the continuity generated by the social practices of human actors; their practical activities embody and enact, but never perfectly replicate its constituent components. This is because Giddens accepts a hermeneutic (interpretive) starting point for the theory of structuration, one that considers the discursive formulation of a rule to be "already an interpretation of it that may in and of itself alter the form of its application," making structure itself a process (hence "structuration") rather than a stable scheme or system.

Together with Bourdieu's theory of practice, and functioning in part as a modification of the more structuralist tenor of his work, Giddens's theory of structuration forms the basis for a rethinking of linguistic turn historiography by de-emphasizing, without abandoning, its semiotic character while highlighting questions of practical consciousness, agency, intentionality, and the power of social actors to reflect on their experiences and thus to perform consciously and knowledgeably in the conduct of their everyday life.

* * *

In offering a preliminary exposition of the main concepts of structuration theory it will be useful to begin from the divisions which have separated functionalism (including systems theory) and structuralism on the one hand from hermeneutics and the various forms of 'interpretative sociology' on the other. Functionalism and structuralism have some notable similarities, in spite of the otherwise marked contrasts that exist between them. Both tend to express a naturalistic standpoint, and both are inclined towards objectivism. Functionalist thought, from Comte onwards, has looked particularly towards biology as the science providing the closest and most compatible model for social science. Biology has been taken to provide a guide to conceptualizing the structure and the functioning of social systems and to analysing processes of evolution via mechanisms of adaptation. Structuralist thought, especially in the writings of Lévi-Strauss, has been hostile to evolutionism and free from biological analogies. Here the homology between social and natural science is primarily a cognitive one in so far as each is supposed to express similar features of the overall constitution of mind. Both structuralism and functionalism strongly emphasize the preeminence of the social whole over its individual parts (i.e., its constituent actors, human subjects).

In hermeneutic traditions of thought, of course, the social and natural sciences are regarded as radically discrepant. Hermeneutics has been the home of that 'humanism' to which structuralists have been so strongly and persistently opposed. In hermeneutic thought, such as presented by Dilthey, the gulf between subject and social object is at its widest. Subjectivity is the preconstituted centre of the experience of culture and history and as such provides the basic foundation of the social or human sciences. Outside the realm of subjective experience, and alien to it, lies the material world, governed by impersonal relations of cause and effect. Whereas for those

122

schools of thought which tend towards naturalism subjectivity has been regarded as something of a mystery, or almost a residual phenomenon, for hermeneutics it is the world of nature which is opaque – which, unlike human activity, can be grasped only from the outside. In interpretative sociologies, action and meaning are accorded primacy in the explication of human conduct; structural concepts are not notably prominent, and there is not much talk of constraint. For functionalism and structuralism, however, structure (in the divergent senses attributed to that concept) has primacy over action, and the constraining qualities of structure are strongly accentuated.

The differences between these perspectives on social science have often been taken to be epistemological, whereas they are in fact also ontological. What is at issue is how the concepts of action, meaning and subjectivity should be specified and how they might relate to notions of structure and constraint. If interpretative sociologies are founded, as it were, upon an imperialism of the subject, functionalism and structuralism propose an imperialism of the social object. One of my principal ambitions in the formulation of structuration theory is to put an end to each of these empire-building endeavours. The basic domain of study of the social sciences, according to the theory of structuration, is neither the experience of the individual actor, nor the existence of any form of societal totality, but social practices ordered across space and time. Human social activities, like some self-reproducing items in nature, are recursive. That is to say, they are not brought into being by social actors but continually recreated by them via the very means whereby they express themselves *as* actors. In and through their activities agents reproduce the conditions that make these activities possible. However, the sort of 'knowledgeability' displayed in nature, in the form of coded programmes, is distant from the cognitive skills displayed by human agents. It is in the conceptualizing of human knowledgeability and its involvement in action that I seek to appropriate some of the major contributions of interpretative sociologies. In structuration theory a hermeneutic starting-point is accepted in so far as it is acknowledged that the description of human activities demands a familiarity with the forms of life expressed in those activities.

It is the specifically reflexive form of the knowledgeability of human agents that is most deeply involved in the recursive ordering of social practices. Continuity of practices presumes reflexivity, but reflexivity in turn is possible only because of the continuity of practices that makes them distinctively 'the same' across space and time. 'Reflexivity' hence should be understood not merely as 'self-consciousness' but as the monitored character of the ongoing flow of social life. To be a human being is to be a purposive agent, who both has reasons for his or her activities and is able, if asked, to elaborate discursively upon those reasons (including lying about them). But terms such as 'purpose' or 'intention', 'reason', 'motive' and so on have to be treated with caution, since their usage in the philosophical literature has very often been associated with a hermeneutical voluntarism, and because they extricate human action from the contextuality of time-space. Human action occurs as a *durée*, a continuous flow of conduct, as does cognition. Purposive action is not composed of an aggregate or series of separate intentions, reasons and motives. Thus it is useful to speak of reflexivity as grounded in the continuous monitoring of action which human beings display and expect others to display. The reflexive monitoring of action depends upon rationalization, understood here as a process rather than a state and as inherently involved in the competence of agents. An ontology of time-space as constitutive of social practices is basic to the conception of structuration, which *begins* from temporality and thus, in one sense, 'history'.

This approach can draw only sparingly upon the analytical philosophy of action, as 'action' is ordinarily portrayed by most contemporary Anglo-American writers. 'Action' is not a combination of 'acts': 'acts' are constituted only by a discursive moment of attention to the *durée* of lived-through experience. Nor can 'action' be discussed in separation from the body, its mediations with the surrounding world and the coherence of an acting self. What I call a *stratification model* of the acting self involves treating the reflexive monitoring, rationalization and motivation of action as embedded sets of processes. The rationalization of action, referring to 'intentionality' as process, is, like the other two dimensions, a routine characteristic of human conduct, carried on in a taken-for-granted fashion. In circumstances of interaction – encounters and episodes – the reflexive monitoring of action typically, and again routinely, incorporates the monitoring of the setting of such interaction. As I shall indicate subsequently, this phenomenon is basic to the interpolation of action within the time-space relations of what I shall call co-presence. The rationalization of action, within the diversity of circumstances of interaction, is the principal basis upon which the generalized 'competence' of actors is evaluated by others. It should be clear, however, that the tendency of some philosophers to equate reasons with 'normative commitments' should be resisted: such commitments comprise only one sector of the rationalization of action. If this is not understood, we fail to understand that norms figure as 'factual' boundaries of social life, to which a variety of manipulative attitudes are possible. One aspect of such attitudes, although a relatively superficial one, is to be found in the commonplace observation that the reasons actors offer discursively for what they do may diverge from the rationalization of action as actually involved in the stream of conduct of those actors.

This circumstance has been a frequent source of worry to philosophers and observers of the social scene – for how can we be sure that people do not dissimulate concerning the reasons for their activities? But it is of relatively little interest compared with the wide 'grey areas' that exist between two strata of processes not accessible to the discursive consciousness of actors. The vast bulk of the 'stocks of knowledge', in Schutz's phrase, or what I prefer to call the *mutual knowledge* incorporated in encounters, is not directly accessible to the consciousness of actors. Most such knowledge is practical in character: it is inherent in the capability to 'go on' within the routines of social life. The line between discursive and practical consciousness is fluctuating and permeable, both in the experience of the individual agent and as regards comparisons between actors in different contexts of social activity. There is no bar between these, however, as there is between the unconscious and discursive consciousness. The unconscious includes those forms of cognition and impulsion which are either wholly repressed from consciousness or appear in consciousness only in distorted form. Unconscious motivational components of action, as psychoanalytic theory suggests, have an internal hierarchy of their own, a hierarchy which expresses the 'depth' of the life history of the individual actor. In saying this I do not imply an uncritical acceptance of the key theorems of Freud's writings. We should guard against two forms of reductionism which those writings suggest or foster. One is a reductive conception of institutions which, in seeking to show the founda-tion of institutions in the unconscious, fails to leave sufficient play for the operation of autonomous social forces. The second is a reductive theory of consciousness which, wanting to show how much of social life is governed by dark currents outside the scope of actors' awareness, cannot adequately grasp the level of control which agents are characteristically able to sustain reflexively over their conduct.

The agent, agency

The stratification model of the agent can be represented as in Figure 6.1. The reflexive monitoring of activity is a chronic feature of everyday action and involves the conduct not just of the individual but also of others. That is to say, actors not only monitor continuously the flow of their activities and expect others to do the same for their own; they also routinely monitor aspects, social and physical, of the contexts in which they move. By the ration-alization of action, I mean that actors – also routinely and for the most part without fuss – maintain a continuing 'theoretical understanding' of the grounds of their activity. As I have mentioned, having such an understanding should not be equated with the discursive giving of reasons for particular items of conduct, nor even with the capability of specifying such reasons discursively. However, it is expected by competent agents of others and is the main criterion of competence applied in day-to-day conduct – that actors will usually be able to explain most of what they do, if asked. [. . .]

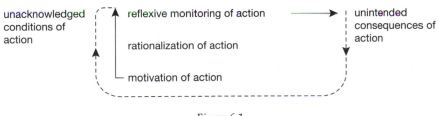

Figure 6.1

125

I distinguish the reflexive monitoring and rationalization of action from its motivation. If reasons refer to the grounds of action, motives refer to the wants which prompt it. However, motivation is not as directly bound up with the continuity of action as are its reflexive monitoring or rationalization. Motivation refers to potential for action rather than to the mode in which action is chronically carried on by the agent. Motives tend to have a direct purchase on action only in relatively unusual circumstances, situations which in some way break with the routine. For the most part motives supply overall plans or programmes – 'projects', in Schutz's term – within which a range of conduct is enacted. Much of our day-to-day conduct is not directly motivated.

While competent actors can nearly always report discursively about their intentions in, and reasons for, acting as they do, they cannot necessarily do so of their motives. Unconscious motivation is a significant feature of human conduct, although I shall later indicate some reservations about Freud's interpretation of the nature of the unconscious. The notion of practical consciousness is fundamental to structuration theory. It is that characteristic of the human agent or subject to which structuralism has been particularly blind. But so have other types of objectivist thought. Only in phenomenology and ethnomethodology, within sociological traditions, do we find detailed and subtle treatments of the nature of practical consciousness. Indeed, it is these schools of thought, together with ordinary language philosophy, which have been responsible for making clear the shortcomings of orthodox social scientific theories in this respect.

[. . .]

It has frequently been supposed that human agency can be defined only in terms of intentions. That is to say, for an item of behaviour to count as action, whoever perpetrates it must intend to do so, or else the behaviour in question is just a reactive response. The view derives some plausibility, perhaps, from the fact that there are some acts which cannot occur unless the agent intends them. Suicide is a case in point. [. . .] However, suicide is not typical of most human acts, in respect of intentions, in so far as it can be said to have occurred only when its perpetrator intended it to occur. Most acts do not have this characteristic.

Some philosophers have argued, however, that for an event in which a human being is involved to count as an example of agency, it is necessary at least that what the person does be intentional under some description, even if the agent is mistaken about that description. An officer on a submarine pulls a lever intending to change course but instead, having pulled the wrong lever, sinks the *Bismarck*. He has done something intentionally, albeit not what he imagined, but thus the *Bismarck* has been sunk through his agency. [. . .]

But even the view that for an event to count as an instance of agency, it must be intentional only under *some* description or another is wrong. It confuses the designation of agency with the giving of act-descriptions; and it mistakes the continued monitoring of an action which individuals carry

126

out with the defining properties of that action as such. Agency refers not to the intentions people have in doing things but to their capability of doing those things in the first place (which is why agency implies power: cf. the *Oxford English Dictionary* definition of an agent, as 'one who exerts power or produces an effect'). Agency concerns events of which an individual is the perpetrator, in the sense that the individual could, at any phase in a given sequence of conduct, have acted differently. Whatever happened would not have happened if that individual had not intervened. Action is a continuous process, a flow, in which the reflexive monitoring which the individual maintains is fundamental to the control of the body that actors ordinarily sustain throughout their day-to-day lives. I am the author of many things I do not intend to do, and may not want to bring about, but none the less *do*. Conversely, there may be circumstances in which I intend to achieve something, and do achieve it, although not directly through my agency. [. . .] But what is it to do something unintentionally? Is it different from bringing about consequences unintentionally? [. . .]

To understand what it is to do something unintentionally, we have first of all to be clear how 'intentional' should be understood. This concept I define as characterizing an act which its perpetrator knows, or believes, will have a particular quality or outcome and where such knowledge is utilized by the author of the act to achieve this quality or outcome. If the characterization of agency given above is correct, we have to separate out the question of what an agent 'does' from what is 'intended' or the intentional aspects of what is done. Agency refers to doing.

[. . .]

Philosophers have used up a great deal of ink attempting to analyse the nature of intentional activity. But from the point of view of the social sciences, it is hard to exaggerate the importance of the unintended consequences of intentional conduct. Merton has provided perhaps the classical discussion of the issue.[1] He points out, entirely correctly, that the study of unintended consequences is fundamental to the sociological enterprise. A given item of activity may have either (a) non-significant or (b) significant consequences; and either (c) singly significant consequences or (d) multiply significant consequences. What is judged 'significant' will depend upon the nature of the study being undertaken or the theory being developed.[2]

[. . .]

Agency and power

What is the nature of the logical connection between action and power? Although the ramifications of the issue are complex, the basic relation involved can easily be pointed to. To be able to 'act otherwise' means being able to intervene in the world, or to refrain from such intervention, with the effect of influencing a specific process or state of affairs. This presumes that to be an agent is to be able to deploy (chronically, in the flow of daily life) a range of causal powers, including that of influencing those deployed by others. Action depends upon the capability of the individual to 'make a difference' to a pre-existing state of affairs or course of events. An agent ceases to be such if he or she loses the capability to 'make a difference', that is, to exercise some sort of power. Many interesting cases for social analysis centre upon the margins of what can count as action – where the power of the individual is confined by a range of specifiable circumstances.[3] But it is of the first importance to recognize that circumstances of social constraint in which individuals 'have no choice' are not to be equated with the dissolution of action as such. To 'have no choice' does not mean that action has been replaced by reaction (in the way in which a person blinks when a rapid movement is made near the eyes). This might appear so obvious as not to need saying. But some very prominent schools of social theory, associated mainly with objectivism and with 'structural sociology', have not acknowledged the distinction. They have supposed that constraints operate like forces in nature, as if to 'have no choice' were equivalent to being driven irresistibly and uncomprehendingly by mechanical pressures [. . .].

Expressing these observations in another way, we can say that action logically involves power in the sense of transformative capacity. In this sense, the most all-embracing meaning of 'power', power is logically prior to subjectivity, to the constitution of the reflexive monitoring of conduct. It is worth emphasizing this because conceptions of power in the social sciences tend faithfully to reflect the dualism of subject and object referred to previously. Thus 'power' is very often defined in terms of intent or the will, as the capacity to achieve desired and intended outcomes. Other writers by contrast, including both Parsons and Foucault, see power as above all a property of society or the social community.

The point is not to eliminate one of these types of conception at the expense of the other, but to express their relation as a feature of the duality of structure. In my opinion, Bachrach and Baratz are right when, in their well-known discussion of the matter, they say that there are two 'faces' of power (not three, as Lukes declares).[4] They represent these as the capability of actors to enact decisions which they favour on the one hand and the 'mobilization of bias' that is built into institutions on the other. This is not wholly satisfactory because it preserves a zero-sum conception of power. Rather than using their terminology we can express the duality of structure in power relations in the following way. Resources (focused via signification and legitimation) are structured properties of social systems, drawn upon and reproduced by knowledgeable agents in the course of interaction. Power is not intrinsically connected to the achievement of sectional interests. In this conception the use of power characterizes not specific types of conduct but all action, and power is not itself a resource. Resources are media through which power is exercised, as a routine element of the instantiation of conduct in social reproduction. We should not conceive of the structures of domination built into social institutions as in some way grinding out 'docile bodies' who behave like the automata suggested by objectivist social science. Power within social systems which enjoy some continuity over time and space presumes regularized relations of autonomy and dependence between actors or collectivities in contexts of social interaction. But all forms of dependence offer some resources whereby those who are subordinate can influence the activities of their superiors. This is what I call the *dialectic of control* in social systems.

Structure, structuration

Let me now move to the core of structuration theory: the concepts of 'structure', 'system' and 'duality of structure'. The notion of structure (or 'social structure'), of course, is very prominent in the writings of most functionalist authors and has lent its name to the traditions of 'structuralism'. But in neither instance is this conceptualized in a fashion best suited to the demands of social theory. Functionalist authors and their critics have given much more attention to the idea of 'function' than to that of 'structure', and consequently the latter has tended to be used as a received notion. But there can be no doubt about how 'structure' is usually understood by functionalists and, indeed, by the vast majority of social analysts – as some kind of 'patterning' of social relations or social phenomena. This is often naively conceived of in terms of visual imagery, akin to the skeleton or morphology of an organism or to the girders of a building. Such conceptions are closely connected to the dualism of subject and social object: 'structure' here appears as 'external' to human action, as a source of constraint on the free initiative of the independently constituted subject. As conceptualized in structuralist and post-structuralist thought, on the other hand, the notion of structure is more interesting. Here it is characteristically thought of not as a patterning of presences but as an intersection of presence and absence; underlying codes have to be inferred from surface manifestations.

These two ideas of structure might seem at first sight to have nothing to do with one another, but in fact each relates to important aspects of the structuring of social relations, aspects which, in the theory of structuration, are grasped by recognizing a differentiation between the concepts of 'structure' and 'system'. In analysing social relations we have to acknowledge both a syntagmatic dimension, the patterning of social relations in time-space involving the reproduction of situated practices, and a paradigmatic dimension, involving a virtual order of 'modes of structuring' recursively implicated in such reproduction. In structuralist traditions there is usually ambiguity over whether structures refer to a matrix of admissible transformations within a set or to rules of transformation governing the matrix. I treat structure, in its most elemental meaning at least, as referring to such rules (and resources). It is misleading, however, to speak of 'rules of transformation' because all rules are inherently transformational. Structure thus refers, in social analysis, to the structuring properties allowing the 'binding' of time-space in social systems, the properties which make it possible for discernibly similar social practices to exist across varying spans of time and space and which lend them 'systemic' form. To say that structure is a 'virtual order' of transformative relations means that social systems, as reproduced social practices, do not have 'structures' but rather exhibit 'structural properties' and that structure exists, as time-space presence, only in its instantiations in such practices and as memory traces orienting the conduct of knowledgeable human agents. This does not prevent us from conceiving of structural properties as hierarchically organized in terms of the time-space extension of the practices they recursively organize. The most deeply embedded structural properties, implicated in the reproduction of societal totalities, I call *structural principles*. Those practices which have the greatest time-space extension within such totalities can be referred to as *institutions*.

To speak of structure as 'rules' and resources, and of structures as isolable sets of rules and resources, runs a distinct risk of misinterpretation because of certain dominant uses of 'rules' in the philosophical literature.

1   Rules are often thought of in connection with games, as formalized prescriptions. The rules implicated in the reproduction of social systems are not generally like this. Even those which are codified as laws are characteristically subject to a far greater diversity of contestations than the rules of games. Although the use of the rules of games such as chess, etc. as prototypical of the rule-governed properties of social systems is frequently associated with Wittgenstein, more relevant is what Wittgenstein has to say about children's play as exemplifying the routines of social life.

2   Rules are frequently treated in the singular, as if they could be related to specific instances or pieces of conduct. But this is highly misleading if regarded as analogous to the operation of social life, in which practices are sustained in conjunction with more or less loosely organized sets.

3   Rules cannot be conceptualized apart from resources, which refer to the modes whereby transformative relations are actually incorporated into the production and reproduction of social practices. Structural properties thus express forms of *domination* and *power*.

4   Rules imply 'methodical procedures' of social interaction, as Garfinkel in particular has made clear. Rules typically intersect with practices in the contextuality of situated encounters: the range of 'ad hoc' considerations which he identifies are chronically involved with the instantiation of rules and are fundamental to the form of those rules. Every competent social actor, it should be added, is *ipso facto* a social theorist on the level of discursive consciousness and a 'methodological specialist' on the levels of both discursive and practical consciousness.

5   Rules have two aspects to them, and it is essential to distinguish these conceptually, since a number of philosophical writers (such as Winch) have tended to conflate them. Rules relate on the one hand to the

constitution of *meaning*, and on the other to the *sanctioning* of modes of social conduct.

I have introduced the above usage of 'structure' to help break with the fixed or mechanical character which the term tends to have in orthodox socio-logical usage. The concepts of system and structuration do much of the work that 'structure' is ordinarily called upon to perform. In proposing a usage of 'structure' that might appear at first sight to be remote from conven-tional interpretations of the term, I do not mean to hold that looser versions be abandoned altogether. 'Society', 'culture' and a range of other forms of sociological terminology can have double usages that are embarrassing only in contexts where a difference is made in the nature of the statements employing them. Similarly, I see no particular objection to speaking of 'class structure', 'the structure of the industrialized societies' and so on, where these terms are meant to indicate in a general way relevant institutional features of a society or range of societies.

One of the main propositions of structuration theory is that the rules and resources drawn upon in the production and reproduction of social action are at the same time the means of system reproduction (the duality of structure). But how is one to interpret such a claim? In what sense is it the case that when I go about my daily affairs my activities incorporate and reproduce, say, the overall institutions of modern capitalism? What rules are being invoked here in any case? Consider the following possible instances of what rules are:

1 'The rule defining checkmate in chess is . . .';
2 A formula: $an = n^2 + n - 1$;
3 'As a rule R gets up at 6.00 every day';
4 'It is a rule that all workers must clock in at 8.00 a.m.'

Many other examples could of course be offered, but these will serve in the present context. In usage (3) 'rule' is more or less equivalent to habit or routine. The sense of 'rule' here is fairly weak, since it does not usually presuppose some sort of underlying precept that the individual is following or any sanction which applies to back up that precept; it is simply something that the person habitually does. Habit is part of routine, and I shall strongly emphasize the importance of routine in social life. 'Rules', as I understand them, certainly impinge upon numerous aspects of routine practice, but a routine practice is not as such a rule.

Cases (1) and (4) have seemed to many to represent two types of rule, constitutive and regulative. To explain the rule governing checkmate in chess is to say something about what goes into the very making of chess as a game. The rule that workers must clock in at a certain hour, on the other hand, does not help define what work is; it specifies how work is to be carried on. As Searle puts it, regulative rules can usually be paraphrased in the form

'Do X', or 'If Y, do X.' Some constitutive rules will have this character, but most will have the form 'X counts as Y', or 'X counts as Y in context C'.[5] That there is something suspect in this distinction, as referring to two types of rule, is indicated by the etymological clumsiness of the term 'regulative rule'. After all, the word 'regulative' already implies 'rule': its dictionary definition is 'control by rules'. I would say of (1) and (4) that they express two aspects of rules rather than two variant types of rule. (1) is certainly part of what chess is, but for those who play chess it has sanctioning or 'regulative' properties; it refers to aspects of play that must be observed. But (4) also has constitutive aspects. It does not perhaps enter into the definition of what 'work' is, but it does enter into that of a concept like 'industrial bureaucracy'. What (1) and (4) direct our attention to are two aspects of rules: their role in the constitution of meaning, and their close connection with sanctions.

Usage (2) might seem the least promising as a way of conceptualizing 'rule' that has any relation to 'structure'. In fact, I shall argue, it is the most germane of all of them. I do not mean to say that social life can be reduced to a set of mathematical principles which is very far from what I have in mind. I mean that it is in the nature of formulae that we can best discover what is the most analytically effective sense of 'rule' in social theory. The formula $an = n^2 + n - 1$ is from Wittgenstein's example of number games.[6] One person writes down a sequence of numbers; a second works out the formula supplying the numbers which follow. What is a formula of this kind, and what is it to understand one? To understand the formula is not to utter it. For someone could utter it and not understand the series; alternatively, it is possible to understand the series without being able to give verbal expression to the formula. Understanding is not a mental process accompanying the solving of the puzzle that the sequence of numbers presents – at least, it is not a mental process in the sense in which the hearing of a tune or a spoken sentence is. It is simply being able to apply the formula in the right context and way in order to continue the series.

A formula is a generalizable procedure – generalizable because it applies over a range of contexts and occasions, a procedure because it allows for the methodical continuation of an established sequence. Are linguistic rules like this? I think they are – much more than they are like the sorts of rule of which Chomsky speaks. And this seems also consonant with Wittgenstein's arguments, or a possible construal of them at any rate. Wittgenstein remarks, 'To understand a language means to be a master of a technique.'[7] This can be read to mean that language use is primarily methodological and that rules of language are methodically applied procedures implicated in the practical activities of day-to-day life. This aspect of language is very important, although not often given much prominence by most followers of Wittgenstein. Rules which are 'stated', as (1) and (4) above, are interpretations of activity as well as relating to specific sorts of activities: all codified rules take this form, since they give verbal expression to what is supposed to be done. But rules are procedures of action, aspects of *praxis*. It is by reference to this that Wittgenstein resolves what he first of all sets up as a 'paradox' of rules and rule-following. This is that no course of action can be said to be guided by a rule because every course of action can be made to accord with that rule. However, if such is the case, it is also true that every course of action can be made to conflict with it. There is a misunderstanding here, a confusing of the interpretation or verbal expression of a rule with following the rule.[8]

Let us regard the rules of social life, then, as techniques or generalizable procedures applied in the enactment/reproduction of social practices. Formulated rules – those that are given verbal expression as canons of law, bureaucratic rules, rules of games and so on – are thus codified interpretations of rules rather than rules as such. They should be taken not as exemplifying rules in general but as specific types of formulated rules, which, by virtue of their overt formulation, take on various specific qualities.[9]

So far these considerations offer only a preliminary approach to the problem. How do formulae relate to the practices in which social actors engage, and what kinds of formulae are we most interested in for general purposes of social analysis? As regards the first part of the question, we can say that awareness of social rules, expressed first and foremost in practical consciousness, is the very core of that 'knowledgeability' which specifically characterizes human agents. As social actors, all human beings are highly 'learned' in respect of knowledge which they possess, and apply, in the production and reproduction of day-to-day social encounters; the vast bulk of such knowledge is practical rather than theoretical in character. As Schutz and many others have pointed out, actors employ typified schemes (formulae) in the course of their daily activities to negotiate routinely the situations of social life. Knowledge of procedure, or mastery of the techniques of 'doing' social activity, is by definition methodological. That is to say, such knowledge does not specify all the situations which an actor might meet with, nor could it do so; rather, it provides for the generalized capacity to respond to and influence an indeterminate range of social circumstances.

Those types of rule which are of most significance for social theory are locked into the reproduction of institutionalized practices, that is, practices most deeply sedimented in time-space. The main characteristics of rules relevant to general questions of social analysis can be described as follows:

intensive	tacit	informal	weakly sanctioned
:	:	:	:
shallow	discursive	formalized	strongly sanctioned

By rules that are intensive in nature, I mean formulae that are constantly invoked in the course of day-to-day activities, that enter into the structuring of much of the texture of everyday life. Rules of language are of this character. But so also, for example, are the procedures utilized by actors in organizing turn-taking in conversations or in interaction. They may be contrasted with rules which, although perhaps wide in scope, have only a superficial impact upon much of the texture of social life. The contrast is an important one, if only because it is commonly taken for granted among social analysts that the more abstract rules – e.g., codified law – are the most influential in the structuring of social activity. I would propose, however, that many seemingly trivial procedures followed in daily life have a more profound influence upon the generality of social conduct. The remaining categories should be more or less self-explanatory. Most of the rules implicated in the production and reproduction of social practices are only tacitly grasped by actors: they know how to 'go on'. *The discursive formulation of a rule is already an interpretation of it*, and, as I have noted, may in and of itself alter the form of its application. Among rules that are not just discursively formulated but are formally codified, the type case is that of laws. Laws, of course, are among the most strongly sanctioned types of social rules and in modern societies have formally prescribed gradations of retribution. However, it would be a serious mistake to underestimate the strength of informally applied sanctions in respect of a variety of mundane daily practices.

[. . .]

I distinguish 'structure' as a generic term from 'structures' in the plural and both from the 'structural properties of social systems'. 'Structure' refers not only to rules implicated in the production and reproduction of social systems but also to resources (about which I have so far not said much but will do so shortly). As ordinarily used in the social sciences, 'structure' tends to be employed with the more enduring aspects of social systems in mind, and I do not want to lose this connotation. The most important aspects of structure are rules and resources recursively involved in institutions. Institutions by definition are the more enduring features of social life. In speaking of the structural properties of social systems I mean their institutionalized features, giving 'solidity' across time and space. I use the concept of 'structures' to get at relations of transformation and mediation which are the 'circuit switches' underlying observed conditions of system reproduction.

Let me now answer the question I originally posed: in what manner can it be said that the conduct of individual actors reproduces the structural properties of larger collectivities? The question is both easier and more difficult to answer than it appears. On a logical level, the answer to it is nothing more than a truism. That is to say, while the continued existence of large collectivities or societies evidently does not depend upon the activities of any particular individual, such collectivities or societies manifestly would cease to be if all the agents involved disappeared. On a substantive level, the answer to the question depends upon issues yet to be broached – those concerning the mechanisms of integration of different types of societal totality. It is always the case that the day-to-day activity of social actors draws upon and reproduces structural features of wider social systems. But 'societies' – as I shall make clear – are not necessarily unified collectivities. 'Social reproduction' must not be equated with the consolidation of social cohesion. The location of actors and of collectivities in different sectors or regions of more encompassing social systems strongly influences the impact of even their habitual conduct upon the integration of societal totalities. Here we reach the limits of linguistic examples which might be used to illustrate the concept of the duality of structure. Considerable illumination of problems of social analysis can be derived from studying the recursive qualities of speech and language. When I produce a grammatical utterance, I draw upon the same syntactical rules as those that utterance helps to produce. But I speak the 'same' language as the other speakers in my language community; we all share the same rules and linguistic practices, give or take a range of relatively minor variations. Such is not necessarily the case with the structural properties of social systems in general. But this is not a problem to do with the concept of the duality of structure as such. It is to do with how social systems, especially 'societies', should be conceptualized.

The duality of structure

Structure(s)	System(s)	Structuration
Rules and resources, or sets of transformation relations, organized as properties of social systems	Reproduced relations between actors or collectivities, organized as regular social practices	Conditions governing the continuity or transmutation of structures, and therefore the reproduction of social systems

Let me summarize the argument thus far. Structure, as recursively organized sets of rules and resources, is out of time and space, save in its instantiations and co-ordination as memory traces, and is marked by an 'absence of the subject'. The social systems in which structure is recursively implicated, on the contrary, comprise the situated activities of human agents, reproduced across time and space. Analysing the structuration of social systems means studying the modes in which such systems, grounded in the knowledgeable activities of situated actors who draw upon rules and resources in the diversity of action contexts, are produced and reproduced in interaction. Crucial to the idea of structuration is the theorem of the duality of structure, which is logically implied in the arguments portrayed above. The constitution of agents and structures are not two independently given sets of phenomena, a dualism, but represent a duality. According to the notion of the duality of structure, the structural properties of social systems are both medium and outcome of the practices they recursively organize. Structure is not 'external' to individuals: as memory traces, and as instantiated in social practices, it is in a certain sense more 'internal' than exterior to their activities in a Durkheimian sense. Structure is not to be equated with constraint but is always both constraining and enabling. This, of course, does not prevent the structured properties of social systems from stretching away, in time and

135

space, beyond the control of any individual actors. Nor does it compromise the possibility that actors' own theories of the social systems which they help to constitute and reconstitute in their activities may reify those systems. The reification of social relations, or the discursive 'naturalization' of the historically contingent circumstances and products of human action, is one of the main dimensions of ideology in social life.

Even the crudest forms of reified thought, however, leave untouched the fundamental significance of the knowledgeability of human actors. For knowledgeability is founded less upon discursive than practical consciousness. The knowledge of social conventions, of oneself and of other human beings, presumed in being able to 'go on' in the diversity of contexts of social life is detailed and dazzling. All competent members of society are vastly skilled in the practical accomplishments of social activities and are expert 'sociologists'. The knowledge they possess is not incidental to the persistent patterning of social life but is integral to it. This stress is absolutely essential if the mistakes of functionalism and structuralism are to be avoided, mistakes which, suppressing or discounting agents' reasons – the rationalization of action as chronically involved in the structuration of social practices – look for the origins of their activities in phenomena of which these agents are ignorant.[10] But it is equally important to avoid tumbling into the opposing error of hermeneutic approaches and of various versions of phenomenology, which tend to regard society as the plastic creation of human subjects. Each of these is an illegitimate form of reduction, deriving from a failure adequately to conceptualize the duality of structure. According to structuration theory, the moment of the production of action is also one of reproduction in the contexts of the day-to-day enactment of social life. This is so even during the most violent upheavals or most radical forms of social change. It is not accurate to see the structural properties of social systems as 'social products' because this tends to imply that pre-constituted actors somehow come together to create them.[11] In reproducing structural properties to repeat a phrase used earlier, agents also reproduce the conditions that make such action possible. Structure has no existence independent of the knowledge that agents have about what they do in their day-to-day activity. Human agents always know what they are doing on the level of discursive consciousness under some description. However, what they do may be quite unfamiliar under other descriptions, and they may know little of the ramified consequences of the activities in which they engage.

The duality of structure is always the main grounding of continuities in social reproduction across time-space. It in turn presupposes the reflexive monitoring of agents in, and as constituting, the *durée* of daily social activity. But human knowledgeability is always bounded. The flow of action continually produces consequences which are unintended by actors, and these unintended consequences also may form unacknowledged conditions of action in a feedback fashion. Human history is created by intentional activities but is not an intended project; it persistently eludes efforts to bring it

136

under conscious direction. However, such attempts are continually made by human beings, who operate under the threat and the promise of the circumstance that they are the only creatures who make their 'history' in cognizance of that fact.

[. . .]

Forms of institution

The division of rules into modes of signifying or meaning constitution and normative sanctions, together with the concept of resources – fundamental to the conceptualization of power – carries various implications which need to be spelled out. What I call the 'modalities' of structuration serve to clarify the main dimensions of the duality of structure in interaction, relating the knowledgeable capacities of agents to structural features. Actors draw upon the modalities of structuration in the reproduction of systems of interaction, by the same token reconstituting their structural properties. The communication of meaning in interaction, it should be stressed, is separable only analytically from the operation of normative sanctions. This is obvious, for example, in so far as language use is itself sanctioned by the very nature of its 'public' character.[12] The very identification of acts or of aspects of interaction – their accurate description, as grounded hermeneutically in the capability of an observer to 'go on' in a form of life – implies the interlacing of meaning, normative elements and power. This is most evident in the not infrequent contexts of social life where what social phenomena 'are', how they are aptly described, is contested. Awareness of such contestation, of divergent and overlapping characterizations of activity, is an essential part of 'knowing a form of life' [. . .].

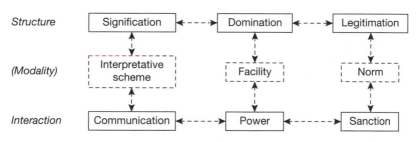

Figure 6.2

The dimensions of the duality of structure are portrayed in Figure 6.2.[13] Human actors are not only able to monitor their activities and those of others in the regularity of day-to-day conduct; they are also able to 'monitor that monitoring' in discursive consciousness. 'Interpretative schemes' are the modes of typification incorporated within actors' stocks of knowledge, applied reflexively in the sustaining of communication. The stocks of knowledge which actors draw upon in the production and reproduction of interaction are the same as those whereby they are able to make accounts, offer reasons, etc.[14] The communication of meaning, as with all aspects of the contextuality of action, does not have to be seen merely as happening 'in' time-space. Agents routinely incorporate temporal and spatial features of encounters in processes of meaning constitution. Communication, as a general element of interaction, is a more inclusive concept than communicative intent (i.e. what an actor 'means' to say or do). There are once more two forms of reductionism to be avoided here. Some philosophers have tried to derive over-all theories of meaning or communication from communicative intent; others, by contrast, have supposed that communicative intent is at best marginal to the constitution of the meaningful qualities of interaction, 'meaning' being governed by the structural ordering of sign systems. In the theory of structuration, however, these are regarded as of equivalent interest and importance, aspects of a duality rather than a mutually exclusive dualism.

The idea of 'accountability' in everyday English gives cogent expression to the intersection of interpretative schemes and norms. To be 'accountable' for one's activities is both to explicate the reasons for them and to supply the normative grounds whereby they may be 'justified'. Normative components of interaction always centre upon relations between the rights and obligations 'expected' of those participating in a range of interaction contexts. Formal codes of conduct, as, for example, those enshrined in law (in contemporary societies at least), usually express some sort of claimed symmetry between rights and obligations, the one being the justification of the other. But no such symmetry necessarily exists in practice, a phenomenon which it is important to emphasize, since both the 'normative functionalism' of Parsons and the 'structuralist Marxism' of Althusser exaggerates the degree to which normative obligations are 'internalized' by the members of societies. Neither standpoint incorporates a theory of action which recognizes human beings as knowledgeable agents, reflexively monitoring the flow of interaction with one another. When social systems are conceived of primarily from the point of view of the 'social object', the emphasis comes to be placed upon the pervasive influence of a normatively co-ordinated legitimate order as an overall determinant or 'programmer' of social conduct. Such a perspective masks the fact that the normative elements of social systems are contingent claims which have to be sustained and 'made to count' through the effective mobilization of sanctions in the contexts of actual encounters. Normative sanctions express structural asymmetries of domination, and the relations of those nominally subject to them may be of various sorts other than expressions of the commitments those norms supposedly engender.

Concentration upon the analysis of the structural properties of social systems, it should be stressed, is a valid procedure only if it is recognized as placing an *epoché* upon – holding in suspension – reflexively monitored social conduct. Under such an *epoché* we may distinguish three structural dimensions of social systems: signification, domination and legitimation.

Structure(s)	Theoretical domain	Institutional order
Signification	Theory of coding	Symbolic orders/modes of discourse
Domination	Theory of resource authorization Theory of resource allocation	Political institutions Economic institutions
Legitimation	Theory of normative regulation	Legal institutions

The connotations of the analysis of these structural properties are indicated in the table above. The theory of coding presumed in the study of structures of signification must look to the extraordinary advances in semiotics which have been pioneered in recent decades. At the same time we have to guard against the association of semiotics with structuralism and with the short-comings of the latter in respect of the analysis of human agency. Signs 'exist' only as the medium and outcome of communicative processes in interaction. Structuralist conceptions of language, in common with similar discussions of legitimation, tend to take signs as the given properties of speaking and writing rather than examining their recursive grounding in the communication of meaning.

Structures of signification always have to be grasped in connection with domination and legitimation. Once more this bears upon the pervasive influence of power in social life. [. . .] Thus – and here we must also reckon with the implications of the writings of Foucault – power is not an inherently noxious phenomenon, not just the capacity to 'say no'; nor can domination be 'transcended' in some kind of putative society of the future, as has been the characteristic aspiration of at least some strands of socialist thought.

What are the connotations of the claim that the semantic has priority over the semiotic rather than vice versa? They can be spelled out, I think, through a comparison of structuralist and post-structuralist conceptions of meaning on the one hand, and that which can be derived from the later Wittgenstein on the other. The foundation of a theory of meaning in 'difference' in which, following Saussure, there are no 'positive values' leads almost inevitably to a view accentuating the primacy of the semiotic. The field of signs, the grids of meaning, are created by the ordered nature of differences which comprise codes. The 'retreat into the code' – whence it is difficult or impossible to re-emerge into the world of activity and event – is a characteristic tactic adopted by structuralist and post-structuralist authors. Such a retreat, however, is not necessary at all if we understand the relational character of the codes that generate meaning to be located in the ordering of social practices, in the very capacity to 'go on' in the multiplicity of contexts of social activity. This is a discovery which Wittgenstein himself surely made, albeit against a very different philosophical backdrop, when he abandoned some of the main parameters of his early writings. Whereas his earlier analysis of language and meaning terminates in paradox – a sort of Indian rope trick, pulling up the ladder after it has been climbed – his later view hugs the ground of routine social practices. Even the most complicated semiotic relations have a grounding in the semantic properties generated by the rule-governed properties of daily activities.

[. . .]

A reiteration of basic concepts[15]

It might be useful at this point to recapitulate some of the basic ideas contained in the preceding chapters. I shall summarize these as a number of points; taken together, they represent the aspects of structuration theory which impinge most generally upon problems of empirical research in the social sciences.

1 All human beings are knowledgeable agents. That is to say, all social actors know a great deal about the conditions and consequences of what they do in their day-to-day lives. Such knowledge is not wholly propositional in character, nor is it incidental to their activities. Knowledgeability embedded in practical consciousness exhibits an extraordinary complexity – a complexity that often remains completely unexplored in orthodox sociological approaches, especially those associated with objectivism. Actors are also ordinarily able discursively to describe what they do and their reasons for doing it. However, for the most part these faculties are geared to the flow of day-to-day conduct. The rationalization of conduct becomes the discursive offering of reasons only if individuals are asked by others why they acted as they did. Such questions are normally posed, of course, only if the activity concerned is in some way puzzling – if it appears either to flout convention or to depart from the habitual modes of conduct of a particular person.

2 The knowledgeability of human actors is always bounded on the one hand by the unconscious and on the other by unacknowledged conditions/ unintended consequences of action. Some of the most important tasks of social science are to be found in the investigation of these boundaries, the signficance of unintended consequences for system reproduction and the ideological connotations which such boundaries have.

3 The study of day-to-day life is integral to analysis of the reproduction of institutionalized practices. Day-to-day life is bound up with the repetitive character of reversible time – with paths traced through time-space and associated with the constraining and enabling features of the body. However, day-to-day life should not be treated as the 'foundation' upon which the more ramified connections of social life are built. Rather, these more far-flung connections should be understood in terms of an interpretation of social and system integration.

4 Routine, psychologically linked to the minimizing of unconscious sources of anxiety, is the predominant form of day-to-day social activity. Most

daily practices are not directly motivated. Routinized practices are the prime expression of the duality of structure in respect of the continuity of social life. In the enactment of routines agents sustain a sense of ontological security.

5   The study of context, or of the contextualities of interaction, is inherent in the investigation of social reproduction. 'Context' involves the following: (a) the time-space boundaries (usually having symbolic or physical markers) around interaction strips; (b) the co-presence of actors, making possible the visibility of a diversity of facial expressions, bodily gestures, linguistic and other media of communication; (c) awareness and use of these phenomena reflexively to influence or control the flow of interaction.

6   Social identities, and the position-practice relations associated with them, are 'markers' in the virtual time-space of structure. They are associated with normative rights, obligations and sanctions which, within specific collectivities, form roles. The use of standardized markers, especially to do with the bodily attributes of age and gender, is fundamental in all societies, notwithstanding large cross-cultural variations which can be noted.

7   No unitary meaning can be given to 'constraint' in social analysis. Constraints associated with the structural properties of social systems are only one type among several others characteristic of human social life.

8   Among the structural properties of social systems, structural principles are particularly important, since they specify overall types of society. It is one of the main emphases of structuration theory that the degree of closure of societal totalities – and of social systems in general – is widely variable. There are degrees of 'systemness' in societal totalities, as in other less or more inclusive forms of social system. It is essential to avoid the assumption that what a 'society' is can be easily defined, a notion which comes from an era dominated by nation-states with clear-cut boundaries that usually conform in a very close way to the administrative purview of centralized governments. Even in nation-states, of course, there are a variety of social forms which cross-cut societal boundaries.

9   The study of power cannot be regarded as a second-order consideration in the social sciences. Power cannot be tacked on, as it were, after the more basic concepts of social science have been formulated. There is no more elemental concept than that of power. However, this does not mean that the concept of power is more essential than any other, as is supposed in those versions of social science which have come under a Nietzschean influence. Power is one of several primary concepts of social science, all clustered around the relations of action and structure. Power is the means of getting things done and, as such, directly implied in human action. It is a mistake to treat power as inherently divisive, but there is no doubt that some of the most bitter conflicts in social life are accurately seen as 'power struggles'. Such struggles can be regarded as to do with efforts

to subdivide resources which yield modalities of control in social systems. By 'control' I mean the capability that some actors, groups or types of actors have of influencing the circumstances of action of others. In power struggles the dialectic of control always operates, although what use agents in subordinate positions can make of the resources open to them differs; very substantially between different social contexts.

10 There is no mechanism of social organization or social reproduction identified by social analysts which lay actors cannot also get to know about and actively incorporate into what they do. In very many instances the 'findings' of sociologists are such only to those not in the contexts of activity of the actors studied. Since actors do what they do for reasons, they are naturally likely to be disconcerted if told by sociological observers that what they do derives from factors that somehow act externally to them. Lay objections to such 'findings' may thus have a very sound basis. Reification is by no means purely characteristic of lay thought.

NOTES

1 Merton, however, favours the term, 'unanticipated' rather than unintended consequences. In my analysis 'intention' presumes knowledge of the likely consequences of action and therefore anticipation. Of course, one can anticipate that something will happen without intending it to happen, but one cannot intend something to happen without anticipating that it might happen. R. K. Merton, 'The unanticipated consequences of purposive social action', *American Sociological Review*, vol. 1, 1936; *idem*, 'Manifest and latent functions', in *Social Theory and Social Structure* (Glencoe, IL: Free Press, 1963).

2 Merton, 'Manifest and latent functions', p. 51.

3 For a further development of this point, see 'Power, the dialectic of control and class structuration', in Anthony Giddens and Gavin Mackenzie, *Social Class and The Division of Labour* (Cambridge: Cambridge University Press, 1982).

4 Peter Bachrach and Morton S. Baratz, 'The two faces of power', *American Political Science Review*, vol. 56, 1962; *Power and Poverty* (New York: Oxford University Press, 1970); Steven Lukes, *Power, a Radical View* (London: Macmillan, 1974). For further discussion of these points, cf. *Central Problems in Social Theory* (London, Berkeley: University of California Press, 1979), pp. 88–94.

5 John R. Searle, *Speech Acts* (Cambridge: Cambridge University Press, 1969), pp. 34–5.

6 Ludwig Wittgenstein, *Philosophical Investigations* (Oxford: Blackwell, 1972), p. 59.

7 Ibid., p. 81.

8 Ibid.

9 Ibid.

10 Cf. Roy Bhaskar, *The Possibility of Naturalism* (Brighton: Harvester, 1979), chapter 2.

11 Ibid., p. 48.

12 Cf. Paul Ziff, *Semantic Analysis* (Ithaca, NY: Cornell University Press, 1960).

13 For this style of representing these relations I am indebted to Derek Gregory; see his *Regional Transformation and Industrial Revolution* (London: Macmillan, 1982), p. 17.

14 Peter Marsh et al., *The Rules of Disorder* (London: Routledge, 1978), p. 15 and *passim*.

15 [This final section was taken from pp. 281–4 of Giddens's original text.]

7

A THEORY OF STRUCTURE

Duality, agency and transformation

William H. Sewell, Jr.

William H. Sewell, Jr., Professor of Political Science and History, interrogates the concept of "structure" that has been in common use among social scientists and structuralists alike, including the linguistic structuralism of Saussure that informs the "linguistic turn." In his opinion, the most fundamental problem with the traditional meanings and uses assigned to "structure" is that they have tended to assume a far too rigid causal determinism in social life, whether from "below," in the form of economic determinism, or from "above," in the form of linguistic determinism. In both instances, an overly systematic account of the operation of structure tends to diminish a belief in the efficacy of human action, or agency, and fails to account for processes of change over time, or historical transformation. Drawing on, while at the same time modifying, the concepts of structure proposed by writers such as Anthony Giddens and Pierre Bourdieu, Sewell agues on behalf of a concept of structure that makes room for the play of human agency; creates the possibility of change and even sudden historical shifts; and overcomes the conceptual division between semiotic/linguistic and material models of structure. By insisting on the existence of a multiplicity of structures and resources within any given culture that both enable and constrain social behavior, and by emphasizing the differential enactment in practice of such cultural schemes by human agents, whose activities never perfectly replicate the underlying structures, Sewell restores an internal dynamic to the concept of structure that explains how it is sustained through human reproduction and at the same time allows for its continuing transformation.

* * *

"Structure" is one of the most important and most elusive terms in the vocabulary of current social science. The concept is central not only in such eponymous schools as structural functionalism, structuralism, and poststructuralism, but in virtually all tendencies of social scientific thought. But if social scientists find it impossible to do without the term "structure," we also find it nearly impossible to define it adequately. Many of us have surely had the experience of being asked by a "naive" student what we mean by structure,

143

and then finding it embarrassingly difficult to define the term without using the word "structure" or one of its variants in its own definition. Sometimes we find what seems to be an acceptable synonym—for example, "pattern"— but all such synonyms lack the original's rhetorical force. When it comes to indicating that a relation is powerful or important it is certainly more convincing to designate it as "structural" than as "patterning."

The term structure empowers what it designates. Structure, in its nominative sense, always implies structure in its transitive verbal sense. Whatever aspect of social life we designate as structure is posited as "structuring" some other aspect of social existence—whether it is class that structures politics, gender that structures employment opportunities, rhetorical conventions that structure texts or utterances, or modes of production that structure social formations. Structure operates in social scientific discourse as a powerful metonymic device, identifying some part of a complex social reality as explaining the whole. It is a word to conjure with in the social sciences. In fact, structure is less a precise concept than a kind of founding or epistemic metaphor of social scientific—and scientific—discourse. For this reason, no formal definition can succeed in fixing the term's meaning: the metaphor of structure continues its essential if somewhat mysterious work in the constitution of social scientific knowledge despite theorists' definitional efforts.

There are, nevertheless, three problems in the current use of the term that make self-conscious theorizing about the meanings of structure seem worthwhile. The most fundamental problem is that structural or structuralist arguments tend to assume a far too rigid causal determinism in social life. Those features of social existence denominated as structures tend to be reified and treated as primary, hard, and immutable, like the girders of a building, while the events or social processes they structure tend to be seen as secondary and superficial, like the outer "skin" of a skyscraper, or as mutable within "hard" structural constraints, like the layout of offices on floors defined by a skeleton of girders. What tends to get lost in the language of structure is the efficacy of human action—or "agency," to use the currently favored term. Structures tend to appear in social scientific discourse as impervious to human agency, to exist apart from, but nevertheless to determine the essential shape of, the strivings and motivated transactions that constitute the experienced surface of social life. A social science trapped in an unexamined metaphor of structure tends to reduce actors to cleverly programmed automatons. A second and closely related problem with the notion of structure is that it makes dealing with change awkward. The metaphor of structure implies stability. For this reason, structural language lends itself readily to explanations of how social life is shaped into consistent patterns, but not to explanations of how these patterns change over time. In structural discourse, change is commonly located outside of structures, either in a telos of history, in notions of breakdown, or in influences exogenous to the system in question. Consequently, moving from questions of stability to questions of change tends to involve awkward epistemological shifts.

144

The third problem is of a rather different order: the term structure is used in apparently contradictory senses in different social scientific discourses, particularly in sociology and anthropology. Sociologists typically contrast "structure" to "culture." Structure, in normal sociological usage, is thought of as "hard" or "material" and therefore as primary and determining, whereas culture is regarded as "soft" or "mental" and therefore as secondary or derived. By contrast, semiotically inclined social scientists, most particularly anthropologists, regard culture as the preeminent site of structure. In typical anthropological usage, the term structure is assumed to refer to the realm of culture, except when it is modified by the adjective "social." As a consequence, social scientists as different in outlook as Theda Skocpol and Marshall Sahlins can be designated as "structuralists" by their respective disciplines. Sociologists and anthropologists, in short, tend to visualize the nature and location of structure in sharply discrepant, indeed mutually incompatible, ways.[1]

In view of all these problems with the notion of structure, it is tempting to conclude that the term should simply be discarded. But this, I think, is impossible: structure is so rhetorically powerful and pervasive a term that any attempt to legislate its abolition would be futile. Moreover, the notion of structure does denominate, however problematically, something very important about social relations: the tendency of patterns of relations to be reproduced, even when actors engaging in the relations are unaware of the patterns or do not desire their reproduction. In my opinion, the notion of structure neither could nor should be banished from the discourse of social science. But it does need extensive rethinking. This article will attempt to develop a theory of structure that overcomes the three cardinal weaknesses of the concept as it is normally employed in social science. The theory will attempt (1) to recognize the agency of social actors, (2) to build the possibility of change into the concept of structure, and (3) to overcome the divide between semiotic and materialist visions of structure. My strategy will be to begin from what I regard as the most promising existing formulations—Anthony Giddens's notion of "the duality of structure" and, at a later point in the argument, Pierre Bourdieu's concept of habitus—and to develop a more adequate theory by means of critique, reformulation, and elaboration.[2]

The duality of structure: a critique and reformulation of Giddens's theory

The most sustained effort at reconceptualizing structure in recent social theory has been made by Anthony Giddens, who has been insisting since the mid-1970s that structures must be regarded as "dual" (Giddens 1976, 1979, 1981, 1984). By this he means that they are "both the medium and the outcome of the practices which constitute social systems" (Giddens 1981, p. 27). Structures shape people's practices, but it is also people's practices that constitute (and reproduce) structures. In this view of things, human agency and structure, far from being *opposed,* in fact *presuppose* each other. Structures are enacted by what Giddens calls "knowledgeable" human agents (i.e., people who know what they are doing and how to do it), and agents act by putting into practice their necessarily structured knowledge. Hence, "structures must not be conceptualized as simply placing constraints on human agency, but as enabling" (Giddens 1976, p. 161). This conception of human agents as "knowledgeable" and "enabled" implies that those agents are capable of putting their structurally formed capacities to work in creative or innovative ways. And, if enough people or even a few people who are powerful enough act in innovative ways, their action may have the consequence of transforming the very structures that gave them the capacity to act. Dual structures therefore are potentially mutable. It is no accident that Giddens calls his theory "the theory of structuration," indicating by this neologism that "structure" must be regarded as a process, not as a steady state.

As a theoretically self-conscious social historian, I find Giddens's notion of the duality of structure particularly congenial. Much of the best social history of the past quarter-century has adopted an implicit theoretical strategy quite consistent with Giddens's theory. Social historians have significantly altered in practice the sociological and anthropological concepts of structure that they began to borrow so avidly in the 1960s and 1970s. Although they were probably writing more from professional instinct than from considered theoretical scruples, social historians have demonstrated how, in a great variety of times and places, structures are in fact dual: how historical agents' thoughts, motives, and intentions are constituted by the cultures and social institutions into which they are born, how these cultures and institutions are reproduced by the structurally shaped and constrained actions of those agents, but also how, in certain circumstances, the agents can (or are forced to) improvise or innovate in structurally shaped ways that significantly reconfigure the very structures that constituted them. [. . .]

What is structure?

But in spite of its promise, Giddens's theory suffers from serious gaps and logical deficiencies that have persisted through the theory's all-too-frequent restatements (for the major statements see Giddens [1976, 1979, 1984]). Most strikingly, "structure"—the central term of Giddens's theory—remains frustratingly underspecified. Unlike most social scientists, he does not leave the term completely undefined and simply allow it to do its accustomed magical work in his readers' minds. Especially in *Central Problems in Social Theory* (1979), he discusses "structure" at some length. But I do not think that the concept of structure he elaborates there or elsewhere is sufficiently clear or robust to serve as the foundation of a theoretical system.

Giddens defines structure formally in several places, including in the glossary to *The Constitution of Society:*

Structure. Rules and resources, recursively implicated in the reproduction of social systems. Structure exists only as memory traces,
the organic basis of human knowledgeability, and as instantiated
in action.

(1984, p. 377)

This far-from-crystalline definition requires some exegesis. The terms "rules
and resources," in spite of their deceptive simplicity, are quite obscure and
will have to be discussed at length. Let us therefore begin with the rest of the
definition, which is arcanely worded but relatively straightforward in
meaning. By "social systems" Giddens means empirically observable, inter-
twining, and relatively bounded social practices that link persons across time
and space. Social systems would encompass what most social scientists mean
by "societies" but would also include social units greater (e.g., the capitalist
world system) or more limited (e.g., the neighborhood community) in scope
than the nation-state. Social systems, according to Giddens, have no existence
apart from the practices that constitute them, and these practices are reproduced by the "recursive" (i.e., repeated) enactments of structures. Structures
are not the patterned social practices that make up social systems, but the
principles that pattern these practices. Structures, therefore, have only what
he elsewhere terms a "virtual" existence (e.g., 1984, p. 17). Structures do not
exist concretely in time and space except as "memory traces, the organic basis
of knowledgeability" (i.e., only as ideas or schemas lodged in human brains)
and as they are "instantiated in action" (i.e., put into practice).

Structures as rules

Structures, then, are "virtual" and are put into practice in the production and
reproduction of social life. But of what do these structures consist? According
to Giddens's definition, they consist of "rules and resources." Giddens's
notion of rules is largely derived from French structuralism. This is especially
clear in *New Rules of Sociological Method* and *Central Problems in Social
Theory.* In both of these he relies heavily on a typically structuralist analogy
with Saussurian linguistics. Giddens likens his own distinction between structure and practice to the Saussurian distinction between *langue* and *parole.*
According to this analogy, structure is to practice as *langue* (the abstract rules
that make possible the production of grammatical sentences) is to *parole*
(speech, or the production of actual sentences; 1976, pp. 118–22). Hence
structure, like *langue,* is a complex of rules with a "virtual" existence, while
practice, like speech, is an enactment of these rules in space and time. [. . .]
However, Giddens leaves his discussion of rules dangling, and he fails to give
examples of rules that underlie any actual social practices. All we know from
Central Problems in Social Theory is that rules are virtual and that they somehow
generate social practices and social systems.

In *The Constitution of Society*, the most recent statement of his theory, Giddens [takes] his cue from Wittgenstein. Giddens there defines rules simply but, in my opinion, with great promise: "Let us regard the rules of social life . . . as generalizable procedures applied in the enactment/reproduction of social life" (1984, p. 21). [. . .] Giddens, however, does not give examples or develop typologies of the sorts of generalizable procedures he has in mind. Consequently, his conception of rules is, if anything, more impoverished in *The Constitution of Society* than it was in *Central Problems in Social Theory* [. . .]. However, I think his Wittgensteinian definition of rules as generalizable procedures can be used as a foundation for a more robust conception.

Throughout his theory, Giddens places a great deal of weight on the notion that actors are *knowledgeable*. It is, presumably, the knowledge of rules that makes people capable of action. But Giddens develops no vocabulary for specifying the *content* of what people know. I would argue that such a vocabulary is, in fact, readily available, but is best developed in a field Giddens has to date almost entirely ignored: cultural anthropology. After all, the usual social scientific term for "what people know" is "culture," and those who have most fruitfully theorized and studied culture are the anthropologists. [. . .]

[. . .] [W]e should, like most anthropologists, think of rules as existing at various levels. Rules nearer the surface may by definition be more "superficial," but they are not necessarily less important in their implications for social life. "The rules of social life" should be thought of as including all the varieties of cultural schemas that anthropologists have uncovered in their research: not only the array of binary oppositions that make up a given society's fundamental tools of thought, but also the various conventions, recipes, scenarios, principles of action, and habits of speech and gesture built up with these fundamental tools. Indeed, the term "rules" is probably not quite the right word, since it tends to imply something like formally stated prescriptions—the sorts of things spelled out in statutes, proverbs, liturgies, constitutions, or contracts.[3] What I mean to get at is not formally stated prescriptions but the informal and not always conscious schemas, metaphors, or assumptions presupposed by such formal statements. I would in fact argue that publicly fixed codifications of rules are actual rather than virtual and should be regarded as *resources* rather than as rules in Giddens's sense. Because of this ambiguity about the meaning of the word "rules," I believe it is useful to introduce a change in terminology. Henceforth I shall use the term "schemas" rather than "rules"—even though this destroys the pleasing alliteration of Giddens's "rules and resources" formula.

The various schemas that make up structures are, to quote Giddens, "generalizable procedures applied in the enactment/reproduction of social life." They are "generalizable" in the sense that they can be applied in or extended to a variety of contexts of interaction. Such schemas or procedures—whether rules of etiquette, or aesthetic norms, or such recipes for group action as the royal progress, grain riot, or democratic vote, or a set of equivalences between wet and dry, female and male, nature and culture, private and public, or the body as a metaphor for hierarchy, or the notion that the human being is composed of a body and a soul—can be used not only in the situation in which they are first learned or most conventionally applied. They can be generalized—that is, transposed or extended—to new situations when the opportunity arises. This *generalizability* or *transposability* of schemas is the reason they must be understood as virtual. To say that schemas are virtual is to say that they cannot be reduced to their existence in any particular practice or any particular location in space and time: they can be actualized in a potentially broad and unpredetermined range of situations.

I agree with Giddens, then, that the rules or schemas making up structures may usefully be conceptualized as having a "virtual" existence, that structures consist of intersubjectively available procedures or schemas capable of being actualized or put into practice in a range of different circumstances. Such schemas should be thought of as operating at widely varying levels of depth, from [. . .] deep structures to relatively superficial rules of etiquette.

Structures as resources

[. . .] Giddens insists that structures are not merely rules, but rules and resources, or "rule-resource sets" (1984, p. 377). But Giddens's concept of resources is even less adequately theorized than his concept of rules.[4] I agree with Giddens that any notion of structure that ignores asymmetries of power is radically incomplete. But tacking an undertheorized notion of resources onto an essentially rule-based notion of structure succeeds merely in confusing things.

In *Central Problems in Social Theory*, Giddens (1979, p. 92) defines resources as "the media whereby transformative capacity is employed as power in the routine course of social interaction." Unless I am missing some subtlety, this obscurely worded definition could be rendered in ordinary English as "resources are anything that can serve as a source of power in social interactions." This seems to me an unexceptional and theoretically uninformative statement of what we usually mean by social resources. Besides this anodyne definition, almost all he tells us about resources is that they can be classified into two types, authoritative and allocative. In *Central Problems in Social Theory*, he defines "authorization" as those "capabilities which generate command over persons" and "allocation" as those "capabilities which generate command over *objects* or other material phenomena" (1979, p. 100). By extension, authoritative resources should be human resources and allocative resources nonhuman resources—which once again seems unexceptional.

I believe that Giddens's classification of resources is potentially useful, but that it needs to be reformulated and put into ordinary English. Resources are of two types, human and nonhuman. Nonhuman resources are objects, animate or inanimate, naturally occurring or manufactured, that can be used to enhance or maintain power; human resources are physical strength, dexterity, knowledge, and emotional commitments that can be used to enhance or maintain power, including knowledge of the means of gaining, retaining, controlling, and propagating either human or nonhuman resources. Both types of resources are media of power and are unevenly distributed. But however unequally resources may be distributed, some measure of both human and nonhuman resources are controlled by all members of society, no matter how destitute and oppressed. Indeed, part of what it means to conceive of human beings as *agents* is to conceive of them as *empowered* by access to resources of one kind or another.

Structures as schemas and resources

Reformulating Giddens's concept of resources does not make it clear how resources and schemas combine to form structures. Here the most glaring problem is Giddens's definition of structures as "virtual." As we have seen, this makes perfect sense for structures conceptualized as rules or schemas. But are *resources* also virtual? It is surprising that Giddens does not seem to have considered the point. The notion of a virtual resource seems particularly doubtful in the case of nonhuman (or in Giddens's terms "allocative") resources. Nonhuman resources would surely include such things as factories owned by capitalists, stocks of weapons controlled by kings or generals, land rented by peasants, or stacks of Hudson Bay blankets accumulated by Kwakiutl chiefs. It is clear that factories, armaments, land, and Hudson Bay blankets have had a crucial weight in shaping and constraining social life in particular times and places, and it therefore seems sensible to include them in some way in a concept of structure. But it is also hard to see how such material resources can be considered as "virtual," since material things by definition exist in space and time. It is, moreover, only in particular times, places, and quantities that such material objects can serve as resources.

The case of human resources is only a little less clear. By definition, human bodies, like any other material objects, cannot be virtual. But what about knowledge and emotional commitments, the mental aspects of human resources? Examples might be the Roman Catholic priest's power to conse-crate the host and hear confession, children's sense of obligation toward their mothers, or the fear and reverence that subjects feel for their king. Unlike factories or Hudson Bay blankets, such resources are not material, or at least not in the same sense. Nevertheless they seem to me actual as opposed to virtual. They exist in what Giddens calls "time-space"; they are observable characteristics of real people who live in particular times and congregate in particular places. And it is their actualization in people's minds and bodies that make them resources. It is not the disembodied concept of the majesty of the king that gives him power, but the fear and reverence felt for him by his actual subjects.

If I am right that all resources are actual rather than virtual, Giddens's notion of structure turns out to be self-contradictory. If structures are virtual, they cannot include both schemas and resources. And if they include both schemas and resources, they cannot be virtual. He, and we, cannot have it both ways. But which way should we have it? The simplest way of conceptualizing structure would be to return to Giddens's starting point in structuralism and to assert that structure refers only to rules or schemas, not to resources, and that resources should be thought of as an *effect* of structures. In this way, structures would retain their virtual quality, and concrete distributions of resources would be seen not as structures but as media animated and shaped by structures, that is, by cultural schemas.

[. . .]

But while we might reasonably speak of human resources as generated by rules or schemas, it is harder to see how nonhuman resources could be conceived of as so generated. Factories, land, and Hudson Bay blankets have material qualities that are certainly not generated by schemas. But it is also true that their condition as resources capable of producing and reproducing disparities in social power is not wholly intrinsic in their material existence. What they amount to as resources is largely a consequence of the schemas that inform their use. To take perhaps the most obvious case, an immense stack of Hudson Bay blankets would be nothing more than a means of keeping a large number of people warm were it not for the cultural schemas that constituted the Kwakiutl potlatch; but given these schemas, the blankets, given away in a potlatch, became a means of demonstrating the power of the chief and, consequently, of acquiring prestige, marriage alliances, military power, and labor services (Boas 1966; Sahlins 1989). In this case, the schemas constituting the potlatch determined the specific value, extent, and effects of Hudson Bay blankets as a resource. But I would argue that this is true of nonhuman resources in general. For example, the extent and kinds of resources generated by a factory will depend on whether it is owned by an individual capitalist or by a workers' cooperative—in other words, on rules defining the nature of property rights and of workplace authority. The resources gained by peasants from the land they use will be determined by the conventions of land tenure, the exigencies of customary law, the sets of obligations owed to kinsmen, and the agricultural techniques employed. Examples could be multiplied at will. Nonhuman resources have a material existence that is not reducible to rules or schemas, but the activation of material things as resources, the determination of their value and social power, is dependent on the cultural schemas that inform their social use.

It is clear, then, that resources can plausibly be thought of as effects of cultural schemas. It therefore would certainly be possible to clean up Giddens's concept of structure by defining structure as schemas with a purely virtual existence, and resources not as coequal elements in structure but as media and outcomes of the operation of structure. But notice that if we adopt this definition, the rhetorical power of the term structure insinuates a single direction of causality. That which is termed structure is, by this act of denomination, granted power over that which is not termed structure. Stocks of material goods and people's knowledge and emotional commitments become inert, mere media for and outcomes of the determinative operations of cultural schemas. If we insist that structures are virtual, we risk lapsing into the de facto idealism that continually haunts structuralism however much its exponents—for example, Lévi-Strauss (1966, p. 130)—protest their materialist credentials and intentions. Schemas—mental structures—become the only form-giving entity, and agents become agents of these mental structures, actors who can only recite preexisting scripts. To define structures in this way threatens, in short, to deny their duality and, consequently, to annihilate the central premise of Giddens's theory.

The duality of schemas and resources

If the duality of structure is to be saved—and as far as I am concerned the notion of duality of structure is the main attraction of Giddens's theory—we must take the other alternative and conceive of structures as having (appropriately) a *dual* character. Structure, then, should be defined as composed simultaneously of schemas, which are virtual, and of resources, which are actual.

If structures are dual in this sense, then it must be true that schemas are the effects of resources, just as resources are the effects of schemas. This seems to me a reasonable claim, one whose plausibility can be demonstrated by a few examples. A factory is not an inert pile of bricks, wood, and metal. It incorporates or actualizes schemas, and this means that the schemas can be inferred from the material form of the factory. The factory gate, the punching-in station, the design of the assembly line: all of these features of the factory teach and validate the rules of the capitalist labor contract. Or take the priest's performance of the Mass. When the priest transforms the host and wine into the body and blood of Christ and administers the host to communicants, the communicants are suffused by a sense of spiritual well-being. Communion therefore demonstrates to the communicants the reality and power of the rule of apostolic succession that made the priest a priest. In short, if resources are instantiations or embodiments of schemas, they therefore inculcate and justify the schemas as well. Resources, we might say, are *read* like texts, to recover the cultural schemas they instantiate. Indeed, texts— whether novels, or statute books, or folktales, or contracts—are resources from the point of view of this theory. They, too, are instantiations of schemas in time-space that can be used by actors to generate power.

If resources are effects of schemas, it is also true that schemas are effects of resources. If schemas are to be sustained or reproduced over time—and without sustained reproduction they could hardly be counted as structural— they must be validated by the accumulation of resources that their enactment engenders. Schemas not empowered or regenerated by resources would eventually be abandoned and forgotten, just as resources without cultural schemas to direct their use would eventually dissipate and decay. Sets of schemas and resources may properly be said to constitute *structures* only when they mutually imply and sustain each other over time.

The transformation of dual structures: out of Bourdieu's habitus

A definition of structure as made up of both schemas and resources avoids both the material determinism of traditional Marxism and the ideal determinism of traditional French structuralism. But how it can enhance our ability to understand transformations of structures is not immediately apparent. Indeed, one could argue that if the enactment of schemas always creates resources that inculcate the schemas, schemas and resources should simply reproduce each other without change indefinitely. The claim that dual structures engender stasis is far from fanciful; such an argument has in fact been made with great panache in Pierre Bourdieu's (1977) widely influential discussion of what he calls "habitus" in *Outline of a Theory of Practice.* Any attempt to argue that duality of structure improves our ability to understand social transformations must confront this argument.[5]

Duality and stasis

Although he uses a different terminology, Bourdieu has powerfully illustrated the mutually sustaining relationship between schemas and resources (what he calls "mental structures" and "the world of objects"). For example, his well-known discussion (Bourdieu 1977) of the Kabyle house shows how the design of the house and the placement of objects in it reproduces funda- mental Kabyle cultural oppositions, such as those between high and low, male and female, fire and water, and light and dark, and thereby patterns all activities conducted in the house in terms of such oppositions. Bourdieu remarks that "all the actions performed in a space constructed in this way are immediately qualified symbolically and function as so many structural exercises through which is built up practical mastery of the fundamental schemes" (Bourdieu 1977, p. 91).

The house is given its shape by the application of schemas ("mental struc- tures" in Bourdieu's vocabulary), and the house in turn inculcates these schemas by assigning tasks, objects, persons, and emotional dispositions to differently coded spaces. As Bourdieu puts it, in his characteristically ornate and paradoxical style,

> The mental structures which construct the world of objects are
> constructed in the practice of a world of objects constructed according
> to the same structures. The mind born of the world of objects does

not rise as a subjectivity confronting an objectivity: the objective universe is made up of objects which are the product of objectifying operations structured according to the very structures which the mind applies to it. The mind is a metaphor of the world of objects which is itself but an endless circle of mutually reflecting metaphors.

(Bourdieu 1977, p. 91)

In many respects, Bourdieu's "theory of practice" is fully compatible with the conception of the duality of structure for which I am arguing in this paper. Bourdieu recognizes the mutual reproduction of schemas and resources that constitutes temporally durable structures—which he calls "habitus." His discussion of habitus powerfully elaborates the means by which mutually reinforcing rule-resource sets constitute human subjects with particular sorts of knowledge and dispositions. Moreover, Bourdieu's Kabyle subjects are not cultural dopes. They are endowed with the capacity to engage in highly autonomous, discerning, and strategic actions. (See, e.g., Bourdieu's discussion of gift exchange and matrimonial strategies [1977, pp. 4–10 and 32–53, respectively].) Bourdieu's Kabyles would seem to be exactly the sort of knowledgeable actors called for by Giddens's theory.

Yet Bourdieu's habitus retains precisely the agent-proof quality that the concept of the duality of structure is supposed to overcome. In Bourdieu's habitus, schemas and resources so powerfully reproduce one another that even the most cunning or improvisational actions undertaken by agents necessarily reproduce the structure. "As an acquired system of generative schemes objectively adjusted to the particular conditions in which it is constituted, the habitus engenders all the thoughts, all the perceptions, and all the actions consistent with those conditions and no others" (Bourdieu 1977, p. 95). Although Bourdieu avoids either a traditional French structuralist ideal determinism or a traditional Marxist material determinism, he does so only by erecting a combined determinism that makes significant social transformations seem impossible.

But is this powerful implication of stasis really warranted? After all, the Kabyle society in which Bourdieu carried out his fieldwork produced a momentous anticolonial revolution shortly after Bourdieu returned to France to analyze his data. It seems to me that, in spite of his devastating attacks on Cartesian and Lévi-Straussian "objectivism" (Bourdieu 1977, esp. pp. 1–30), Bourdieu's own theory has fallen victim to an impossibly objectified and over-totalized conception of society. Only in the idealized world constructed by the social scientific observer could habitus engender "all the thoughts, all the perceptions, and all the actions" consistent with existing social conditions "and no others." In the world of human struggles and strategems, plenty of thoughts, perceptions, and actions consistent with the reproduction of existing social patterns fail to occur, and inconsistent ones occur all the time.

154

Why structural change is possible

It is, of course, entirely proper for Bourdieu to insist on the strong reproductive bias built into structures—that is the whole point of the structure
concept and part of what makes the concept so essential for theorizing social
change. After all, as Renato Rosaldo (1980) and Marshall Sahlins (1981, 1985)
have brilliantly demonstrated, the same reproductive biases of structures that
explain the powerful continuities of social relations also make it possible to
explain the paths followed in episodes of social change. What gets Bourdieu
off the track is his unrealistically unified and totalized concept of habitus,
which he conceptualizes as a vast series of strictly homologous structures
encompassing all of social experience. Such a conceptualization, which
Bourdieu in fact shares roughly with many structurally inclined theorists,
cannot explain change as arising from within the operation of structures.
It is characteristic that many structural accounts of social transformation
tend to introduce change from outside the system and then trace out the
ensuing structurally shaped changes, rather than showing how change is
generated by the operation of structures internal to a society. In this respect,
Marshall Sahlins's (1981) analysis of how Captain Cook's voyages affected
the Hawaiians is emblematic. It is my conviction that a theory of change
cannot be built into a theory of structure unless we adopt a far more multiple,
contingent, and fractured conception of society—and of structure. What is
needed is a conceptual vocabulary that makes it possible to show how the
ordinary operations of structures can generate transformations. To this end,
I propose five key axioms: the multiplicity of structures, the transposability
of schemas, the unpredictability of resource accumulation, the polysemy of
resources, and the intersection of structures.

The multiplicity of structures Societies are based on practices that derive
from many distinct structures, which exist at different levels, operate in
different modalities, and are themselves based on widely varying types and
quantities of resources. While it is common for a certain range of these structures to be homologous, like those described by Bourdieu in *Outline of a Theory
of Practice*, it is never true that all of them are homologous. Structures tend
to vary significantly between different institutional spheres, so that kinship
structures will have different logics and dynamics than those possessed by
religious structures, productive structures, aesthetic structures, educational
structures, and so on. There is, moreover, important variation even within a
given sphere. For example, the structures that shape and constrain religion
in Christian societies include authoritarian, prophetic, ritual, and theoretical
modes. These may sometimes operate in harmony, but they can also lead to
sharply conflicting claims and empowerments. The multiplicity of structures
means that the knowledgeble social actors whose practices constitute a society
are far more versatile than Bourdieu's account of a universally homologous
habitus would imply: social actors are capable of applying a wide range of
different and even incompatible schemas and have access to heterogeneous
arrays of resources.

The transposability of schemas Moroever, the schemas to which actors have access can be applied across a wide range of circumstances. This is actually recognized by Bourdieu, but he has not, in my opinion, drawn the correct conclusions from his insight. Schemas were defined above as generalizable or transposable procedures applied in the enactment of social life. The term "generalizable" is taken from Giddens; the term "transposable," which I prefer, is taken from Bourdieu.[6] At one point Bourdieu defines habitus as "a system of lasting transposable dispositions which, integrating past experiences, functions at every moment as a *matrix of perceptions, appreciations, and actions* and makes possible the achievement of infinitely diversified tasks, thanks to analogical transfers of schemes permitting the solution of similarly shaped problems" (1977, p. 83; emphasis in original).

The slippage in this passage occurs in the final phrase, "permitting the solution of similarly shaped problems." Whether a given problem is similarly shaped enough to be solved by analogical transfers of schemes cannot be decided in advance by social scientific analysts, but must be determined case by case by the actors, which means that there is no fixed limit to the possible transpositions. This is in fact implied by the earlier phrase, "makes possible the achievement of infinitely diversified tasks." To say that schemas are transposable, in other words, is to say that they can be applied to a wide and not fully predictable range of cases outside the context in which they are initially learned. This fits with what we usually mean by knowledge of a rule or of some other learned procedure. In ordinary speech one cannot be said to really *know* a rule simply because one can apply it mechanically to repeated instances of the same case. Whether we are speaking of rules of grammar, mathematics, law, etiquette, or carpentry, the real test of knowing a rule is to be able to apply it successfully in *unfamiliar* cases. Knowledge of a rule or a schema by definition means the ability to transpose or extend it—that is, to apply it creatively. If this is so, then *agency*, which I would define as entailing the capacity to transpose and extend schemas to new contexts, is inherent in the knowledge of cultural schemas that characterizes all minimally competent members of society.[7]

The unpredictability of resource accumulation But the very fact that schemas are by definition capable of being transposed or extended means that the resource consequences of the enactment of cultural schemas is never entirely predictable. A joke told to a new audience, an investment made in a new market, an offer of marriage made to a new patriline, a cavalry attack made on a new terrain, a crop planted in a newly cleared field or in a familiar field in a new spring—the effect of these actions on the resources of the actors is never quite certain. Investment in a new market may make the entrepreneur a pauper or a millionaire, negotiation of a marriage with a new patriline may result in a family's elevation in status or its extinction in a feud, planting a crop in the familiar field may result in subsistence, starvation, or plenty. Moreover, if the enactment of schemas creates unpredictable quantities and qualities of resources, and if the reproduction of schemas depends on their

156

continuing validation by resources, this implies that schemas will in fact be differentially validated when they are put into action and therefore will potentially be subject to modification. A brilliantly successful cavalry attack on a new terrain may change the battle plans of subsequent campaigns or even theories of military tactics; a joke that draws rotten tomatoes rather than laughter may result in the suppression of a category of jokes from the comedian's repertoire; a succession of crop failures may modify routines of planting or plowing.[8]

The polysemy of resources The term polysemy (or multiplicity of meaning) is normally applied to symbols, language, or texts. Its application to resources sounds like a contradiction in terms. But, given the concept of resources I am advocating here, it is not. Resources, I have insisted, embody cultural schemas. Like texts or ritual performances, however, their meaning is never entirely unambiguous. The form of the factory embodies and therefore teaches capitalist notions of property relations. But, as Marx points out, it can also teach the necessarily social and collective character of production and thereby undermine the capitalist notion of private property. The new prestige, wealth, and territory gained from the brilliant success of a cavalry charge may be attributed to the superior discipline and élan of the cavalry officers and thereby enhance the power of an aristocratic officer corps, or it may be attributed to the commanding general and thereby result in the increasing subordination of officers to a charismatic leader. Any array of resources is capable of being interpreted in varying ways and, therefore, of empowering different actors and teaching different schemas. Again, this seems to me inherent in a definition of agency as the capacity to transpose and extend schemas to new contexts. Agency, to put it differently, is the actor's capacity to reinterpret and mobilize an array of resources in terms of cultural schemas other than those that initially constituted the array.

The intersection of structures One reason arrays of resources can be interpreted in more than one way is that structures or structural complexes intersect and overlap. The structures of capitalist society include both a mode of production based on private property and profit and a mode of labor organization based on workplace solidarity. The factory figures as a crucial resource in both of these structures, and its meaning and consequences for both workers and managers is therefore open and contested. The intersection of structures, in fact, takes place in both the schema and the resource dimensions. Not only can a given array of resources be claimed by different actors embedded in different structural complexes (or differentially claimed by the same actor embedded in different structural complexes), but schemas can be borrowed or appropriated from one structural complex and applied to another. Not only do workers and factory owners struggle for control of the factory, but Marx appropriates political economy for the advancement of socialism.

Structures, then, are sets of mutually sustaining schemas and resources that empower and constrain social action and that tend to be reproduced by that social action. But their reproduction is never automatic. Structures are at risk, at least to some extent, in all of the social encounters they shape—because structures are multiple and intersecting, because schemas are transposable, and because resources are polysemic and accumulate unpredictably. Placing the relationship between resources and cultural schemas at the center of a concept of structure makes it possible to show how social change, no less than social stasis, can be generated by the enactment of structures in social life.

Agency

Such enactments of structures imply a particular concept of agency—one that sees agency not as opposed to, but as constituent of, structure. To be an agent means to be capable of exerting some degree of control over the social relations in which one is enmeshed, which in turn implies the ability to transform those social relations to some degree. As I see it, agents are empowered to act with and against others by structures: they have knowledge of the schemas that inform social life and have access to some measure of human and nonhuman resources. Agency arises from the actor's knowledge of schemas, which means the ability to apply them to new contexts. Or, to put the same thing the other way around, agency arises from the actor's control of resources, which means the capacity to reinterpret or mobilize an array of resources in terms of schemas other than those that constituted the array. Agency is implied by the existence of structures.

I would argue that a capacity for agency—for desiring, for forming intentions, and for acting creatively—is inherent in all humans. But I would also argue that humans are born with only a highly generalized capacity for agency, analogous to their capacity to use language. Just as linguistic capacity takes the form of becoming a competent speaker of some particular language—French, or Arabic, or Swahili, or Urdu—agency is formed by a specific range of cultural schemas and resources available in a person's particular social milieu. The specific forms that agency will take consequently vary enormously and are culturally and historically determined. But a capacity for agency is as much a given for humans as the capacity for respiration.

[. . .]

It is equally important, however, to insist that the agency exercised by different persons is far from uniform, that agency differs enormously in both kind and extent. What kinds of desires people can have, what intentions they can form, and what sorts of creative transpositions they can carry out vary dramatically from one social world to another depending on the nature of the particular structures that inform those social worlds. Without a notion of heaven and hell a person cannot strive for admission into paradise; only in a modern capitalist economy can one attempt to make a killing on the futures market; if they are denied access to the public sphere, women's ambitions will be focused on private life. Agency also differs in extent, both between and within societies. Occupancy of different social positions—as defined, for example, by gender, wealth, social prestige, class, ethnicity, occupation, generation, sexual preference, or education—gives people knowledge of different schemas and access to different kinds and amounts of resources and hence different possibilities for transformative action. And the scope or extent of agency also varies enormously between different social systems, even for occupants of analogous positions. The owner of the biggest art gallery in St. Louis has far less influence on American artistic taste than the owner of the biggest gallery in Los Angeles; the president of Chad has far less power over global environmental policy than the president of Russia. Structures, in short, empower agents differentially, which also implies that they embody the desires, intentions, and knowledge of agents differentially as well. Structures, and the human agencies they endow, are laden with differences in power.

Finally, I would insist that agency is collective as well as individual. [. . .] I [. . .] see agency as profoundly social or collective. The transpositions of schemas and remobilizations of resources that constitute agency are always acts of communication with others. Agency entails an ability to coordinate one's actions with others and against others, to form collective projects, to persuade, to coerce, and to monitor the simultaneous effects of one's own and others' activities. Moreover, the extent of the agency exercised by individual persons depends profoundly on their positions in collective organizations. To take the extreme case, a monarch's personal whims or quarrels may affect the lives of thousands (see, e.g., Sahlins 1991). But it is also true that the agency of fathers, executives, or professors is greatly expanded by the places they occupy in patriarchal families, corporations, or universities and by their consequent authority to bind the collectivity by their actions. Agency, then, characterizes all persons. But the agency exercised by persons is collective in both its sources and its mode of exercise. Personal agency is, therefore, laden with collectively produced differences of power and implicated in collective struggles and resistances.

Varieties of structures

The concept of structure I elaborate in this article is very general and therefore could be applied to structures of widely differing character—ranging in import from structures that shape and constrain the development of world military power to those that shape and constrain the joking practices of a group of Sunday fishing buddies or the erotic practices of a single couple. This immense range in the scope and character of the structures to which this article's concepts can be applied is appropriate, given the premise that all social action is shaped by structures. But it suggests a need for some means of distinguishing the character and dynamics of different sorts of structures. I will offer no detailed typology—both because space is short and because I feel that typologies should arise out of concrete analyses of social change and reproduction. Instead, I shall simply indicate two important dimensions along which structures vary: depth, which refers to the schema dimension of structure, and power, which refers to the resource dimension. I shall try to demonstrate that thinking in terms of depth and power can help to illuminate the very different dynamics and durabilities of [two] important types of structures: those of language [and] states [. . .].

Depth has long been a key metaphor of linguistic and structuralist discourse. To designate a structure as "deep" implies that it lies beneath and generates a certain range of "surface" structures, just as structures underlie and generate practices. In structuralist discourse, deep structures are those schemas that can be shown to underlie ordinary or "surface" structures, in the sense that the surface structures are a set of transformations of the deep structures. Thus the structural schemas for the performance of a fertility ritual may be shown to be particular transformations of a deeper set of oppositions between wet and dry or male and female that also underlie structures informing other institutionally distinct practices—from housebuilding, to personal adornment, to oratory. Consequently, deep structural schemas are also pervasive, in the sense that they are present in a relatively wide range of institutional spheres, practices, and discourses. They also tend to be relatively unconscious, in the sense that they are taken-for-granted mental assumptions or modes of procedure that actors normally apply without being aware that they are applying them.

Different structures also vary enormously in the resources, and hence the power, that they mobilize. Military structures or structures shaping state finance create massive concentrations of power, whereas the grammatical structures of a language or the structures shaping schoolchildren's play create much more modest power concentrations. Structures also differ in the kinds of power they mobilize. For example, the power created by apostolic succession is based primarily (although far from exclusively) on persuasion, while that created by the military government of a conquering army is based primarily on coercion.

Language I believe that thinking about structures in terms of their depth and power can lead to insights about the structures' durability and dynamics. Consider, for example, linguistic structures, which scholars in many disciplines have used as the prime example of structure in general. Linguistic structures, which of course tend to be remarkably durable, actually fall at extremes on the dimensions of both power and depth. Linguistic structures are unusually deep. Intricate phonological, morphological, syntactical, and semantic structures underlie every sentence. Sentences, in turn, are aggregated into meaningful utterances or texts in accord with the discursive structures of rhetoric, narrative, metaphor, and logic. And all of these layered linguistic structures underlie the multitude of structures that rely at least in part on speech and writing—which is to say the immense preponderance of all structures.

Yet the *power* of linguistic structures is unusually slight. The enactment of phonological, morphological, syntactical, and semantic structures in speech or writing in itself has relatively modest resource effects. It confirms the speaker's membership in a linguistic community and reinforces the schemas that make the generation of grammatical sentences possible. Assuming that an utterance is made to other competent speakers of the language, the speaking of a grammatical sentence in itself creates no significant power disparities but rather establishes an equality among the conversants. Language, of course, serves as a medium for all kinds of enactments of power relations, but at the level of phonology, morphology, syntax, and semantics, it is as close as we are likely to get to a neutral medium of exchange. This relative neutrality with respect to power helps to account for the other peculiarity of linguistic structures: their extraordinary durability. If the enactment of linguistic schemas serves only to sustain the linguistic empowerment of speakers without sharply shifting resources toward some speakers and away from others, then no one has much incentive to engage in innovations that would transform linguistic structures.

If it is true that linguistic structures are much less implicated in power relations and much deeper and more durable than most structures, it follows that we should be wary of the widespread tendency to use linguistic structures as a paradigm for structures in general. Although the elegance of the linguistic model may set an enviable standard, structures that operate nearer the surface of social life and that are more directly implicated in power relations may have very different principles and dynamics. One danger that arises from accepting the linguistic model uncritically is a tendency to think of structures as composed purely of schemas, while ignoring the resource dimension. In studying the syntactic structures of languages, where the enactment of schemas has minor power consequences, it does not matter much if the resource aspect of structure is neglected. But when we try to make sense of the arenas of life more permeated by power relations, it may be downright crippling to apply the linguistic analogy and conceptualize structures purely as schemas.

States Particularly poor candidates for the linguistic analogy would be state or political structures, which commonly generate and utilize large concentrations of power and which are usually relatively near the surface of social life. State and political structures are consciously established, maintained, fought over, and argued about rather than taken for granted as if they were unchangeable features of the world. Although one might initially imagine that large power concentrations would tend to assure a structure's durability, this may not actually be true. Although centralized states with immense coercive power impose high costs on those who would challenge them, it is far from clear that centralized and coercive states have generally proved more durable than relatively decentralized or uncoercive states. [...] One might argue that state structures are relatively mutable precisely because the massiveness (power) and obviousness (lack of depth) of their resource effects make them natural targets for open struggles.

But if most political structures are characterized by both high power and low depth, an inverse relationship between power and depth is by no means necessary. There are some political structures with immense power implications that are nevertheless relatively deep, that have become "second nature" and are accepted by all (or nearly all) political actors as essentially power-neutral, taken-for-granted means to political ends. Such structures also appear to be unusually durable. This would appear to be true of political structures as diverse as the American constitutional system, the French public bureaucracy, or the English community legal structures whose persistence Margaret Somers (1986) has traced from the 14th to the mid-19th century. Durability, then, would appear to be determined more by a structure's depth than by its power. [. . .] In some cases, structures can combine depth with great power and, consequently, can shape the experiences of entire societies over many generations.

Conclusion

Beginning from the premise that structure is an unavoidable epistemic metaphor in the social sciences, I have tried to specify how that metaphor should be understood. Structures, I have argued, are constituted by mutually sustaining cultural schemas and sets of resources that empower and constrain social action and tend to be reproduced by that action. Agents are empowered by structures, both by the knowledge of cultural schemas that enables them to mobilize resources and by the access to resources that enables them to enact schemas. This differs from ordinary sociological usage of the term because it insists that structure is a profoundly cultural phenomenon and from ordinary anthropological usage because it insists that structure always derives from the character and distribution of resources in the everyday world. Structure is dynamic, not static; it is the continually evolving outcome and matrix of a process of social interaction. Even the more or less perfect reproduction of structures is a profoundly temporal process that requires resourceful and innovative human conduct. But the same resourceful agency that sustains the reproduction of structures also makes possible their transformation—by means of transpositions of schemas and remobilizations of resources that make the new structures recognizable as transformations of the old. Structures, I suggest, are not reified categories we can invoke to explain the inevitable shape of social life. To invoke structures as I have defined them here is to call for a critical analysis of the dialectical interactions through which humans shape their history.

NOTES

1 This bifurcation of the meaning of structure especially inhibits communication between two groups of social scientists whose current projects seem convergent but who have thus far paid little attention to one another: the growing band of sociologists who are examining the cultural dimensions of social life and the anthropologists who are insisting on the importance of power and practice in understanding culture. For an assessment of the mushrooming field of cultural sociology, see Lamont and Wuthnow (1990). For trends in current anthropology, see the remarks of Ortner (1984, pp. 144–60).

2 It is not my purpose to develop a full critique or appreciation of Giddens or Bourdieu. The critical literature on both is growing rapidly. Held and Thompson (1989) and Bryant and Jary (1991) include not only a wide range of critiques of Giddens's work by prominent scholars but also useful bibliographical listings of previous critiques. On Bourdieu, see DiMaggio (1979), Brubaker (1985), Lamont and Lareau (1988), and Wacquant (1989). The last of these contains extensive references to critical works on Bourdieu.

3 For a particularly convincing critique of the notion of "rule," see Bourdieu (1977, pp. 1–29).

4 Giddens's concept of rules has occasionally been criticized, most recently by Thompson (1989), but to my knowledge no one has systematically criticized his paired concept of resources.

5 Some of Bourdieu's more recent work, esp. *Homo Academicus* (1988), which is a study of the French professoriat in the events of 1968, deals more directly with change. I do not think, however, that Bourdieu has considered the question of how habitus itself might *generate* change. In *Homo Academicus*, e.g., change arises from sources external to the habitus he is analyzing—fundamentally from the immense rise in the population of students in French universities in the 1960s. The concept of habitus is used to argue that the professors' responses to the crisis was wholly determined by their location in the "academic field." *Homo Academicus* seems to indicate that Bourdieu has not overcome the lack of agency inherent in the concept of habitus elaborated in *Outline of a Theory of Practice*.

6 To generalize a rule implies stating it in more abstract form so that it will apply to a larger number of cases. The verb "transpose" implies a concrete application of a rule to a new case, but in such a way that the rule will have subtly different forms in each of its applications. This is implied by three of the *Oxford English Dictionary's* (1971, s.v. "transpose") definitions: "To remove from one place or time to another; to transfer, shift," "to alter the order of or the position of in a series . . . to interchange," and, in music, "to put into a different key." *Transposer*, in French (which was of course the language in which Bourdieu wrote), also has an even more appropriate meaning: "faire changer de forme ou de contenu en faisant passer dans un autre domaine," (to cause something to change in form or content by causing it to pass into another domain, *Le Petit Robert* [1984, s.v. "transposer"]). I would like my use of *transpose* to be understood as retaining something of this French meaning.

7 Here my thinking has been influenced by Goran Therborn (1980, esp. pp. 15–22).

8 Although Marshall Sahlins (1981, 1985) does not explicitly include resources in his definition of structure, my argument here runs closely parallel to his. Sahlins argues that "in action in the world—technically, in acts of reference—the cultural categories acquire new functional values" because the categories are "burdened with the world" (1985, p. 138). This burdening of categories with the world is a matter of schemas being changed by the unanticipated effects of action on the resources that sustain the schemas.

REFERENCES

Bourdieu, Pierre. 1977. *Outline of a Theory of Practice.* Cambridge: Cambridge University Press.

—— 1988. *Homo Academicus,* translated by Peter Collier. Stanford, Calif.: Stanford University Press.

Boas, Franz. 1966. *Kwakiutl Ethnography,* edited by Helen Codere. Chicago: University of Chicago Press.

Brubaker, Rogers. 1985. "Rethinking Classical Social Theory: The Sociological Vision of Pierre Bourdieu." *Theory and Society* 14: 745–75.

Bryant, Christopher G. A., and David Jary, eds. 1991. *Giddens' Theory of Structuration: A Critical Appreciation.* London: Routledge.

DiMaggio, Paul. 1979. "Review Essay: On Pierre Bourdieu." *American Journal of Sociology* 84: 1460–74.

Giddens, Anthony. 1976. *New Rules of Sociological Method: A Positive Critique of Interpretive Sociologies.* London: Hutchinson.

—— 1979. *Central Problems in Social Theory: Action, Structure and Contradiction in Social Analysis.* Berkeley and Los Angeles: University of California Press.

—— 1981. *A Contemporary Critique of Historical Materialism.* Volume 1: *Power, Property and the State.* London: Macmillan.

—— 1984. *The Constitution of Society: Outline of the Theory of Structuration.* Berkeley and Los Angeles: University of California Press.

Held, David, and John B. Thompson, eds. 1989. *Social Theory of Modern Societies: Anthony Giddens and His Critics.* Cambridge: Cambridge University Press.

Lamont, Michèle, and Annette Lareau. 1988. "Cultural Capital: Allusions, Gaps, and Glissandos in Recent Theoretical Development." *Sociological Theory* 6: 153–68.

Lamont, Michèle, and Robert Wuthnow. 1990. "Betwixt and Between: Recent Cultural Sociology in Europe and the United States." Pp. 287–315 in *Frontiers of Social Theory: The New Synthesis,* edited by George Ritzer. New York: Columbia University Press.

Lévi-Strauss, Claude. 1966. *The Savage Mind.* Chicago: University of Chicago Press.

Ortner, Sherry B. 1984. "Theory in Anthropology since the Sixties." *Comparative Studies in Society and History* 26: 126–66.

Oxford English Dictionary. 1971. *The Compact Edition of the Oxford English Dictionary.* Oxford: Oxford University Press.

Le Petit Robert. 1984. *Le Petit Robert: Dictionnaire alphabétique et analogique de la langue française.* Paris: Le Robert.

Rosaldo, Renato. 1980. *Ilongot Headhunting, 1883–1974: A Study in Society and History.* Stanford, Calif.: Stanford University Press.

Sahlins, Marshall. 1981. *Historical Metaphors and Mythical Realities.* Ann Arbor: University of Michigan Press.

—— 1985. *Islands of History.* Chicago: University of Chicago Press.

—— 1989. "The Cosmology of Capitalism: The Trans-Pacific Sector of the World System." *Proceedings of the British Academy for 1988.*

—— 1991. "The Return of the Event, Again; With Reflections on the Beginnings of the Great Fijian War of 1843 to 1855 between the Kingdoms of Bau and Rewa." Pp. 37–100 in *Clio in Oceania: Toward a Historical Anthropology,* edited by A. Biersack. Washington, D.C.: Smithsonian.

Somers, Margaret Ramsay. 1986. "The People and the Law: The Place of the Public Sphere in the Formation of English Popular Identity." Ph.D. dissertation. Harvard University, Department of Sociology.

Therborn, Goran. 1980. *The Ideology of Power and the Power of Ideology.* London: Verso.

Thompson, John B. 1989. "The Theory of Structuration." Pp. 56–76 in *Social Theory of Modern Societies: Anthony Giddens and His Critics*, edited by D. Held and J. B. Thompson. Cambridge: Cambridge University Press.

Wacquant, Loïc. 1989. "Towards a Reflexive Sociology: A Workshop with Pierre Bourdieu." *Sociological Theory* 7: 26–63.

8

HOW TO BE AN
INTENTIONALIST

Mark Bevir

One of the major problems currently under debate in linguistic turn historiography derives from what theorists identify as its tendency to emphasize the unconscious, semiotically constructed nature of human behavior, the effect of which is to destroy any foundation for a theory of human agency or intentionality. If all behavior is largely governed by unconscious forces, there can be no ground upon which a concept of agency can be accepted. Mark Bevir, an intellectual historian and philosopher, begins by asking whether we can "still be intentionalists in a postfoundational age?" In this article, which represents both a summary of the larger argument found in his recent book, The Logic of the History of Ideas, *and a response to criticism of that book by Vivienne Brown ("On Some Problems with Weak Intentionalism for Intellectual History,") Bevir seeks to fashion a postfoundational theory of intentionality, in particular as it applies to questions of intellectual history. Accepting the basic insight of poststructuralism (or what he calls "the new textualism"), namely that there is no unmediated access to concepts or reality independent of their linguistic (or textual) construction, Bevir nonetheless seeks to rehabilitate the subjective perspective of historical persons and their mental acts of consciousness. He does this by arguing for the unconstrained character of individual meaning-making, postulating an "intentional theory of meaning," which he qualifies as a "weak intentionalism" since it is always conditioned, although not compelled, by the cultural legacies—the intellectual traditions and social inheritances—within which thinkers must, of necessity, operate and which, therefore, inevitably exercise influence on them. Bevir's theory of "weak intentionality" rests on the philosophical argument that (1) actions in the world can be inferred to be guided by beliefs, without which such actions would not be taken; and (2) the existence of beliefs, which are at the very least provisionally true for those who hold and act upon them, in turn implies the existence of intentional states. Hence social behavior itself, which here includes such things as writing and reading intellectual works, indicates that intentions exist in the minds of individuals, and indeed have meanings that are specific to individuals alone, since, he argues, "meanings are always meanings for specific individuals." It is this last point that compels Bevir to qualify his restored intentionalism as "weak," since it can only be established on the basis of individual beliefs and aims.*

Among the revisionists represented in this volume, Bevir goes farthest toward the rehabilitation of the individual in his theory of a freely operating, conscious intentionality by means of which he seeks, as he says in The Logic of the History of Ideas, *to "grapple with concepts tied to the creativity of the individual subject— concepts such as agency, intentionality and intuition" (p. 126). In this, he comes close to reviving liberal conceptions of the individual considered as the source and generator of social and intellectual meaning.*

* * *

[...]

One strand within the linguistic turn in the human sciences has emphasized the inescapability of textuality: it has made familiar what once were shocking phrases, such as everything is text or "there is no 'outside' to the text."[1] Two of the themes conveyed by these phrases are widely shared by participants in the many diverse strands that make up the linguistic turn. The first theme is a postfoundationalism that implies that all experience and reasoning is theory-laden, as opposed to being concerned with a given object. The second theme is a consequent view of individuals as inherently embedded within social traditions or languages. A third theme conveyed by such phrases is, however, notably more contentious even among those effected by the linguistic turn. This final theme is the idea that historians are trapped in texts so that they cannot access, or appeal to, objects outside texts. According to what we might label "new textualism," texts – whether written or not – gain meaning only from a chain of signifiers that takes us from text to text without any possibility of our ever bringing this chain to an end by invoking an intention, action, or other object.[2] What should we make of this new textualism? Can we still be intentionalists in a postfoundational age? Can we reject the third theme even if we accept – as I do – the first two? Vivienne Brown raises these issues for me, and I am grateful to her for so doing. In what follows, I hope fruitfully to address them, as well as her specific questions. [...]

Outside the text

The distinction between intentionalism and the new textualism is often confused with that between foundationalism and postfoundationalism. Really, we need not equate the two distinctions. To be intentionalists, we need counter only the new textualist view that historians cannot legitimately appeal to intentions in order to bring the alleged play of signifiers to a close; we do not also have to repudiate either postfoundational epistemology or the view that individuals are inherently socially embedded. To rethink the distinction between intentionalism and the new textualism in this way is to raise the possibility of postfoundational intentionalism.

Postfoundational intentionalists share the first of the three themes charac-terizing the new textualism – we cannot have the pure experience or pure reason we would need to give our knowledge secure foundations. All experi-ences, including those of texts, are theory-laden: we, at least in part, construct their content through the prior theories we bring to bear upon them. This shared postfoundationalism supports a particular account of the historian's relation to the text. Historians have before them various relics from the past: we can call such a relic, as it is prior to our interpreting it, "the text as a phys-ical object." When historians interpret a text, they ascribe to it a meaning that derives, at least in part, from their prior theories: to indicate the constructed aspect of interpretation, we can call this "the meaning of a text for us."[3] Because historians thus, at least in part, construct the meaning a text has for them, we cannot describe them as mere recorders of a pristine intention or past exhibited by a text.

But it is at this point that postfoundational intentionalists part company with new textualists. New textualists imply that a postfoundational account of the historian's relationship to the text precludes any appeal to objects outside texts. They argue that because we cannot record a past exhibited by texts, we remain trapped within a world of texts – those we read and those we construct in our readings; we cannot access other objects, such as inten-tional states, in order to fix, illuminate, or explain textual meanings.[4] Any interpretation that pursues such an object to ground or gives meaning to a text is, they continue, a misconceived, and perhaps unethical, repression of the slippages, playfulness, and difference inherent in textuality. In contrast, postfoundational intentionalists seek to provide a justification for appealing to objects, specifically intentional states, which are outside texts. They invoke not only the text as a physical object, as well as the meaning of a text for us, but also the intentional states of individuals in the past.

How might we justify appealing to objects outside the text while accepting a postfoundational account of the historian's relationship to the text? My answer appeals to philosophical reasoning to defend commitments to the existence of objects belonging to general classes, and to inference to the best explanation to defend postulating particular instances of these general classes. Postfoundationalism implies that all our experiences, and so all our concepts and beliefs, are laden with our theories in a way that precludes our taking them as straightforward representations of the world. Nonetheless, whenever we act, we thereby commit ourselves to beliefs as provisionally true or adequate to the world. For example, if we feel hungry, go to a café, order a sandwich, pay in cash, and eat it, we commit ourselves to belief in the exist-ence of certain objects – such as bread and money – and about the nature of these objects – such as that food mitigates hunger, that others accept author-ized coins in exchange for commodities, and that we can act for reasons of our own. Philosophy can go to work on the beliefs our actions thus commit us to. It can analyze the implications of these beliefs so as to provide an account of the classes of objects with which we populate the world and the forms of reasoning appropriate to such objects. For example, our commitment to bread suggests we populate the world with physical objects, our commitment to money suggests we populate it with objects that acquire significance through inter-subjective beliefs, and our commitment to our being able to act for reasons of our own suggests we populate it with other intentional states. In this way, philosophical analysis of the beliefs embedded in our actions provides us with good reason to believe in the existence of objects belonging to certain general classes, including intentional states.

While philosophical reflection on the beliefs embedded in our actions provides us with good reasons for postulating the existence of objects belonging to certain general classes, it cannot legitimate our postulating particular instances of these classes. It allows us to claim that people have intentional states, but not to ascribe particular webs of belief to, say, Hobbes and Locke. It may appear that postfoundationalism implies that we have access only to our interpretations of texts, not to any intentional state of the author or reader. But this appearance is deceiving; postfoundationalists can justify ascribing a particular web of beliefs to an author or reader as a case of inference to the best explanation. Because we have good reason to populate the world with intentional states such as beliefs, we are justified in assuming a particular individual held a particular web of beliefs. Although historians obviously do not have direct access to this web of beliefs, they can justify ascribing a web to someone by saying that doing so best explains, or makes sense of, the evidence. For example, philosophy gives us grounds for assuming Hobbes had beliefs that he sought to convey in *Leviathan*, and this assumption raises the question of what these beliefs were; historians then can answer this question by saying that ascribing such and such beliefs rather than others to Hobbes best makes sense of the facts on which we agree. Inference to the best explanation thus provides the justification for postulating particular intentional states or webs of belief as those held by individuals in the past.

Although we can thus justify appeals to objects outside the text, we still have to acknowledge the theory-laden, and so provisional, nature of any knowledge we claim to have of such objects. Knowledge cannot be certain – based on appeals to pure facts. It must be provisional – justified by an anthropological epistemology that provides criteria in terms of which to compare different interpretations, that is, different sets of postulated historical objects.[5] Perhaps the new textualists want only to insist on this provisionality. If this is so, however, they have to allow for the existence of a world outside the text, in which case it seems to be incumbent upon them to say more than they have to date about what objects populate this world. Do they, for example, believe we should populate this world, at least provisionally, with intentional states? If they do not, what philosophical psychology do they offer as an alternative to that which dominates our daily practices?

Postfoundational intentionalism allows that historians do not have direct access to the past but rather confront a range of texts that they actively interpret. It differs from the new textualism in allowing historians, as part of their interpretations of texts, to postulate intentional states, and other historical objects, and thereby bring to a provisional halt the process of interpretation. The justification for historians postulating objects outside texts derives not from an alleged experience of such objects, but from inference to the best explanation within the context of philosophical commitments entailed by our beliefs. Philosophical reflection gives historians a justification for postulating objects of the general class they do – for example, intentional states such as beliefs. Inference to the best explanation provides them with a justification for postulating a particular set of such objects – for example, a particular web of beliefs as that held by an individual in the past.

Beliefs as intentional states

We have found that postfoundationalists need not conclude that there is no outside to the text. On the contrary, they can defend historians' postulating objects outside of the text by reference to, first, philosophical commitments to general classes of objects, and, second, inference to the best explanation with respect to particular objects belonging to the relevant general classes. To defend postfoundational intentionalism, we need also to establish that intentional states, notably beliefs, are the general class of object that give meaning to texts. My procedural individualism, or weak intentionalism, is an attempt to do just this.

Having established the possibility of escaping the text to postulate intentional states, we should clarify what it means to say that meanings are intentional. [. . .] [M]y weak intentionalism stands in contrast to a strong intentionalism that reduces all meanings to the prior purposes of authors. I use the term "intentional" to indicate that an object exists in or for the mind. My weak intentionalism consists of the claim that meanings only exist in or for a mind – meanings are always meanings for specific individuals; it also consists of a procedural individualism, according to which, when historians claim a text meant such and such, they should be able to specify for whom it did so, whether author or reader. All meanings arise from the intentional states, notably the beliefs, which individuals attach to texts. To defend this procedural individualism, we need to argue that meanings are always meanings for individuals, not innate or emergent properties of texts or disembodied languages. However, rather than repeating these arguments here – arguments Brown does not question – I want to turn to the questions she does raise, questions that allow me to continue to discuss the nature of the extra-textual objects invoked by postfoundational intentionalism.[6]

I prefaced my response to Brown's questions with a discussion of postfoundational intentionalism because many of them seem to me to embody confusion about the status of the beliefs that I would have historians invoke.

Brown appears to think that the only options on offer are new textualism and foundationalist intentionalism, and, as a result, she thinks I must be committed to taking at least some of these beliefs to be given by, or present in, texts themselves. In contrast, I am suggesting that all these beliefs – whether expressed or actual – are postulates made by historians.

Brown asks, what are expressed beliefs? Postfoundational intentionalists should reply that they are the beliefs people hoped to express by saying or doing whatever they did. Although historians never have direct access to such beliefs, they legitimately can postulate them as part of their interpretation of the texts before them. Indeed, because historians can study only what Brown calls the text itself, they can justify postulating the expressed beliefs they do only by saying that doing so best makes sense of the text itself. The text itself, however, does not possess agency in the sense of being able to express beliefs. On the contrary, procedural individualism clearly implies that texts only acquire a meaning if individuals ascribe one to them. While people can ascribe a meaning to a text for all sorts of reasons, moreover, historians surely do so in order to attain knowledge of the past, that is, to postulate objects that we have good reason to believe really existed in the past. Historians thus seek to ascribe to a text the meaning somebody in the past ascribed to it. Of course, historians do not have direct access to the expressed beliefs they thus postulate: there is nothing outside textuality to which they might appeal to justify postulating the expressed beliefs they do. As we have seen, however, they can still justify their interpretation – their attribution of expressed beliefs to someone in the past – as an inference to the best explanation.

Postfoundational intentionalism implies that texts do not express beliefs, but rather are objects on the basis of which historians attribute beliefs to people from the past. As such, we cannot parse my distinction between expressed and actual beliefs by referring simply to meanings allegedly inherent within texts. Brown goes awry, then, in equating actual beliefs with those expressed by the text itself, in contrast to the beliefs expressed by the author. My distinction between expressed and actual beliefs is, rather, one between two types of belief that historians might postulate as objects that existed in the past. Actual beliefs are those individuals hold and act upon.[7] Expressed beliefs are those they want to convey by saying what they do: for example, politicians who actually believe government mismanagement caused a depression might nonetheless say that the recession is a product of a global downturn in an attempt to express the belief that the government could not prevent it.

Brown's confusion over the nature of the distinction between expressed and actual beliefs arises, I suspect, because she thinks the text alone could provide evidence, and so express, actual beliefs contrary to those expressed by the author. Hence, she asks, "on what grounds may historians conclude that the beliefs an author expressed in a text differed from his or her actual beliefs?"[8] Postfoundational intentionalists should reply by emphasizing the holistic nature of historical interpretation. The evidence for disjunctures between actual and expressed beliefs typically derives not so much from the text itself as from other texts. Typically we distinguish between people's actual and expressed beliefs either because their expressed beliefs do not match with their actions or because we find an odd pattern across a pertinent range of utterances and actions. It is these mismatches and patterns that encourage us to postulate insincerity, the unconscious, and irrationality. Perhaps, however, someone will ask, what justifies historians postulating actual beliefs as "hidden" objects to explain such mismatches and patterns? Once more, postfoundational intentionalists should appeal here to inference to the best explanation in the context of the philosophical commitments embedded within our beliefs.

Some answers

Brown asks three specific questions of my postfoundational intentionalism. In my view, these questions also show her oscillating exclusively between foundationalism and new textualism. On the one hand, the sort of given experiences invoked by foundationalists appear to be the only grounds on which she allows historians to claim knowledge of objects. On the other, she follows the new textualists in denying that texts can provide us with such experiences of intentional states. Postfoundational intentionalism enables us to break out of the restrictions of such a dichotomy.

Brown's first question is, "how is it that the beliefs expressed by the work constitute a *historical* meaning when they are different from the beliefs expressed by the historical individual" (p. 203)? So phrased, the question rests on her confusion over the nature of expressed and actual beliefs. For postfoundational intentionalists, only an individual, not a work, expresses beliefs. What makes meanings historical is that they are meanings for specific individuals; that is to say, they are the meanings specific individuals attached to the text as a physical object at sometime in the past. Such historical meanings consist of expressed beliefs, which might or might not be in accord with the actual beliefs of the individual concerned. In either case, the historian ascribes the beliefs to the individual as part of a creative act of interpretation, not because the beliefs are simply given in the text. The historian is justified in so ascribing beliefs to people because of a combination of philosophical commitments and inference to the best explanation.

Historians can postulate both expressed and actual beliefs as those that people held in the past. Sometimes, moreover, the actual beliefs they ascribe are ones they take people to have held unconsciously. These unconscious beliefs are, however, historical in the same sense as the expressed and actual beliefs we already have considered: that is to say, they are objects that historians postulate as having had a real existence in time. What makes these beliefs historical is the fact that we ascribe to them a temporal existence in the past. When historians ascribe meanings to texts, therefore, they do so by appealing to objects external to those texts – to beliefs, which might be sincere or

insincere, conscious or unconscious, rational or irrational. Although historians only have access to the text, they still can legitimately postulate beliefs
external to the text in order to ascribe a meaning to it.

Brown's second question concerns the ontological status of these beliefs. In
reply, of course, postfoundational intentionalists should say that these beliefs
are objects we postulate, but that we postulate them as having a real existence. Underlying Brown's question, however, there seems to be a reluctance
to ascribe real existence to objects that historians postulate but to which they
have no direct access. While such reluctance befits foundationalists who
believe in pure experience, postfoundationalists should respond to it by
pointing out that in their view we do not have unmediated access to any
object, so all objects to which we ascribe real existence are ones we postulate.
Postfoundationalism implies that because all our experiences are laden with
our theories, we have access only to our interpretations of the world, not to
real objects. Nonetheless, within our interpretations we rightly ascribe a real
existence to some objects – the keyboard and computer screen in front of me
– on the basis of inference to the best explanation in the context of the philosophical commitments embedded in our practices. The case of intentional
states, including actual and expressed beliefs, is no different from these
objects. We postulate them as real objects within our interpretations of the
world.

Although the foregoing account of the ontological status of beliefs applies
to the unconscious just as readily as to the conscious, it does not address
Brown's question as to what criteria differentiate the two, given that historians only have one type of evidence – texts in themselves. This question
too has a foundationalist ring to it. It suggests that we can differentiate
objects only if they correspond to varied types of evidence. In contrast,
postfoundationalism implies that because all knowledge is theory-laden,
the justification for distinguishing two kinds of objects depends on doing
so helping us to make sense of the evidence. Postfoundational intentionalists thus should reply to Brown by saying that historians should invoke
unconscious beliefs when doing so enables them to offer a more compelling
account of the past. The relevant criteria are not attached to the evidence,
but rather to the practice in which we judge rival historical narratives. We
do not distinguish conscious and unconscious beliefs as atomized units
inherent in the evidence. Instead, we introduce both types of belief as and
when doing so gives an accurate, comprehensive, consistent, open, fruitful,
and progressive account of the past.

Brown's third question concerns the relationship of objectivity in intellectual history and in natural science. To begin, Brown suggests that historians
can compare rival historical interpretations only with each other, not with
extra-textual objects. I agree with her here since I invoke extra-textual objects
only as postulates made in interpretations. Thereafter, however, Brown
contrasts objectivity in history, so understood, with the objectivity in the
natural sciences, where, she implies, we can compare interpretations with a

fixed reality. Once again, her position gets too close to foundationalism. Postfoundationalists surely should deny that natural scientists, as well as historians, have pure experiences of an independent reality. In my view, historians and natural scientists alike have theory-laden experiences which they interpret by postulating a range of objects as having a real existence independent of their interpretations. Because these objects are postulates, neither natural scientists nor historians can compare their interpretations with some sort of external fact of the matter. Rather, natural scientists and historians alike can arrive at objective knowledge only through a suitable comparison of the rival merits of the various interpretations on offer. The knowledge at which they thus arrive will be theory-laden and provisional, rather than given and certain, but because they have good reasons for accepting it as true, it still constitutes objective knowledge for them.

Implications

I hope my responses to Brown's questions have opened novel lines of thought rather than merely restating arguments already made. The most obvious new line of thought is the evaluation of new textualism. In addition, my responses suggest that we should think of the beliefs that historians ascribe to people in the past not as present in text themselves, but as objects historians postulate as those that best make sense of the texts. This analysis of the beliefs historians ascribe to people coheres with several philosophical trends of recent years. Of particular interest to me is what I take to be its fit with my anthropological epistemology, according to which historical knowledge is justified not by reference to pure facts but in terms of a comparison between rival historical narratives – rival sets of postulates – in relation to appropriate epistemic criteria. More generally, it fits with the broad drift in the philosophy of mind from mentalism toward positions, such as analytic behaviorism, which analyze mental states as objects we postulate to make sense of action or to bridge a gap between input and output.

Postfoundational intentionalism not only coheres with certain philosophical trends, it also offers a distinctive view of the relationship of history and theory. On the one hand, postfoundational intentionalism suggests that historians can continue much as before: they still can go outside texts to invoke intentions and other historical objects that call a provisional halt to the process of interpretation. Equally though, it implies that they cannot neglect theory – sticking their heads in the sand like ostriches. Historians should acknowledge that their interpretations are saturated with their particular theories so that they need to offer some kind of defense of these theories. Nor should they seek to defend their theories by saying that these illuminate their material: such a defense cannot work since their theories are already implicated in their construction of their material. Instead, historians are required by intellectual rigor and honesty to develop, or at least gesture toward, a philosophical analysis that defends the theories and concepts they deploy;

this is so no matter how natural or straightforward these theories and concepts might appear to them. If the implications of postfoundational intentionalism should prove at all fruitful, then much of the credit should, of course, go to Brown for raising such pertinent issues.

NOTES

1 J. Derrida, *Of Grammatology*, transl. G. Spivak (Baltimore: Johns Hopkins University Press, 1976), 158. Although this textualism is now some thirty years old, and in parts of the human sciences a dominant orthodoxy, I am calling it the "new textualism" to distinguish it from the older view that the meaning of a text is inherent within it as an independent, idealized object.

2 "A text . . . is no longer a finished corpus of writing, some content enclosed in a book or its margins, but a differential network, a fabric of traces referring endlessly to something other than itself, to other differential traces." J. Derrida, "Living On: Borderlines," in H. Bloom *et al.*, *Deconstruction and Criticism* (New York: Seabury Press, 1979), 84.

3 Originally I reserved the word "text" for the "text as a physical object" and used "work" to refer to "the meaning a text has for someone," since doing so helped me to highlight my view that texts do not have any meaning in themselves. M. Bevir, *The Logic of the History of Ideas* (Cambridge: Cambridge University Press, 1999), 57–59.

4 "All those boundaries that form the running border of what used to be called a text, of what we once thought this word could identify, i.e. the supposed end and beginning of a work, the unity of a corpus, the title, the margins, the signatures, the referential realm outside the frame, and so forth [have been subject to] a sort of overrun that spoils all these boundaries and divisions and forces us to extend the accredited concept, the dominant notion of a 'text'." Derrida, "Living On: Borderlines," 83.

5 Bevir, *Logic*, 96–106.

6 For the relevant arguments, see especially ibid., 31–77.

7 Although I am eliding the differences between actual beliefs in cases of the unconscious and irrationality with those in cases of insincerity, I do not think unpacking the differences among the three cases would add to my response to Brown. For a fuller analysis of the specifics of each case, see ibid., 265–308.

8 I have rewritten Brown's question (pp. 205–206 above) to reflect my correction to her account of my distinction between expressed and actual beliefs.

Part III

EXPERIENCE
AND PRACTICE

9

OUTLINE OF THE THEORY OF PRACTICE

Structures and the habitus

Pierre Bourdieu

Pierre Bourdieu's Outline of the Theory of Practice *is frequently used by the authors represented in this collection as the basis for rethinking "linguistic turn" historiography in terms of concepts of agency, experience, and practice. In this seminal work, originally published in French in 1972, Bourdieu set out to examine the theoretical and social conditions that make objective knowledge possible by specifying the mode of production and functioning through which social actors exercise their practical mastery of the underlying schemes and codes of any given cultural configuration. In particular, Bourdieu wanted to frame a theory of practice sensitive to the ambiguities, equivocations, and indeterminacy of life as it is actually lived, thereby permitting the investigator to move, as he claimed, from the "mechanics of the model to the dialectic of strategies." For this reason, he focused on the strategies and tactics employed by social actors to negotiate social norms explicitly governing practice, so as to uncover the fundamental logic of practice as a logic distinct from that of a culture's underlying codes. In that sense, Bourdieu is interested in how culture is used by individuals in pursuit of goals and interests, thereby opening a space for intentionality and agency. An additional benefit of a focus on strategies and the realization of cultural models through practice, Bourdieu believed, was the recovery of time and temporal duration for consideration by the social scientist, a dimension previously obliterated by the concentration on timeless structures and models. For Bourdieu, what is most important is to understand how underlying cultural schemes work themselves out, in and through time, by means of actual social practices, which disclose actors' practical mastery of the symbolism of social interaction. Only in this way, he claimed, is it possible "to restore to practice its practical truth."*

The key concept in Bourdieu's formulation of a theory of practice is habitus, *which he defines as a deep structure generative of all thought and behavior, one that orients practice without producing it. In the* Outline of the Theory of Practice, *he defines* habitus *as composed of systems of durable, transposable dispositions, "an acquired system of generative schemes objectively adjusted to the particular conditions in which it is constituted; the habitus engenders all the thoughts, all the perceptions, and all the actions consistent with those conditions, and no others." It is an "immanent law*

179

... *[a]* lex insita *laid down in each agent by his earliest upbringing," one that "makes coherence and necessity out of accident and contingency," that, in effect, turns history into nature. Thus, in keeping with his early structuralist leanings, Bourdieu empha-sizes the unconscious nature of such schemes, which are subjective but not individual. Rather, the cultural schemes installed by the* habitus *are laid down in the earliest stages of life as basic dispositions, or orientations, and operate equally as bodily dispos-itions and mental operations that function, according to his metaphor, as "maps" of the individual's social worlds, generating thoughts, perceptions, expressions, and actions limited by the historically and socially existing conditions under which they are produced. Thus, while Bourdieu attempts to stress the relatively free and ambiguous nature of social strategies and tactics performed by individuals, who never simply reproduce their initial conditioning, social actors are in the end wholly governed by the generative schemes initially acquired via the cultures they inhabit which, as the citation at the beginning of this paragraph makes clear, allow only those behaviors and thoughts consistent with the culture's basic norms and institutions, "and no others." Although Bourdieu later attempted to modify his position in favor of a more open-ended understanding of agents' interpretive and social practices, most historians have taken the* Outline of the Theory of Practice *as the basis for their discussion of his work, hence the reason for its republication here.*

* * *

[...]

The structures constitutive of a particular type of environment (e.g. the material conditions of existence characteristic of a class condition) produce *habitus*, systems of durable, transposable *dispositions*,[1] structured structures predisposed to function as structuring structures, that is, as principles of the generation and structuring of practices and representations which can be objectively "regulated" and "regular" without in any way being the product of obedience to rules, objectively adapted to their goals without presupposing a conscious aiming at ends or an express mastery of the operations necessary to attain them and, being all this, collectively orchestrated without being the product of the orchestrating action of a conductor.

Even when they appear as the realization of the explicit, and explicitly stated, purposes of a project or plan, the practices produced by the habitus, as the strategy-generating principle enabling agents to cope with unforeseen and ever-changing situations, are only apparently determined by the future. If they seem determined by anticipation of their own consequences, thereby encouraging the finalist illusion, the fact is that, always tending to reproduce the objective structures of which they are the product, they are determined by the past conditions which have produced the principle of their produc-tion, that is, by the actual outcome of identical or interchangeable past practices, which coincides with their own outcome to the extent (*and only to the extent*) that the objective structures of which they are the product are prolonged in the structures within which they function. Thus, for example, in the interaction between two agents or groups of agents endowed with the same habitus (say A and B), everything takes place as if the actions of each of them (say, a_1 for A) were organized in relation to the reactions they call forth from any agent possessing the same habitus (say, b_1, B's reaction to a_1) so that they objectively imply anticipation of the reaction which these reactions in turn call forth (say a_2, the reaction to b_1). But the teleological description according to which each action has the purpose of making possible the reaction to the reaction it arouses (individual A performing action a_1, e.g. a gift or challenge, in order to make individual B produce action b_1, a counter-gift or riposte, so as to be able to perform action a_2, a stepped-up gift or challenge) is quite as naive as the mechanistic description which presents the action and the riposte as moments in a sequence of programmed actions produced by a mechanical apparatus. The habitus is the source of these series of moves which are objectively organized as strategies without being the product of a genuine strategic intention – which would presuppose at least that they are perceived as one strategy among other possible strategies.[2]

It is necessary to abandon all theories which explicitly or implicitly treat practice as a mechanical reaction, directly determined by the antecedent conditions and entirely reducible to the mechanical functioning of pre-established assemblies, "models" or "rôles" – which one would, moreover, have to postulate in infinite number, like the chance configurations of stimuli capable of triggering them from outside, thereby condemning oneself to the grandiose and desperate undertaking of the anthropologist, armed with fine positivist courage, who recorded 480 elementary units of behaviour in twenty minutes' observation of his wife in the kitchen.[3] But rejection of mechanistic theories in no way implies that, in accordance with another obligatory option, we should bestow on some creative free will the free and wilful power to constitute, on the instant, the meaning of the situation by projecting the ends aiming at its transformation, and that we should reduce the objective intentions and constituted significations of actions and works to the conscious and deliberate intentions of their authors.

[. . .]

It is, of course, never ruled out that the responses of the habitus may be accompanied by a strategic calculation tending to carry on quasi-consciously the operation the habitus carries on in a quite different way, namely an estimation of chances which assumes the transformation of the past effect into the expected objective. But the fact remains that these responses are defined first in relation to a system of objective potentialities, immediately inscribed in the present, things to do or not to do, to say or not to say, in relation to a *forthcoming* reality which – in contrast to the future conceived as "absolute possibility" (*absolute Möglichkeit*), in Hegel's sense, projected by the pure project of a "negative freedom" – puts itself forward with an urgency and a claim to existence excluding all deliberation. To eliminate the need to resort *def.*

to "rules", it would be necessary to establish in each case a complete description (which invocation of rules allows one to dispense with) of the relation between the habitus, as a <u>socially constituted system of cognitive</u> and <u>motivating structures</u>, and the socially structured situation in which the agents' *interests* are defined, and with them the objective functions and subjective motivations of their practices. It would then become clear that, as Weber indicated, the juridical or customary rule is never more than a *secondary principle* of the determination of practices, intervening when the primary principle, interest, fails.[4]

[. . .]

Because the dispositions durably inculcated by objective conditions (which science apprehends through statistical regularities as the probabilities objectively attached to a group or class) engender aspirations and practices objectively compatible with those objective requirements, the most improbable practices are excluded, either totally without examination, as *unthinkable*, or at the cost of the *double negation* which inclines agents to make a virtue of necessity, that is, to refuse what is anyway refused and to love the inevitable. The very conditions of production of the ethos, *necessity made into a virtue*, are such that the expectations to which it gives rise tend to ignore the restriction to which the validity of any calculus of probabilities is subordinated, namely that the conditions of the experiments should not have been modified. Unlike scientific estimations, which are corrected after each experiment in accordance with rigorous rules of calculation, practical estimates give <u>disproportionate weight</u> to <u>early experiences</u>: the structures characteristic of a determinate type of conditions of existence, through the economic and social necessity which they bring to bear on the relatively autonomous universe of family relationships, or more precisely, through the mediation of the specifically familial manifestations of this external necessity (sexual division of labour, domestic morality, cares, strife, tastes, etc.), produce the structures of the habitus which become in turn the basis of perception and appreciation of all subsequent experience. Thus, as a result of the *hysteresis effect* necessarily implied in the logic of the constitution of habitus, practices are always liable to incur negative sanctions when the environment with which they are actually confronted is too distant from that to which they are objectively fitted. This is why generation conflicts oppose not age-classes separated by natural properties, but habitus which have been produced by different *modes of generation*, that is, by conditions of existence which, in imposing <u>different</u> definitions of the <u>impossible</u>, the <u>possible</u>, and the <u>probable</u>, cause one group to experience as <u>natural</u> or <u>reasonable practices</u> or aspirations which another group finds unthinkable or scandalous, and vice versa.

Structures, habitus and practices

def.

The habitus, the durably installed generative principle of regulated improvisations, produces practices which tend to reproduce the regularities

immanent in the objective conditions of the production of their generative
principle, while adjusting to the demands inscribed as objective potentialities
in the situation, as defined by the cognitive and motivating structures making
up the habitus. It follows that these practices cannot be directly deduced either
from the objective conditions, defined as the instantaneous sum of the stimuli
which may appear to have directly triggered them, or from the conditions
which produced the durable principle of their production. These practices can
be accounted for only by relating the objective *structure* defining the social
conditions of the production of the habitus which engendered them to the
conditions in which this habitus is operating, that is, to the *conjuncture* which,
short of a radical transformation, represents a particular state of this structure. In practice, it is the habitus, history turned into nature, i.e. denied as
such, which accomplishes practically the relating of these two systems of relations, in and through the production of practice. The "unconscious" is never
anything other than the forgetting of history which history itself produces by
incorporating the objective structures it produces in the second natures of
habitus: ". . . in each of us, in varying proportions, there is part of yesterday's
man; it is yesterday's man who inevitably predominates in us, since the
present amounts to little compared with the long past in the course of which
we, were formed and from which we result. Yet we do not sense this man of
the past, because he is inveterate in us; he makes up the unconscious part of
ourselves. Consequently we are led to take no account of him, any more than
we take account of his legitimate demands. Conversely, we are very much
aware of the most recent attainments of civilization, because, being recent,
they have not yet had time to settle into our unconscious."[5]

[. . .]

Each agent, wittingly or unwittingly, willy nilly, is a producer and repro-
ducer of objective meaning. Because his actions and works are the product
of a *modus operandi* of which he is not the producer and has no conscious
mastery, they contain an "objective intention", as the Scholastics put it, which
always outruns his conscious intentions. The schemes of thought and expression he has acquired are the basis for the *intentionless invention* of regulated
improvisation. Endlessly overtaken by his own words, with which he maintains a relation of "carry and be carried", as Nicolaï Hartmann put it, the
virtuoso finds in the *opus operatum* new triggers and new supports for
the *modus operandi* from which they arise, so that his discourse continuously
feeds off itself like a train bringing along its own rails.[6] If witticisms surprise
their author no less than their audience, and impress as much by their retrospective necessity as by their novelty, the reason is that the *trouvaille* appears
as the simple unearthing, at once accidental and irresistible, of a buried
possibility. It is because subjects do not, strictly speaking, know what they
are doing that what they do has more meaning than they know. The habitus
is the universalizing mediation which causes an individual agent's practices,
without either explicit reason or signifying intent, to be none the less
"sensible" and "reasonable". That part of practices which remains obscure in

the eyes of their own producers is the aspect by which they are objectively adjusted to other practices and to the structures of which the principle of their production is itself the product.[7]

One of the fundamental effects of the orchestration of habitus is the production of a commonsense world endowed with the *objectivity* secured by consensus on the meaning (*sens*) of practices and the world, in other words the harmonization of agents' experiences and the continuous reinforcement that each of them receives from the expression, individual or collective (in festivals, for example), improvised or programmed (commonplaces, sayings), of similar or identical experiences. The homogeneity of habitus is what – within the limits of the group of agents possessing the schemes (of production and interpretation) implied in their production – causes practices and works to be immediately intelligible and foreseeable, and hence taken for granted. This practical comprehension obviates the "intention" and "intentional transfer into the Other" dear to the phenomenologists, by dispensing, for the ordinary occasions of life, with close analysis of the nuances of another's practice and tacit or explicit inquiry ("What do you *mean*?") into his intentions. Automatic and impersonal, significant without intending to signify, ordinary practices lend themselves to an understanding no less automatic and impersonal: the picking up of the objective intention they express in no way implies "reactivation" of the "lived" intention of the agent who performs them.[8] "Communication of consciousnesses" presupposes community of "unconsciouses" (i.e. of linguistic and cultural competences). The deciphering of the objective intention of practices and works has nothing to do with the "reproduction" (*Nachbildung*, as the early Dilthey puts it) of lived experiences and the reconstitution, unnecessary and uncertain, of the personal singularities of an "intention" which is not their true origin.

The objective homogenizing of group or class habitus which results from the homogeneity of the conditions of existence is what enables practices to be objectively harmonized without any intentional calculation or conscious reference to a norm and mutually adjusted *in the absence of any direct interaction* or, *a fortiori*, explicit co-ordination. [. . .] If the practices of the members of the same group or class are more and better harmonized than the agents know or wish, it is because, as Leibniz puts it, "following only [his] own laws", each "nonetheless agrees with the other".[9] The habitus is precisely this immanent law, *lex insita*, laid down in each agent by his earliest upbringing, which is the precondition not only for the co-ordination of practices but also for practices of co-ordination, since the corrections and adjustments the agents themselves consciously carry out presuppose their mastery of a common code and since undertakings of collective mobilization cannot succeed without a minimum of concordance between the habitus of the mobilizing agents (e.g. prophet, party leader, etc.) and the dispositions of those whose aspirations and world-view they express.

So it is because they are the product of dispositions which, being the internalization of the same objective structures, are objectively concerted that the practices of the members of the same group or, in a differentiated society, the same class are endowed with an objective meaning that is at once unitary and systematic, transcending subjective intentions and conscious projects whether individual or collective.[10] To describe the process of objectification and orchestration in the language of *interaction* and mutual adjustment is to forget that the interaction itself owes its form to the objective structures which have produced the dispositions of the interacting agents and which allot them their relative positions in the interaction and elsewhere. Every confrontation between agents in fact brings together, in an *interaction* defined by the *object-ive structure* of the relation between the groups they belong to (e.g. a boss giving orders to a subordinate, colleagues discussing their pupils, academics taking part in a symposium), systems of dispositions (carried by "natural persons") such as a linguistic competence and a cultural competence and, through these habitus, all the objective structures of which they are the product, structures which are active only when *embodied* in a competence acquired in the course of a particular history (with the different types of bilingualism or pronunciation, for example, stemming from different modes of acquisition).[11]

Thus, when we speak of class habitus, we are insisting, against all forms of the occasionalist illusion which consists in directly relating practices to properties inscribed in the situation, that "interpersonal" relations are never, except in appearance, *individual-to-individual* relationships and that the truth of the interaction is never entirely contained in the interaction. This is what social psychology and interactionism or ethnomethodology forget when, reducing the objective structure of the relationship between the assembled individuals to the conjunctural structure of their interaction in a particular situation and group, they seek to explain everything that occurs in an exper-imental or observed interaction in terms of the experimentally controlled characteristics of the situation, such as the relative spatial positions of the participants or the nature of the channels used. In fact it is their present and past positions in the social structure that biological individuals carry with them, at all times and in all places, in the form of dispositions which are so many marks of *social position* and hence of the social distance between objective positions, that is, between social persons conjuncturally brought together (in physical space, which is not the same thing as social space) and correlatively, so many reminders of this distance and of the conduct required in order to "keep one's distance" or to manipulate it strategically, whether symbolically or actually, to reduce it (easier for the dominant than for the dominated), increase it, or simply maintain it (by not "letting oneself go", not "becoming familiar", in short, "standing on one's dignity", or on the other hand, refusing to "take liberties" and "put oneself forward", in short "knowing one's place" and staying there).

Even those forms of interaction seemingly most amenable to description in terms of "intentional transfer into the Other", such as sympathy, friendship, or love, are dominated (as class homogamy attests), through the harmony of habitus, that is to say, more precisely, the harmony of ethos and tastes – doubt-less sensed in the imperceptible cues of body *hexis* – by the objective structure of the relations between social conditions. The illusion of mutual election or predestination arises from ignorance of the social conditions for the harmony of aesthetic tastes or ethical leanings, which is thereby perceived as evidence of the ineffable affinities which spring from it.

In short, the habitus, the product of history, produces individual and collec-tive practices, and hence history, in accordance with the schemes engendered by history. The system of dispositions – a past which survives in the present and tends to perpetuate itself into the future by making itself present in practices structured according to its principles, an internal law relaying the continuous exercise of the law of external necessities (irreducible to immediate conjunctural constraints) – is the principle of the continuity and regularity which objectivism discerns in the social world without being able to give them a rational basis. And it is at the same time the principle of the transformations and regulated revolutions which neither the extrinsic and instantaneous deter-minisms of a mechanistic sociologism nor the purely internal but equally punctual determination of voluntarist or spontaneist subjectivism are capable of accounting for.

It is just as true and just as untrue to say that collective actions produce the event or that they are its product. The conjuncture capable of transforming practices objectively co-ordinated because subordinated to partially or wholly identical objective necessities, into *collective action* (e.g. revolutionary action) is constituted in the dialectical relationship between, on the one hand, a *habitus*, understood as a system of lasting, transposable dispositions which, integrating past experiences, functions at every moment as a *matrix of percep-tions, appreciations, and actions* and makes possible the achievement of infinitely diversified tasks, thanks to analogical transfers of schemes permitting the solution of similarly shaped problems, and thanks to the unceasing correc-tions of the results obtained, dialectically produced by those results, and on the other hand, an *objective event* which exerts its action of conditional stimulation calling for or demanding a determinate response, only on those who are disposed to constitute it as such because they are endowed with a determinate type of dispositions (which are amenable to reduplication and reinforcement by the "awakening of class consciousness", that is, by the direct or indirect possession of a discourse capable of securing symbolic mastery of the practically mastered principles of the class habitus). Without ever being totally co-ordinated, since they are the product of "causal series" char-acterized by different structural durations, the dispositions and the situa-tions which combine synchronically to constitute a determinate conjuncture are never wholly independent, since they are engendered by the objective structures, that is, in the last analysis, by the economic bases of the social formation in question. The hysteresis of habitus, which is inherent in the social conditions of the reproduction of the structures in habitus, is doubtless one of the foundations of the structural lag between opportunities and the dispositions to grasp them which is the cause of missed opportunities and, in particular, of the frequently observed incapacity to think historical crises in categories of perception and thought other than those of the past, albeit a revolutionary past.

If one ignores the dialectical relationship between the objective structures and the cognitive and motivating structures which they produce and which tend to reproduce them, if one forgets that these objective structures are themselves products of historical practices and are constantly reproduced and transformed by historical practices whose productive principle is itself the product of the structures which it consequently tends to reproduce, then one is condemned to reduce the relationship between the different social agencies (*instances*), treated as "different translations of the same sentence" – in a Spinozist metaphor which contains the truth of the objectivist language of "articulation" – to the logical formula enabling any one of them to be derived from any other. The unifying principle of practices in different domains which objectivist analysis would assign to separate "sub-systems", such as matrimonial strategies, fertility strategies, or economic choices, is nothing other than the habitus, the locus of practical realization of the "articulation" of fields which objectivism (from Parsons to the structuralist readers of Marx) lays out side by side without securing the means of discovering the real principle of the structural homologies or relations of transformation objectively established between them (which is not to deny that the structures are objectivities irreducible to their manifestation in the habitus which they produce and which tend to reproduce them). [. . .]

Just as the opposition of language to speech as mere execution or even as a preconstructed object masks the opposition between the objective relations of the language and the dispositions making up linguistic competence, so the opposition between the structure and the individual against whom the structure has to be won and endlessly rewon stands in the way of construction of the dialectical relationship between the structure and the dispositions making up the habitus.

[. . .]

The habitus is the product of the work of inculcation and appropriation necessary in order for those products of collective history, the objective structures (e.g. of language, economy, etc.) to succeed in reproducing themselves more or less completely, in the form of durable dispositions, in the organisms (which one can, if one wishes, call individuals) lastingly subjected to the same conditionings, and hence placed in the same material conditions of existence. Therefore sociology treats as identical all the biological individuals who, being the product of the same objective conditions, are the supports of the same habitus: social class, understood as a system of objective determinations, must be brought into relation not with the individual or with the "class" as a *population*, i.e. as an aggregate of enumerable, measurable biological individuals, but with the class habitus, the system of dispositions (partially) common to all products of the same structures. Though it is impossible for *all* members of the same class (or even two of them) to have had the same experiences, in the same order, it is certain that each member of the same class is more likely than any member of another class to have been confronted with the situations most frequent for the members of that class. The objective structures which science apprehends in the form of statistical regularities (e.g. employment rates, income curves, probabilities of access to secondary education, frequency of holidays, etc.) inculcate, through the direct or indirect but always convergent experiences which give a social environment its *physiognomy*, with its "closed doors", "dead ends", and limited "prospects", that "art of assessing likelihoods", as Leibniz put it, of anticipating the objective future, in short, the sense of reality or realities which is perhaps the best-concealed principle of their efficacy.

In order to define the relations between class, habitus, and the organic individuality which can never entirely be removed from sociological discourse, inasmuch as, being given immediately to immediate perception (*intuitus personae*), it is also socially designated and recognized (name, legal identity, etc.) and is defined by a *social trajectory* strictly speaking irreducible to any other, the habitus could be considered as a subjective but not individual system of internalized structures, schemes of perception, conception, and action common to all members of the same group or class and constituting the precondition for all objectification and apperception: and the objective co-ordination of practices and the sharing of a world-view could be founded on the perfect impersonality and interchangeability of singular practices and views. But this would amount to regarding all the practices or representations produced in accordance with identical schemes as impersonal and substitutable, like singular intuitions of space which, according to Kant, reflect none of the peculiarities of the individual ego. In fact, it is in a relation of homology, of diversity within homogeneity reflecting the diversity within homogeneity characteristic of their social conditions of production, that the singular habitus of the different members of the same class are united; the homology of world-views implies the systematic differences which separate singular world-views, adopted from singular but concerted standpoints. Since the history of the individual is never anything other than a certain specification of the collective history of his group or class, *each individual system of dispositions* may be seen as a *structural variant* of all the other group or class habitus, expressing the difference between trajectories and positions inside or outside the class. "Personal" style, the particular stamp marking all the products of the same habitus, whether practices or works, is never more than a *deviation* in relation to the *style* of a period or class so that it relates back to the common style not only by its conformity – like Phidias, who, according to Hegel, had no "manner" – but also by the difference which makes the whole "manner".

The principle of these individual differences lies in the fact that, being the product of a chronologically ordered series of structuring determinations, the habitus, which at every moment structures in terms of the structuring experiences which produced it the structuring experiences which affect its structure, brings about a unique integration, dominated by the earliest experiences, of the experiences statistically common to the members of the same class. Thus, for example, the habitus acquired in the family underlies the structuring of school experiences (in particular the reception and assimilation of the specifically pedagogic message), and the habitus transformed by schooling, itself diversified, in turn underlies the structuring of all subsequent experiences (e.g. the reception and assimilation of the messages of the culture industry or work experiences), and so on, from restructuring to restructuring.

Springing from the encounter in an integrative organism of relatively independent causal series, such as biological and social determinisms, the habitus makes coherence and necessity out of accident and contingency: for example, the equivalences it establishes between positions in the division of labour and positions in the division between the sexes are doubtless not peculiar to societies in which the division of labour and the division between the sexes coincide almost perfectly. In a class society, all the products of a given agent, by an essential *overdetermination*, speak inseparably and simultaneously of his class – or, more precisely, his position in the social structure and his rising or falling trajectory – and of his (or her) body – or, more precisely, all the properties, always socially qualified, of which he or she is the bearer – sexual properties of course, but also physical properties, praised, like strength or beauty, or stigmatized.

The dialectic of objectification and embodiment

So long as the work of education is not clearly institutionalized as a specific, autonomous practice, and it is a whole group and a whole symbolically structured environment, without specialized agents or specific moments, which exerts an anonymous, pervasive pedagogic action, the essential part of the *modus operandi* which defines practical mastery is transmitted in practice, in its practical state, without attaining the level of discourse. The child imitates not "models" but other people's actions. Body *hexis* speaks directly to the motor function, in the form of a pattern of postures that is both individual and systematic, because linked to a whole system of techniques involving the body and tools, and charged with a host of social meanings and values: in all societies, children are particularly attentive to the gestures and postures which, in their eyes, express everything that goes to make an accomplished adult – a way of walking, a tilt of the head, facial expressions, ways of sitting and of using implements, always associated with a tone of voice, a style of speech, and (how could it be otherwise?) a certain subjective experience. But the fact that schemes are able to pass from practice to practice without going through discourse or consciousness does not mean that acquisition of the habitus comes down to a question of mechanical learning by trial and error. Unlike an incoherent series of figures, which can be learnt only gradually, through repeated attempts and with continuous predictable progress, a numerical series is mastered more easily because it contains a structure which makes it unnecessary to memorize all the numbers one by one: in verbal products such as proverbs, sayings, maxims, songs, riddles, or games; in objects, such as tools, the house, or the village; or again, in practices such as contests of honour, gift exchanges, rites, etc., the material which the Kabyle child has to assimilate is the product of the systematic application of principles coherent in practice,[12] which means, that in all this endlessly redundant material, he has no difficulty in grasping the *rationale* of what are clearly series and in making it his own in the form of a principle generating conduct organized in accordance with the same rationale.

[. . .]

Between apprenticeship through simple familiarization, in which the apprentice insensibly and unconsciously acquires the principles of the "art" and the art of living – including those which are not known to the producer of the practices or works imitated, and, at the other extreme, explicit and express transmission by precept and prescription, every society provides for *structural exercises* tending to transmit this or that form of practical mastery. Such are the riddles and ritual contests which test the "sense of ritual language" and all the games, often structured according to the logic of the wager, the challenge or the combat (duels, group battles, target-shooting, etc.), which require the boys to set to work, in the mode of "let's pretend", the schemes generating the strategies of honour?[13] Then there is daily participation in gift exchanges and all their subtleties, which the boys derive from their rôle as messengers and, more especially, as intermediaries between the female world and the male world. There is silent observation of the discussions in the men's assembly, with their effects of eloquence, their rituals, their strategies, their ritual strategies, and strategic uses of ritual. There are the interactions with their relatives, which lead them to explore the structured space of objective kin relationships in all directions by means of *reversals* requiring the person who saw himself and behaved as a nephew of his father's brother to see himself and behave as a paternal uncle towards his brother's son, and thus to acquire mastery of the transformational schemes which permit the passage from the system of dispositions attached to one position to the system appropriate to the symmetrically opposite position. There are the lexical and grammatical commutations ("I" and "you" designating the same person according to the relation to the speaker) which instill the sense of the interchangeability of positions and of reciprocity as well as a sense of the limits of each. And, at a deeper level, there are the relationships with the mother and the father, which, by their dyssymmetry in antagonistic complementarity, constitute one of the opportunities to internalize, inseparably, the schemes of the *sexual division of labour* and of the *division of sexual labour*.

But it is in the dialectical relationship between the body and a space structured according to the mythico-ritual oppositions that one finds the form par excellence of the structural apprenticeship which leads to the em-bodying of the structures of the world, that is, the appropriating by the world of a body thus enabled to appropriate the world. In a social formation in which the absence of the symbolic-product-conserving techniques associated with literacy retards the objectification of symbolic and particularly cultural capital, inhabited space – and above all the house – is the principal locus for the objectification of the generative schemes; and, through the intermediary of the divisions and hierarchies it sets up between things, persons, and practices, this tangible classifying system continuously inculcates and reinforces the taxonomic principles underlying all the arbitrary provisions of this culture.[14] Thus, as we have seen, the opposition between the sacred of the right hand and the sacred of the left hand, between *nif* and *ḥaram*, between man, invested with protective, fecundating virtues, and woman, at once sacred and charged with maleficent forces, and, correlatively, between religion (male) and magic (female), is reproduced in the spatial division between male space, with the place of assembly, the market, or the fields, and female space, the house and its garden, the retreats of *ḥaram*. To discover how this spatial organization (matched by a temporal organization obeying the same logic) governs practices and representations – far beyond the frequently described rough divisions between the male world and the female world, the assembly and the fountain, public life and intimacy – and thereby contributes to the durable imposition of the schemes of perception, thought, and action, it is necessary to grasp the dialectic of objectification and embodiment in the privileged locus of the space of the house and the earliest learning processes.

This analysis of the relationship between the objectified schemes and the schemes incorporated or being incorporated presupposes a structural analysis of the social organization of the internal space of the house and the relation of this internal space to external space, an analysis which is not an end in itself but which, precisely on account of the (dangerous) affinity between objectivism and all that is already objectified, is the only means of fully grasping the structuring structures which, remaining obscure to themselves, are revealed only in the objects they structure. The house, an *opus operatum*, lends itself as such to a deciphering, but only to a deciphering which does not forget that the "book" from which the children learn their vision of the world is read with the body, in and through the movements and displacements which make the space within which they are enacted as much as they are made by it.

The interior of the Kabyle house, rectangular in shape, is divided into two parts by a low wall: the larger of these two parts, slightly higher than the other, is reserved for human use; the other side, occupied by the animals, has a loft above it. A door with two wings gives access to both rooms. In the upper part is the hearth and, facing the door, the weaving loom. The lower, dark, nocturnal part of the house, the place of damp, green, or raw objects – water jars set on the benches on either side of the entrance to the stable or against the "wall of darkness", wood, green fodder – the place too of natural beings – oxen and cows, donkeys and mules – and natural activities – sleep, sex, birth – and also of death, is opposed to the high, light-filled, noble place of humans and in particular of the guest, fire and fire-made objects, the lamp, kitchen utensils, the rifle – the attribute of the manly point of honour (*nif*) which protects female honour (*ḥurma*) – the loom, the symbol of all protection, the place also of the two specifically cultural activities performed within the house, cooking and weaving. The meaning objectified in things or places is fully revealed only in the practices structured according to the same schemes which are organized in relation to them (and vice versa). The guest to be honoured (*qabel*, a verb also meaning "to stand up to", and "to face the east") is invited to sit in front of the loom. The opposite wall is called the wall of darkness, or the wall of the invalid: a sick person's bed is placed next to it. The washing of the dead takes place at the entrance to the stable. The low dark part is opposed to the upper part as the female to the male: it is the most intimate place within the world of intimacy (sexuality, fertility). The opposition between the male and the female also reappears in the opposition between the "master" beam and the main pillar, a fork open skywards.

Thus, the house is organized according to a set of homologous oppositions – fire: water :: cooked: raw :: high: low :: light: shade :: day: night :: male: female :: *nif* : *ḥurma*:: fertilizing: able to be fertilized. But in fact the same oppositions are established between the house as a whole and the rest of the universe, that is, the male world, the place of assembly, the fields, and the market. It follows that each of these two parts of the house (and, by the same token, each of the objects placed in it and each of the activities carried out in it) is in a sense qualified at two degrees, first as female (nocturnal, dark, etc.) insofar as it partakes of the universe of the house, and secondarily as male or female insofar as it belongs to one or the other of the divisions of that universe. Thus, for example, the proverb "Man is the lamp of the outside, woman the lamp of the inside" must be taken to mean that man is the true light, that of the day, and woman the light of darkness, dark brightness; and we also know that she is to the moon as man is to the sun. But one or the other of the two systems of oppositions which define the house, either in its internal organization or in its relationship with the external world, is brought to the foreground, depending on whether the house is considered from the male point of view or the female point of view: whereas for the man, the house is not so much a place he enters as a place he comes out of, movement inwards properly befits the woman.[15]

All the actions performed in a space constructed in this way are immediately qualified symbolically and function as so many structural exercises through which is built up practical mastery of the fundamental schemes, which organize magical practices and representations: going in and coming out, filling and emptying, opening and shutting, going leftwards and going rightwards, going westwards and going eastwards, etc. Through the magic of a world of objects which is the product of the application of the same schemes to the most diverse domains, a world in which each thing speaks metaphorically of all the others, each practice comes to be invested with an objective meaning, a meaning with which practices – and particularly rites –

have to reckon at all times, whether to evoke or revoke it. The construction of the world of objects is clearly not the sovereign operation of consciousness which the neo-Kantian tradition conceives of; the mental structures which construct the world of objects are constructed in the practice of a world of objects constructed according to the same structures.[16] The mind born of the world of objects does not rise as a subjectivity confronting an objectivity: the objective universe is made up of objects which are the product of objectifying operations structured according to the very structures which the mind applies to it. The mind is a metaphor of the world of objects which is itself but an endless circle of mutually reflecting metaphors.

quite self-replicating

All the symbolic manipulations of body experience, starting with displacements within a mythically structured space, e.g. the movements of going in and coming out, tend to impose the *integration* of the body space with cosmic space by grasping in terms of the same concepts (and naturally at the price of great laxity in logic) the relationship between man and the natural world and the complementarity and opposed states and actions of the two sexes in the division of sexual work and sexual division of work, and hence in the work of biological and social reproduction. For example, the opposition between movement outwards towards the fields or the market, towards the production and circulation of goods, and movement inwards, towards the accumulation and consumption of the products of work, corresponds symbolically to the opposition between the male body, self-enclosed and directed towards the outside world, and the female body, resembling the dark, damp house, full of food, utensils, and children, which is entered and left by the same inevitably soiled opening.[17]

The opposition between the *centrifugal*, male orientation and the *centripetal*, female orientation, which, as we have seen, is the true principle of the organization of domestic space, is doubtless also the basis of the relationship of each of the sexes to their "psyche", that is, to their bodies and more precisely to their sexuality. As in every society dominated by male values – and European societies, which assign men to politics, history, or war and women to the hearth, the novel, and psychology, are no exception – the specifically male relation to sexuality is that of *sublimation*, the symbolism of honour tending at once to refuse any direct expression of sexuality and to encourage its transfigured manifestation in the form of manly prowess: the men, who are neither conscious of nor concerned with the female orgasm but seek the affirmation of their potency in repetition rather than prolongation of the sexual act, are not unaware that, through the intermediary of the female gossip that they both fear and despise, the eyes of the group always threaten their intimacy. As for the women, it is true to say, with Erikson, that male domination tends to "restrict their verbal consciousness"[18] so long as this is taken to mean not that they are forbidden all talk of sex, but that their discourse is dominated by the male values of virility, so that all reference to specifically female sexual "interests" is excluded from this aggressive and shame-filled cult of male potency.

doubtful

193

[. . .] The child constructs its *sexual identity,* the major element in its social identity, at the same time as it constructs its image of the division of work between the sexes, out of the same socially defined set of inseparably biological and social indices. In other words, the awakening of consciousness of sexual identity and the incorporation of the dispositions associated with a determinate social definition of the social functions incumbent on men and women come hand in hand with the adoption of a socially defined vision of the sexual division of labour.

[. . .]

It is not hard to imagine the weight that must be brought to bear on the construction of self-image and world-image by the opposition between masculinity and femininity when it constitutes the fundamental principle of division of the social and symbolic world. As is emphasized by the twofold meaning of the word *nif,* sexual potency inseparable from social potency, what is imposed through a certain social definition of maleness (and, by derivation, of femaleness), is a political mythology which governs all bodily experiences, not least sexual experiences themselves. Thus, the opposition between male sexuality, public and sublimated, and female sexuality, secret and, so to speak, "alienated" (with respect to Erikson's "utopia of universal genitality", i.e. the "utopia of full orgasmic reciprocity") is only a specification of the opposition between the extraversion of politics or public religion and the introversion of psychology or private magic, made up for the most part of rites aimed at domesticating the male partners.

Bodily *hexis* is political mythology realized, *em-bodied,* turned into a permanent disposition, a durable manner of standing, speaking, and thereby of *feeling* and *thinking.* The oppositions which mythico-ritual logic makes between the male and the female and which organize the whole system of values reappear, for example, in the gestures and movements of the body, in the form of the opposition between the straight and the bent, or between assurance and restraint. "The Kabyle is like the heather, he would rather break than bend." The man of honour's pace is steady and determined. His way of walking, that of a man who knows where he is going and knows he will arrive in time, whatever the obstacles, expresses strength and resolution, as opposed to the hesitant gait (*thikli thamahmahth*) announcing indecision, half-hearted promises (*awal amahmah*), the fear of commitments and the incapacity to fulfil them. At the same time it is a *measured* pace: it contrasts as much with the haste of the man who "throws his feet up as high as his head", "walks along with great strides", "dances" – running being weak and frivolous conduct – as it does with the sluggishness of the man who "trails along". The manly man stands up straight and honours the person he approaches or wishes to welcome by looking him right in the eyes; ever on the alert, because ever threatened, he lets nothing that happens around him escape him, whereas a gaze that is up in the clouds or fixed on the ground is the mark of an irresponsible man, who has nothing to fear because he has no responsibilities in his group. Conversely, a woman is expected to walk with a slight

194

stoop, looking down, keeping her eyes on the spot where she will next put her foot, especially if she happens to have to walk past the *thajma'th*; her gait must avoid the excessive swing of the hips which comes from a heavy stride; she must always be girdled with the *thimehremth*, a rectangular piece of cloth with yellow, red, and black stripes worn over her dress, and take care that her headscarf does not come unknotted, revealing her hair. In short, the specifically feminine virtue, *lahia*, modesty, restraint, reserve, orients the whole female body downwards, towards the ground, the inside, the house, whereas male excellence, *nif*, is asserted in movement upwards, outwards, towards other men.

If all societies and, significantly, all the "totalitarian institutions", in Goffman's phrase, that seek to produce a new man through a process of "deculturation" and "reculturation" set such store on the seemingly most insignificant details of *dress, bearing*, physical and verbal *manners*, the reason is that, treating the body as a memory, they entrust to it in abbreviated and practical, i.e. mnemonic, form the fundamental principles of the arbitrary content of the culture. The principles em-bodied in this way are placed beyond the grasp of consciousness, and hence cannot be touched by voluntary, deliberate transformation, cannot even be made explicit; nothing seems more ineffable, more incommunicable, more inimitable, and, therefore, more precious, than the values given body, *made* body by the transubstantiation achieved by the hidden persuasion of an implicit pedagogy, capable of instilling a whole cosmology, an ethic, a metaphysic, a political philosophy, through injunctions as insignificant as "stand up straight" or "don't hold your knife in your left hand".[19] The logic of scheme transfer which makes each technique of the body a sort of *pars totalis*, predisposed to function in accordance with the fallacy *pars pro toto*, and hence to evoke the whole system of which it is a part, gives a very general scope to the seemingly most circumscribed and circumstantial observances. The whole trick of pedagogic reason lies precisely in the way it extorts the essential while seeming to demand the insignificant: in obtaining the respect for form and forms of respect which constitute the most visible and at the same time the best-hidden (because most "natural") manifestation of submission to the established order, the incorporation of the arbitrary abolishes what Raymond Ruyer calls "lateral possibilities", that is, all the eccentricities and deviations which are the small change of madness. The concessions of *politeness* always contain *political* concessions. The term *obsequium* used by Spinoza to denote the "constant will" produced by the conditioning through which "the State fashions us for its own use and which enables it to survive"[20] could be reserved to designate the public testimonies of recognition which every group expects of its members (especially at moments of co-option), that is, the symbolic taxes due from individuals in the exchanges which are set up in every group between the individuals and the group. Because, as in gift exchange, the exchange is an end in itself, the tribute demanded by the group generally comes down to a matter of trifles, that is, to symbolic rituals (rites of passage, the ceremonials of etiquette, etc.), formalities and formalisms which "cost nothing" to perform and seem such "natural" things to demand ("It's the least one can do . . ."; "It wouldn't cost him anything to . . .") that abstention amounts to a refusal or a challenge.[21]

Through the habitus, the structure which has produced it governs practice, not by the processes of a mechanical determinism, but through the mediation of the orientations and limits it assigns to the habitus's operations of invention.[22] As an acquired system of generative schemes objectively adjusted to the particular conditions in which it is constituted, the habitus engenders all the thoughts, all the perceptions, and all the actions consistent with those conditions, and no others. This paradoxical product is difficult to conceive, even inconceivable, only so long as one remains locked in the dilemma of determinism and freedom, conditioning and creativity [. . .]. Because the habitus is an endless capacity to engender products – thoughts, perceptions, expressions, actions – whose limits are set by the historically and socially situated conditions of its production, the conditioned and conditional freedom it secures is as remote from a creation of unpredictable novelty as it is from a simple mechanical reproduction of the initial conditionings.[23]

NOTES

1 The word *disposition* seems particularly suited to express what is covered by the concept of habitus (defined as a system of dispositions). It expresses first the *result of an organizing action*, with a meaning close to that of words such as structure; it also designates a *way of being*, a *habitual state* (especially of the body) and, in particular, a *predisposition, tendency, propensity*, or *inclination*. [The semantic cluster of "disposition" is rather wider in French than in English, but as this note – translated literally – shows, the equivalence is adequate. Translator.]

2 The most profitable strategies are usually those produced, on the hither side of all calculation and in the illusion of the most "authentic" sincerity, by a habitus objectively fitted to the objective structures. These strategies without strategic calculation procure an important secondary advantage for those who can scarcely be called their authors – the social approval accruing from apparent disinterestedness.

3 "Here we confront the distressing fact that the sample episode chain under analysis is a fragment of a larger segment of behavior which in the complete record contains some 480 separate episodes. Moreover, it took only twenty minutes for these 480 behavior stream events to occur. If my wife's rate of behavior is roughly representative of that of other actors, we must be prepared to deal with an inventory of episodes produced at the rate of some 20,000 per sixteen-hour day per actor . . . In a population consisting of several hundred actor-types, the number of different episodes in the total repertory must amount to many millions during the course of an annual cycle" (M. Harris, *The Nature of Cultural Things* (New York: Random House, 1964), pp. 74–5).

4 See the whole chapter entitled "Rechtsordnung, Konvention und Sitte", in which Max Weber analyses the differences and transitions between custom, convention, and law (*Wirtschaft und Gesellschaft* (Cologne and Berlin: Kiepenhauer und Witsch, 1964), vol. I, pp. 240–50, esp. pp. 246–9; English trans. "Law, Convention and Custom", *Economy and Society*, ed. G. Roth and C. Wittich (New York: Bedminster Press, 1968), 1, pp. 319–33).

5 E. Durkheim, *L'évolution pedagogique en France* (Paris: Alcan, 1938), p. 16.

6 R. Ruyer, *Paradoxes de la conscience et limites de l'automatisme* (Paris: Albin Michel, 1966), p. 136.
7 This universalization has the same limits as the objective conditions of which the principle generating practices and works is the product. The objective conditions exercise simultaneously a universalizing effect and a particularizing effect, because they cannot homogenize the agents whom they determine and whom they constitute into an objective group, without distinguishing them from all the agents produced in different conditions.
8 One of the merits of subjectivism and moralism is that the analyses in which it condemns, as inauthentic, actions subject to the objective solicitations of the world (e.g. Heidegger on everyday existence and *"das Man"* or Sartre on the "spirit of seriousness") demonstrate, *per absurdum,* the impossibility of the authentic existence that would gather up all pregiven significations and objective determinations into a project of freedom. The *purely ethical* pursuit of authenticity is the privilege of the leisured thinker who can afford to dispense with the economy of thought which "inauthentic" conduct allows.
9 C. W. Leibniz, "Second éclaircissement du système de la communication des substances", (1696), in *Oeuvres philosophiques,* ed. P. Janet (Paris: de Lagrange, 1866), vol. II, p. 548.
10 Were such language not dangerous in another way, one would be tempted to say, against all forms of subjectivist voluntarism, that class unity rests fundamentally on the "class unconscious". The awakening of "class consciousness" is not a primal act constituting the class in a blaze of freedom; its sole efficacy, as with all actions of symbolic reduplication, lies in the extent to which it brings to consciousness all that is implicitly assumed in the unconscious mode in the class habitus.
11 This takes us beyond the false opposition in which the theories of acculturation have allowed themselves to be trapped, with, on the one hand, *the realism of the structure* which represents cultural or linguistic contacts as contacts between cultures or languages, subject to generic laws (e.g. the law of the restructuring of borrowings) and specific laws (those established by analysis of the structures specific to the languages or cultures in contact) and on the other hand the *realism of the element,* which emphasizes the contacts between the *societies* (regarded as populations) involved or, at best, the structures of the relations between those societies (domination, etc.).
12 If illiterate societies seem to have a particular bent for the structural games which fascinate the anthropologist, their purpose is often quite simply mnemonic: the remarkable homology to be observed in Kabylia between the structure of the distribution of the families in the village and the structure of the distribution of graves in the cemetery (Aït Hichem, Tizi Hibel) clearly makes it easier to locate the traditionally anonymous graves (with expressly transmitted landmarks added to the structural principles).
13 Thus, in the game of *qochra,* which the children play in early spring, the cork ball (the *qochra*) which is fought for, passed and defended, is the practical equivalent of woman. In the course of the game the players must both defend themselves against it and, possessing it, defend it against those trying to take it away. At the start of the match, the leader of the game repeatedly asks, "Whose daughter is she?" but no one will volunteer to be her father and protect her: a daughter is always a liability for men. And so lots have to be drawn for her, and the unlucky player who gets her must accept his fate. He now has to protect the ball against the attacks of all the others, while at the same time trying to pass it on to another player; but he can only do so in an honourable, approved way. A player whom the "father" manages to touch with his stick, telling him "She's your daughter", has to acknowledge defeat, like a man temporarily obliged to a socially inferior family from whom he has taken a wife. For the suitors the temptation is to take the prestigious course of abduction, whereas the father wants a marriage that will free him from

guardianship and allow him to re-enter the game. The loser of the game is excluded from the world of men; the ball is tied under his shirt so that he looks like a girl who has been got pregnant.

14 It is said that formerly the women used to go to market alone; but they are so talk-ative that the market went on until the market time of the following week. So the men turned up one day with sticks and put an end to their wives' gossiping . . . It can be seen that the "myth" "explains" the present division of space and work by invoking the "evil nature" of women. When a man wants to say that the world is topsy-turvy, he says that "the women are going to market".

15 A full presentation of the analysis of the internal structure of the Kabyle house, of which it has only been possible to give the indispensable outline here, can be found in P. Bourdieu, *Esquisse d'une théorie de la pratique* (Paris and Geneva: Librairie Droz, 1972), pp. 45–69.

16 This means to say that the "learning by doing" hypothesis, associated with the name of Arrow (see K. J. Arrow, "The Economic Implications of Learning by Doing", *Review of Economic Studies*, 29, 3, no. 80 (June 1962), pp. 155–73) is a particular case (whose particularity needs to be specified) of a very general law: every made product – including symbolic products such as works of art, games, myths, etc. – exerts by its very functioning, particularly by the use made of it, an educative effect which helps to make it easier to acquire the dispositions necessary for its adequate use.

17 Erikson's analyses of the Yoruk might be interpreted in the same light (see E. H. Erikson, "Observations on the Yoruk: Childhood and World Image" (University of California Publications in American Archaeology and Ethnology, vol. 35, no. 10, Berkeley: University of California Press, 1943), pp. 257–302).

18 E. H. Erikson, "Childhood and Tradition in Two American Tribes", in *The Psycho-analytic Study of the Child* (New York: International Universities Press 1945), vol. I, pp. 319–50.

19 Every group entrusts to bodily automatisms those principles most basic to it and most indispensable to its conservation. In societies which lack any other recording and objectifying instrument, inherited knowledge can survive only in its embodied state. Among other consequences, it follows that it is never detached from the body which bears it and which – as Plato noted – can deliver it only at the price of a sort of gymnastics intended to evoke it: *mimesis*. The body is thus continuously mingled with all the knowledge it reproduces, which can never have the objectivity and distance stemming from objectification in writing.

20 A. Matheron, *Individu et société chez Spinoza* (Paris: Editions de Minuit, 1969), p. 349.

21 Thus, practical mastery of what are called the rules of politeness, and in particular the art of adjusting each of the available formulae (e.g. at the end of a letter) to the different classes of possible addressees, presupposes the implicit mastery, hence the recognition, of a set of oppositions constituting the implicit axiomatic of a determin-ate political order: in the example considered these are (in France) the opposition between men and women, the former requiring "homage", the latter "salutations" or "sentiments"; the opposition between the older and the younger; the opposition between the personal, or private, and the impersonal – with administrative or busi-ness letters; and finally the hierarchical opposition between superiors, equals, and inferiors, which governs the subtle grading of marks of respect.

22 One of the reasons for the use of the term habitus is the wish to set aside the common conception of habit as a mechanical assembly or preformed programme as Hegel does when in the *Phenomenology of Mind* he speaks of "habit as dexterity".

23 For a sociological application of these analyses, see P. Bourdieu, "Avenir de class et causalité du probable", *Revue Française de Sociologie*, 15, (January-March 1974), pp. 3–42. [. . .]

10

THE EVIDENCE OF EXPERIENCE

Joan Scott

Feminist historian Joan Scott's classic essay, "The Evidence of Experience," many times reprinted, extends the semiotic principle that there is no unmediated access to reality—that language, in the form of available discourses, prefigures our perception of the world—to the heart of the traditional historian's notion of historical trans-parency, the evidence of experience. For most historians, from Herodotus on, evidence (a word derived from the Latin videre, to see), typically functions as the bedrock of historical truth and objectivity, since it is grounded in the testimony of those who actually experience "what happened." The essay opens with Samuel Delany's account of a visit to a homosexual bathhouse, an experience that, in its powerful visibility, persuaded him of the "fact" of homosexuality as a mass move-ment, shaping the shared lives of millions of men and women, in contrast to the view of homosexuals at the time as "isolated" marginal figures. Delany's reliance on the "truth" of the evidence provided by his experience of the bathhouse is analogous to the historian's belief in a referential notion of evidence that presents it as a "reflection of the real."

Scott deploys the account to contest its implicit commitment to a referential concep-tion of evidence, buttressed by being grounded in individual experience. As she states, "what could be truer, after all, than a subject's own account of what he or she has lived through?" Yet, such an account of experience precludes any consideration of its constructed nature: of how subjects are constituted in the first place, and about how perception ("vision," producing "evidence") is structured by discourse and history. In short, it denies the very principles informing a semiotic understanding of history and the subject as socially constructed in language. Indeed, in the debates that attended the introduction of the "linguistic turn," "experience" became the ultimate term on which traditional historians took their stand in opposition to its claims.

The essay offers a rapid review of the way that "experience" came to function as the key concept grounding the authenticity of historical evidence as the source of historians' knowledge of the past and as the place where forces external to the historical subject operated.

In contesting this view of experience, Scott insists that to understand the histor-ically contingent ways that experience is constituted, "we need to attend to the historical processes that, through discourse, position subjects and produce their experience." It is not, she asserts, "individuals who have experience, but subjects who are constituted through experience." On this view, treating the emergence of identity "as a discursive event is not to introduce a new form of linguistic determinism, nor to deprive subjects of agency." Rather, it is to refuse to separate experience from language and to "insist instead on the productive quality of discourse," which constitutes subjects discursively, and hence constructs their experience. If "experience is the subject's history," then "language is the site of history's enactment." "Historical explanation cannot, therefore, separate the two."

Scott's position represents a logical articulation of "linguistic turn" historiography, one that is consistent with its basic semiotic principles. Yet few of the historians represented in this collection still share her belief that experience is itself a linguistic event, preferring to see language as the place where experience is made meaningful via a creative appropriation of the conditions of daily life, rather than created. And a problem remains for Scott in understanding how historical change occurs, how inherited languages or discourses become inadequate to explain the vast variety of empirical realities or experiences presented for interpretation, how, in short, life sometimes seems to outrun the capacity of culture to account for it.

* * *

Becoming visible

There is a section in Samuel Delany's magnificent autobiographical meditation, *The Motion of Light in Water*, that dramatically raises the problem of writing the history of difference, the history, that is, of the designation of "other," of the attribution of characteristics that distinguish categories of people from some presumed (and usually unstated) norm.[1]

Delany (a gay man, a black man, a writer of science fiction) recounts his reaction to his first visit to the St. Marks bathhouse in 1963. He remembers standing on the threshold of a "gym-sized room" dimly lit by blue bulbs. The room was full of people, some standing, the rest

> an undulating mass of naked, male bodies, spread wall to wall.
>
> My first response was a kind of heart-thudding astonishment, very close to fear.
>
> I have written of a space at certain libidinal saturation before. That was not what frightened me. It was rather that the saturation was not only kinesthetic but visible.[2]

Watching the scene establishes for Delany a "fact that flew in the face" of the prevailing representation of homosexuals in the 1950s as "isolated perverts," as subjects "gone awry." The "apprehension of massed bodies" gave him (as it does, he argues, anyone, "male, female, working or middle class") a "sense of political power":

200

what *this* experience said was that there was a population – not of individual homosexuals . . . not of hundreds, not of thousands, but rather of millions of gay men, and that history had, actively and already, created for us whole galleries of institutions, good and bad, to accommodate our sex.

(*M*, p. 174)

The sense of political possibility is frightening and exhilarating for Delany. He emphasizes not the discovery of an identity, but a sense of participation in a movement; indeed, it is the extent (as well as the existence) of these sexual practices that matters most in his account. Numbers – massed bodies – constitute a movement and this, even if subterranean, belies enforced silences about the range and diversity of human sexual practices. Making the movement visible breaks the silence about it, challenges prevailing notions, and opens new possibilities for everyone. Delany imagines, even from the vantage of 1988, a future utopian moment of genuine sexual revolution, "once the AIDS crisis is brought under control."

[. . .]

The point of Delany's description, indeed of his entire book, is to document the existence of those institutions in all their variety and multiplicity, to write about and thus to render historical what has hitherto been hidden from history. [. . .] In this conceptualization, the visible is privileged; writing is then put at its service.[3] Seeing is the origin of knowing. Writing is reproduction, transmission – the communication of knowledge gained through (visual, visceral) experience.

This kind of communication has long been the mission of historians documenting the lives of those omitted or overlooked in accounts of the past. It has produced a wealth of new evidence previously ignored about these others and has drawn attention to dimensions of human life and activity usually deemed unworthy of mention in conventional histories. It has also occasioned a crisis for orthodox history by multiplying not only stories but subjects, and by insisting that histories are written from fundamentally different – indeed irreconcilable – perspectives or standpoints, none of which is complete or completely "true." Like Delany's memoir, these histories have provided evidence for a world of alternative values and practices whose existence gives the lie to hegemonic constructions of social worlds, whether these constructions vaunt the political superiority of white men, the coherence and unity of selves, the naturalness of heterosexual monogamy, or the inevitability of scientific progress and economic development. The challenge to normative history has been described, in terms of conventional historical understandings of evidence, as an enlargement of the picture, a correction to oversights resulting from inaccurate or incomplete vision, and it has rested its claim to legitimacy on the authority of experience, the direct experience of others, as well as of the historian who learns to see and illuminate the lives of those others in his or her texts.

201

Documenting the experience of others in this way has been at once a highly successful and limiting strategy for historians of difference. It has been successful because it remains so comfortably within the disciplinary framework of history, working according to rules that permit calling old narratives into question when new evidence is discovered. The status of evidence is, of course, ambiguous for historians. On the one hand, they acknowledge that "evidence only counts as evidence and is only recognized as such in relation to a potential narrative, so that the narrative can be said to determine the evidence as much as the evidence determines the narrative."[4] On the other hand, historians' rhetorical treatment of evidence and their use of it to falsify prevailing interpretations, depends on a referential notion of evidence which denies that it is anything but a reflection of the real.[5] Michel de Certeau's description is apt. Historical discourse, he writes,

> gives itself credibility in the name of the reality which it is supposed to represent, but this authorized appearance of the "real" serves precisely to camouflage the practice which in fact determines it. Representation thus disguises the praxis that organizes it.[6]

When the evidence offered is the evidence of "experience," the claim for referentiality is further buttressed – what could be truer, after all, than a subject's own account of what he or she has lived through? It is precisely this kind of appeal to experience as uncontestable evidence and as an originary point of explanation – as a foundation on which analysis is based – that weakens the critical thrust of histories of difference. By remaining within the epistemological frame of orthodox history, these studies lose the possibility of examining those assumptions and practices that excluded considerations of difference in the first place. They take as self-evident the identities of those whose experience is being documented and thus naturalize their difference. They locate resistance outside its discursive construction and reify agency as an inherent attribute of individuals, thus decontextualizing it. When experience is taken as the origin of knowledge, the vision of the individual subject (the person who had the experience or the historian who recounts it) becomes the bedrock of evidence on which explanation is built. Questions about the constructed nature of experience, about how subjects are constituted as different in the first place, about how one's vision is structured – about language (or discourse) and history – are left aside. The evidence of experience then becomes evidence for the fact of difference, rather than a way of exploring how difference is established, how it operates, how and in what ways it constitutes subjects who see and act in the world.[7]

To put it another way, the evidence of experience, whether conceived through a metaphor of visibility or in any other way that takes meaning as transparent, reproduces rather than contests given ideological systems – those that assume that the facts of history speak for themselves and those that rest on notions of a natural or established opposition between, say, sexual practices and social conventions, or between homosexuality and hetero-sexuality. Histories that document the "hidden" world of homosexuality, for example, show the impact of silence and repression on the lives of those affected by it and bring to light the history of their suppression and exploitation. But the project of making experience visible precludes critical examination of the workings of the ideological system itself, its categories of representation (homosexual/heterosexual, man/woman, black/white as fixed immutable identities), its premises about what these categories mean and how they operate, and of its notions of subjects, origin, and cause. Homosexual practices are seen as the result of desire, conceived as a natural force operating outside or in opposition to social regulation. In these stories homo-sexuality is presented as a repressed desire (experience denied), made to seem invisible, abnormal, and silenced by a "society" that legislates heterosexuality as the only normal practice.[8] Because this kind of (homosexual) desire cannot ultimately be repressed – because experience is there – it invents institutions to accommodate itself. These institutions are unacknowledged but not invis-ible; indeed, it is the possibility that they can be seen that threatens order and ultimately overcomes repression. Resistance and agency are presented as driven by uncontainable desire; emancipation is a teleological story in which desire ultimately overcomes social control and becomes visible. History is a chronology that makes experience visible, but in which categories appear as nonetheless ahistorical: desire, homosexuality, heterosexuality, femininity, masculinity, sex, and even sexual practices become so many fixed entities being played out over time, but not themselves historicized. Presenting the story in this way excludes, or at least understates, the historically variable interrelationship between the meanings "homosexual" and "heterosexual," the constitutive force each has for the other, and the contested and changing nature of the terrain that they simultaneously occupy. *this is actually a very small claim!*

[...]

The project of making experience visible precludes analysis of the work-ings of this system and of its historicity; instead, it reproduces its terms. We come to appreciate the consequences of the closeting of homosexuals and we understand repression as an interested act of power or domination; alterna-tive behaviors and institutions also become available to us. What we don't have is a way of placing those alternatives within the framework of (histor-ically contingent) dominant patterns of sexuality and the ideology that supports them. We know they exist, but not how they have been constructed; we know their existence offers a critique of normative practices, but not the extent of the critique. Making visible the experience of a different group exposes the existence of repressive mechanisms, but not their inner workings or logics; we know that difference exists, but we don't understand it as rela-tionally constituted. For that we need to attend to the historical processes that, through discourse, position subjects and produce their experiences. It is not individuals who have experience, but subjects who are constituted through experience. Experience in this definition then becomes not the origin

A straw-man —
who doesn't know
(historical) influence
that ideas (historical) Schemes: Psych 101
perceptions?

of our explanation, not the authoritative (because seen or felt) evidence that grounds what is known, but rather that which we seek to explain, that about which knowledge is produced. To think about experience in this way is to historicize it as well as to historicize the identities it produces. This kind of historicizing represents a reply to the many contemporary historians who have argued that an unproblematized "experience" is the foundation of their practice; it is a historicizing that implies critical scrutiny of all explanatory categories usually taken for granted, including the category of "experience."

The authority of experience

History has been largely a foundationalist discourse. By this I mean that its explanations seem to be unthinkable if they do not take for granted some primary premises, categories, or presumptions. These foundations (however varied, whatever they are at a particular moment) are unquestioned and unquestionable; they are considered permanent and transcendent. As such they create a common ground for historians and their objects of study in the past and so authorize and legitimize analysis; indeed, analysis seems not to be able to proceed without them.[9] In the minds of some foundationalists, in fact, nihilism, anarchy, and moral confusion are the sure alternatives to these givens, which have the status (if not the philosophical definition) of eternal truths.

Historians have had recourse to many kinds of foundations, some more obviously empiricist than others. What is most striking these days is the determined embrace, the strident defense, of some reified, transcendent category of explanation by historians who have used insights drawn from the sociology of knowledge, structural linguistics, feminist theory, or cultural anthropology to develop sharp critiques of empiricism. This turn to foundations even by antifoundationalists appears, in Fredric Jameson's characterization, as "some extreme form of the return of the repressed."[10]

"Experience" is one of the foundations that has been reintroduced into historical writing in the wake of the critique of empiricism; unlike "brute fact" or "simple reality," its connotations are more varied and elusive. It has recently emerged as a critical term in debates among historians about the limits of interpretation and especially about the uses and limits of post-structuralist theory for history. In these debates those most open to interpretive innovation – those who have insisted on the study of collective mentalities, of economic, social, or cultural determinations of individual behavior, and even of the influences of unconscious motives on thought and action – are among the most ardent defenders of the need to attend to "experience." Feminist historians critical of biases in "male-stream" histories and seeking to install women as viable subjects, social historians insisting on the materialist basis of the discipline on the one hand and on the "agency" of individuals or groups on the other, and cultural historians who have brought symbolic analysis to the study of behavior, have joined political historians whose stories privilege the purposive actions of rational actors and intellectual historians who maintain that thought originates in the minds of individuals. All seem to have converged on the argument that experience is an "irreducible" ground for history.

The evolution of "experience" appears to solve a problem of explanation for professed anti-empiricists even as it reinstates a foundational ground. For this reason it is interesting to examine the uses of "experience" by historians. Such an examination allows us to ask whether history can exist without foundations and what it might look like if it did.

In *Keywords* Raymond Williams sketches the alternative senses in which the term *experience* has been employed in the Anglo-American tradition. These he summarizes as "(i) knowledge gathered from past events, whether by conscious observation or by consideration and reflection; and (ii) a particular kind of consciousness, which can in some contexts be distinguished from 'reason' or 'knowledge.'"[11] Until the early eighteenth century, he says, experience and experiment were closely connected terms, designating how knowledge was arrived at through testing and observation (here the visual metaphor is important). In the eighteenth century, experience still contained this notion of consideration or reflection on observed events, of lessons gained from the past, but it also referred to a particular kind of consciousness. This consciousness, in the twentieth century, has come to mean a "full and active 'awareness,'" including feeling as well as thought (*K*, p. 127). The notion of experience as subjective witness, writes Williams, is "offered not only as truth, but as the most authentic kind of truth," as "the ground for all (subsequent) reasoning and analysis" (*K*, p. 128). According to Williams, experience has acquired another connotation in the twentieth century different from these notions of subjective testimony as immediate, true, and authentic. In this usage it refers to influences external to individuals – social conditions, institutions, forms of belief or perception – "real" things outside them that they react to, and does not include their thought or consideration.[12]

In the various usages described by Williams, "experience," whether conceived as internal or external, subjective or objective, establishes the prior existence of individuals. When it is defined as internal, it is an expression of an individual's being or consciousness; when external, it is the material on which consciousness then acts. Talking about experience in these ways leads us to take the existence of individuals for granted (experience is something people have) rather than to ask how conceptions of selves (of subjects and their identities) are produced.[13] It operates within an ideological construction that not only makes individuals the starting point of knowledge, but that also naturalizes categories such as man, woman, black, white, heterosexual, and homosexual by treating them as given characteristics of individuals.

Teresa de Lauretis's redefinition of experience exposes the workings of this ideology. "Experience," she writes, is the process by which, for all social beings, subjectivity is constructed. Through that process one places oneself or is placed in social reality, and so perceives and comprehends as subjective (referring to, originating in, oneself) those relations – material, economic, and interpersonal – which are in fact social and, in a larger perspective, historical.[14]

The process that de Lauretis describes operates crucially through differentiation; its effect is to constitute subjects as fixed and autonomous, and who are considered reliable sources of a knowledge that comes from access to the real by means of their experience.[15] When talking about historians and other students of the human sciences it is important to note that this subject is both the object of inquiry – the person one studies in the present or the past – and the investigator him- or herself – the historian who produces knowledge of the past based on "experience" in the archives or the anthropologist who produces knowledge of other cultures based on "experience" as a participant observer.

The concepts of experience described by Williams preclude inquiry into processes of subject-construction; and they avoid examining the relationships between discourse, cognition, and reality, the relevance of the position or situatedness of subjects to the knowledge they produce, and the effects of difference on knowledge. Questions are not raised about, for example, whether it matters for the history they write that historians are men, women, white, black, straight, or gay; instead, as de Certeau writes, "the authority of the 'subject of knowledge' [is measured] by the elimination of everything concerning the speaker" ("H," p. 218). His knowledge, reflecting as it does something apart from him, is legitimated and presented as universal, accessible to all. There is no power or politics in these notions of knowledge and experience.

[. . .]

Another, very different use of "experience" can be found in E. P. Thompson's *Making of the English Working Class*, the book that revolutionized social and labor history. Thompson specifically set out to free the concept of "class" from the ossified categories of Marxist structuralism. For this project "experience" was a key concept. "We explored," Thompson writes of himself and his fellow New Left historians, "both in theory and in practice, those junction-concepts (such as 'need', 'class', and 'determine') by which, through the missing term, 'experience', structure is transmuted into process, and the subject re-enters into history."[16]

Thompson's notion of experience joined ideas of external influence and subjective feeling, the structural and the psychological. This gave him a mediating influence between social structure and social consciousness. For him experience meant "social being" – the lived realities of social life, especially the affective domains of family and religion and the symbolic dimensions of expression. This definition separated the affective and the symbolic from the economic and the rational. "People do not only experience their own experi-ence as ideas, within thought and its procedures," he maintained, "they also experience their own experience as *feeling*" ("PT," p. 171). This statement grants importance to the psychological dimension of experience, and it allows Thompson to account for agency. Feeling, Thompson insists, is "handled" culturally as "norms, familial and kinship obligations and reciprocities, as values or (through more elaborated forms) within art and religious beliefs" ("PT," p. 171). At the same time it somehow precedes these forms of expression and so provides an escape from a strong structural determination: "For any living generation, in any 'now,'" Thompson asserts, "the ways in which they 'handle' experience defies prediction and escapes from any narrow definition of determination" ("PT," p. 171).[17]

dítto Bourdieu

And yet in his use of it, experience, because it is ultimately shaped by relations of production, is a unifying phenomenon, overriding other kinds of diversity. Since these relations of production are common to workers of different ethnicities, religions, regions, and trades they necessarily provide a common denominator and emerge as a more salient determinant of "experi-ence" than anything else. In Thompson's use of the term, experience is the start of a process that culminates in the realization and articulation of social consciousness, in this case a common identity of class. It serves an integrat-ing function, joining the individual and the structural, and bringing together diverse people into that coherent (totalizing) whole which is a distinctive sense of class.[18] "'Experience' (we have found) has, in the last instance, been generated in 'material life', has been structured in class ways, and hence 'social being' has determined 'social consciousness'" ("PT," p. 171). In this way unequivocal and uniform identity is produced through objective circum-stances and there is no reason to ask how this identity achieved predominance – it had to.

?

The unifying aspect of experience excludes whole realms of human activity by simply not counting them as experience, at least not with any consequences for social organization or politics. When class becomes an overriding iden-tity, other subject-positions are subsumed by it, those of gender, for example (or, in other instances of this kind, of history, race, ethnicity, and sexuality). The positions of men and women and their different relationships to politics are taken as reflections of material and social arrangements rather than as products of class politics itself; they are part of the "experience" of capitalism. Instead of asking how some experiences become more salient than others, how what matters to Thompson is defined as experience, and how differ-ences are dissolved, experience becomes itself cumulative and homogenizing, providing the common denominator on which class consciousness is built.

[...]

In Thompson's account class is finally an identity rooted in structural rela-tions that preexist politics. What this obscures is the contradictory and contested process by which class itself was conceptualized and by which diverse kinds of subject-positions were assigned, felt, contested, or embraced.

As a result, Thompson's brilliant history of the English working class, which set out to historicize the category of class, ends up essentializing it. The ground may seem to be displaced from structure to agency by insisting on the subjectively felt nature of experience, but the problem Thompson sought to address isn't really solved. Working-class "experience" is now the ontological foundation of working-class identity, politics, and history.[19]

This kind of use of experience has the same foundational status if we substitute "women's" or "black" or "lesbian" or "homosexual" for "working-class" in the previous sentence. Among feminist historians, for example, "experience" has helped to legitimize a critique of the false claims to object-ivity of traditional historical accounts. Part of the project of some feminist history has been to unmask all claims to objectivity as an ideological cover for masculine bias by pointing out the shortcomings, incompleteness, and exclusiveness of mainstream history. This has been achieved by providing documentation about women in the past that calls into question existing inter-pretations made without consideration of gender. But how do we authorize the new knowledge if the possibility of all historical objectivity has been questioned? By appealing to experience, which in this usage connotes both reality and its subjective apprehension – the experience of women in the past and of women historians who can recognize something of themselves in their foremothers.

Judith Newton, a literary historian writing about the neglect of feminism by contemporary critical theorists, argues that women, too, arrived at the critique of objectivity usually associated with deconstruction or the new historicism. This feminist critique came "straight out of reflection on our own, that is, women's experience, out of the contradictions we felt between the different ways we were represented even to ourselves, out of the inequities we had long experienced in our situations."[20] Newton's appeal to experience seems to bypass the issue of objectivity (by not raising the question of whether feminist work can be objective) but it rests firmly on a foundational ground (experience). In her work the relationship between thought and experience is represented as transparent (the visual metaphor combines with the visceral) and so is directly accessible, as it is in historian Christine Stansell's insistence that "social practices," in all their "immediacy and entirety," constitute a domain of "sensuous experience" (a prediscursive reality directly felt, seen, and known) that cannot be subsumed by "language."[21] The effect of these kinds of statements, which attribute an indisputable authenticity to women's experience, is to establish incontrovertibly women's identity as people with agency. It is also to universalize the identity of women and thus to ground claims for the legitimacy of women's history in the shared experience of historians of women and those women whose stories they tell. In addition, it literally equates the personal with the political, for the lived experience of women is seen as leading directly to resistance to oppression, that is, to femin-ism.[22] Indeed, the possibility of politics is said to rest on, to follow from, a preexisting women's experience.

[. . .]

[I]t is precisely the discursive character of experience that is at issue for some historians because attributing experience to discourse seems somehow to deny its status as an unquestionable ground of explanation. This seems to be the case for John Toews, who wrote a long article in the *American Historical Review* in 1987 called "Intellectual History after the Linguistic Turn: The Autonomy of Meaning and the Irreducibility of Experience." The term *linguistic turn* is a comprehensive one used by Toews to refer to approaches to the study of meaning that draw on a number of disciplines, but especially on theories of language "since the primary medium of meaning was obviously language."[23] The question for Toews is how far linguistic analysis has gone and should go, especially in view of the post-structuralist challenge to foundationalism. Reviewing a number of books that take on questions of meaning and its analysis, Toews concludes that

> the predominant tendency [among intellectual historians] is to adapt traditional historical concerns for extralinguistic origins and reference to the semiological challenge, to reaffirm in new ways that, in spite of the relative autonomy of cultural meanings, human subjects still make and remake the worlds of meaning in which they are suspended, and to insist that these worlds are not creations *ex nihilo* but responses to, and shapings of, changing worlds of experience ultimately irreducible to the linguistic forms in which they appear.
>
> ("IH," p. 882)

By definition, he argues, history is concerned with explanation; it is not a radical hermeneutics, but an attempt to account for the origin, persistence, and disappearance of certain meanings "at particular times and in specific sociocultural situations" ("IH," p. 882). For him explanation requires a separation of experience and meaning: experience is that reality which demands meaningful response. "Experience," in Toews's usage, is taken to be so self-evident that he never defines the term. This is telling in an article that insists on establishing the importance and independence, the irreducibility of "experience." The absence of definition allows experience to resonate in many ways, but it also allows it to function as a universally understood category – the undefined word creates a sense of consensus by attributing to it an assumed, stable, and shared meaning.

Experience, for Toews, is a foundational concept. While recognizing that meanings differ and that the historian's task is to analyze the different meanings produced in societies and over time, Toews protects "experience" from this kind of relativism. In doing so he establishes the possibility for objective knowledge and for communication among historians, however diverse their positions and views. This has the effect (among others) of removing historians from critical scrutiny as active producers of knowledge.

The insistence on the separation of meaning and experience is crucial for Toews, not only because it seems the only way to account for change, but also because it protects the world from "the hubris of wordmakers who claim to be makers of reality" ("IH," p. 906). Even if Toews here uses "wordmakers" metaphorically to refer to those who produce texts, those who engage in signification, his opposition between "words" and "reality" echoes the distinction he makes earlier in the article between language (or meaning) and experience. This opposition guarantees both an independent status for human agents and the common ground on which they can communicate and act. It produces a possibility for "intersubjective communication" among individuals despite differences between them, and also reaffirms their existence as thinking beings outside the discursive practices they devise and employ.

[. . .]

Toews's "experience" thus provides an object for historians that can be known apart from their own role as meaning makers and it then guarantees not only the objectivity of their knowledge, but their ability to persuade others of its importance. Whatever diversity and conflict may exist among them, Toews's community of historians is rendered homogeneous by its shared object (experience). [. . .] In Toews's article no disagreement about the meaning of the term *experience* can be entertained, since experience itself lies somehow outside its signification. For that reason, perhaps, Toews never defines it.

Even among those historians who do not share all of Toews's ideas about the objectivity or continuous quality of history writing, the defense of "experience" works in much the same way: it establishes a realm of reality outside of discourse and it authorizes the historian who has access to it. The evidence of experience works as a foundation providing both a starting point and a conclusive kind of explanation, beyond which few questions can or need to be asked. And yet it is precisely the questions precluded – questions about discourse, difference, and subjectivity, as well as about what counts as experience and who gets to make that determination – that would enable us to historicize experience, and to reflect critically on the history we write about it, rather than to premise our history on it.

Historicizing "experience"

Gayatri Chakravorty Spivak begins an essay addressed to the Subaltern Studies collective with a contrast between the work of historians and literary scholars:

> A historian confronts a text of counterinsurgency or gendering where the subaltern has been represented. He unravels the text to assign a new subject-position to the subaltern, gendered or otherwise.
>
> A teacher of literature confronts a sympathetic text where the gendered subaltern has been represented. She unravels the text to make visible the assignment of subject-positions . . .

The performance of these tasks, of the historian and the teacher of literature, must critically "interrupt" each other, bring each other to crisis, in order to serve their constituencies; especially when each seems to claim all for its own.[24]

Spivak's argument here seems to be that there is a difference between history and literature that is both methodological and political. History provides categories that enable us to understand the social and structural positions of people (as workers, subalterns, and so on) in new terms, and these terms define a collective identity with potential political (maybe even revolutionary, but certainly subversive) effects. Literature relativizes the categories history assigns, and exposes the processes that construct and position subjects. In Spivak's discussion, both are critical operations, although she clearly favors the deconstructive task of literature.[25] Although her essay has to be read in the context of a specific debate within Indian historiography, its general points must also be considered. In effect, her statements raise the question of whether historians can do other than construct subjects by describing their experience in terms of an essentialized identity.

Spivak's characterization of the Subaltern Studies historians' reliance on a notion of consciousness as a "*strategic* use of positivist essentialism" doesn't really solve the problem of writing history either, since whether it's strategic or not, essentialism appeals to the idea that there are fixed identities, visible to us as social or natural facts.[26] A refusal of essentialism seems particularly important once again these days within the field of history, as disciplinary pressure builds to defend the unitary subject in the name of his or her "experience." Neither does Spivak's invocation of the special political status of the subaltern justify a history aimed at producing subjects without interrogating and relativizing the means of their production. In the case of colonial and postcolonial peoples, but also of various others in the West, it has been precisely the imposition of a categorical (and universal) subject-status (*the* worker, *the* peasant, *the* woman, *the* black) that has masked the operations of difference in the organization of social life. Each category taken as fixed works to solidify the ideological process of subject-construction, making the process less rather than more apparent, naturalizing rather than analyzing it.

It ought to be possible for historians (as for the teachers of literature Spivak so dazzlingly exemplifies) to "make visible the assignment of subject-positions," not in the sense of capturing the reality of the objects seen, but of trying to understand the operations of the complex and changing discursive processes by which identities are ascribed, resisted, or embraced, and which processes themselves are unremarked and indeed achieve their effect because they are not noticed. To do this a change of object seems to be required, one that takes the emergence of concepts and identities as historical events in need of explanation. This does not mean that one dismisses the *effects* of such concepts and identities, nor that one does not explain behavior in terms of their operations. It does mean assuming that the appearance of a new

211

histories should do history of categories

identity is not inevitable or determined, not something that was always there simply waiting to be expressed, not something that will always exist in the form it was given in a particular political movement or at a particular historical moment. [. . .]

Treating the emergence of a new identity as a discursive event is not to introduce a new form of linguistic determinism, nor to deprive subjects of agency. It is to refuse a separation between "experience" and language and to insist instead on the productive quality of discourse. Subjects are constituted discursively, but there are conflicts among discursive systems, contradictions within any one of them, multiple meanings possible for the concepts they deploy.[27] And subjects do have agency. They are not unified, autonomous individuals exercising free will, but rather subjects whose agency is created through situations and statuses conferred on them. Being a subject means being "subject to definite conditions of existence, conditions of endowment of agents and conditions of exercise."[28] These conditions enable choices, although they are not unlimited. Subjects are constituted discursively and experience is a linguistic event (it doesn't happen outside established meanings), but neither is it confined to a fixed order of meaning. Since discourse is by definition shared, experience is collective as well as individual. Experience can both confirm what is already known (we see what we have learned to see) and upset what has been taken for granted (when different meanings are in conflict we readjust our vision to take account of the conflict or to resolve it – that is what is meant by "learning from experience," though not everyone learns the same lesson or learns it at the same time or in the same way). Experience is a subject's history. Language is the site of history's enactment. Historical explanation cannot, therefore, separate the two.

The question then becomes how to analyze language, and here historians often (though not always and not necessarily) confront the limits of a discipline that has typically constructed itself in opposition to literature. [. . .] The kind of reading I have in mind would not assume a direct correspondence between words and things, nor confine itself to single meanings, nor aim for the resolution of contradiction. It would not render process as linear, nor rest explanation on simple correlations or single variables. Rather it would grant to "the literary" an integral, even irreducible, status of its own. To grant such status is not to make "the literary" foundational, but to open new possibilities for analyzing discursive productions of social and political reality as complex, contradictory processes.

[. . .]

Conclusion

Reading for "the literary" does not seem at all inappropriate for those whose discipline is devoted to the study of change. It is not the only kind of reading I am advocating, although more documents than those written by literary figures are susceptible to such readings. Rather it is a way of changing the focus and the philosophy of our history, from one bent on naturalizing "experience" through a belief in the unmediated relationship between words and things, to one that takes all categories of analysis as contextual, contested, and contingent. How have categories of representation and analysis – such as class, race, gender, relations of production, biology, identity, subjectivity, agency, experience, even culture – achieved their foundational status? What have been the effects of their articulations? What does it mean for historians to study the past in terms of these categories and for individuals to think of themselves in these terms? What is the relationship between the salience of such categories in our own time and their existence in the past? [. . .] The history of these concepts (understood to be contested and contradictory) then becomes the evidence by which "experience" can be grasped and by which the historian's relationship to the past he or she writes about can be articulated. This is what Foucault meant by genealogy:

> If interpretation were the slow exposure of the meaning hidden in an origin, then only metaphysics could interpret the development of humanity. But if interpretation is the violent or surreptitious appro-priation of a system of rules, which in itself has no essential meaning, in order to impose a direction, to bend it to a new will, to force its participation in a different game, and to subject it to secondary rules, then the development of humanity is a series of interpretations. The role of genealogy is to record its history: the history of morals, ideals, and metaphysical concepts, the history of the concept of liberty or of the ascetic life; as they stand for the emergence of different inter-pretations, they must be made to appear as events on the stage of historical process.[29]

Experience is not a word we can do without, although, given its usage to essentialize identity and reify the subject, it is tempting to abandon it alto-gether. But *experience* is so much a part of everyday language, so imbricated in our narratives that it seems futile to argue for its expulsion. It serves as a way of talking about what happened, of establishing difference and similarity, of claiming knowledge that is "unassailable."[30] Given the ubiquity of the term, it seems to me more useful to work with it, to analyze its operations and to redefine its meaning. This entails focussing on processes of identity produc-tion, insisting on the discursive nature of "experience" and on the politics of its construction. Experience is at once always already an interpretation *and* something that needs to be interpreted. What counts as experience is neither self-evident nor straightforward; it is always contested, and always therefore political. The study of experience, therefore, must call into question its originary status in historical explanation. This will happen when histor-ians take as their project *not* the reproduction and transmission of knowledge said to be arrived at through experience, but the analysis of the production of that knowledge itself. Such an analysis would constitute a genuinely nonfoundational history, one which retains its explanatory power and its interest in change but does not stand on or reproduce naturalized categories. It also cannot guarantee the historian's neutrality, for deciding which categories to historicize is inevitably political, necessarily tied to the historian's recognition of his or her stake in the production of knowledge. Experience is, in this approach, not the origin of our explanation, but that which we want to explain. This kind of approach does not undercut politics by denying the existence of subjects; it instead interrogates the processes of their creation and, in so doing, refigures history and the role of the historian and opens new ways for thinking about change.[31]

No – this suggests that all categories must be historical

NOTES

1 For an important discussion of the "dilemma of difference," see Martha Minow. "Justice Engendered," foreword to "The Supreme Court, 1986 Term," *Harvard Law Review* 101 (Nov. 1987): 10–95.

2 Samuel R. Delany, *The Motion of Light in Water: Sex and Science Fiction Writing in the East Village, 1957–1965* (New York, 1988), p. 173; hereafter abbreviated M.

3 On the distinction between seeing and writing in formulations of identity, see Homi K. Bhabha, "Interrogating Identity," in *Identity: The Real Me,* ed. Lisa Appignanesi (London, 1987), pp. 5–11.

4 Lionel Gossman, *Towards a Rational Historiography,* Transactions of the American Philosophical Society, n.s. 79, pt. 3 (Philadelphia, 1989). p. 26.

5 On the "documentary" or "objectivist" model used by historians, see Dominick LaCapra, "Rhetoric and History," *History and Criticism* (Ithaca, N.Y., 1985), pp. 15–44.

6 Michel de Certeau, "History: Science and Fiction," in *Heterologies: Discourse on the Other,* trans. Brian Massumi (Minneapolis, 1986), p. 203; hereafter abbreviated "H."

7 Vision, as Donna Haraway points out, is not passive reflection. "All eyes, including our own organic ones, are active perceptual systems, building in translations and specific ways of seeing – that is, ways of life" (Donna Haraway, "Situated Knowledges: The Science Question in Feminism and the Privilege of Partial Perspective," *Feminist Studies* 14 [Fall 1988]: 583). In another essay she pushes the optical metaphor further: "The rays from my optical device diffract rather than reflect. These diffracting rays compose *interference* patterns, not reflecting images … A diffraction pattern does not map where differences appear, but rather where the *effects* of differences appear" (Haraway, "The Promises of Monsters: Reproductive Politics for Inappropriate/d Others," typescript). In this connection, see also Minnie Bruce Pratt's discussion of her eye that "has only let in what I have been taught to see," in her "Identity: Skin Blood Heart," in Ely Bulkin, Pratt, and Barbara Smith, *Yours in Struggle: Three Feminist Perspectives on Anti-Semitism and Racism* (Brooklyn, N.Y., 1984), and the analysis of Pratt's autobiographical essay by Biddy Martin and Chandra Talpade Mohanty, "Feminist Politics: What's Home Got to Do with It?" in *Feminist Studies/Critical Studies,* ed. Teresa de Lauretis (Bloomington, Ind., 1986), pp. 191–212.

8 On the disruptive, antisocial nature of desire, see Leo Bersani, *A Future for Astyanax: Character and Desire in Literature* (Boston, 1976).

9 I am grateful to Judith Butler for discussions on this point.

10 Fredric Jameson, "Immanence and Nominalism in Postmodern Theory," *Postmodernism, or, the Cultural Logic of Late Capitalism* (Durham, N.C., 1991), p. 199.

11 Raymond Williams, *Keywords: A Vocabulary of Culture and Society,* rev. ed. (New York, 1985), p. 126; hereafter abbreviated K.

12 On the ways knowledge is conceived "as an assemblage of accurate representations," see Richard Rorty, *Philosophy and the Mirror of Nature* (Princeton, N.J., 1979), esp. p. 163.

13 Bhabha puts it this way: "*To see* a missing person, or *to look* at Invisibleness, is to emphasize the subject's *transitive* demand for a *direct* object of self-reflection; a point of presence which would maintain its privileged enunciatory position *qua subject*" (Bhabha, "Interrogating Identity," p. 5).

14 De Lauretis, *Alice Doesn't: Feminism, Semiotics, Cinema* (Bloomington, Ind., 1984), p. 159.

15 Gayatri Chakravorty Spivak describes this as "positing a metalepsis":

> A subject-effect can be briefly plotted as follows: that which seems to operate as a subject may be part of an immense discontinuous network . . . of strands that may be termed politics, ideology, economics, history, sexuality, language, and so on . . . Different knottings and configurations of these strands, determined by heterogeneous determinations which are themselves dependent upon myriad circumstances, produce the effect of an operating subject. Yet the continuist and homogenist deliberative consciousness symptomatically requires a continuous and homogeneous cause for this effect and thus posits a sovereign and determining subject. This latter is, then, the effect of an effect, and its positing a metalepsis, or the substitution of an effect for a cause.
>
> (Gayatri Chakravorty Spivak, *In Other Worlds: Essays in Cultural Politics* (New York, 1987), p. 204)

16 E. P. Thompson, "The Poverty of Theory or an Orrery of Errors," *The Poverty of Theory and Other Essays* (New York, 1978), p. 170; hereafter abbreviated "PT."

17 Williams's discussion of "structures of feeling" takes on some of these same issues in a more extended way. See Williams, *The Long Revolution* (New York, 1961), and the interview about it in his *Politics and Letters: Interviews with New Left Review* (1979; London, 1981), pp. 133–74. I am grateful to Chun Lin for directing me to these texts.

18 On the integrative functions of "experience," see Judith Butler, *Gender Trouble: Feminism and the Subversion of Identity* (New York, 1990), pp. 22–25.

19 For a different reading of Thompson on experience, see William H. Sewell, Jr., "How Classes Are Made: Critical Reflections on E. P. Thompson's Theory of Working-class Formation," in *E. P. Thompson: Critical Debates*, ed. Harvey J. Kay and Keith McClelland (Philadelphia, 1990), pp. 50–77. I also have benefitted from Sylvia Schafer's "Writing about 'Experience': Workers and Historians Tormented by Industrialization," typescript.

20 Judith Newton, "History as Usual? Feminism and the 'New Historicism,'" *Cultural Critique* 9 (Spring 1988): 93.

21 Christine Stansell, "A Response to Joan Scott," *International Labor and Working-Class History*, no. 31 (Spring 1987): 28. Often this kind of invocation of experience leads back to the biological or physical "experience" of the body. See, for example, the arguments about rape and violence offered by Mary E. Hawkesworth, "Knowers, Knowing, Known: Feminist Theory and Claims of Truth," *Signs* 14 (Spring 1989): 533–57.

22 This is one of the meanings of the slogan "the personal is the political." Personal knowledge, that is, the experience of oppression is the source of resistance to it. This is what Mohanty calls "the feminist osmosis thesis: females are feminists by association and identification with the experiences which constitute us as female" (Mohanty, "Feminist Encounters: Locating the Politics of Experience," *Copyright* 1 [Fall 1987]: 82). See also an important article by Katie King, "The Situation of Lesbianism as Feminism's Magical Sign: Contests for Meaning and the U.S. Women's Movement, 1968–1972," *Communication* 9 (1986): 65–91.

23 John E. Toews, "Intellectual History after the Linguistic Turn: The Autonomy of Meaning and the Irreducibility of Experience," *American Historical Review* 92 (Oct. 1987): 881; hereafter abbreviated "IH."

24 Spivak, "A Literary Representation of the Subaltern: A Woman's Text from the Third World," *In Other Worlds*, p. 241.

25 Her argument is based on a set of oppositions between history and literature, male and female, identity and difference, practical politics and theory, and she repeatedly privileges the second set of terms. These polarities speak to the specifics of the debate she is engaged in with the (largely male) Subaltern Studies collective, historians working within a Marxist, especially Gramscian, frame.

26 Spivak, "Subaltern Studies: Deconstructing Historiography," *In Other Worlds*, p. 205. See also Spivak (with Rooney), "In a Word. *Interview*," *differences* 1 (Summer 1989): 124–54, esp. p. 128. On essentialism, see Diana Fuss, *Essentially Speaking: Feminism, Nature and Difference* (New York, 1989).

27 For discussions of how change operates within and across discourses, see James J. Bono, "Science, Discourse, and Literature: The Role/Rule of Metaphor in Science," in *Literature and Science: Theory and Practice*, ed. Stuart Peterfreund (Boston, 1990), pp. 59–89. See also, Mary Poovey, *Uneven Developments: The Ideological Work of Gender in Mid-Victorian England* (Chicago, 1988), pp. 1–23.

28 Parveen Adams and Jeff Minson, "The 'Subject' of Feminism," *m/f*, no. 2 (1978), p. 52. On the constitution of the subject, see Foucault, *The Archaeology of Knowledge*, trans. A. M. Sheridan Smith (New York, 1972), pp. 95–96; Felicity A. Nussbaum, *The Autobiographical Subject: Gender and Ideology in Eighteenth Century England* (Baltimore, 1989); and Peter de Bolla, *The Discourse of the Sublime: Readings in History, Aesthetics, and the Subject* (New York, 1989).

29 Foucault, "Nietzsche, Genealogy, History," *Language, Counter-Memory, Practice: Selected Essays and Interviews,* trans. Donald F. Bouchard and Sherry Simon, ed. Bouchard (Ithaca, N.Y., 1977), pp. 151–52.

30 Ruth Roach Pierson, "Experience, Difference, and Dominance in the Writings of Women's History," typescript.

31 For an important attempt to describe a post-structuralist history, see de Bolla, "Disfiguring History," *Diacritics* 16 (Winter 1986): 49–58.

11

THE PRACTICE
OF EVERYDAY LIFE
"Making do": uses and tactics

Michel de Certeau

Michel de Certeau, French ethnologist, historian of ideas and a member of the Freudian school of Paris, dedicates his book on The Practice of Everyday Life *to "the ordinary man," whom he characterizes as "the murmuring voice of societies." In it, he aims to produce what he calls "a science of singularity, that is to say, a science of the relationship that links everyday pursuits to particular circumstances." The focus here is on the practices of ordinary people and the ways in which they use, or in de Certeau's provocative terminology, "consume" social representations and normative modes of social behavior. These practices of consumption are tantamount to "ways of operating," or doing things, and for de Certeau they should not be considered as passive forms of social activity. Rather, in "using" and "consuming" culture, ordinary persons are engaged, at the most basic level on which life is lived, in a "making," a poiesis, but a "hidden one, because it does not manifest itself through its own products, but rather through its ways of using the products imposed by a dominant economic order." To "consume" (or use) culture is, therefore, also to engage in its production, although this production takes place in the interstices of normative schemes of action and representation, and thus largely fails to leave a trace. The purpose of the book is to make explicit the combined systems that operate to compose a "culture" and to illuminate the modes of action within a given culture that are characteristic of ordinary people, those who practice and perform it. In their practices, ordinary persons adopt strategies and tactics that enable them to reclaim autonomy from the all-pervasive forces of economics, politics, and culture in general. Thus, as is true for a large number of the authors represented in this volume, de Certeau is attempting to theorize the relationship between the structural elements of culture and the practices that both enact and modify them.*

Although de Certeau focusses on the individual's practices that compose everyday life—walking, cooking, talking, and the like—the reader should not assume that he returns to a concept of the individual as social science or liberal humanism formerly had envisaged him. On this point de Certeau is absolutely clear. He insists:

The examination of practices does not imply a return to individuality. The social atomism which over the past three centuries has served as the historical axiom of social analysis posits an elementary unit—the individual—on the basis of which groups are supposed to be formed and to which they are supposed to be always reducible. This axiom . . . plays no part in this study. Analysis shows that a relation (always social) determines its terms, and not the reverse, and that each individual is a locus in which an incoherent (and often contradictory) plurality of such relational determinations interact.

Thus, for de Certeau, culture is and remains a public order, even in its most ordinary and private instantiations in practice.

The chapter reproduced in part here—Chapter III on "'Making Do': Uses and Tactics" presents the core of de Certeau's analysis of the ways that ordinary individuals tactically employ elements of the imposed systems in which they live their daily lives and thus exercise their agency as users and interpreters of culture. Like Marshall Sahlins, de Certeau adopts a Saussurean framework for his analysis, using "enunciation" (parole) as a heuristic model by which to understand the practical activity of individual social actors. In this light, practice—"ways of operating," "doing," "acting," "making"—discloses the means by which agents enact their cultures in loosely regulated, improvised ways, achieving through "use" the tactical, strategic, and personal aims that are realized within a culture's normative spaces.

* * *

[. . .]

Use, or consumption

In the wake of the many remarkable works that have analyzed "cultural products," the system of their production,[1] the geography of their distribution and the situation of consumers in that geography,[2] it seems possible to consider these products no longer merely as data on the basis of which statistical tabulations of their circulation can be drawn up or the economic functioning of their diffusion understood, but also as parts of the repertory with which users carry out operations of their own. Henceforth, these facts are no longer the data of our calculations, but rather the lexicon of users' practices. Thus, once the images broadcast by television and the time spent in front of the TV set have been analyzed, it remains to be asked what the consumer *makes* of these images and during these hours. The thousands of people who buy a health magazine, the customers in a supermarket, the practitioners of urban space, the consumers of newspaper stories and legends – what do they make of what they "absorb," receive, and pay for? What do they do with it?

[. . .]

In reality, a rationalized, expansionist, centralized, spectacular, and clamorous production is confronted by an entirely different kind of production, called "consumption" and characterized by its ruses, its fragmentation (the result of the circumstances), its poaching, its clandestine nature, its tireless but quiet activity, in short by its quasi-invisibility, since it shows itself not in its own products (where would it place them?) but in an art of using those imposed on it.

The cautious yet fundamental inversions brought about by consumption in other societies have long been studied. Thus the spectacular victory of Spanish colonization over the indigenous Indian cultures was diverted from its intended aims by the use made of it: even when they were subjected, indeed even when they accepted their subjection, the Indians often used the laws, practices, and representations that were imposed on them by force or by fascination to ends other than those of their conquerors; they made something else out of them; they subverted them from within – not by rejecting them or by transforming them (though that occurred as well), but by many different ways of using them in the service of rules, customs, or convictions foreign to the colonization which they could not escape.[3] They metaphorized the dominant order: they made it function in another register. They remained other within the system which they assimilated and which assimilated them externally. They diverted it without leaving it. Procedures of consumption maintained their difference in the very space that the occupier was organizing.

Is this an extreme example? No, even if the resistance of the Indians was founded on a memory tattooed by oppression, a past inscribed on their body.[4] To a lesser degree, the same process can be found in the use made in "popular" milieus of the cultures diffused by the "elites" that produce language. The imposed knowledge and symbolisms become objects manipulated by practitioners who have not produced them. The language produced by a certain social category has the power to extend its conquests into vast areas surrounding it, "deserts" where nothing equally articulated seems to exist, but in doing so it is caught in the trap of its assimilation by a jungle of procedures rendered invisible to the conqueror by the very victories he seems to have won. However spectacular it may be, his privilege is likely to be only apparent if it merely serves as a framework for the stubborn, guileful, everyday practices that make use of it. What is called "popularization" or "degradation" of a culture is from this point of view a partial and caricatural aspect of the revenge that utilizing tactics take on the power that dominates production. In any case, the consumer cannot be identified or qualified by the newspapers or commercial products he assimilates: between the person (who uses them) and these products (indexes of the "order" which is imposed on him), there is a gap of varying proportions opened by the use that he makes of them.

Use must thus be analyzed in itself. There is no lack of models, especially so far as language is concerned; language is indeed the privileged terrain on which to discern the formal rules proper to such practices. Gilbert Ryle, borrowing Saussure's distinction between *langue* (a system) and *parole* (an

219

act), compared the former to a fund of *capital* and the latter to the *operations* it makes possible: on the one hand, a stock of materials, on the other, trans- actions and uses.[5] In the case of consumption, one could almost say that production furnishes the capital and that users, like renters, acquire the right to operate on and with this fund without owning it. But the comparison is valid only for the relation between the knowledge of a language and "speech acts." From this alone can be derived a series of questions and categories which have permitted us, especially since Bar-Hillel's work, to open up within the study of language (*semiosis* or *semiotics*) a particular area (called *pragmatics*) devoted to use, notably to *indexical expressions,* that is, "words and sentences of which the reference cannot be determined without knowledge of the context of use."[6]

We shall return later to these inquiries which have illuminated a whole region of everyday practices (the use of language); at this point, it suffices to note that they are based on a problematics of enunciation. By situating the act in relation to its circumstances, "contexts of use" draw attention to the traits that specify the act of speaking (or practice of language) and are its effects. Enunciation furnishes a model of these characteristics, but they can also be discovered in the relation that other practices (walking, resid- ing, etc.) entertain with non-linguistic systems. Enunciation presupposes: (1) a *realization* of the linguistic system through a speech act that actualizes some of its potential (language is real only in the act of speaking); (2) an *appropriation* of language by the speaker who uses it; (3) the postulation of an interlocutor (real or fictive) and thus the constitution of a relational *contract* or allocution (one speaks to someone); (4) the establishment of a *present* through the act of the "I" who speaks, and conjointly, since "the present is properly the source of time," the organization of a temporality (the present creates a before and an after) and the existence of a "now" which is the presence to the world.[7]

These elements (realizing, appropriating, being inscribed in relations, being situated in time) make of enunciation, and secondarily of use, a nexus of circumstances, a nexus adherent to the "context" from which it can be distin- guished only by abstraction. Indissociable from the present *instant,* from particular circumstances and from a *faire* (a peculiar way of doing things, of producing language and of modifying the dynamics of a relation), the speech act is at the same time a use *of* language and an operation performed *on* it. We can attempt to apply this model to many non-linguistic operations by taking as our hypothesis that all these uses concern consumption.

We must, however, clarify the nature of these operations from another angle, not on the basis of the relation they entertain with a system or an order, but insofar as *power relationships* define the networks in which they are inscribed and delimit the circumstances from which they can profit. In order to do so, we must pass from a linguistic frame of reference to a polemological one. We are concerned with battles or games between the strong and the weak, and with the "actions" which remain possible for the latter.

Strategies and tactics

Unrecognized producers, poets of their own affairs, trailblazers in the jungles of functionalist rationality, consumers produce something resembling the *lignes d'erre* described by Deligny.[8] They trace "indeterminate trajectories" that are apparently meaningless, since they do not cohere with the constructed, written, and prefabricated space through which they move. They are sentences that remain unpredictable within the space ordered by the organizing techniques of systems. Although they use as their *material* the *vocabularies* of established languages (those of television, newspapers, the supermarket, or city planning), although they remain within the framework of prescribed *syntaxes* (the temporal modes of schedules, paradigmatic organizations of places, etc.), these "traverses" remain heterogeneous to the systems they infiltrate and in which they sketch out the guileful ruses of *different* interests and desires. They circulate, come and go, overflow and drift over an imposed terrain, like the snowy waves of the sea slipping in among the rocks and defiles of an established order.

Statistics can tell us virtually nothing about the currents in this sea theoretically governed by the institutional frameworks that it in fact gradually erodes and displaces. Indeed, it is less a matter of a liquid circulating in the interstices of a solid than of different *movements* making use of the elements of the terrain. Statistical study is satisfied with classifying, calculating, and tabulating these elements – "lexical" units, advertising words, television images, manufactured products, constructed places, etc. – and they do it with categories and taxonomies that conform to those of industrial or administrative production. Hence such study can grasp only the material used by consumer practices – a material which is obviously that imposed on everyone by production – and not the *formality* proper to these practices, their surreptitious and guileful "movement," that is, the very activity of "making do." The strength of these computations lies in their ability to divide, but this ana-lytical ability eliminates the possibility of representing the tactical trajectories which, according to their own criteria, select fragments taken from the vast ensembles of production in order to compose new stories with them.

What is counted is *what* is used, not the *ways* of using. Paradoxically, the latter become invisible in the universe of codification and generalized transparency. Only the effects (the quantity and locus of the consumed products) of these waves that flow in everywhere remain perceptible. They circulate without being seen, discernible only through the objects that they move about and erode. The practices of consumption are the ghosts of the society that carries their name. Like the "spirits" of former times, they constitute the multiform and occult postulate of productive activity.

In order to give an account of these practices, I have resorted to the category of "trajectory."[9] It was intended to suggest a temporal movement through space, that is, the unity of a diachronic *succession* of points through which it passes, and not the *figure* that these points form on a space that is supposed to be synchronic or achronic. Indeed, this "representation" is insufficient, precisely because a trajectory is drawn, and time and movement are thus reduced to a line that can be seized as a whole by the eye and read in a single moment, as one projects onto a map the path taken by someone walking through a city. However useful this "flattening out" may be, it transforms the *temporal* articulation of places into a *spatial* sequence of points. A graph takes the place of an operation. A reversible sign (one that can be read in both directions, once it is projected onto a map) is substituted for a practice indissociable from particular moments and "opportunities," and thus irreversible (one cannot go backward in time, or have another chance at missed opportunities). It is thus a mark *in place of* acts, a relic in place of performances: it is only their remainder, the sign of their erasure. Such a projection postulates that it is possible to take the one (the mark) for the other (operations articulated on occasions). This is a *quid pro quo* typical of the reductions which a functionalist administration of space must make in order to be effective.

A distinction between *strategies* and *tactics* appears to provide a more adequate initial schema. I call a *strategy* the calculation (or manipulation) of power relationships that becomes possible as soon as a subject with will and power (a business, an army, a city, a scientific institution) can be isolated. It postulates a *place* that can be delimited as its *own* and serve as the base from which relations with an *exteriority* composed of targets or threats (customers or competitors, enemies, the country surrounding the city, object-ives and objects of research, etc.) can be managed. As in management, every "strategic" rationalization seeks first of all to distinguish its "own" place, that is, the place of its own power and will, from an "environment." A Cartesian attitude, if you wish: it is an effort to delimit one's own place in a world bewitched by the invisible powers of the Other. It is also the typical attitude of modern science, politics, and military strategy.

The establishment of a break between a place appropriated as one's own and its other is accompanied by important effects, some of which we must immediately note:

1 The "proper" is *a triumph of place over time.* It allows one to capitalize acquired advantages, to prepare future expansions, and thus to give oneself a certain independence with respect to the variability of circum-stances. It is a mastery of time through the foundation of an autonomous place.

2 It is also a mastery of places through sight. The division of space makes possible a *panoptic practice* proceeding from a place whence the eye can transform foreign forces into objects that can be observed and measured, and thus control and "include" them within its scope of vision.[10] To be able to see (far into the distance) is also to be able to predict, to run ahead of time by reading a space.

3   It would be legitimate to define the *power of knowledge* by this ability to transform the uncertainties of history into readable spaces. But it would be more correct to recognize in these "strategies" a specific type of knowledge, one sustained and determined by the power to provide oneself with one's own place. Thus military or scientific strategies have always been inaugurated through the constitution of their "own" areas (autonomous cities, "neutral" or "independent" institutions, laboratories pursuing "disinterested" research, etc.). In other words, *a certain power is the precondition of this knowledge* and not merely its effect or its attribute. It makes this knowledge possible and at the same time determines its characteristics. It produces itself in and through this knowledge.

By contrast with a strategy (whose successive shapes introduce a certain play into this formal schema and whose link with a particular historical configuration of rationality should also be clarified), a *tactic* is a calculated action determined by the absence of a proper locus. No delimitation of an exteriority, then, provides it with the condition necessary for autonomy. The space of a tactic is the space of the other. Thus it must play on and with a terrain imposed on it and organized by the law of a foreign power. It does not have the means to *keep to itself*, at a distance, in a position of withdrawal, foresight, and self-collection: it is a maneuver "within the enemy's field of vision," as von Bülow put it,[11] and within enemy territory. It does not, therefore, have the options of planning general strategy and viewing the adversary as a whole within a district, visible, and objectifiable space. It operates in isolated actions, blow by blow, it takes advantage of "opportunities" and depends on them, being without any base where it could stockpile its winnings, build up its own position, and plan raids. What it wins it cannot keep. This nowhere gives a tactic mobility, to be sure, but a mobility that must accept the chance offerings of the moment, and seize on the wing the possibilities that offer themselves at any given moment. It must vigilantly make use of the cracks that particular conjunctions open in the surveillance of the proprietary powers. It poaches in them. It creates surprises in them. It can be where it is least expected. It is a guileful ruse.

In short, a tactic is an art of the weak. Clausewitz noted this fact in discussing deception in his treatise *On War*. The more a power grows, the less it can allow itself to mobilize part of its means in the service of deception: it is dangerous to deploy large forces for the sake of appearances; this sort of "demonstration" is generally useless and "the gravity of bitter necessity makes direct action so urgent that it leaves no room for this sort of game." One deploys his forces, one does not take chances with feints. Power is bound by its very visibility. In contrast, trickery is possible for the weak, and often it is his only possibility, as a "last resort": "The weaker the forces at the disposition of the strategist, the more the strategist will be able to use deception."[12] I translate: the more the strategy is transformed into tactics.

Clausewitz also compares trickery to wit: "Just as wit involves a certain legerdemain relative to ideas and concepts, trickery is a sort of legerdemain relative to acts."[13] This indicates the mode in which a tactic, which is indeed a form of legerdemain, takes an order by surprise. The art of "pulling tricks" involves a sense of the opportunities afforded by a particular occasion. Through procedures that Freud makes explicit with reference to wit,[14] a tactic boldly juxtaposes diverse elements in order suddenly to produce a flash shedding a different light on the language of a place and to strike the hearer. Cross-cuts, fragments, cracks and lucky hits in the framework of a system, consumers' ways of operating are the practical equivalents of wit.

Lacking its own place, lacking a view of the whole, limited by the blindness (which may lead to perspicacity) resulting from combat at close quarters, limited by the possibilities of the moment, a tactic is determined by the *absence of power* just as a strategy is organized by the postulation of power. [. . .]

In sum, strategies are actions which, thanks to the establishment of a place of power (the property of a proper), elaborate theoretical places (systems and totalizing discourses) capable of articulating an ensemble of physical places in which forces are distributed. They combine these three types of places and seek to master each by means of the others. They thus privilege spatial relationships. At the very least they attempt to reduce temporal relations to spatial ones through the analytical attribution of a proper place to each particular element and through the combinatory organization of the movements specific to units or groups of units. The model was military before it became "scientific." Tactics are procedures that gain validity in relation to the pertinence they lend to time – to the circumstances which the precise instant of an intervention transforms into a favorable situation, to the rapidity of the movements that change the organization of a space, to the relations among successive moments in an action, to the possible intersections of durations and heterogeneous rhythms, etc. In this respect, the difference corresponds to two historical options regarding action and security (options that moreover have more to do with constraints than with possibilities): strategies pin their hopes on the resistance that the *establishment of a place* offers to the erosion of time; tactics on a clever utilization of time, of the opportunities it presents and also of the play that it introduces into the foundations of power. Even if the methods practiced by the everyday art of war never present themselves in such a clear form, it nevertheless remains the case that the two ways of acting can be distinguished according to whether they bet on place or on time.

The rhetorics of practice, ancient ruses

Various theoretical comparisons will allow us better to characterize the tactics or the polemology of the "weak." The "figures" and "turns" analyzed by *rhetoric* are particularly illuminating in this regard. Freud already noticed this fact and used them in his studies on wit and on the forms taken by the return of the repressed within the field of an order: verbal economy and condensation, double meanings and misinterpretations, displacements and alliterations, multiple uses of the same material, etc.[15] There is nothing surprising about these homologies between practical ruses and rhetorical movements. In relation to the legalities of syntax and "proper" sense, that is, in relation to the general definition of a "proper" (as opposed to what is not "proper"), the good and bad tricks of rhetoric are played on the terrain that has been set aside in this way. They are manipulations of language relative to occasions and are intended to seduce, captivate, or invert the linguistic position of the addressee.[16] Whereas grammar watches over the "propriety" of terms, rhetorical alterations (metaphorical drifts, elliptical condensations, metonymic miniaturizations, etc.) point to the use of language by speakers in particular situations of ritual or actual linguistic combat. They are the indexes of consumption and of the interplay of forces. They depend on a problematics of enunciation. In addition, although (or because) they are excluded in principle from scientific discourse, these "ways of speaking" provide the analysis of "ways of operating" with a repertory of models and hypotheses. After all, they are merely variants within a general semiotics of tactics. To be sure, in order to work out that semiotics, it would be necessary to review arts of thinking and acting other than the one that the articulation of a certain rationality has founded on the delimitation of a proper. [. . .]

I am not concerned directly here with the constitution of such a semiotics, but rather with suggesting some ways of thinking about everyday practices of consumers, supposing from the start that they are of a tactical nature. Dwelling, moving about, speaking, reading, shopping, and cooking are activities that seem to correspond to the characteristics of tactical ruses and surprises: clever tricks of the "weak" within the order established by the "strong," an art of putting one over on the adversary on his own turf, hunter's tricks, maneuverable, polymorph mobilities, jubilant, poetic, and warlike discoveries.

Perhaps these practices correspond to an ageless art which has not only persisted through the institutions of successive political orders but goes back much farther than our histories and forms strange alliances preceding the frontiers of humanity. These practices present in fact a curious analogy, and a sort of immemorial link, to the simulations, tricks, and disguises that certain fishes or plants execute with extraordinary virtuosity. The procedures of this art can be found in the farthest reaches of the domain of the living, as if they managed to surmount not only the strategic distributions of historical institutions but also the break established by the very institution of consciousness. They maintain formal continuities and the permanence of a memory without language, from the depths of the oceans to the streets of our great cities.

In any event, on the scale of contemporary history, it also seems that the generalization and expansion of technocratic rationality have created, between the links of the system, a fragmentation and explosive growth of these practices which were formerly regulated by stable local units. Tactics

are more and more frequently going off their tracks. Cut loose from the traditional communities that circumscribed their functioning, they have begun to
wander everywhere in a space which is becoming at once more homogeneous
and more extensive. Consumers are transformed into immigrants. The system
in which they move about is too vast to be able to fix them in one place, but
too constraining for them ever to be able to escape from it and go into exile
elsewhere. There is no longer an elsewhere. Because of this, the "strategic"
model is also transformed, as if defeated by its own success: it was by
definition based on the definition of a "proper" distinct from everything else;
but now that "proper" has become the whole. It could be that, little by little,
it will exhaust its capacity to transform itself and constitute only the space
(just as totalitarian as the cosmos of ancient times) in which a cybernetic
society will arise, the scene of the Brownian movements of invisible and innu-
merable tactics. One would thus have a proliferation of aleatory and
indeterminable manipulations within an immense framework of socioeconomic constraints and securities: myriads of almost invisible movements, playing on the more and more refined texture of a place that is even,
continuous, and constitutes a proper place for all people. Is this already the
present or the future of the great city?

[. . .]

The imaginary landscape of an inquiry is not without value, even if it is
without rigor. It restores what was earlier called "popular culture," but it does
so in order to transform what was represented as a matrix-force of history
into a mobile infinity of tactics. It thus keeps before our eyes the structure of
a social imagination in which the problem constantly takes different forms
and begins anew. It also wards off the effects of an analysis which necessarily
grasps these practices only on the margins of a technical apparatus, at the
point where they alter or defeat its instruments. It is the study itself which
is marginal with respect to the phenomena studied. The landscape that represents these phenomena in an imaginary mode thus has an overall corrective
and therapeutic value in resisting their reduction by a lateral examination. It
at least assures their presence as ghosts. This return to another scene thus
reminds us of the relation between the experience of these practices and what
remains of them in an analysis. It is evidence, evidence which can only be
fantastic and not scientific, of the disproportion between everyday tactics and
a strategic elucidation. Of all the things everyone does, how much gets written
down? Between the two, the image, the phantom of the expert but mute body,
preserves the difference.

NOTES

1 See in particular A. Huet *et al.*, *La Marchandise culturelle* (Paris: CNRS, 1977), which
  is not satisfied merely with analyzing products (photos, records, prints), but also
  studies a system of commercial repetition and ideological reproduction.
2 See, for example, *Pratiques culturelles des Français* (Paris: Secrétariat d'Etat à la Culture
  – SER, 1974), 2 vol. Alvin Toffler, *The Culture Consumers* (Baltimore: Penguin, 1965),

remains fundamental and pioneering, although it is not statistically based and is limited to mass culture.

3 See, for example, on the subject of the Aymaras of Peru and Bolivia, J.-E. Monast, *On les croyait Chrétiens: les Aymaras* (Paris: Cerf, 1969).

4 See M. de Certeau, "La Longue marche indienne," in *Le Réveil indien en Amérique latine,* ed. Yves Materne and DIAL (Paris: Cerf, 1976), 119–135.

5 G. Ryle, "Use, Usage and Meaning," in *The Theory of Meaning,* ed. G. H. R. Parkinson (Oxford: Oxford University Press, 1968), 109–116. A large part of the volume is devoted to use.

6 Richard Montague, "Pragmatics," in *La Philosophie contemporaine,* ed. Raymond Klibansky (Firenze: La Nuova Italia, 1968), I, 102–122. Y. Bar-Hillel thus adopts a term of C. S. Peirce, of which the equivalents are, in B. Russell, "ego-centric particulars"; in H. Reichenbach, "token-reflexive expressions"; in N. Goodman, "indicator words"; in W. V. Quine, "non-eternal sentences"; etc. A whole tradition is inscribed in this perspective. Wittgenstein belongs to it as well, the Wittgenstein whose slogan was "Don't ask for the meaning; ask for the use" in reference to normal use, regulated by the institution that is language.

7 See Emile Benveniste, *Problèmes de linguistique générale* (Paris: Gallimard, 1974), II, 79–88.

8 Fernand Deligny, *Les Vagabonds efficaces* (Paris: Maspero, 1970), uses this word to describe the trajectories of young autistic people with whom he lives, writings that move through forests, wanderings that can no longer make a path through the space of language.

9 Ibid.

10 According to John von Neumann and Oskar Morgenstern, *Theory of Games and Economic Behaviour,* 3rd ed. (New York: John Wiley, 1964), "there is only strategy when the other's strategy is included."

11 "Strategy is the science of military movements outside of the enemy's field of vision; tactics, within it" (von Bülow).

12 Karl von Clausewitz, *Vom Kriege;* see *De la guerre* (Paris: Minuit, 1955), 212–213; *On War,* trans. M. Howard and P. Paret (Princeton: Princeton University Press, 1976). This analysis can be found moreover in many other theoreticians, ever since Machiavelli. See Y. Delahaye, "Simulation et dissimulation," *La Ruse (Cause Commune* 1977/1) (Paris: UGE 10/18, 1977), 55–74.

13 Clausewitz, *De la guerre,* 212.

14 S. Freud, *Jokes and their Relation to the Unconscious,* trans. J. Strachey (London: The Hogarth Press and the Institute of Psychoanalysis, 1960).

15 Freud, *Jokes and their Relation to the Unconscious,* on the techniques of wit.

16 See S. Toulmin, *The Uses of Argument* (Cambridge: Cambridge University Press, 1958); Perelman and Ollbrechts-Tyteca, *Traité de l'argumentation;* J. Dubois *et al., Rhétorique générale* (Paris: Larousse, 1970); etc.

12

LANGUAGE AND THE SHIFT FROM SIGNS TO PRACTICES IN CULTURAL INQUIRY

Richard Biernacki

In this article sociologist Richard Biernacki criticizes the model of culture offered in linguistic turn historiography by indicating the manner in which it relied upon a "formalizing" premise which assumed that human meaning is generated by the formal relations among signs in a sign system, and then proceeds to consider the operation of such linguistic signs as a natural, "essential" part of the world, rather than as historically generated modes of understanding, a phenomenon he dubs the linguistic turn's "essentializing premise." In Biernacki's view, the combined workings of the "formalizing" and "essentializing" premises hid from the investigator's view the ways that agents themselves produce meanings in the context of performing social practices, rather than simply enacting a pre-existing discursive code or sign system as earlier semiotic views of culture had suggested. By embedding culture in material and social practices possessing diverse logics, he seeks to demonstrate that the pragmatics of sign usage comprise a structure and generator of meaning in their own right, interdependent with but not identical to the system of signs upon which they draw. It is through the diversity of cultural practices that signs come to seem experientially real for their users. Biernacki's desire to locate the production of meaning at the intersection of language and material practice represents a dominant tendency in the rethinking of linguistic turn historiography that pushes it in the direction of "Practice Theory."

* * *

[. . .]

The new cultural history has become both preeminent and old. A quarter century has now passed since the phrase "linguistic turn" entered our vocabulary of inquiry. [. . .] [A] just-issued collection of essays on method in cultural history and historical sociology, edited by two early practitioners of cultural method in historical inquiry, Lynn Hunt and Victoria Bonnell, suggests that some are troubled by the role of culture in historical inquiry in the current phase of consolidation "after the revolution." The very title of their collection,

Beyond the Cultural Turn, raises the question "What next?" Above all, Hunt and Bonnell conclude, many analysts at the current juncture share a general unease "with a definition of culture as entirely systematic, symbolic, or linguistic."[1] Recent historical works on the embodied culture of material life and on the use of culture in practice represent efforts to rethink the constituents of culture and how culture fits into social context – without returning, however, to the notion that the economic or political logic of that context determines a culture's themes and organization.[2]

From my perspective, this most recent emphasis on embedding culture in its practical context evinces a stirring that seems likely to lead historical researchers to cede two premises that gave rise to the cultural turn in the first place. Rather than moving away from culture as a tool of illumination, however, historians are likely to renew their understanding of how culture "works" in action. I will evaluate, quickly and provocatively, the advantages and limitations of the most widely employed model of culture that the cultural turn in historical investigations made familiar; then I tentatively offer examples of an alternate approach to culture, one focused on the implicit ties between representations and practices. In the current state of play, I suggest, investigators have much to gain from typifying the organization of the use of signs in ongoing practices *as a structure in its own right,* rather than focusing primarily on abstracting the systematic relations among signs in a separate, purely semiotic reality. Not only would such an alternative approach to culture capture the meanings generated through the execution of practices that are not discernible from reading the signs or symbols *of* practice; it would also help to resolve some of the disabling limitations in the new cultural history's tools of explanation.

For movements so rich as the new cultural history or cultural-historical sociology, it would be reckless to suppose there has been any kind of consensus about what culture is or how to study it.[3] Nonetheless, it is helpful to consider two of the assumptions that were at least the most widely shared and whose fusion, I suspect, powered the extraordinary period of invention in historical studies during the 1980s. These assumptions promoted the establishment of a new, if diverse canon of cultural histories that has come to include the works of such investigators as Robert Darnton, Lynn Hunt, Joan Scott, Carlo Ginzburg, and William Sewell, Jr.

The formalizing premise

The most important assumption, which I will call the "formalizing premise," is *that meaning is generated by the synchronic relations among signs in a "sign system."* Darnton, Hunt, Scott, Ginzburg, and Sewell have not only adopted this assumption in their craft. They have articulated it in their methodological reflections.[4] To capture cultural meanings, they argue, investigators ought to isolate the contrasts and systematic relations among the signs employed in a semiotic community. It is worth emphasizing how far this assumption can be stretched without losing its role. In the craft of research it does not block practitioners from portraying the messy, multilayered processes of social action. But it leads investigators to assume that their job ultimately is to abstract out of this historical flow of action the networks of analogy and difference among signs at discrete junctures and to analyze those networks as a separate semiotic dimension. In the hands of the early Michel Foucault, most famously, this approach resulted in static but architecturally elegant presentations of the relations of signification.[5] Lynn Hunt introduced a more dynamic perspective in her analyses of the sequences of political change in the French Revolution. She showed how the agents' conduct complied with the placement of political emblems into general narrative forms of comedy, tragedy, and romance.[6]

More recently, investigators have sought to underscore departures from the assumption that culture is fixed or ordered by making culture part of a story of "symbolic conflict," "transgression," and "cultural subversion." Yet these recent emphases on slippage in a culture's coherence underscore how enduring the formalist premise remains.[7] Joan Scott's emphasis on the instability of meanings and their tactical transformations, for instance, still draws on the notion that the overarching relations among signs at a given moment generates cultural meaning. Scott searches for relations of significance across whole constellations of intersecting discourses, even if those relations are driven by locally contingent, discrepant undertakings.[8] In a similar rethinking of the stability of culture as a "system," William Sewell has asked how sign systems are open to transformation and remain structures with their own powers of cohesion as generators of meaning. To combine those perspectives on structure and change, he proposes we rethink culture as a kind of code that is both realized and transformed in practice. Although Sewell's rich project is still taking shape, he has set out by defining practice derivatively, as a peculiar historical instantiation of an inherited code. "To engage in cultural practice," he reasons, "is to make use of a semiotic code to do something in the world."[9] In keeping with the formalist premise that culture should be grasped as a sign system, he designates the synchronically defined, intellectual code – not the *processes* of putting it to work – as comprising the *structure* of a culture.

The notion of culture as a sign system exhilarated investigators by suggesting that human action could be elucidated as a kind of text.[10] But an implication of the textual analogy was to divide the agents' self-understanding of their conduct (the text) from its execution (the doing), and to make their self-understanding the chief object of cultural analysis. The division took place because investigators reasoned that if cultural meanings emerge from interdependencies among signs, practice generates meaning as it is reflected on in turn as itself a sign in relation to other signs. Researchers supposed that agents experience the meaning of practice as the apprehension and composition of sign statements about the world or about their conduct in it. The conception of culture as "sign system" worked against analyzing the generation of meaning in the processual actions in which agents not only reflect upon, but *occupy* the world and organize and execute their practices in it. The reception of Pierre Bourdieu's work on body *hexis* reinforced this unfortunate narrowing of focus. For it suggested to many a kind of dualism between the textual and the material, between what was graspable as an intellectual form and what remained inaccessibly corporeal. What lay outside the logic of sign reading seemed either impenetrable to verbal representation or functioned by principles that could not be brought into relation with models of discursive thought.[11]

Theorizing culture as sign system also set up a hierarchy between sign and practice that paralleled that between a general cultural structure and a contextually unique, eventful use of that structure. Practice comprised simply the manipulation of signs in specific statements. This notion of culture rendered practice and the system of signs complementary but not coequal. Investigators absorbed the pragmatics of using signs into their historically particular accounts of each discrete setting, rather than theorizing those pragmatics as a component of cultural structure in their own right.

Investigators also organized their histories around the assumption *that culture creates unanticipated consequences for agents because social reality is constituted by the semantic relations among signs.* Every powerful form of historical inquiry includes formulas for narrating the tragedy of the unintended effects of human agency. In the new cultural history, sign systems produced those miscarriages. Signs mislead agents about the situational consequences of action by conveying a counterproductive reading of the world. Incidental changes in the network of signs may also activate larger metaphoric transfers which the agents did not anticipate and which may even undermine their attempts at the self-interested deployment of those signs. Sewell shows, for instance, how French Enlightenment thinkers who classified humankind as *part of* nature rather than as spiritual beings *counterposed* to nature accidentally turned upside down the place of manual labor in the hierarchy of social honor and, by implication, recoded the sources of authority and the grounds for organizing the professions.[12] With the model of culture as sign reading, the pathos of historical action derives as much from intellectual maneuvering to master the representation of social relations as from the coercive capacities of social relations.[13]

The essentializing premise

The second of the two major assumptions that came together in the 1980s could well be termed the "essentializing premise." By this I mean to suggest how cultural investigators *mistook the concepts of "sign" and "sign reading" for parts of the natural furniture of the world,* rather than as historically generated "ways of seeing." Clifford Geertz's statement of principle in *The Interpretation of Cultures* proved phenomenally influential in legitimating this move.

231

"As interworked systems of construable signs," Geertz wrote, "culture is not a power, something to which social events, behaviors, institutions, or processes can be causally attributed; it is a context, something within which they can be intelligibly – that is, thickly – described."[14] Geertz disallowed any form of illumination that would put culture on the same plane as other elements with which it might be compared (it "is not a power"). In my view, however, there is a contradiction here that had to be suppressed at all cost: the formal theory of meaning focused on sign and sign system as natural constituents violates the principle that all concepts are conjured by convention. To call on the title of one of Geertz's books, the paradigm of the sign system is the only exception to the rule that every principle is "local knowledge."[15] This naturalizing move emerges in Geertz's nonchalance about the nomenclature employed to think about interpretation of meanings. Whereas some linguists see high stakes in the technical distinctions we make about types of signs and about how they work, Geertz's quips about the lack of real differences among the terms establishes that whatever the choice of label, something like the sign is so fundamentally part of the world, it cannot be colored by the vouchers we adopt.[16] Cultural historians and sociologists followed Geertz in reifying the concept of a sign system as a naturally given dimension of social reality.[17] At the same time they were ready to acknowledge the tentative status of their diagnoses of particular sign systems and the possibility of multiple, even irreconcilable reconstructions by historians of those systems.[18]

The cultural turn took place when historical investigators found that they could persuasively combine the formalizing and the essentializing premises: the proposal that culture consists of a (partially) cohesive, intelligible system of signs fused with the proposal that our general notion of a sign system reflects a basic and irreducible sphere of being. Nowadays, the union seems so natural and inevitable a part of the scholarly landscape, it is difficult to conceive the two premises separately. But the first assumption in isolation, exemplified in Saussure's work, yields a formal theory of semantics for artificially delimited linguistic units, the kind handled by philologists in ancient texts stripped of a life-context. On its own Saussure's model never seemed to present a competitive form of historical explanation for complex social contexts. After all, how could a bookish view of semantics alone compete with the more relevant conjecture that the motors of conduct – the interests and values that decide how agents *orient* themselves to signs – were generated by the institutions of, say, government or class? The second assumption in isolation, the essentializing premise, asserted the primacy or autonomy of culture in historical processes, but lacked a means for justifying this sovereignty. Combining it with the formalist premise solved this problem by making a sign system constitutive and definitive of agents' conduct.

Each of the two assumptions shores up the inadequacies of the other. In taking over a Saussurian-affiliated theory of sign systems, the formalizing premise had inherited the problem of analyzing how agents use signs to indicate or to "refer to" processes in the social world. That problem arises because the signifieds called to life by the signs are not of the world of give-and-take interaction. They are only concepts within an idealized sign system, defined by their interdependencies in a separate and closed semiotic domain. How, in the terms of this model, do agents take the pure signifieds of that sign system and use them to index things and to make things happen in their world of action? Saussure recognized this as a distinct and important question, one he thought did not have to be addressed in a theory of structure.[19] His mode of exposition from dictionary examples enabled him to devote his enterprise to the philologist's analysis of tokens of language isolated from any context of utterance. More specifically, he relegated the question of how agents connect signifieds with their world of practice and social interaction to a haphazard event of *parole*, comparatively unsuited for theoretical analysis.[20] This distance between sign system and context of action might have been expected to make Saussure's approach unhelpful and uncongenial for historians, who remain among the paramount investigators of irreducible contexts. But the essentializing premise of the cultural turn patched up this distance between the sign in a formally conceived semiotic system and the agent's use of signs as tools of maneuver and reference in the world. By suggesting that the sign is not a philosopher's artifact but the constituent of a real firmament, and that the world consists of signs "all the way down," it collapsed categorical distinctions between signs and action in the world, as well as between signifieds and what they problematically index in the world. Cultural investigators associated their constructs of "signifieds" with the historical universe itself. Agents, actions, and processes *were* now the signs and signifieds by which they revealed themselves in history. Bruno Latour drew on this naturalizing reduction when he claimed that diagnostic machinery in laboratories that produce signs in the form of data and readouts do thereby "speak" and exercise a genuine agency.[21]

On its own the essentializing move was similarly problematic. The new cultural historians had customarily objected to the search for realist foundations for history, but they replaced one ultimate ground – economic conditions and social structure, which the social historians and materialist Marxists had reified – with another, named "culture" or "sign system." The formalist premise suppressed that contradictory continuity. We usually classify a "sign system" as belonging to the category of a figure, and as such it appears an insubstantial construct, a mere form. Culture, Geertz insists, remains a *mot*, not a *chose*, even if indispensable and grounding.[22] The ethereal, unreal connotations of "sign system" camouflaged its function of denoting a prerequisite material that served as the putative underpinning of history. In the conduct of inquiry, neither of the two premises – neither the formalizing nor the essentializing – could work without the other, but together they created a new conception of historical analysis.

The turn in method

The fusion of the formalist and essentializing premises licensed rich and novel methodological moves. In retrospect it is easy to quibble with their soundness, but they enabled historians to launch dazzling new genres of research.

1   Historical investigators used the marriage of the two assumptions to show that the decipherment of meaning is not the explication of subjective meanings or states of consciousness locked away in the heads of individual agents. Instead cultural investigators extracted a semiotic code (or at least a model of partial consistencies) from public symbols and conventions. The code is independent of the ideas in the head of any individual. As Geertz always emphasized, the analyst does not have to perceive what agents perceive, only the shared conventions the agents perceive with.[23] That is sufficient for the investigator to explain how the agents use the conventions so as to carry on their own thought or performances. Perhaps only the marriage of the formalist and essentializing premises could have so naturally legitimated the pursuit of the putative code, not of individuals' fluid consciousness and thoughts, as the grasping of the tenable foundation to historical process. The abstracted code for studying meaning became more substantial than the agents' thinking itself. Historians were relieved of the interminable evidentiary game of guessing the inward intentions in agents' sayings. They had a rationale for limiting themselves to the accessible conventions by which those sayings were structured – or, more exactly, to examples sufficient to support the invention of a putatively shared model of their meanings. Likewise sociologists who had been influenced by the Weberian and Parsonian views of culture were now fortunate they no longer had to stake inquiries into culture on the agents' "ultimate values." Those final commitments had not only proven difficult to document and measure; worse yet, since the constraints and ethical contradictions of actual social settings skewed the agents' pursuit of ultimate values, these values had begun to appear to be related only tangentially to the agents' observed decision-making and courses of action.[24]

2   The new combination of premises gave investigators a license to relate any piece of culture to another. If meaning is generated by an approximate coherence in a sign system that reaches across local sites of practice, then investigators can start with any fragment and move with it to a perspective on a larger cultural system. [. . .] The essentializing premise helped imply that the underlying qualities connecting the textual fragments into a whole were not conjured by the act of interpretation, but present in the minutiae themselves, and indeed necessary for each detail to have developed at all.[25] For historians of distant and partially non-literate locales who were challenged in their research by the skewed production and preservation of documentation, the license to start with whatever limited and opaque sources remained at hand, and to follow their noses, proved exhilarating. By supposing individual thought is constituted by the use of codes in semiotic communities,

investigators received an unprecedented authority to move from the rare, accidentally preserved writings of individuals to deductions about the codes and counter-codes of communities at large.[26]

3   The combination of premises gave investigators a means of making culture both an explanatory foundation and a device for conceiving the metamorphosing power of actions and events. To appreciate the culturally transformative power of the contingent in history, an analyst needs to begin with an orderly dissection – a model, if you will – of how a field of signs fits together, if incompletely, at an initial historical juncture. That is the only means of appreciating how a local, even incidental event can trigger far-reaching changes in a cognitive framework. The view of culture as a set of mutually dependent signs satisfied that requirement for identifying a kind of fundamental (if potentially unstable) structure and its built-in possibilities for eventful change. Earlier understandings of culture as a collection of values and norms had explained change as a largely gradual, inevitable product of social evolution;[27] or, alternatively, had focused only on massive interventions (such as sudden contact between civilizations) or on the deliberately creative genius of individuals. The methods of the cultural turn created a new understanding of how the outcomes of historical processes are both deeply structured by culture *and* contingent on conjunctures of local events. William Sewell's analysis of the transformative power of the taking of the Bastille in the French Revolution represents the most sophisticated among recent attempts to apply these dual insights. Sewell shows how the inherited ambiguity of the term "le peuple" – which referred to the sovereignty of the citizenry at large as well as to the poor commoners of the streets – contained the potential for the innovation of interpreting the mob action of the Bastille as the legitimate inauguration of a new regime through "revolution."[28]

[. . .]

The incomplete premises of the model of culture as a sign system

[A] broad difficulty concealed in the cultural turn is that its principal, Saussurean-affiliated model of sign systems as a distinct and irreducible realm is untenable as an account of how cultural meaning is generated. Of course, linguists such as R. Rommetveit and V. N. Voloshinov had made this point long ago by offering more pragmatic, context-dependent analyses of how language conveys meaning.[29] But their philosophies have not dislodged the Saussurean account because it is all too easy for historians to see the critiques as calling only for supplements to the fashionable way of doing cultural analysis. If the meanings of signs also depend on how they are used in the moment in a particular, often unpredictable social context, researchers can take this as suggesting only that the sign system is *inflected* by "history" and "politics" to produce specific meanings. Historical investigators retain the notion that the synchronically and formally defined sign system provides an adequate general structure for cultural meaning in a community, and they view the particulars of practice in context as historical instantiations of that structure.[30]

Rather than try to argue here that another philosophy of cultural meaning more "accurately" captures the way signification works, it is simpler to accept the formalist model on its terms and to reason about how it breaks down by its own procedures. Once we develop formal models of the generation of cultural meaning out of contrasts among signs, we inaugurate a divide between statements and their significance: meaning, as is often said, is no longer immanent in expression. The divide in place, a verbal disclosure cannot contain a meaning, it can only stand at a distance for something. This shifts the agenda of questions we pursue to grasp how culture works. If meaning is at a remove from form, a model of culture has to acknowledge as a separate order of logic the principles that agents employ for bridging that deferral in major types of practice or types of social context. [. . .]

To sum up so far, I propose that aside from dissecting the content or structure of sign systems, the analyst also classify the means by which agents connect representations to practice as they engage in social conduct. What is "cultural" about cultural analysis, then, is not inclusion of a particular dimension that is foundational of the setting – a pure realm of signifying signs – but analysis of the mode by which the agents executing a practice come to operate in a meaningful and symbolically "real" world. The definition of culture as a foundational sign system won cultural analysts a pyrrhic victory. They re-encoded as "signs" the fundamental constituents of social life – the self, emotion, labor, individual interest, and more – without having to show how lending those categories a status as "cultural" resulted in different accounts of the efficient mechanisms responsible for particular historical outcomes. To the contrary, the essentialist premise ironically facilitated application of rational choice and socioeconomic logics. By supposing that the signs the agents used to interpret and negotiate the social world corresponded unproblematically to the signs that *comprised* the social world, cultural analysts unintentionally authorized utilitarian explanations of outcomes. For agents could be seen as following exclusively instrumental or material interest in the world – relabeled as a sign – yet their conduct could illustrate at the same time the proviso that culture is constitutive of the action and the scene "in the last instance."[31] By contrast, if we think of culture as resting on the *ties* between two levels – an order of representations *and* an order of practice that connects representation to a context of social exchange – we can concentrate the analysis on variation in those types of ties.

[. . .]

A [. . .] type of relation between representation and practice can be illustrated through my comparative research into nineteenth-century German and British weaving mills, in *The Fabrication of Labor*.[32] In this model, the tie between representation and practice is figured by the trope of irony.

The practice depends for its execution on an initial, constitutive representation of the essence of the practice which the very execution of the practice comments upon and ironizes (without assuming an "objective" perspective, however, from which to classify the representation as false). Weavers in both Germany and Britain were paid by piece-rate scales that gauged the quantity of output. When posted as written texts on the factory walls, these schedules all appeared to gauge the same object: *cloth* turned in. Surely one could expect nothing else from a piece-rate scale! The British piece-rate scales represented the value of different fabrics by their density given a fixed length of cloth, whereas the German scales portrayed the value of different fabrics by the number of weft insertions made per fixed length. The weavers in both lands used the schedules to maximize earnings, not to conform to a premise about the transfer of labor. Yet from daily application of the representations to equate diverse types of output, the British weavers learned that value fluctuated according to the dimension of the cloth, whereas the German weavers learned that value fluctuated according to the process of inserting the weft threads. By accustoming themselves to different ways of comparing the value of their fabrics, German weavers perceived the motions of labor, British weavers the yards of output, as the denominator of labor as a quantifiable substance.[33] Weavers in each country could not "read" the divergent messages about labor through the signs of the piece-rate systems posted on the wall; they received those messages as a process, as weavers day by day experienced the transmission of abstract labor in the expenditure of labor power – in Germany – or as labor concretized in finished products – in Britain.

In this example of piece-rates, [. . .] a representation – the systematic codification of the rules of turning in diverse types of finished cloth for a wage – is requisite for the exchange to proceed. Yet agents could not decipher the conditions for equating diverse kinds of weaving work as general labor from the piece-rate scales themselves. As verbal characterizations, the schedules equate payment with the same object, cloth, and nothing more. But practice implicitly changes the status of what is affirmed in signs. In execution, the German system, by making the expenditure of labor power in inserting weft threads the unit of abstract labor, changes on a figural level what is affirmed on the literal level of the scale. It turns cloth into only a token for the actual unit of value, the expenditure of labor *power*. The British system, too, turns out to convey the meaning of abstract labor, not merely to measure cloth as it claims. By ironizing the piece-rate scales, the unfolding of practice makes us skeptical of the ability of representation to secure the meaning of agents' experience. By contrast with the trope of metaphor in Marx's story, the representation of products as autonomous bearers of value, though based on a limited perspective, is nonetheless a mirror adequate to the producers' experience of their practice.[34]

Let me finish by pulling out the implications of [this] example and suggesting how exploration might proceed. In [this example], the structure of culture is defined by how signs fit into a context of practice, not by an analytically separate realm of semiotic relations. [The] relations between representations and practices offer a means for explaining how the use of symbols can make them seem experientially real. Neither the original linguistic turn nor the older, Marxist-inspired emphasis on practice focused on this experience as an unsolved puzzle. Not every set of beliefs seems definitive of the world just because it is so applied. For example, the state socialist regimes of Eastern Europe succeeded in institutionalizing their language of collective production and association as the lingua franca of public life. Ethnographers have also shown in remarkable detail how parts of Communist ideology – such as the emphasis on production as the basis of social relations and as the creator of value – became natural givens among the working populations.[35] Yet other parts of that ideology, such as the emphasis on collective authority over the generation of wealth, were never accepted as genuine or as taken-for-granted wisdom. Simple reiteration in the everyday life of collectivized farms or factories did not suffice. The representations encoded social relations, but did not seem experientially faithful or natural. Pascal's dictum for religion, made famous by Althusser and other Marxist analysts for all of ideology in practice, was "Kneel down, move your lips in prayer, and you will believe."[36] The dictum asserts that practice is crucial, but does not explain why, because it fails to offer a comparative hypothesis about the failure of symbols in many instances to do their mystifying work.[37]

Although comparative studies are required to pursue this riddle, the models of relations between practice and representation offer a preliminary conjecture. In [. . .] the payment systems in *The Fabrication of Labor*, the beliefs supported by practice are implicit suppositions of practice the agents need to "fill in" the execution of the practice, and they can support second-order signs that index the real execution of a practice. [. . .] [I]mplicit practical assumptions that ephemeral work activities can be fitted to metrics of value enable weavers to organize their tasks in time and to attach the signs of the piecerate scales to quantities of abstract labor. [. . .] [T]hese kinds of tacit pragmatic suppositions can center larger clusters of practices and beliefs. To elucidate for the case of the piece-rate scales, the assumptions about the form in which human labor was abstracted into comparable quantities structured the German and British workers' entire response to industrial employment. It created national differences in the understanding of time, in the organization of factory space, in the articulation of strike demands, and in the reception of ideologies of exploitation in the labor movements. Most importantly, it served as the unspoken basis for workers' conduct even when alternative courses of action might have been recommended.[38] Even as workers' beliefs about religion, politics, and the family underwent substantial change in each country in the course of the nineteenth century, these assumptions about the metric of abstract labor, reproduced as a pragmatic assumption, remained uncannily stable until the shock of the First World War.[39] [. . .]

[. . .] [T]he pragmatic assumptions that become so influential are not necessarily seen as "sacred," because they are anchored by the execution of practice rather than by their cognitive or normative import. In consequence, the stability of cultural elements does not depend on the iteration or resonance of signs across multiple domains of conduct. Conversely, deep cultural changes in one domain may not echo across others. The coherence of culture has to be tested rather than assumed. In Germany and Britain, state regulators in the First World War intervened without ado to dramatically modify payment systems for textile workers. In each country the constellation of industrial techniques and labor relations that revolved around a particular metric of abstract labor suddenly came apart without an amplifying sense of crisis in other locales. [. . .] Investigators who seek to analyze a culture's contingent fixity and coherence must focus initially on the connections between representations and practice *in situ*, rather than only on global associations among representations.

Just as the new cultural history drew on analogies with language to appreciate semantic relations, so a rethinking of culture in operation can draw on models of language in *use* to appreciate how practice naturalizes cultural categories. In fact, we can take the case of language as an object of popular reflection to contrast disbelief about the realism of signs with the experienced realism of the principles used to put the signs to work. It is now almost folk knowledge to claim that any language is an arbitrary construct, not a faithful telescope of the structure of the world. Despite that "fictive" status, however, the users of a language still experience as foundational the implicit principles by which they use the signs of that language to reference the world. [. . .] However conventional or unbelievable the signs we manipulate may seem, the principles by which we enact their use can seem foundationally real.[40] Conversely, a belief may appear specious if it is not an implicit organizing principle of practice, however genuine our commitment to the belief may be. Some analysts have concluded that the failure of the Communist ideology of human relations to take root as an accepted piece of reality in Eastern European societies originated in its unsuitability for adapting agents to everyday contingencies of conduct, rather than in lack of popular commitment to that ideology as a social philosophy. Or, to illustrate the reverse relation, Americans in opinion polls reject as myth the proposition that an individual's ability and effort guarantee personal occupational success, at least when surveyors direct respondents' attention to particular examples. Yet the individualistic principle of success resurfaces as a general cliché, even among the disadvantaged, because they must adopt that principle to negotiate their way in market society as formally self-sufficient persons.[41]

The counter-proposals of culture in practice

Three propositions sum up the differences between this model of culture in practice versus the most widespread (though scarcely monolithic) model of culture as a sign system with which the new cultural history began.

239

1   *Cultural meaning is generated in the ties between practice and representation.* Historical analysts are adding a cluster of new metaphors about how "culture" works – as a tool kit, as know-how, as a repertoire for applying the body – beside the older metaphors of culture as the reading or decoding of signs.[42] The new imagery draws on the premise that neither the organization of a practice nor its experienced import for agents are derivable from the semantic interdependencies among signs in a system. The pragmatic dimension of culture comprises a structure and a typifiable constituent of meaning in its own right. By analyzing the pragmatic *relations* between signs and the organization of practice, we move away from a purely discursive notion of culture without, however, counterposing "corporeal" practice as a binary opposite that is inaccessible and essentially dissimilar to language. As I sought to illustrate by calling on Whorf and on the elementary literary tropes, we can dissect the relations between representation and practice with the incomparable analytic resources of the linguists.

2   *The agents' relations to the signs they put to work decides whether applying a cultural metaphor to illuminate conduct offers explanatory advantages over competing sociohistorical theory.* In some kinds of transactions, the agents are severely restricted in the institutional settings in which they can employ signs, are unable to play with or vary the use of signs in that setting, or even lack resources for reading the signs' nuances. A corporate executive's exercise of a stock option represents one such transaction. The means of using the sign, the stock option, are relatively explicit and determinate. In this instance, it is more difficult for an account that treats the stock option as a sign to offer a systematic, empirically diverging, and more accurate prediction or explanation of exchanges.[43] But when cultural categories – such as the "economic signs" of labor and capital – are deployed in environments where the *use* of symbols is less formalized and insulated (such as the messy province of manufacture proper),[44] cultural accounts illustrate unique patterns in the use of signs that exclusively utilitarian or material-economic accounts are poorly equipped to explain. The pragmatics of the agents' use of symbols decides whether resorting to the artifices of cultural analysis offers an epistemological gain. In this enterprise, [. . .] *embedding* the functioning of signs in a larger practical or social context bolsters our ability to highlight distinctive cultural organizations of practice. [. . .] [T]he model of practice incorporates the social context via the implicit principles agents call on to use signs [. . .]. Since culture is identified through its pragmatics in an institutional context, the problem of reductionism – when a separate, abstracted semiotic structure is repositioned against its institutional background – does not recur as a necessary, irresolvable issue.

3   *A leading cause of the miscarriage of human agency is the very belief that the purpose of cultural categories is to represent the world.* The new cultural history

remained captive to this misleading belief by making the representational function of language supremely responsible for tragedy. But in the alternative sketched here, categories of a culture may reflect the implicit means for carrying out practices or for putting signs to work; they may be based, that is, more on doing than on thinking. [. . .]

Of course the approach to cultural inquiry outlined by these propositions raises a larger agenda of questions. Does each kind of relation between practice and representation, [. . .] contain its own distinctive dynamics of cultural change? [. . .] Does each trope that connects practice and representation in an analysis also entail a specific kind of narrative emplotment of history? When is misrecognition or lack of awareness of the implicit assumptions of practice a constitutive part of a life-world, and when does insight into those implicit assumptions lead to a restructuring of the life-world? In developing responses to these questions, the agents' own models of the relation between language and the world will prove crucial to the play between representation and practice in their culture. May we as self-analysts become more aware of that paradox in the ongoing life of our investigations.

NOTES

1 Editors' introduction, *Beyond the Cultural Turn*, ed. Victoria Bonnell and Lynn Hunt (Berkeley, 1999), 26.
2 Recent exemplars include Chandra Mukerji, *Territorial Ambitions and the Gardens at Versailles* (Cambridge, 1997); Ken Alder, *Engineering the Revolution: Arms and Enlightenment in France, 1763–1815* (Princeton, 1997); Adrian Johns, *The Nature of the Book: Print and Knowledge in the Making* (Chicago, 1998), especially chapter two.
3 For an example of a more unconventional approach that highlighted cultural meaning as the product of fluid social interaction, see John R. Hall, "Social Interaction, Culture, and Historical Studies," in *Symbolic Interaction and Cultural Studies*, ed. Howard S. Becker and Michal M. McCall (Chicago, 1990), 31–32.
4 Robert Darnton, "The Symbolic Element in History," *Journal of Modern History* 58 (1986), 218–234; *The New Cultural History*, ed. Lynn Hunt (Berkeley, 1989), "Introduction: History, Culture, and Text," 16–17; Joan Scott, *Gender and the Politics of History* (New York, 1988), 59–60; Carlo Ginzburg, *Ecstasies: Deciphering the Witches' Sabbath* (New York, 1992), 23, 30; William Sewell, Jr., "The Concept(s) of Culture," in *Beyond the Cultural Turn*, ed. Bonnell and Hunt, 35–61. In cultural sociology, perhaps the most stringent analysis of the syntax of symbols, drawing on Saussure, is Karen A. Cerulo, *Identity Designs: The Sights and Sounds of a Nation* (New Brunswick, N.J., 1995).
5 Michel Foucault, *The Order of Things. An Archaeology of the Human Sciences* (New York, 1971).
6 Lynn Hunt, *Politics, Culture, and Class in the French Revolution* (Berkeley, 1984), 34–39.
7 Analysts may position deviance and creativity as parts of a cohesive sign system. See the critiques by Catherine Gallagher and Stephen Greenblatt in *Practicing the New Historicism* (Chicago, 2000), 12–13 and by William M. Reddy, *Money and Liberty in Modern Europe. A Critique of Historical Understanding* (Cambridge, 1987), 39.
8 Scott's notion of cultural meaning draws, I think, on what William Sewell has termed "thin" coherence among cultural elements. Sewell's synthetic review of changes in

investigators' understandings of culture, "The Concept(s) of Culture," convincingly demonstrates continued reliance on a concept of culture as a sign system. See *Beyond the Cultural Turn,* ed. Bonnell and Hunt, 35–61.

9 Sewell, "The Concept(s) of Culture," in *Beyond the Cultural Turn,* ed. Bonnell and Hunt, 51.

10 In Darnton's the *Great Cat Massacre,* for example, the analysis culminates by showing how Parisian journeymen in revolt could manipulate ritual signs as dextrously as poets could words. Robert Darnton, *The Great Cat Massacre and Other Episodes in French Cultural History* (New York, 1984), 101.

11 As illustration, see Bourdieu's oft-repeated assertion that the logic of practice "has nothing in common with intellectual work, that it consists of an activity of practical construction . . . that ordinary notions of thought, consciousness, knowledge prevent us from adequately thinking." In Pierre Bourdieu and Loïc Wacquant, *An Invitation to Reflexive Sociology* (Chicago, 1992), 121. On the reception of Bourdieu's divide between thought and practice, see Paul Connerton, *How Societies Remember* (Cambridge, 1989), 94–95.

12 William Sewell, Jr., *Work and Revolution in France: The Language of Labor from the Old Regime to 1848* (Cambridge, 1980), 23–24, 71.

13 See, for illustration, Lynn Hunt, review essay of *Penser la révolution française, History and Theory* 20 (1981), 320; and the treatment of language as a broker of history in Gareth Stedman Jones, "Rethinking Chartism," in his *Languages of Class: Studies in English Working Class History, 1832–1982* (Cambridge, 1983).

14 Clifford Geertz, *The Interpretation of Cultures* (New York, 1973), 14.

15 It is worth noting how Geertz's naturalizing of culture as a fundament is confirmed by his stance toward those outside the culturalist fold. He often wrote that the ultimate goal of anthropology was to promote dialogue between different communities in the world. Yet he rejected dialogue between himself and those outside his own paradigm. For instance, he treated the metaphors of culture-skeptics as inadmissible *a priori* and blacklisted the enterprise of social explanation as "social physics" (Clifford Geertz, *Local Knowledge: Further Essays in Interpretive Anthropology* [New York, 1983], 3). Geertz described the acceptance of the cultural paradigm as a kind of conversion process: you are either inside the flock or you are lost outside of it. His illiberal stance is evident in how he narrates the rise of interpretive studies. In 1972 he wrote that "Even Marxists are quoting Cassirer; even positivists, Kenneth Burke" (*The Interpretation of Cultures,* 29). Geertz portrays the ongoing shift to the study of symbols as a wondrous process of conversion. "The woods are full of eager interpreters," Geertz concludes in *Local Knowledge* (21). His essays in every climate from the 1960s through the 1990s assert that the conversions are ongoing and will continue. The eventless teleology implies that practices of inquiry grow by natural assent to general truth, rather than by empirical contest and messy debate over historical riddles.

16 Geertz, *Local Knowledge,* 21; Clifford Geertz, *Available Light: Anthropological Reflections on Philosophical Topics* (Princeton, 2000), 17.

17 I attempted to trace historians' naturalizing of the concept of the sign system in Richard Biernacki, "Method and Metaphor after the New Cultural History," in *Beyond the Cultural Turn,* ed. Bonnell and Hunt, 64,

18 John E. Toews portrayed the acceptance of a multiplicity of interpretations of a historical process as a form of anti-essentialism in "Historiography as Exorcism: Conjuring Up 'Foreign Worlds' and Historicizing Subjects," *Theory and Society* 27 (August, 1998), 593. In my view, however, it is easy to imagine scientists who agree among themselves that their concepts reflect the essence of the world, while disagreeing only on key measurements made with those concepts in a particular context.

19 For a swift exposition of Saussure's view of the use of language to make reference to the world, see Benjamin Lee, "Peirce, Frege, Saussure, and Whorf: The Semiotic

Mediation of Ontology," in *Semiotic Meditation: Sociocultural and Psychological Perspectives*, ed. E. Mertz and R. Parmentier (Orlando, Fla., 1985), 113.

20 Ferdinand Saussure, *Course in General Linguistics* (New York, 1959), 15, 18.

21 Bruno Latour, *We Have Never Been Modern* (Cambridge, Mass., 1993), 23. Margaret Jacob shows how Latour's equation of natural with human agency rests on a naturalized concept of the sign in "Science Studies after Social Construction," in *Beyond the Cultural Turn*, ed. Bonnell and Hunt, 106.

22 Geertz, *Available Light*, 12.

23 As Geertz famously put it, "Culture is public because meaning is." Geertz, *The Interpretation of Cultures*, 12. For his most recent formulation, see *Available Light*, 16.

24 Ann Swidler, "Culture in Action: Symbols and Strategies," *American Sociological Review* 51 (April, 1986), 275, 280.

25 I try to develop this point from a different perspective in "Method and Metaphor after the New Cultural History," in *Beyond the Cultural Turn*, ed. Bonnell and Hunt, 70–71.

26 Carlo Ginzburg, *The Cheese and the Worms: The Cosmos of a Sixteenth-Century Miller* (Baltimore, 1980).

27 See, illustratively, Robert Nisbet, *Social Change and History* (Oxford, 1969), 264ff.

28 William Sewell, "Historical Events as Transformations of Structures: Inventing Revolution at the Bastille," *Theory and Society* 25 (December, 1996), 863.

29 R. Rommetveit, *On Message Structure: A Framework for the Study of Language and Communication* (New York, 1974); V. N. Voloshinov, *Marxism and the Philosophy of Language* [1929] (Cambridge, Mass., 1986).

30 Sonya O. Rose, "Cultural Analysis and Moral Discourses," in *Beyond the Cultural Turn*, ed. Bonnell and Hunt, 223. For a brilliant critique of this method of haphazardly patching up the model of language, see Michael Silverstein, "Language Structure and Linguistic Ideology," in *The Elements: A Parasession on Linguistic Units and Levels*, ed. Paul Clyne *et al.* (Chicago Linguistic Society, 1979).

31 Consider, for example, the commendations the notion of the "moral economy" received even after the behavior it designated was reexplained as rational price bargaining. For references, see Richard Biernacki, *The Fabrication of Labor: Germany and Britain, 1640–1914* (Berkeley, 1995), 18, note 47.

32 Biernacki, *The Fabrication of Labor*, chapter two.

33 The mathematics of the two systems of payment were indeed distinct: in the German system there is a linear increase in payment as the density of the cloth into which one thousand weft threads are inserted declines; whereas in Britain there was a linear increase in payment with increases in the density of cloth.

34 For an analysis of representations that are complete for practical experience but partial as theories, see John Torrance, *Karl Marx's Theory of Ideas* (Cambridge, 1995), 158, 165.

35 Martha Lampland, *The Object of Labor* (Chicago, 1995).

36 Louis Althusser, *Lenin and Philosophy and Other Essays* (London, 1971), 168.

37 For an example of the failure of mass ritual to cast its spell, consider the imperial German government's unsuccessful effort to make Sedan Day a significant holiday for Germans in Württemberg after 1871. Alon Confino, *The Nation as Local Metaphor: Württemberg, Imperial Germany, and National Memory, 1871–1918* (Chapel Hill, N.C., 1997), 84–85.

38 For illustration, see Biernacki, *The Fabrication of Labor*, 52.

39 Ibid., 433–434.

40 In this pragmatic view of culture, the unspoken status of an assumption *per se* does not grant that assumption its stability, experienced realism, or organizing power. But the principles of pragmatics are, to be sure, often unspoken or virtually irretrievable among the agents themselves, partly because these principles are only about

relations in processes, not necessarily about separable things, and partly because their role is to organize conduct rather than to represent it.

41 Ann Swidler, "Inequality in American Culture: The Persistence of Voluntarism," *American Behavioral Scientist* 35 (March, 1992), 606–629.
42 Swidler, "Culture in Action," 277.
43 The rich sociological literature on the meaning of distinct kinds of money-like currencies, from stock options to household "pin money," has not yielded distinctive predictions so far about the creation and use of these currencies. Economists have already shown that individuals or households will segregate their monies by frequency of receipt and expenditure and by whether the expenditure is a relative luxury, the better to regulate their consumption rationally. Cultural sociologists are unacquainted with these parallel accounts. Compare Viviana Zelizer's fascinating "Payments and Social Ties," *Sociological Forum* 11 (1996) with congruent rational choice explanations in Richard Thaler, "Mental Accounting and Consumer Choice," *Marketing Science* 4 (1985), 199–201.
44 Biernacki, *The Fabrication of Labor*, chapter eleven.

13

TOWARD A THEORY OF SOCIAL PRACTICES

A development in culturalist theorizing

Andreas Reckwitz

In this article German sociologist Andreas Reckwitz analyzes a variety of current strands in contemporary social theory that focus on questions of social practice and notions of embodiment, which he then groups under the rubric of "Practice Theory." The article shows the roots of these ideas in the work of authors as diverse as sociologists Pierre Bourdieu and Anthony Giddens, philosophers Michel Foucault, Charles Taylor, and the late writings of Ludwig Wittgenstein, together with work done on ethnomethodology in anthropology and the notion of the "performative" by scholars such as Harold Garfinkel and Judith Butler respectively. Reckwitz shows how "Practice Theory" repositions ideas of the social and the body with respect to questions of mind, things, knowledge, discourse, structure/process, and the agent, in contrast to three alternative forms of social and cultural theory, which he labels "mentalism," "textualism," and "intersubjectivism."

Reckwitz acknowledges that "Practice Theory" as such has scarcely attained the status of a definable body of thought possessing a unified theoretical orientation or method. Nonetheless, he argues that all the thinkers discussed share a strong commitment to an examination of daily routines and enactments of social life, or what Michel de Certeau called "the practice of everyday life," in his book of the same title. Reckwitz claims that despite its reliance on earlier forms of social theory, present in the literature since the 1970s, if not earlier (as in the case of Wittgenstein and others), "Practice Theory" still represents something new in terms of the social-theoretical vocabulary it offers social analysts, which amounts to "a novel picture of the social and of human agency." By comparing "Practice Theory" with the alternative social and cultural theories on which it draws but which it seeks to modify, Reckwitz works out the novel claims embedded in the concept of practice and the specific ways in which it construes concepts of the mind/body, human action and agency, and cultural interpretation. Indeed, he sees "Practice Theory" as an example of a more general cultural theory, but differing from the latter in its treatment of ideas of the body, mind, things, knowledge, discourse, and agency.

Reckwitz offers the most comprehensive guide currently available to new trends in social theorizing. His article provides the organizing theme of the present volume insofar as "practicing history" has led historians, of late, to commit themselves to "theorizing practice."

* * *

[...]

In the complex landscape of contemporary social theories after the 'interpretative turn' of the 1970s, 'practice theories' or 'theories of social practices' have formed a conceptual alternative that seems attractive to an audience dissatisfied with both classically modern and high-modern types of social theories,[1] but that, at the same time, has never been systematically elaborated. We can find elements of a theory of social practices in the work of a multitude of social theorists in the last third of the twentieth century who are of diverse theoretical origin: Pierre Bourdieu has explicitly pursued the project of a 'praxeology' since *Outline of a Theory of Practice* (1972) up to his latest *Cartesian Meditations* (1997), a project which at least at the beginning was still influenced to a considerable degree by structuralism. Anthony Giddens (1979, 1984) develops his version of practice theory in the framework of a 'theory of structuration', heavily influenced by late Wittgenstein. Michel Foucault, who in his works of the 1960s and 1970s tried out a number of diverse theoretical options between structuralism, post-structuralism and a Nietzschean theory of the body, arrives in his late works on ancient ethics (1984a, b) at a framework of analysing the relations between bodies, agency, knowledge and understanding that can likewise be understood as 'praxeological'. In empirical sociology, cultural studies and anthropology it is above all works in the wake of Harold Garfinkel's ethnomethodology (1984 [1967]), Judith Butler's 'performative' gender studies (1990) and Bruno Latour's science studies (1991) that can be understood as members of the praxeological family of theories. In social philosophy Charles Taylor's neo-hermeneutical model of embodied agency and the self-interpreting animal (1993a, b) follows a 'praxeological' path. Eventually, Theodore Schatzki outlined in *Social Practices. A Wittgensteinian Approach to Human Activity and the Social* (1996) a social philosophy explicitly focused on the practice concept.[2]

Upon first consideration, it might not be clear why the common label of 'practice theories' is justified to embrace these diverse authors, apart from certain rather diffuse affinities. The turn to practices seems to be tied to an interest in the 'everyday' and 'life-world'; all the authors in question are influenced by the interpretative or cultural turn in social theory; finally, it seems that late Wittgenstein and, to a lesser degree, early Heidegger are common philosophical points of reference (which are, however, hardly ever systematically scrutinized).[3] Yet these are rather superficial commonalities. One might even suspect that the 'practice theorists' are hardly more than well-disguised successors to the time-honoured sociological tradition of a theory of action as it was founded by Max Weber: After all, 'practices' form structures of action which in some way are treated by all kinds of social theories stemming from the tradition of action theory.

The lack of theoretically systematic analysis displayed by some of the practice theorists should, however, not lead to their hasty dismissal. Rather, there are good reasons to argue that there is something new in the social-theoretical vocabulary the practice theorists offer. They do form a family of theories which, in certain basic ways, differs from other, classical types of social theory. The task of this article is to work out more precisely the points at which a theory of social practices can be distinguished from its theoretical alternatives, and how its basic vocabulary thus amounts to a novel picture of the social and of human agency.[4] To that end, however, it is necessary to build up 'ideal types' of theories which hardly correspond to the variability and distinctiveness of 'real' authors. I will use an idealized model of practice theory which leans partly on different and largely common elements of Bourdieu, Giddens, late Foucault, Garfinkel, Latour, Taylor or Schatzki, ignoring the peculiarities of the single authors, and which is partly of programmatic character.[5] Similarly, I confront this ideal type of practice theory with idealized theoretical alternatives: the model of the homo economicus and the homo sociologicus, but in particular with culturalist mentalism, textualism and intersubjectivism. Only by working out these theoretical differences can one succeed in approaching the identity of practice theories (an identity, which is doubtless still not highly stable).

My argument will follow four steps: My point of departure is that practice theories provide a specific form of what I will label 'cultural theories'. Consequently, I will first very briefly elucidate how cultural theories basically differ from the two classical vocabularies of social theory: that of the homo economicus and that of the homo sociologicus. Cultural theories, including practice theory, are founded upon a different form of explaining and understanding action, namely by having recourse to symbolic structures of meaning. Although practice theory is an example of cultural theory, not all cultural theories are practice theories. Rather, one can distinguish between four forms of cultural theories: culturalist mentalism, textualism, intersubjectivism and practice theory. On a very basic level, these schools of thought offer opposing locations of the social and conceptualize the 'smallest unit' of social theory differently: in minds, discourses, interactions and 'practices'. Thus, it becomes possible to work out in some detail the new conceptualization that elementary social-theoretical terms experience in practice theory in comparison with the three other, 'intellectualist' versions of cultural theories. These differences concern the ideas of body, mind, things, knowledge, discourse, structure/process and the agent. In the end, I will briefly discuss the 'effects' of practice theory.[6]

Practice theory as cultural theory

Practice theory – as it is exemplified in authors such as Bourdieu, Giddens, late Foucault, Garfinkel, Latour, Taylor or Schatzki – is a type of cultural theory. What does that mean? Since its emergence with Scottish moral philosophy at the end of the eighteenth century, modern social theory has developed three fundamentally different forms of explaining action and social order: The first option – which was that of the Scottish utilitarianists themselves, but which reaches to contemporary Rational Choice Theory – is that of a purpose-oriented theory of action. The second vocabulary, which Durkheim and Parsons presented as the proper perspective of 'sociology', is a norm-oriented theory of action. These two classical social-theoretical perspectives understand one another as opposing conceptual options – but they both have been challenged by a third vocabulary, which has emerged as a result of the 'culturalist' revolutions in twentieth-century social philosophy. These 'cultural theories' are rooted primarily in structuralism and semiotics, phenomenology and hermeneutics, and in Wittgensteinian language game philosophy. Influenced by structuralism, cultural theories in the social sciences reach from Claude Lévi-Strauss to Michel Foucault and Pierre Bourdieu; influenced by phenomenology and hermeneutics, they embrace Alfred Schütz, Harold Garfinkel and (in a very specific way) Niklas Luhmann; in the wake of Wittgensteinian philosophy, they contain the works of Jürgen Habermas and Anthony Giddens. What distinguishes all these diverse cultural theorists from the two classical figures of the 'homo economicus' and the 'homo sociologicus' is their way of grasping the conditions of human action and social order. The model of the homo economicus explains action by having recourse to individual purposes, intentions and interests; social order is then a product of the combination of single interests. The model of the homo sociologicus explains action by pointing to collective norms and values, i.e. to rules which express a social 'ought'; social order is then guaranteed by a normative consensus. In contrast, the newness of the cultural theories consists in explaining and understanding actions by reconstructing the symbolic structures of knowledge which enable and constrain the agents to interpret the world according to certain forms, and to behave in corresponding ways. Social order then does not appear as a product of compliance of mutual normative expectations, but embedded in collective cognitive and symbolic structures, in a 'shared knowledge' which enables a socially shared way of ascribing meaning to the world. From the point of view of cultural theory, the seemingly opposed classical figures of the homo economicus and homo sociologicus share a common 'blind spot': They both dismiss the implicit, tacit or unconscious layer of knowledge which enables a symbolic organization of reality. The basic distinctions and schemes of this knowledge lay down which desires are regarded as desirable and which norms are considered to be legitimate; morever, these cognitive-symbolic structures (of which language is a prominent example) reproduce a social order even in cases in which a normative consensus does not exist.[7]

All practice theorists are examples of cultural theory in this sense: Their vocabularies stand opposed to both the purpose-oriented and the norm-oriented models of explaining action (which, needless to say, are anything but discarded in the current discussion). They all highlight the significance of shared or collective symbolic structures of knowledge in order to grasp both action and social order. Yet, this conceptual strategy is not an exclusive possession of practice theory. Not all cultural theorists are practice theorists. Therefore, to understand practice theory we require a second set of distinctions.

Four versions of cultural theory: mentalism, textualism, intersubjectivism, practice theory

The field of cultural theories, that is, of social theories which explain or understand action and social order by referring to symbolic and cognitive structures and their 'social construction of reality' (Berger/Luckmann) is highly complex. Practice theory represents a subtype of cultural theory. There are a number of differences between a theory of social practices and other forms of cultural theory, but the most important and very elementary one – which then leads us to all the other differences – is that practice theory situates the social in a different realm from those of other cultural theories. The 'place' of the social here is different. Simultaneously, this means that the 'smallest unit' of social theory and social analysis in practice theory is conceptualized differently.

Where is the social 'localized'? [. . .] [C]lassical social theory above all offered two answers to this question. The model of the homo economicus placed the social on the level of the intended or unintended product of subjective interests – a common will or distribution of values on 'markets' – whereas the model of the homo sociologicus situated the social in a consensus of norms and roles. The smallest unit of social analysis, then, is respectively, single actions or normative structures. Of course, for cultural theories the 'locus' of the social must be connected with symbolic and cognitive structures of knowledge. Yet, this general idea can amount to rather diverse solutions: culturalist mentalism (in an objectivist and a subjectivist version), culturalist textualism, intersubjectivism – and practice theory.

One branch of cultural theories – in fact, that with the longest tradition – locates the social or collective in human mind. Mind is the place of the ocial because mind is the place of knowledge and meaning structures – this is the basic idea of culturalist mentalism. The social can be found, so to speak, in the 'head' of human beings. The 'smallest unit' of social analysis, then, is mental structures. Culturalist mentalism appears in two different branches, an objectivist and a subjectivist. It is classical structuralism as it was developed first by de Saussure (1995 [1916]) and later on in anthropology by Lévi-Strauss (1950, 1989 [1962]), that exemplifies the objectivist branch

249

of a mentalist theory of culture in a paradigmatic way. For structuralism human behaviour is an 'effect' of symbolic structures in the 'unconscious' mind. Therefore, these unconscious symbolic systems must be the smallest unit and final aim of social analysis. Here, the social is the mental; the social and psychological level turn out to be identical. It seems hardly misleading to regard cognitive psychology (including cognitive linguistics) as the empirical discipline that carries out this structuralist programme in a systematic way.

If Claude Lévi-Strauss's structuralism provides the prototype of an 'objectivist' and 'scientistic' version of mentalism in cultural theory, then Alfred Schütz's social phenomenology, as it is developed in *Der sinnhafte Aufbau der sozialen Welt* (1991 [1932]) can be regarded as prototype of a mentalist 'subjectivism'. If structuralism represents one theoretical root of mentalism in cultural theory, then phenomenology represents its second source. For social phenomenology, the aim of social analysis is to take over the 'subjective perspective', i.e. to reconstruct the sequence of mental acts of consciousness which are located 'inside' and are directed in the form of phenomenological 'intentionality' at outward objects to which the consciousness ascribes meanings. The social then is – as Husserl elucidated it classically in his fifth *Cartesianische Meditationen* (1992 [1931]) – the subjective *idea* of a common world of meanings. So the social is located here in the mind as well, even if 'mind' now turns out to be something quite different: not unconscious cognitive structures, but the sequence of intentional acts in consciousness. The aim of social-as-cultural analysis from the point of view of social phenomenology, then, is to describe the subjective acts of (mental) interpretations of the agents and their schemes of interpretation.

[...] Culturalist mentalism provides an influential – negative – backdrop against which practice theory situates itself. Yet, apart from practice theory, there are still two other versions of cultural theory which gain their profile against mentalism – and which are themselves targets of a theory of social practices: textualism and intersubjectivism.

For culturalist textualism, symbolic structures are not situated 'inside' the mind. Instead, they have their place 'outside' – in chains of signs, in symbols, discourse, communication (in a specific sense) or 'texts'. In order to explain the structurality of the social world, one need not climb down into the inwardness of mental qualities, but rather must stay on the level of signs and texts in their 'publicness' (Geertz): here symbolic structures must be located. The social cannot be anchored on the psychological level of minds (including a 'conscience collective'), but only on the (by definition) extrasubjective level of signs in their 'materiality' (Foucault). 'Mental' qualities, then, turn out to be nothing more than very specific *concepts* within discourse *about* something which is described as mental. Culturalist textualism (no doubt an awkward label, but there is no conventionally shared concept in sight) has emerged in the last third of the twentieth century as a result of a basic critique of mentalism, in both its phenomenological and its structuralist strand. It is anti-foundationalist in its elementary doubt that we can find a last 'foundation' of social analysis in the human mind.

[. . .] Culturalist textualism in its radical anti-mentalism and understanding of mental attributes as conceptual ascriptions in discourse (including the localization of knowledge and the social beyond bodily acts) thus represents a second mode of thinking within cultural theories against which practice theory gains its profile.

Finally, there remains the specific outlook on the social offered by culturalist intersubjectivism. Intersubjectivism locates the social in interactions – the paradigmatic case is the use of ordinary language. The social thus has the structure of 'intersubjectivity': In their speech acts, the agents refer to a non-subjective realm of semantic propositions and of pragmatic rules concerning the use of signs. Sociality can be nowhere other than in a constellation of symbolic interactions between agents. Intersubjectivism has likewise emerged as a product of a critique of mentalism, here understood as the tradition of a theory of consciousness. For intersubjectivists, mentalism has misunderstood the qualities of language: Instead, language represents a sort of 'world 3' (Popper) of propositions and rules irreducible to psychological factors. At the same time, however, intersubjectivism, classically formulated in Jürgen Habermas's 'theory of communicative action' (1988a, b [1981]), does not follow the radical anti-subjectivism of the textualists. It is agents endowed with minds who interact with one another: The agents internalize and use the contents and patterns of the oversubjective, 'objective' realm of meanings in their mutual speech-acts. Interaction is thus a process of a transference of meanings which have been internalized in the mind. It is obvious that intersubjectivism cannot conceal a certain proximity to the model of rule-governed behaviour of the homo sociologicus – but this one is given a decidedly 'linguistic' turn. At any rate, the intersubjectivist identification of the social with interrelations between agents – itself a target of textualism – provides a third negative background of practice theory.

Practice theory does not place the social in mental qualities, nor in discourse, nor in interaction. To say that it places the social in 'practices' and that it treats practices as the 'smallest unit' of social analysis is at first nothing more than tautological. One needs to clarify what practices are. First of all, it is necessary to distinguish between 'practice' and 'practices' (in German there is the useful difference between Praxis and Praktiken). 'Practice' (Praxis) in the singular represents merely an emphatic term to describe the whole of human action (in contrast to 'theory' and mere thinking). 'Practices' in the sense of the theory of social practices, however, is something else. A 'practice' (Praktik) is a routinized type of behaviour which consists of several elements, interconnected to one other: forms of bodily activities, forms of mental activities, 'things' and their use, a background knowledge in the form of understanding, know-how, states of emotion and motivational knowledge.

A practice – a way of cooking, of consuming, of working, of investigating, of taking care of oneself or of others, etc. – forms so to speak a 'block' whose existence necessarily depends on the existence and specific interconnectedness of these elements, and which cannot be reduced to any one of these single elements. Likewise, a practice represents a pattern which can be filled out by a multitude of single and often unique actions reproducing the practice (a certain way of consuming goods can be filled out by plenty of actual acts of consumption). The single individual – as a bodily and mental agent – then acts as the 'carrier' (*Träger*) of a practice – and, in fact, of many different practices which need not be coordinated with one another. Thus, she or he is not only a carrier of patterns of bodily behaviour, but also of certain routinized ways of understanding, knowing how and desiring. These conventionalized 'mental' activities of understanding, knowing how and desiring are necessary elements and qualities of a practice in which the single individual participates, not qualities of the individual. Moreover, the practice as a 'nexus of doings and sayings' (Schatzki) is not only understandable to the agent or the agents who carry it out, it is likewise understandable to potential observers (at least within the same culture). A practice is thus a routinized way in which bodies are moved, objects are handled, subjects are treated, things are described and the world is understood. To say that practices are 'social practices' then is indeed a tautology: A practice is social, as it is a 'type' of behaving and understanding that appears at different locales and at different points of time and is carried out by different body/minds. Yet, this does not necessarily presuppose 'interactions' – i.e. the social in the sense of the intersubjectivists – and nor does it remain on the extra-mental and extra-corporal level of discourses, texts and symbols, i.e. the social in the sense of the textualists.

Body, mind, things, knowledge, discourse, structure/process, the agent and the shifted status of these in practice theory

There is a certain danger of trivializing practice theory. At first sight, its approach might seem relatively close to everyday talking about 'agents' and their behaviour. In fact, this is not the case. Although praxeological 'new speak' is highly modest in its terminology [. . .], it implies a considerable shift in our perspective on body, mind, things, knowledge, discourse, structure/process and the agent. One could point out the philosophical background of practice theory, above all Ludwig Wittgenstein's late works (1984a,b [1953, 1969]) and Martin Heidegger's early philosophy (1986 [1927]) and their radical attempts to reverse common philosophical and everyday vocabularies – and in fact, we find everything that is original in practice theory already in the work of these authors. Yet, it seems more promising to contrast the specific way in which practice theory and the other versions of cultural theory conceptualize certain social-theoretical key terms in order to clarify the praxiological world view – again in the form of theoretical ideal-types.

Body

At the core of practice theory lies a different way of seeing the body. Practices are routinized bodily activities; as interconnected complexes of behavioural acts they are movements of the body. A social practice is the product of training the body in a certain way: when we learn a practice, we learn to be bodies in a certain way (and this means more than to 'use our bodies'). A practice can be understood as the regular, skilful 'performance' of (human) bodies. This holds for modes of handling certain objects as well as for 'intellectual' activities such as talking, reading or writing. The body is thus not a mere 'instrument' which 'the agent' must 'use' in order to 'act', but the routinized actions are themselves bodily performances (which does not mean that a practice consists only of these movements and of nothing more, of course). These bodily activities then include also routinized mental and emotional activities which are – on a certain level – bodily, as well. The conclusion: if practices are the site of the social, then routinized bodily performances are the site of the social and – so to speak – of 'social order'. They give the world of humans its visible orderliness.

For the other versions of cultural theory, bodies are not the site of the social, but are rather epiphenomena or instruments. For mentalism, there is an unequivocal, neo-Cartesian inside – outside distinction between mind and body. The 'outward' behaviour may necessarily be tied to bodily acts; the proper place of the social and of the cultural is, however, in the 'inside' of the mind. The body thus gains the status of an epiphenomenon: it carries out what mind – unconscious categories or acts of consciousness – has prescribed. There is a causal priority of thinking to bodily acting. Nevertheless, the body can in a very specific way achieve a central status in mentalism: Objectivist mentalism can come to the conclusion that mental structures are at the end of the day identical with structures of the brain.

In textualism, the body provides one of the objects which can become a symbol, a theme of discourse. We talk about the body and interpret it in a certain way; thus the body is an object of cultural meanings just as other – concrete or abstract – objects are. In intersubjectivism, there might be a certain sense of the 'bodily' basis of action as it proceeds from the constellation of 'agents'. Yet, as action here is primarily identified with symbolic interaction, it is simple to identify behaviour with norm-following symbolic acts, not with bodily routines. So, at the end of the day in the constellation of intersubjectivity (and very similarly to the textualists), the body appears primarily as a referent of propositions just as other objects do.

Mind

Social practices are sets of routinized bodily performances, but they are at the same time sets of mental activities. They necessarily imply certain routinized ways of understanding the world, of desiring something, of knowing how to to do something. For practice theory, this is not a contradiction: A practice such as, say, playing football consists of a routinized set of bodily perform- ances. Yet, within the practice these bodily performances are necessarily connected with certain know-how, particular ways of interpretation (of the other players' behaviour, for example), certain aims (most of all, of course, to win the game) and emotional levels (a particular tension) which the agents, as carriers of the practice, make use of, and which are routinized as well. Without these mental and bodily activities, we could not imagine a practice of 'playing football'. For practice theory, a social practice consists of certain bodily *and* certain mental activities. If somebody 'carries' (and 'carries out') a practice, he or she must take over both the bodily and the mental patterns that constitute the practice. These mental patterns are not the 'possession' of an individual 'deep inside', but part of the social practice. Thus, it is not at all incorrect, but must be properly understood when we say that for practice theory not only are bodily routines the place of the social, but that mental routines and their 'knowledge' are also the place of the social: the mental routines and their knowledge are integral parts and elements of practices. A 'practice' thus crosses the distinction between the allegedly inside and outside of mind and body.

[. . .]

Things

For practice theory, objects are necessary components of many practices – just as indispensable as bodily and mental activities. Carrying out a practice very often means using particular things in a certain way. It might sound trivial to stress that in order to play football we need a ball and goals as indis- pensable 'resources'. Maybe it is less trivial, meanwhile – after studies of the history of communicative media – to point out that writing, printing and electronic media 'mould' social (here, above all, discursive) practices, or, better, they enable and limit certain bodily and mental actitivities, certain knowledge and understanding as elements of practices (cf. Kittler, 1985; Gumbrecht, 1988). When particular 'things' are necessary elements of certain practices, then, contrary to a classical sociological argument, subject–subject relations cannot claim any priority over subject–object relations, as far as the production and reproductions of social order(liness) is concerned. The stable relation between agents (body/minds) and things within certain practices reproduces the social, as does the 'mutually' stable relation between several agents in other practices. Moreover, one can assume that most social prac- tices consist of routinized relations between several agents (body/minds) and objects. At any rate, the social is also to be located in practices in which single agents deal with objects (besides, also in practices in which a single agent deals only with himself, with neither other subjects nor objects) and in this sense also the objects – television sets, houses and brownies – are the place of the social insofar as they are necessary components of social practices. There is no necessary link between the observability of social orderliness and 'intersubjectivity'.

Basically, the other types of cultural theory share a common viewpoint on things: namely, that they are primarily objects of knowledge and thus a cultural symbol. In mentalism, the symbolic categories or intentional interpretations are 'about objects' (just as Kantian categories were). In textualism and intersubjectivism respectively the discourses or the propositions produce these objects as meaningful entities or make statements about them. The things are not used, they are known and interpreted, they are objects of the knowing subject (even if the subject might be replaced by discourse or the intersubjective community). Of course, in practice theory things also appear as always-already-interpreted – but here they are things to be handled and constitutive elements of forms of behaviour.

Knowledge

A specific social practice contains specific forms of knowledge. For practice theory, this knowledge is more complex than 'knowing that'. It embraces ways of understanding, knowing how, ways of wanting and of feeling that are linked to each other within a practice. In a very elementary sense, in a practice the knowledge is a particular way of 'understanding the world', which includes an understanding of objects (including abstract ones), of humans, of oneself. This way of understanding is largely implicit and largely historically-culturally specific – it is this form of interpretation that holds together already for the agent herself (the carrier of the practice) the single acts of her own behaviour, so that they form parts of a practice. This way of understanding is a collective, shared knowledge – but not in the sense of a mere sum of the content of single minds: Just as the bodily activities are 'social' as a consequence of their stable reproduction beyond the limits of space, time and single individuals, their 'corresponding' forms of understanding must be 'collective' – right from the beginning, they are necessary components of a practice as a non-subjective pattern. The practice of falling in love with someone in the sense of 'Romantic love' for instance consists – as a culturally understandable practice – of a pattern of routinized (bodily) behaviour and of a certain way of understanding (oneself and another person). Single agents in their single mind/bodies then – independent of one another -'take over' the practice, and thus also its interpretative perspective. Yet, the knowledge that is a constitutive element of a practice is not only a way of understanding; it is – in connection with that – also a know-how and a certain way of wanting and feeling. Every practice contains a know-how knowledge of ethno-methods.

Every practice implies a particular routinized mode of intentionality, i.e. of wanting or desiring certain things and avoiding others. And, finally, every practice contains a certain practice-specific emotionality (even if that means a high control of emotions). Wants and emotions thus do not belong to individuals but – in the form of knowledge – to practices.

The status of knowledge in other cultural theories is not absolutely, but relatively, different. In general, they downplay the know-how and motivational, as well as, to a lesser extent, the understanding-enabling character of knowledge. In objectivist mentalism, knowledge is identified with unconscious systems of distinctions that have effects on behaviour and do not contribute to the agent's understanding (treated as a potentially ideological epiphenomenon here). The textualist concept of knowledge has a similarly 'intellectualist' tendency: Here, knowledge is by definition not ascribed to minds or bodies, but to texts, discourses or communication; a 'code', then, that produces certain chains of signs. The concepts of knowledge in mentalist subjectivism and intersubjectivism are closer to practice theory. Here knowledge is presented as the background of understanding on the part of the agent. However, in the first case there is a tendency toward an emphatic individualization of knowledge which seems separate from collective bodily routines. In the second case, knowledge is above all a background for communication, not for practices in general. At any rate, these approaches do not work within the idea that a social practice is a two-sided block of patterns of bodily behaviour and patterns of knowledge and understanding. Rather, they attribute behaviour and knowledge to two different realms.

Discourse/Language

In practice theory – in contrast to textualism and intersubjectivism – discourse and language lose their omnipotent status. Discursive practices are one type of practices among others. Discursive practices embrace different forms in which the world is meaningfully constructed in language or in other sign-systems. At any rate, discursive practices must, as practices, be more than chains of signs or 'communication' (in the sense of Luhmann), but they are not identical to speech-acts. A discursive practice also contains bodily patterns, routinized mental activities – forms of understanding, know-how (here including grammar and pragmatic rules of use), and motivation – and above all, objects (from sounds to computers) that are linked to each other. However, this is not a structural difference to other, non-discursive practices. Practice theory must stress that 'language exists only in its (routinized) use': in discursive practices the participants ascribe, in a routinized way, certain meanings to certain objects (which thus become 'signs') to understand other objects, and above all, in order to do something.

In objectivist mentalism, language is primarily understood as a mental set of competences which is thus untied from the discursive practice of language use – 'parole' appears as an actualization of 'langue'.[8] Textualism identifies the entire realm of the social with texts, signs, symbols or communication. Moreover, it understands these discourses as extra-mental and extra-bodily patterns. The concept of speech-acts in intersubjectivism contains some similarities to 'discursive practices'. But there are two differences: The concept of discursive practices does not imply the idea of 'transferring meanings from ego to alter' – rather, every practice already contains a routinized, non-subjective way of understanding, so that there is nothing to be transferred (a process which in intersubjectivism must remain opaque). Moreover, practice theory does not share with intersubjectivism the priorization of 'communicative action' over other forms of action.

Structure/Process

For practice theory, the nature of social structure consists in routinization. Social practices are routines: routines of moving the body, of understanding and wanting, of using things, interconnected in a practice. Structure is thus nothing that exists solely in the 'head' or in patterns of behavior: One can find it in the routine nature of action. Social fields and institutionalized complexes – from economic organizations to the sphere of intimacy – are 'structured' by the routines of social practices. Yet the idea of routines necessarily implies the idea of a temporality of structure: Routinized social practices occur in the sequence of time, in repetition; social order is thus basically social reproduction. For practice theory, then, the 'breaking' and 'shifting' of structures must take place in everyday crises of routines, in constellations of interpretative interdeterminacy and of the inadequacy of knowledge with which the agent, carrying out a practice, is confronted in the face of a 'situation'.

In objectivist mentalism, structure is tied to the existence of oversubjective mental categories. Structure exists in this sense 'beyond time', it is a stock of structures in mind whereas 'process' appears as the infinite actualization and application of the structures in action. From this point of view, it becomes highly difficult to conceptualize processes that 'break up' the structures. In contrast, intersubjectivism regards social structure primarily according to a paradigm of a 'consensus' of meanings. Social structure manifests itself in an agreement between subjects/agents to believe the same. One must see the 'breaking' of structure, then, primarily in a constellation of dissent, in a disagreement between speakers. The idea of structure/process in textualism, finally, comes nearest to that in practice theory: Here, structure consists in the autopoiesis of codes in a sequence of discursive events (early Foucault and Luhmann are very similar in this regard). Structure is thus temporal and always implies the possibility of breaking down in 'new events' which do not conform to the code. However, these discursive sequences are not bodily-mental routines in the sense of practice theory, and the accidental emergence of new events is not identical with a constellation of interpretative indeterminacy and pragmatic innovation in a crisis of practice.

The agent/Individual

The agent stands at the centre of classical theories of action. Here he presents himself either as the self-interested figure of the homo economicus, or as the norm-following and role-playing actor of the homo sociologicus. In the former case, the social world seems first and foremost to be populated by independent individuals who confront one another with their decisions. In the latter case, the social world is first and foremost a system of normative rules and expectations, to which agents/actors as rule-following figures conform (or become 'deviant'). In practice theory, agents are body/minds who 'carry' and 'carry out' social practices. Thus, the social world is first and foremost populated by diverse social practices which are carried by agents. Agents, so to speak, 'consist in' the performance of practices (which includes – to stress the point once more – not only bodily, but also mental routines). As carriers of a practice, they are neither autonomous nor the judgemental dopes who conform to norms: They understand the world and themselves, and use know-how and motivational knowledge, according to the particular practice. There is a very precise place for the 'individual' – as distinguished from the agent – in practice theory (though hitherto, practice theorists have hardly treated this question): As there are diverse social practices, and as every agent carries out a multitude of different social practices, the individual is the unique crossing point of practices, of bodily-mental routines.[9]

[. . .]

The effects of practice theory

We hardly need mention that practice theory is not 'true' (in the sense of corresponding to the 'facts'), nor are the other versions of social and cultural theory 'false' (or vice versa). After all, social theories are vocabularies necessarily underdetermined by empirical 'facts'. As vocabularies they never reach the bedrock of a real social world, but offer contingent systems of interpretation which enable us to make certain empirical statements (and exclude other forms of empirical statements). The pertinent questions, then, are: Where does a certain vocabulary lead us? What are its effects? What are the effects of practice theory? There are two sorts of effects to be distinguished. On the one hand, a social-theoretical vocabulary is a heuristic device, a sensitizing 'framework' for empirical research in the social sciences. It thus opens up a certain way of seeing and analysing social phenomena. On the other hand, as vocabularies social theories mould and change 'our' self-understanding.[10] Even without being applied in empirical research, social theories provide us with a certain way of defining our position as human beings in a social world, which inevitably implies a political and ethical dimension. Above all, social theories (and social philosophies alike) provide cultural traditions of grasping ourselves – and frequently they are ways of breaking with cultural traditions of human self-perception, changing them and opening up 'new' possibilities of self-understanding.

Understood as a heuristic device, practice theory – in comparison with social-theoretical alternatives – is handicapped in one point: Hitherto, it has not offered a theoretical 'system' which could compete in complexity with Parsons's homo sociologicus, Luhmann's constructivist theory of social systems, Habermas's theory of communicative action or the theories of cognitive psychology. So, if one is looking for a systematized 'new speak', practice theory and the tentative praxeological remarks of Bourdieu, Giddens, late Foucault, Garfinkel, Latour, Butler or Taylor might not be the first place to look.[11] But even if we do not find a full-blown 'grand theory' here, we can estimate the heuristic effects of practice theory, as it is has already been employed in such diverse fields as science studies, gender studies and organizational studies. The general effect of *cultural* theories in contrast to the classical and still influential models of a homo economicus and homo sociologicus consists in bringing to light the sphere of the symbolic and the cognitive and in asking how these structures give meaning to the world in a contingent way. *Practice* theory, however, prevents cultural theory from following the path of 'culturalism' or 'idealism'. Other versions of cultural theory tend toward an 'intellectualization' of culture by taking as a point of departure very specific entities: either mind or consciousness as in the tradition of Western, post-Cartesian philosophy; or texts and communicative action, i.e. the use of symbols and language. Practice theory thus has a double-effect: Compared to mentalism, it does not invite the analysis of mental phenomena 'as such', but the exploration of the embeddedness of the mental activities of understanding and knowing in a complex of doings, thus, the analysis of the interconnectedness of bodily routines of behaviour, mental routines of understanding and knowing and the use of objects. Compared to textualism and intersubjectivism, practice theory does not encourage the regard of institutional complexes solely as spheres of discourse, communication or communicative action, but their consideration as routinized body/knowledge/things-patterns of which discursive practices (understood in the sense elucidated above) are components. The way, for instance, that organizational, gender or science studies change their outlook under the influence of practice theory can be imagined even if one does not know the works that actually are influenced by it.[12] There is a considerable heuristic difference between whether we are, for instance, encouraged to analyse the 'mental maps' that scientists, men/women or members of an organization use; to explore scientific discourses, gender discourse or 'organization as communication'; or whether our interest is directed to reconstruct how gender, science or organization is produced by a nexus of (non-discursive and discursive) practices as body/knowledge/things-complexes.

Not only the model figures of classically modern social theory, the homo economicus and the homo sociologicus, but also the 'high-modern' theories of culture in mentalism, textualism and intersubjectivism imply a rigid formal rationalization of what human agency and social order are. From the point of view of practice theory, Charles Taylor and Pierre Bourdieu make very clear this tendency of 'hyperintellectualization' and situate themselves in opposition to it. Taylor (1985a [1971], 1985b) has again and again reconstructed the tradition of 'rationalism' in modern philosophical and social thought. This tradition has in diverse ways narrowed our understanding of human agency and the social. Above all, the traditions of atomism and mentalism, rooted already in early modernity, have promoted the understanding of a 'disengaged subject' and marginalized the importance of the 'significance feature', i.e. the importance of practical understanding. In the form of his critique of the 'scholastic habitus', Bourdieu (1997, ch. 2) has arrived at a similar judgement: modern social theory and social philosophy have a tendency to present human agency as a highly reflexive and formally rational enterprise which resembles to an amazing extent the self-images of modern intellectuals and their life-world – in the form of calculating or duty-obeying agents, in the form of consciousness or mental machines, of dominating texts or conversation.[13]

In fact, it seems that practice theory revises the hyperrational and intellectualized picture of human agency and the social offered by classical and high-modern social theories. Practice theory 'decentres' mind, texts and conversation. Simultaneously, it shifts bodily movements, things, practical knowledge and routine to the centre of its vocabulary. The 'hyperrationalism' of mentalism consists in encouraging us to understand ourselves not as agents, but either as systems of unconscious mental categories or as intentional streams of individual consciousness. Intersubjectivism invites us to understand ourselves as participants in the highly specific constellation of conversational acts. Textualism calls upon us to regard the social world as a chain of discourses, symbols and communication – all of them preferred intellectual motives – thus, as an unintended play of meanings, distinct from 'agents'. Practice theory, in contrast, encourages a shifted self-understanding. It invites us to regard agents as carriers of routinized, oversubjective complexes of bodily movements, of forms of interpreting, knowing how and wanting and of the usage of things. [. . .]

Practice theory should develop more philosophical perseverance and at the same time not give up its embeddedness in empirical social and cultural analysis. Then, in future the hitherto loose network of praxeological thinking might yield some interesting surprises.

NOTES

1 'Classically modern social theories' embrace the paradigms of the homo economicus and of the homo sociologicus (see section 1). The label 'high-modern social theories' in this context refers to 'universalist' and 'intellectualist' versions of cultural theory as we find them in mentalism, intersubjectivism and textualism (see section 2).

2 Not all of the authors in question use the term 'practice theory' themselves. The term is important in the work of Bourdieu and Schatzki. In contrast, Stephen Turner (1994) gives the label a different meaning which I do not follow: He describes all cultural

theories as practice theories (concerning the concept of cultural theory and its difference to practice theory see sections 1 and 2 of this article).

3 Practice theory in this sense stands in a rather loose relation to the tradition of classical American pragmatism in the work of Dewey, James or Mead. Yet, the relationship between practice theories and Hans Joas's neo-pragmatism deserves a closer analysis.

4 The task in this article is thus not to argue in favour of practice theories (although such a positive evaluation forms my background), but, more basically, to make plain what practice theories are in comparison with other conceptual options.

5 Therefore, in my presentation of the approach and its particular aspects, I will not give references to single texts or passages of single authors; the task is to develop a programmatic ideal type of a 'practice theory'.

6 A closer critical analysis of the relationship between cultural theories and the two classical figures of homo economicus and homo sociologicus, above all, however, a detailed reconstruction of the emergence of practice theory as a result of a transformation of structuralist and interpretative cultural theories and their mentalist assumptions can be found in my *Die Transformation der Kulturtheorien. Zur Entwicklung eines Theorieprogramms* (2000).

7 Classical instances of such a critique of the homo economicus and the homo sociologicus from the angle of cultural theories are the works of Schütz, Goffman, Cicourel, Taylor and Bourdieu.

8 Subjectivist mentalism, i.e. phenomenology, is characterized by the well-known difficulty of how one can grasp language while remaining in the 'subjective perspective'. I do not address this classical topic in greater detail here.

9 It is Simmel who invented the idea of defining the individual as a crossing-point of different social spheres; see Simmel (1992 [1908], ch. 6). However, Simmel understands the social in the form of 'social circles', i.e. of networks, not in the sense of complexes of social practices.

10 Generally, this idea has been developed by Richard Rorty (Rorty, 1989).

11 Yet Schatzki (1996) has begun such a systematic elaboration in a highly fruitful way, though from the perspective of social philosophy.

12 Examples of empirical studies influenced by practice theory can be found in science studies (Knorr-Cetina, 1981), in gender studies (Butler, 1990 and Hirschauer, 1993), and in organizational studies (Ortmann, 1995).

13 In this context, it can be instructive to situate practice theory and the other social and cultural-theoretical paradigms in the context of the debate on 'modernism' and 'postmodernism'. In general, we can define 'modernist' social theories as theories which support strong concepts of rationality towards human action and social order whereas theories which are sceptical towards modernism weaken these criteria of rationality. In this sense, the paradigms of the homo economicus and of the homo sociologicus represent classical types of social-theoretical modernism. In general, cultural theories relativize the rationalist models of the interest-following or the norm-following transparent agent by situating action in implicit or unconscious, collective symbolic structures. However, the exact relation towards modernism in mentalism, intersubjectivism, textualism and practice theory differs. Structuralism, phenomenology and Habermas's intersubjectivism follow a sort of critical modernism which searches for 'hidden' universal structures of human culture (in mind, consciousness or interaction). Both textualism and practice theory are opposed to these universalizing models and stress cultural contingency and historicity. Textualism chooses the path of 'postmodernism', which stresses the discursive or semiotic 'constructedness' of all entities. For practice theory, this focus on signs, texts and discourse secretly tends to become high-modernist. For practice theory, only the new focus on the groundedness of human action in bodily routines

and in practical understanding is suitable to remain aloof from modernist models of the social and of the agent. Wittgenstein, Heidegger and hermeneutics are philosophical forerunners of such a project.

REFERENCES

Bourdieu, Pierre (1972) *Esquisse d'une théorie de la pratique, précédé de trois études d'éthnologie kabyle.* Geneva: Droz.

—— (1997) *Méditations pascaliennes.* Paris: Seuil.

Foucault, Michel (1984a) *L'usage du plaisir. L'histoire de la sexualité,* Vol. II. Paris: Gallimard.

—— (1984b) *Le souci de soi. L'histoire de la sexualité,* Vol. III. Paris: Gallimard.

Garfinkel, Harold (1984 [1967]) *Studies in Ethnomethodology.* Cambridge: Polity Press.

Giddens, Anthony (1979) *Central Problems in Social Theory. Action, Structure and Contradiction in Social Analysis.* London: Macmillan.

—— (1984) *The Constitution of Society. Outline of the Theory of Structuration.* Cambridge: Polity Press.

Gumbrecht, Hans-Ulrich, ed. (1988) *Materialität der Kommunikation.* Frankfurt/Main: Suhrkamp.

Habermas, Jürgen (1988a [1981]) *Theorie des kommunikativen Handelns, Erster Band: Handlungsrationalität und gesellschaftliche Rationalisierung.* Frankfurt/Main: Suhrkamp.

—— (1988b [1981]) *Theorie des kommunikativen Handelns, Zweiter Band: Zur Kritik der funktionalistischen Vernunft.* Frankfurt/Main: Suhrkamp.

Heidegger, Martin (1986 [1927]) *Sein und Zeit.* Tübingen: Niemeyer.

Hirschauer, Stefan (1999 [1993]) *Die soziale Konstruktion der Transsexualität: über die Medizin und den Geschlechtswechsel.* Frankfurt/Main: Suhrkamp.

Husserl, Edmund (1992 [1931]) 'Cartesianische Meditationen. Eine Einleitung in die Phänomenologie', *Gesammelte Schriften* 8. Hamburg: Meiner.

Kittler, Friedrich (1985) *Aufschreibesysteme 1800/1900.* Munchen: Fink.

Knorr-Cetina, Karin (1981) *The Manufacture of Knowledge. An Essay on the Constructivist and Contextual Nature of Science.* Oxford: Pergamon Press.

Latour, Bruno (1991) *Nous n'avons jamais été modernes. Essai d' anthropologie symétrique.* Paris: La Découverte.

Lévi-Strauss, Claude (1950) 'Introduction à l'oeuvre de Marcel Mauss', in Marcel Mauss (1950) *Sociologie et Anthropologie,* pp. ix–lii. Paris: PUF.

—— (1989 [1962]) *The Savage Mind.* London: Weidenfeld.

Ortmann, Günter (1995) *Formen der Produktion. Organisation und Rekursivität.* Opladen: Westdeutscher Verlag.

Reckwitz, Andreas (2000) *Die Transformation der Kulturtheorien. Zur Enrwicklung eines Theorieprogramms.* Weilerswist: Velbrück Wissenschaft.

Rorty, Richard (1989) *Contingency, Irony, and Solidarity.* Cambridge: Cambridge University Press.

Saussure, Ferdinand de (1995 [1916]) *Cours de linguistique générale.* Paris: Payot.

Schatzki, Theodore (1996) *Social Practices. A Wittgensteinian Approach to Human Activity and the Social.* Cambridge: Cambridge University Press.

Schütz, Alfred (1991 [1932]) *Der sinnhafte Aufbau der sozialen Welt. Eine Einleitung in die verstehende Soziologie.* Frankfurt/Main: Suhrkamp.

Simmel, Georg (1992 [1908]) *Soziologie. Untersuchungen über die Formen der Vergesellschaftung. Gesamtausgabe vol. 11.* Frankfurt/Main: Suhrkamp.

Taylor, Charles (1985a [1971]) 'What is Human Agency?', in *Human Agency and Language, Philosophical Papers 1,* pp. 15–44. Cambridge: Cambridge University Press.

—— (1985b) 'Self-interpreting Animals', in *Human Agency and Language, Philosophical Papers 1,* pp. 45–76. Cambridge: Cambridge University Press.

—— (1993a) 'Engaged Agency and Background in Heidegger', in Charles Guignon (ed.) *The Cambridge Companion to Heidegger,* pp. 317–36. Cambridge: Cambridge University Press.

—— (1993b) 'To Follow a Rule ...', in Craig Calhoun *et al.* (eds) *Bourdieu: Critical Perspectives,* pp. 45–60. Cambridge: Polity Press.

Turner, Stephen P. (1994) *The Social Theory of Practices. Tradition, Tacit Knowledge and Presuppositions.* Cambridge: Polity Press.

Wittgenstein, Ludwig (1984a [1953]) 'Philosophische Untersuchungen', in *Werkausgabe,* Vol. 1. Frankfurt/Main: Suhrkamp [written 1945–9].

—— (1984b [1969]) 'Über Gewißheit', in *Werkausgabe,* Vol. 8. Frankfurt/Main: Suhrkamp [written 1949–51].

BIBLIOGRAPHY

General readings

Anchor, Robert, "The Quarrel Between Historians and Postmodernists," *History and Theory*, 38 (1999): 111–121.

Appleby, Joyce, "One Good Turn Deserves Another: Moving Beyond the Linguistic: A Response to David Harlan," *American Historical Review*, 94 (1989): 1326–1332.

Cabrera, Miguel A., *Postsocial History: An Introduction*, trans. Marie McMahon, foreword by Patrick Joyce (Boulder, CO, New York and Toronto, 2004).

Chartier, Roger, "Intellectual History or Sociocultural History? The French Trajectories," in Dominick LaCapra and Steven L. Kaplan, eds, *Modern European Intellectual History: Reappraisals and New Perspectives* (Ithaca, NY and London, 1982): 13–46.

Chartier, Roger, *Cultural History: Between Practices and Representations*, trans. Lydia G. Cochrane (Ithaca, NY, 1988).

Chartier, Roger, "The World as Representation," in Jacques Revel and Lynn Hunt, eds, "Introduction," *Histories: French Constructions of the Past*, Vol. I "Postwar French Thought," trans. Arthur Goldhammer *et al.* (New York, 1995): 544–558.

Cohen, Sande and Sylvère Lotringer, "Introduction," in *French Theory in America* (New York and London, 2001): 1–9.

Derrida, Jacques, "Structure, Sign and Play in the Discourse of the Human Sciences," in *Writing and Difference*, trans. Alan Bass (Chicago, 1978): 278–293.

Harlan, David, "Intellectual History and the Return of Literature," *American Historical Review*, 94 (1989): 581–609.

Harrington, Austin, "Meanings and Interests in the History of Ideas," in "Constructing the Past: Review Symposium of Bevir's *The Logic of the History of Ideas*," *History of the Human Sciences*, 15 (2002): 109–114.

Hunt, Lynn, Joyce Appleby, and Margaret C. Jacob, *Telling the Truth About History* (New York and London, 1994).

Jay, Martin, "Should Intellectual History Take a Linguistic Turn? Reflections on the Habermas-Gadamer Debate," in Dominick LaCapra and Steven L. Kaplan, eds, *Modern European Intellectual History: Reappraisals and New Perspectives* (Ithaca, NY and London, 1982): 86–110.

Jenkins, Keith, ed., *The Postmodern History Reader* (London and New York, 1997).

Jenkins, Keith, "A Postmodern Reply to Perez Zagorin," *History and Theory*, 39 (2000): 181–200.

Joyce, Patrick, "History and Postmodernism," *Past and Present*, 133 (1991): 204–209.

Joyce, Patrick, "More Secondary Modern than Postmodern," *Rethinking History*, 5 (2001): 367–382.

Kramer, Lloyd, "Literature, Criticism and Historical Imagination: The Literary Challenge of Hayden White and Dominick LaCapra," in Lynn Hunt, ed., *The New Cultural History* (Berkeley and Los Angeles, 1980): 97–128.

Munslow, Alun, "Editorial," *Rethinking History: The Journal of Theory and Practice*, 1 (1997): 1–20.

Revel, Jacques and Lynn Hunt, eds, "Introduction," *Histories French Constructions of the Past*, Vol. I "Postwar French Thought," trans. Arthur Goldhammer *et al.* (New York, 1995): 1–63.

Roberts, David D., "Postmodern Continuities: Difference, Dominance, and the Question of Historiographic Renewal," *History and Theory*, 37 (1998): 388–400.

Rorty, Richard, ed., *The Lingustic Turn: Essays in Philosophical Method with Two Retrospective Essays* (Chicago and London, 1992).

Ross, Dorothy, "The New and Newer Histories: Social Theory and Historiography in an American Key," in Anthony Molho and Gordon S. Wood, eds *Imagined Histories: American Historians Interpret the Past*, (Princeton, 1998): 85–106.

Spiegel, Gabrielle M., "History, Historicism and the Social Logic of the Text in the Middle Ages," *Speculum*, 65 (1990): 59–86.

Spiegel, Gabrielle M., "History and Post-modernism," *Past and Present*, 135 (1992): 194–208.

Spiegel, Gabrielle M., "Towards a Theory of the Middle Ground: Historical Writing in the Age of Postmodernism," in *Historia a Debate*, Vol. 1 (Santiago de Compostela, 1995): 169–176.

Spiegel, Gabrielle M., *The Past as Text: The Theory and Practice of Medieval Historiography* (Baltimore, 1997).

Toews, John E., "Perspectives on 'The Old History and the New': A Comment," *American Historical Review*, 94 (1989): 693–698.

Toews, John E., "A New Philosophy of History? Reflections on Postmodern Historicizing," *History and Theory*, 36 (1997): 235–248.

White, Hayden, *Metahistory* (Baltimore and London, 1973).

Zagorin, Perez, "History, the Referent, and Narrative: Reflections on Postmodernism Now," *History and Theory*, 38 (1999): 1–24

Discourse/Social and cultural history

Biernacki, Richard, "Method and Metaphor after the New Cultural History," in Victoria E. Bonnell and Lynn Hunt, eds, *Beyond the Cultural Turn* (New Directions in the Study of Society and Culture) (Berkeley, 1999): 62–92.

Biernacki, Richard and Jennifer Jordan, "The Place of Space in the Study of the Social," in Patrick Joyce, ed., *The Social in Question: New Bearings in History and the Social Sciences* (London and New York, 2002): 133–150.

Biersack, Aletta, "Local Knowledge, Local History: Geertz and Beyond," in Lynn Hunt, ed., *The New Cultural History* (Berkeley, 1989): 72–96.

Bonnell, Victoria E. and Lynn Hunt, eds, *Beyond the Cultural Turn* (New Directions in the Study of Society and Culture) (Berkeley, 1999): 1–32.

Brantlinger, Patrick, "A Response to *Beyond the Cultural Turn*," *American Historical Review*, 107 (2002): 1500–1511.

Cabrera, Miguel A., "On Language, Culture and Social Action," *History and Theory*, 40 (2001): 82–100.

Dirks, Nicholas B., "Is Vice Versa? Historical Anthropologies and Anthropological Histories," in Terrence J. McDonald, ed., *The Historic Turn in the Human Sciences* (Ann Arbor, 1996): 17–51.

Eley, Geoff, "Is All the World a Text?: From Social History to the History of Society Two Decades Later," in Terrence J. McDonald, ed., *The Historic Turn in the Human Sciences* (Ann Arbor, 1996): 193–243.

Eley, Geoff and Keith Nield, "Starting Over: The Present, the Post-Modern and the Moment of Social History," in Keith Jenkins, ed., *The Postmodern History Reader* (London and New York, 1997): 366–379.

Geertz, Clifford, "The Growth of Culture and the Evolution of Mind," in *The Interpretation of Cultures* (New York, 1973): 55–83.

Geertz, Clifford, "Religion as a Cultural System," in *The Interpretation of Cultures* (New York, 1973): 87–125.

Geertz, Clifford, "Thick Description: Toward an Interpretive Theory of Culture," in *The Interpretation of Cultures* (New York, 1973): 3–30.

Handler, Richard, "Cultural Theory in History Today," *American Historical Review*, 107 (2002): 1512–1520.

Joyce, Patrick, "The Imaginary Discontents of Social History: A Note of Response to Mayfield and Thorne, and Lawrence and Taylor," *Social History*, 18 (1) (1993): 81–85.

Joyce, Patrick, "The End of Social History?" in Keith Jenkins, ed., *The Postmodern History Reader* (London and New York, 1997): 341–365.

Joyce, Patrick, ed., *The Social in Question: New Bearings in History and the Social Sciences* (London and New York, 2002).

Kirk, Neville, "History, Language, Ideas and Postmodernism: A Materialist View," *Social History*, 19 (1994): 221–240.

Lorenz, Chris, "Some Afterthoughts on Culture and Explanation in Historical Inquiry," *History and Theory*, 39 (2000): 348–363.

Megill, Allan, "Recounting the Past: 'Description,' Explanation, and Narrative in Historiography," *American Historical Review*, 94 (1989): 627–653.

O'Brien, Patricia, "Michel Foucault's History of Culture," in Lynn Hunt, ed., *The New Cultural History* (Berkeley, 1989): 25–46.

Ortner, Sherry B., ed., *The Fate of Culture Geertz and Beyond* (Berkeley, 1999).

Suny, Ronald Grigor, "Back and Beyond: Reversing the Cultural Turn?," *American Historical Review*, 107 (2002): 1476–1499.

Walters, Ronald G., "Signs of the Times: Clifford Geertz and Historians," *Social Research*, 47 (3) (Autumn 1980): 537–556.

White, Hayden, "Afterword," in Victoria E. Bonnell and Lynn Hunt, eds, *Beyond the Cultural Turn* (New Directions in the Study of Society and Culture) (Berkeley, 1999): 315–324.

Self, subjectivity and agency

Allen, James Smith, "Navigating the Social Sciences: A Theory for the Meta-History of Emotions" (Review essay of William Reddy, *The Navigation of Feeling: A Framework for the History of Emotions*), *History and Theory*, 42 (2003): 82–93.

Bevir, Mark, *The Logic of the History of Ideas* (Cambridge, 1999).

Bevir, Mark, "Author's Introduction" and "A Reply to Critics," in "Constructing the Past: Review Symposium of Bevir's *The Logic of the History of Ideas*," *History of the Human Sciences*, 15 (2002): 99–101, 126–133.

Bevir, Mark, "How to be an Intentionalist," *History and Theory*, 41 (2002): 209–217.

Brown, Vivienne, "On Some Problems with Weak Intentionalism for Intellectual History," *History and Theory*, 41 (2002): 198–208.

Cabrera, Miguel, A., "Linguistic Approach or Return to Subjectivism? In Search of an Alternative to Social History," *Social History*, 24 (1991): 74–89.

Erickson, Mark, "What do Normative Accounts Tell Us," in "Constructing the Past: Review Symposium of Bevir's *The Logic of the History of Ideas*," *History of the Human Sciences*, 15 (2002): 102–109.

Ermarth, Elizabeth Deeds, "Agency in the Discursive Condition," *History and Theory*, 40 (2001): 34–58.

Fitzhugh, Michael L. and William H. Leckie, Jr., "Agency, Postmodernism and the Causes of Change," in *History and Theory*, 40 (2001): 59–81.

Foucault, Michel, "Nietzsche, Genealogy, History," in *Language, Counter-memory, Practice: Selected Essays and Interviews by Michel Foucault*, edited and with an introduction by Donald F. Bouchard (Ithaca, NY, 1977): 139–164.

Harrington, Austin, "Meanings and Interests in the History of Ideas," in "Constructing the Past: Review Symposium of Bevir's *The Logic of the History of Ideas*," *History of the Human Sciences*, 15 (2002): 109–114.

Merleau-Ponty, Maurice, *The Visible and the Invisible*, ed. Claude Lefort, trans. Alphonso Lingis (Evanston, IL, 1968).

Reckwitz, Andreas, "The Constraining Power of Cultural Schemes and the Liberal Model of Beliefs," in "Constructing the Past: Review Symposium of Bevir's *The Logic of the History of Ideas*," *History of the Human Sciences*, 15 (2002): 115–125.

Reddy, William M., "The Logic of Action: Indeterminacy, Emotion and Historical Narrative," *History and Theory*, 40 (2001): 10–33.

Sewell, Jr., William H., "A Theory of Structure: Duality, Agency, and Transformation," *American Journal of Sociology*, 98 (1992): 1–29.

Shaw, David Gary, "Happy in Our Chains? Agency and Language in the Postmodern Age," *History and Theory*, 40 (2001): 1–9.

Smith, Jay, "No More Language Games: Words, Beliefs, and the Political Culture of Early Modern France," *American Historical Review*, 102 (1997): 1413–1440.

Smith, Jay, "Between *Discourse* and *Experience*: Agency and Ideas in the French Pre-Revolution," *History and Theory*, 40 (2001): 116–142.

Experience and practice

Biernacki, Richard, "Language and the Shift from Signs to Practices in Cultural Inquiry," *History and Theory*, 30 (2000): 289–310.

Bourdieu, Pierre, *Outline of the Theory of Practice*, trans. Richard Nice (Cambridge, 1977).

Bourdieu, Pierre, *The Logic of Practice* (Stanford, CA, 1990).

Canning, Kathleen, "Feminist History after the Linguistic Turn: Historicizing Discourse and Experience," *Signs*, 19 (2) (1994): 368–404.

Censer, Jack, "Social Twists and Linguistic Turns: Revolutionary Historiography a Decade after the Bicentennial," *French Historical Studies*, 22 (1999): 139–167.

de Certeau, Michel, *The Practice of Everyday Life*, trans. Steven Rendall (Berkeley, 1984).

de Lauretis, Teresa, "Semiotics and Experience," in *Alice Doesn't: Feminism, Semiotics, Cinema* (Bloomington, IN, 1984): 158–186

Editorial, "Tentons l'Expérience," *Annales ESC*, 44 (1989): 1317–1323.

Giddens, Anthony, *The Constitution of Society: Outline of the Theory of Structuration* (Berkeley, 1986).

Lepetit, Bernard, ed., *Les Formes de l'Expérience: Un Autre Histoire Sociale* (Paris, 1995).

Reckwitz, Andreas, "Toward a Theory of Social Practices: A Development in Culturalist Theorizing," *European Journal of Social Theory*, 5 (2) (2002): 243–263.

Revel, Jacques, "L'Institution et le Social," in *Les Formes de l'Expérience: Une Autre Histoire Sociale*, Bernard Lepetit, ed. (Paris, 1995): 63–84.

Rouse, Joseph "Vampires: Social Constructivism, Realism and Other Philosophical Undead," (Review essay of André Kukla, *Social Constructivism and the Philosophy of Science*, and Ian Hacking, *The Social Construction of What?*), *History and Theory*, 41 (2002): 60–78.

Sahlins, Marshall, *Islands of History* (Chicago and London, 1985).

Sahlins, Marshall, "Individual Experience and Cultural Order," in *Culture in Practice Selected Essays* (New York, 2000): 277–291.

Sahlins, Marshall, "The Return of the Event, Again," in *Culture in Practice Selected Essays* (New York, 2000): 293–351.

Schatzki, Theodore, *Social Practices: A Wittgensteinian Approach to Human Activity and the Social* (Cambridge, 1996).

Scott, Joan Wallach, "History in Crisis? The Others' Side of the Story," *American Historical Review*, 94 (1989): 680–692.

Scott, Joan, "The Evidence of Experience," *Critical Inquiry* (Summer, 1991): 773–797.

Scott, Joan, "Deconstructing Equality-Versus-Difference: Or, the Uses of Poststructuralist Theory for Feminism," *Feminist Studies*, 14 (1988): 33–50.

Sewell, William H., Jr., "Historical Events as Transformations of Structures: Inventing Revolution at the Bastille," *Theory and Society*, 25 (1996): 841–881.

Toews, John E., "Intellectual History after the Linguistic Turn: The Autonomy of Meaning and the Irreducibility of Experience," *American Historical Review*, 92 (1987): 879–907.

INDEX